Competitive Governments explores in a systematic way the hypothesis that governments are internally competitive, that they are competitive in their relations with one another and in their relations with other institutions in society that, like them, supply consuming households with goods and services. Professor Breton contends that competition not only serves to bring the political system to an equilibrium but that it also leads to a revelation of the households' true demand functions for publicly provided goods and services and to the molding of a link between the quantities and the qualities demanded and supplied and the taxprices paid for these goods and services. In the real world where information is costly, the links may not be first-best, but they will be efficient if competition is vigorous.

Competitive governments

Competitive governments

An economic theory of politics and public finance

ALBERT BRETON
University of Toronto

CAMBRIDGE
UNIVERSITY PRESS

Published by the Press Syndicate of the University of Cambridge
The Pitt Building, Trumpington Street, Cambridge CB2 1RP
40 West 20th Street, New York, NY 10011-4211, USA
10 Stamford Road, Oakleigh, Melbourne 3166, Australia

First published 1996

Printed in the United States of America

Library of Congress Cataloging-in-Publication Data
Breton, Albert.
Competitive governments : an economic theory of politics and public
finance / Albert Breton.
p. cm.
ISBN 0-521-48102-3 (hardcover)
1. Finance, Public. 2. Public goods. 3. Government competition. I.
Title.
HJ131.B74 1996
336 – dc20   95-12463
                                                                  CIP

A catalog record for this book is available from the British Library.

ISBN 0-521-48102-3 Hardback

for Margot

Contents

Preface   *page* xi

Part I   Compound governments

1   The conceptual framework   3
    1.1   Goods and services defined   5
    1.2   Models of government   9
    1.3   Concepts of efficiency   17
    1.4   Requisites of democracy   24
    1.5   Competition   30
    1.6   Assembling the building blocks   34

2   Demand and its revelation   37
    2.1   Utility maximization   42
          i.   Taxprices   43
          ii.   Free-riding   44
          iii.   Substitution   46
    2.2   Demand revelation   48
          i.   Motivation   49
          ii.   Mechanism   52
    2.3   Demand lobbies   57
          i.   Aggregation and the interaction of demand lobbies
                 with centers of power   59
          ii.   Shirking by lobby members   61
          iii.   Reverse shirking by lobby managers   64
          iv.   Collusion and rent-seeking   65
    2.4   The Wicksellian Connection   66
    2.5   Conclusion   69

3   Checks and balances   70
    3.1   Compound governments   71
    3.2   Definitions and assumptions   74
          i.   Checking and balancing   75
          ii.   Checking instruments illustrated   76
    3.3   A formal model and some implications   79

3.4 The Wicksellian Connection anew   87
3.5 A digression on American exceptionalism   90
3.6 Balanced governments   93
3.7 Conclusion   95

4 Budgetary processes   96
   4.1 The budgetary process of parliamentary governments   98
        i.   Stylized structure   98
        ii.   The model   101
   4.2 The budgetary process of congressional governments   111
        i.   Stylized structure   112
        ii.   The model   114
   4.3 The Wicksellian Connection once again   118
   4.4 Conclusion   121

5 Consent, suffrage, and support   122
   5.1 A model of political consent   123
        i.   A *Vox Dei* dispensation model   125
        ii.   A *Vox Populi* dispensation model   129
   5.2 Introducing suffrage and support   134
   5.3 Collusion and breakdown   141
   5.4 The Wicksellian Connection once more   146
   5.5 Conclusion   146

6 Hierarchy and bureaucracy   148
   6.1 The problem defined   149
   6.2 Models of inefficient bureaus   155
        i.   The principal–agent model   155
        ii.   The discretionary power model   162
   6.3 Models of efficient bureaus and bureaucracies   167
        i.   Single bureaus   167
        ii.   Bureaucracies   176
   6.4 Conclusion   178

Part II Governmental systems

7 A retrospective overview   181
   7.1 More definitions   183
   7.2 Vertical competition   184
   7.3 Horizontal competition   190
   7.4 Conclusion   194

8 The organization of governmental systems   196
   8.1 The standard explanation   197

8.2 An alternative explanation 203
  i. Technology 204
  ii. Coordination costs 209
    a. Origin 209
    b. Nature 210
    c. Effects 212
  iii. Contractual enforcement costs 213
  iv. Caveats 222
    a. Information costs 222
    b. Collusion 223
8.3 The constitutional factor 223
8.4 The Wicksellian Connection remembered 226
8.5 Conclusion 227

9 Competition, stability, and central governments 228
9.1 The inducements to compete 229
  i. Tiebout's potential entry and exit mechanism 230
  ii. Salmon's external benchmark mechanism 233
9.2 Some empirical evidence on intergovernmental competition 235
  i. Indices of policy and program diffusion 235
  ii. Estimates of political mobility 238
  iii. Analysis of price rivalry 239
9.3 Horizontal competition and stability 240
  i. Policy and program diffusion 241
  ii. Political mobility 243
  iii. Price rivalry 245
9.4 Vertical competition and stability 245
9.5 Securing stability 248
  i. Why use monitors? 249
  ii. Monitoring horizontal competition 250
    a. Prohibitions and standards 250
    b. Regional policies 251
    c. Intergovernmental grants 254
  iii. Monitoring vertical competition 258
    a. Bicameralism 259
    b. Intrastate federalism 260
    c. Constitutional entrenchment 261
9.6 The Wicksellian Connection reconsidered 262
9.7 Conclusion 262

10 The world order 264
10.1 International competition 267

10.2 International regimes   271
10.3 The European Union   275
10.4 Conclusion   276

Part III   Socio-political structures

11   The size of the nonmarket sector   279
     11.1 Nonprofit organizations   280
     11.2 An alternative perspective   282
     11.3 Goods are goods   284
     11.4 Conclusion   285

12   The growth of governments   286
     12.1 The determinants of supply   288
           i.   Some preliminaries   289
           ii.   Differential productivity growth of conventional
                 inputs   293
           iii. Differential growth in the capacity to control
                 free-riding   295
           iv.   Differential growth in the ability to acquire
                 information   302
     12.2 Equilibrium and growth   304
     12.3 Conclusion   308

     Conclusion   311

Appendices

A.   Long-term budget deficits   315

B.   The power of "small" groups   318

C.   The independence of judiciaries   321

D.   Information and pressure   326

E.   An empirical Wicksellian Connection?   328

F.   Overlap and duplication   331

G.   Structure and stability of federal states   334

     References   337

     Name index   363

     Subject index   369

Preface

Critics of my first book – *The Economic Theory of Representative Government* (1974) – pointed to some of the mistakes and imprecisions it contained, criticisms that I have, on the whole, accepted and made mine. However, except for a few reviews (I note those of Migué, 1974, and Oates, 1975), the two main weaknesses of the monograph were not really identified. That this should have been so is easy to understand. The author of the book as well as his critics were all functioning within the period's *Zeitgeist,* one that was quite simple given the age of the still nameless budding discipline of Public Choice or Economics of Politics. These two weaknesses eventually came to dominate my thinking on the subject. They were first, the lack of a well-defined equilibrium for the various forces and influences that I thought were important elements for an understanding of politics and, in particular, for an eventual positive analysis of the public finances of political jurisdictions. There was, second, the lack of a tractable mechanism that would insure that equilibrium outcomes, properly identified, would be reached.

To a degree, both failures were the consequence of the assumption, which pervaded the thinking of the period and the whole of my monograph, that governments are monopolies. The book did discuss, albeit no more than as an afterthought, federalism and, therefore, a structure in which more than one government exists, but the sway of the monopoly assumption was so great that it prevented me from pursuing the idea that intergovernmental relations in federal states are generally competitive. Jean-Luc Migué (1974), in his thoughtful review article of the monograph, criticized me for having too wholeheartedly embraced the monopoly assumption, but I felt that I could not accept his criticism because I thought that what he was urging me to accept was the presupposition that democratic politics was competitive because of the existence of competitive elections. I have always thought that a "good" theory of elections and of electoral contests is absolutely essential for an understanding of democratic politics, but I could not resign myself then, any more than I can today after twenty additional years of observation and study of governments and of political behaviors, to a reduction and identification of democratic politics to electoral contests.

It was not until I worked with Ronald Wintrobe on bureaucracy that I began to understand that the driving mechanism in political life – the force that propels the system toward equilibrium and that must be placed at the center of the stage in models of politics – is the same as that which regulates economic life, namely, competition. Dropping the monopoly assumption to explore that of competition requires, among other things, that we turn our attention toward supply and toward the institutions that make up the supply side. It is no longer possible to parade a theory of politics in which governments have no existence. That is being recognized by an increasing number of scholars among whom I mention Kenneth Shepsle (1975), Morris Fiorina (1982), Barry Weingast and William Marshall (1988), and John Ferejohn and Charles Shipan (1990). Such a shift does not reduce the *absolute* importance of elections in democratic politics, but it does diminish their *relative* weight, if only because of the crucial role played by centers of power that are not elected in the production and supply of goods and services by governmental centers of power (for a definition of goods and services, see Chapter 1, Section 1.1).

If elections have a prominent place in what follows, the focus is certainly on supply and on the competition that organizes the relations between supply sources. More precisely, the study explores some of the implications of the assumption that politics is competitive. In addition, it seeks to establish that the equilibrium toward which competition drives the political system is one that possesses, at least at the limit, the characteristics of the equilibrium Knut Wicksell described in his classic 1896 paper and which Erik Lindahl explored more deeply in his also classic 1919 contribution.

The whole exercise has taken many years. During that time, I have accumulated debts that a brief acknowledgment cannot possibly repay. Still, this is virtually the only mode of indemnification available to a debtor in this type of relationship when creditors are numerous. I therefore wish to express my profound gratitude, first, to my colleagues of the Villa Colombella Group – Gianluigi Galeotti (Roma, La Sapienza), Pierre Salmon (Bourgogne), and Ronald Wintrobe (Western Ontario) – who have read all the substantive chapters of the book, sometimes more than once, and have provided me with such good comments, criticisms, and observations that it was only with great trepidation that I sometimes decided that I could not accept some of their suggestions. I must also thank in a very special way my friend and erstwhile co-author, Anthony Scott, who has lavished comments and remarks – all of them thoughtful and demanding – on many parts of earlier drafts and especially on the chapters of Part II on which he has had a profound influence.

At the risk of forgetting some persons who have, either verbally but often in writing, made comments on one chapter or the other, on papers that, transformed, have subsequently become chapters and, in a number of instances, on sets of chapters, I wish to thank by name Gérard Bélanger, the late Jean Bénard, Michele Bernasconi, Richard Bird, Robert Bish, Geoffrey Brennan, Raymond Breton, Thomas Courchene, Robert Deacon, Stéphan Dupré, Angela Fraschini, Brian Galligan, Emilio Gerelli, Scott Gordon, Douglas Hartle, Peter Ibbott, Daphne Kenyon, Jean-Dominique Lafay, Louis Lévy-Garboua, Andrea Mancini, Carla Marchese, Allan Maslove, William Niskanen, Alan Peacock, Ilde Rizzo, Kimberly Scharf, Jean Tirole, Cliff Walsh, Stanley Winer, and Robert Young. I am also grateful for the excellent comments of two anonymous referees. I need not add that none of these persons are responsible for remaining errors and for the positions I have finally adopted.

I am also thankful to participants in seminars or workshops held at the Advisory Council on Intergovernmental Relations (in Washington), at the Center for Study of Public Choice in George Mason University, at the Federalism Research Centre in the Australian National University, at the Liberty Fund Workshop in the University of Victoria (British Columbia), at the Université de Bourgogne (in Dijon), at the Université de Paris I – Panthéon-Sorbonne, at Queen's University (in Kingston), at the University of Toronto, at the University of Western Ontario (in London), and at the University of Windsor, where at one time or another I have presented materials now incorporated in what follows, often in radically revised form consequent on the comments and criticisms of seminar or workshop participants. Chapters 2 and 4 were presented, in rather different cloth, at Villa Colombella Seminars. I am also grateful to the participants at these Seminars for discussions that have been rewarding.

I have also greatly benefited from the obligation to present my evolving thoughts in a more or less orderly fashion in an Economics of Politics course given yearly at the University of Toronto and given also at the Université de Paris I–Panthéon-Sorbonne and at the Institut d'Etudes Politiques de Paris. I am grateful to all my students – in Canada and in France – for their comprehension and patience, but especially for their questions and comments.

There have been many drafts of all the chapters that follow. For their efficiency and good grace in typing and retyping all of these, I wish to thank Jennifer Johnson, Kitty Legault, Agnes Miller, Dorothy Vreeker, and Irene Wyka. I am also very grateful to my daughter Françoise Breton for collating the Reference section of the book and for checking it out – a time-consuming and ungrateful task that was flawlessly performed.

I would also like to thank in a very special way Scott Parris, the Economics editor at Cambridge University Press, for his considerate attention, competence, and efficiency in dealing with a succession of editorial problems. He has, in the process, not only served as catalyst for improvements to the final product, but he has made my task in dealing with these problems much easier than it would otherwise have been.

I owe special thanks to the Connaught Foundation of the University of Toronto for granting me a Senior Fellowship in the Social Sciences in 1986–7, thus allowing me to take a year away from teaching to begin, on a full-time basis, the planning and writing of the book. I am also grateful to the Social Sciences and Humanities Research Council of Canada for providing me over all the years I have been engaged in this project with funds to purchase typing services and research assistance. Finally, I wish to thank in a special way the Lynde and Harry Bradley Foundation for the funds granted to the Villa Colombella Group, funds that have allowed me over the past few years to work severally and collectively with members of the Group on all of the various parts of the book.

Nothing in this book has been published before in the form it has taken in the chapters that follow. I have, however, used some material from previously published papers of mine. For permission to do so, I wish to thank the *Canadian Journal of Economics,* the *European Journal of Political Economy* (Elsevier Science B.V.), Kluwer Academic Publishers, The School of Policy Studies at Queen's University, the University of Toronto Press, and the Urban Institute in Washington.

PART I

Compound governments

CHAPTER 1

The conceptual framework

The first and overriding objective of the whole of this study is an exploration of some of the implications and requirements of the assumption, which I endeavor to buttress empirically, that governments are competitive – that each one individually is internally competitive, that they compete among themselves, and, last but not least, that they compete with other institutions in society that are, like them, engaged in the provision of goods and services. That intra-, inter-, and extragovernmental competition, in the process of driving politics to equilibrium outcomes, acts as a preference, or demand, revelation mechanism for government-supplied as well as for nongovernment–nonmarket-provided goods and services. It does this by building links or connections between the taxation (revenue) and the spending decisions that governments and nongovernment–nonmarket agents, as suppliers of goods and services, have to make.

As is well known, Wicksell (1896) and Lindahl (1919), followed by generations of prominent students of the Public Finance model they developed, have recognized that if genuine links or connections were to emerge between revenue and expenditure decisions and if true demand functions were as a result to be revealed, the public (collective) provision of goods and services would be efficient. Wicksell's seminal idea and its further development therefore provides the foundation for the theory of Politics and Public Finance suggested in the pages that follow. To rephrase the opening sentence of this chapter, the first and overriding objective of this study is an exploration of some of the implications and requirements of the assumption that governments are competitive in a Wicksell–Lindahl frame of reference and that this competition leads to the molding of a connection between taxing and spending decisions and to the revelation of the citizenry's demand functions for nonmarket-provided goods and services. I will henceforth call this connection the Wicksellian Connection.

Competition in political as in economic affairs is a powerful force. If it *implies* the emergence of a Wicksellian Connection, it also *requires* a reexamination of a number of prominent concepts that have wide currency in the economic analysis of politics. As the discussion in this and the next chapter in particular will make clear, when the supply of goods and services is regulated by competition, the meaning that is often attached to concepts such as wealth

3

and income redistribution, interest- and pressure-group politics, and free-riding as well as the significance given to the presence of (pure or impure Samuelsonian) public goods, is quite different from the meaning associated with these concepts in a framework in which the supply side is not competitive.

It is useful to begin by delineating the domain from which I will choose analytical building blocks and hence the conceptual framework of the Wicksellian theory of Politics and Public Finance I will propose. That is not as easy as it would appear at first sight. A look at the literature of Public Choice or Economics of Politics and at those of Public Economics, Welfare Economics, and Political Science rapidly reveals that these various literatures house many models of government, many concepts of efficiency (in public affairs), several different approaches to democracy, and at least two distinct theories of voting. This is hardly surprising given the histories and preoccupations of the various disciplines.

In choosing one model of government, one concept of efficiency, one approach to democracy, and one theory of voting from the variety at my disposal, I have been governed by the necessity to assemble the selected building blocks in one consistent whole – a whole also capable of incorporating the reality of competition and able to yield a theory that can shed new light on Politics and Public Finance and particularly on the *public finances of real-world governments*. The proposed theory is intended to be primarily positive or descriptive, even though it will embody the essentially normative concept of efficiency. It will be easier to explain the role of that concept after the discussion of some of the different versions of it that one finds in the literature. At this point, let me simply note that I follow standard practice: I seek to establish that certain hypotheses and mechanisms satisfactorily account for what we observe in the real world, and on the basis of theories that build on and incorporate these hypotheses and mechanisms and demonstrate that the outcomes they generate are efficient (or inefficient), I conclude to efficiency (or inefficiency). I return to this question at the end of Section 1.3.

Throughout, I proceed on the assumption that governments are concerned with the production and supply of goods and services and with their financing, but with nothing else. The main objection to this assumption is that governments redistribute income and wealth, and that redistribution is neither a good nor a service. In Section 1.1, I address this objection by suggesting that in competitive democratic societies redistribution is necessarily preference-based and therefore a service demanded by citizens. Then, in Section 1.2, I introduce seven models of government and opt for one of them.[1] Section 1.3

1. As the reader will discover, seven is an arbitrary number. It is easy to regroup concepts and doctrines or to subdivide them differently than I have done. What counts in the end is the help a particular classification gives to the formulation of a basic conceptual framework.

presents four separate concepts of efficiency and again chooses one. The fourth section is constructed differently. It argues, on what are essentially neo-Madisonian lines (a rationale for the affix to Madisonian will become apparent shortly), that two conditions or requisites must be satisfied if a political regime is to be identified as democratic: First, at least one important and real decision-making center of power (historically, the legislative or the executive branch) that is constitutive of the apparatus of government must be popularly elected.[2] Second, competition must regulate the relations of all the autonomous and quasi-autonomous centers of power – in particular, the nonelected centers – that make up governments and governmental systems.[3,4] I will argue in addition that the two conditions must be satisfied simultaneously. Section 1.4 also shows how the model of government and the concept of efficiency I have chosen blend with the neo-Madisonian theory of democracy. In Section 1.5, I begin the task, which will be completed only at the end of this volume, of defining competition and of identifying some of the actions and behaviors that are attached to it when it is manifested in politics. Section 1.6 concludes by providing a chapter-by-chapter outline of the content of Part I of the book, the part that focuses on intragovernmental competition in compound governments.

1.1.   Goods and services defined

Because of a persistent ambiguity that characterizes the subject, it is necessary – before addressing the matter of income redistribution – to begin by saying a few words about the "ordinary" goods and services supplied by governments. Some of the confusion has its origin, no doubt, in a normative–positive conundrum of conventional Public Economics: that some goods and services are but should not, while others are not but should, be supplied by governments. I am not concerned with what governments should or should not provide but only with what they do in fact supply. Providing useful abstract definitions in this domain is almost impossible. The most effective communication strategy is to offer a list that illustrates the variety of goods and services that governments at different times and places actually supply. I offer the

2. Accordingly, a *parliamentary monarchy,* as exists in England, satisfies this condition, whereas a *constitutional monarchy* – a regime in which "cabinet ministers are . . . servants of the monarch" (Schumpeter, 1975, p. 270) and, as a consequence, a regime in which electorates and parliaments can be overruled by the monarch – does not. This first condition does not, therefore, depart from convention.
3. This expression is defined in footnote 17 of this chapter. In a nutshell, it refers to the totality of governments that constitute the political system of a society.
4. From a descriptive point of view, we could therefore say that the greater the competition and the larger the number of centers of power that share in the competition, the more democratic the regime.

following in more or less haphazard order: justice (laws, courts, legal aid, police officers, prisons and so on), injustice (delays, harassment, false arrests, brutality, etc.), national defense, war, low and high unemployment, price stability and inflation, anti- and proabortion laws, environmental protection and pollution, free and protected foreign trade, marketing boards, light-houses, traffic signals, zoning, busing, refuse collection, snow removal, street lighting, daycare centers, unemployment insurance, old-age pensions, museum exhibits, theater productions, building codes, air, maritime, road and rail transportation, hospital services, schooling, mining, broadcasting, oil exploration, censorship, racism, discrimination, nationalism, anti-Semitism and concentration camps. This list could be easily extended. I hope, however, that it makes two points. First, that in addition to goods and services that standard textbooks, say, would regard as "wholesome" or "beneficial," governments *de facto* also supply goods and services that the same textbooks would take to be "harmful" or "bad." It is likely that the supply of some of the second kind of goods and services is more abundant in dictatorships than in democracies, but it must be stressed, and this is the second point, that when these goods and services are supplied by democratic governments, as they sometimes are, it is necessary in a model based on a doctrine of self-interested actors and embodied in a neo-Madisonian theory of democracy to assume that the goods and services supplied are arguments in the utility functions of some citizens. They are, in other words, supplied only because they are demanded. This being clear, I now turn my attention to redistribution.

The assumption (often tacit) that governments are principally if not exclu-sively engaged in redistribution (even when they appear to be busy laying sewers, censoring movies, criminalizing abortion, and auditing taxpayers) is basic to a number of widely cited economic models of politics. As examples, I note Tullock's (1967) theory of rent-seeking, Stigler's (1971) theory of eco-nomic regulation, Meltzer and Richard's (1981) theory of the extended fran-chise, and Becker's (1983) theory of pressure groups. Scholars – like all free citizens – have the liberty to choose and to examine the implications of any assumptions and therefore to construct any models they want. The test of a model's worth is the improvement it permits in our understanding of the real world and, for reformers, in the guidance it provides to recommendations and action.

Even if models founded on the exploitation of fellow citizens by means of rent-seeking, capture, and "takings" – the basis of the models listed in the preceding paragraph – have shed light on some aspects of politics, they have obscured the essential. They have done this by representing politics as an essentially zero-sum – or even a negative-sum – enterprise, a view that is inescapable when redistribution is seen as the alpha and omega of politics and the product of rent-seeking, capture, and takings. It is a view that makes fools of us all by insisting that, incapable of doing anything about the way it is played, we all freely choose to engage in this kind of political game decade after decade.

If instead we choose to think of politics as producing on the average positive-sum outcomes and if at the same time we eschew the organicist, despotic-but-benevolent, or monolithic conceptions of government identified in Section 1.2, we are compelled to seek a rationale for redistribution in the preferences of citizens as these preferences are conceived and rationalized in conventional neoclassical economics. Doing so denies validity to the claim sometimes made that governments intervene in the distribution of income because they want to redistribute a larger amount than citizens do, because, *ceteris paribus,* if it is citizens and not some outside (benevolent or malevolent) power that wills redistribution, the volume observed will be mandated by these citizens. As with ordinary goods and services, the quantity and quality actually supplied may differ from that desired (see Chapter 2), but that "fact" is irrelevant in deciding if redistribution is or is not based on the preferences of citizens.

When probing the preferences of citizens for redistribution, it is natural to turn one's mind to altruism or, in more technical terms, to the interdependence of utility functions of all or of a subgroup of individuals in a given context. (For models based on that assumption, see among many Boulding, 1962; Vickrey, 1962; and Hochman and Rodgers, 1969). Altruism is without doubt a powerful preferences-based rationale for income redistribution. In a recent survey of the literature on the subject, Harold Hochman (1992, p. 9) speculates that "distributional preferences which center on utility interdependence . . . across time and generations . . . underlie certain social concerns with environmental issues, like depletion of the ozone layer, the survival of endangered species, and global warming." I concur and emphasize that even if we often lack a convincing test that would make it possible to distinguish behaviors that are truly altruistic from those that are essentially self-interested but camouflaged in altruism, it is still possible to put a fairly heavy burden on that concept to explain the redistribution we observe. Other preferences-based rationales are available. I look at three of them and conclude that, together with altruism, they provide a strong explanation for the redistribution we observe in the world.

In *The Calculus of Consent,* James Buchanan and Gordon Tullock (1962, pp. 192–5), on the basis of commonly accepted assumptions about the preferences of citizens and about the likely high cost of enforcing private contracts in this domain, argue that some redistribution can be rationalized as "income insurance" collectively provided but anchored in the preferences of individuals. More recently, Louis Lévy-Garboua (1991) in a thought-provoking model different from that of Buchanan and Tullock but with roots in the same preoccupation, has shown, *inter alia,* that if citizens are assumed to have a demand for self-insurance against certain risks because they believe that their own final position in the distribution of income will be determined by unpredictable events, as if through the drawing of a social lottery, and if that demand for self-insurance is formulated by all citizens under a binding Rousseauesque social contract, these citizens will want some income redistribution as a way to satisfy that demand. (For other developments in the same general frame of reference, see Polinsky, 1974, and Zeckhauser, 1974). All these models, incidentally, provide robust microeconomic foundations for a long tradition of writings that goes back at least to William Beveridge's (1942, 1945) rationalization of redistribution as "social insurance."

Addressing an altogether different preoccupation, Gary Becker and Kevin Murphy (1988), building on some earlier work of Becker (1967), show that if the relations of parents and children are assumed to be embodied in incomplete contracts – contracts whose terms can be monitored by the contracting parties but cannot be verified by a third party and cannot therefore be legally enforced – and in addition if it is assumed that children cannot commit to eventually compensate their parents for investments in the children's well-being, parents who plan to make gifts to their children, leave them bequests, or do both will invest optimally in these children because "they can force even selfish children to repay them for expenditure on . . . human capital" (Becker and Murphy 1988, p. 5) by simply withholding all or part of the gifts and/or bequests. Parents who are too poor to make gifts or bequests do not have that option and may not, as a consequence, optimally invest in their children. An (implicit) intergenerational "social compact" mediated by governments can remedy the contractual failure. In Becker and Murphy's (1988, p. 9) words "[t]axes on adults help finance efficient investments in children. In return, adults receive public pensions and medical payments when old. This compact tries to achieve for poorer and middle-level families what richer families tend to achieve without government help; namely, efficient levels of investment in children and support for elderly parents." (See Appendix A for an application of the Becker–Murphy model to the problem of long-term budget deficits.)

The third and last preferences-based rationale for redistribution to be noted in these pages is provided by the work of a number of scholars studying various aspects of the relationship between property rights and the distribution of income and wealth (Johnsen, 1986; Allen, 1991). Recently Curtis Eaton and William White (1991) – apparently unaware of Buchanan's (1975) pioneering analysis of the same problem – have proposed an elegant game-theoretic model that nicely captures an aspect of the question. In a two-person, two-period economy in which each person can consume, plant, and harvest or steal corn, Eaton and White show that the distribution of wealth or of initial endowments can be in some circumstances an important complement to legal enforcement mechanisms supporting property rights, when an enforcement mechanism is defined by two variables: the probability of being apprehended after a theft and the size of the sanction – the amount to be restituted if apprehended. The point is that, as their model is set up, efficiency requires that in the first period both persons plant their corn, but whether they do so depends on the cost of enforcing property rights, which in turn depends on the distribution of wealth. At the end of their paper, Eaton and White (1991, p. 350) note that many students of regulation have pointed to the fact that small operators in, say, oil fields and the fisheries often receive "favorable treatment" by regulators. They also note that "the standard interpretation" of that treatment is based on "equity concerns and political lobbying." They then conclude by saying that although they do not rule out these possibilities, another explanation exists, "namely that enforcement costs may be lower when small operators are given more to lose." (Remarkably, many years before, Beveridge, 1945, had placed on the title page of his report a quotation taken from Charlotte Brontë's *Shirley* that reads: "Misery generates hate" and, no doubt, theft as an emanation of that hatred.) (See Appendix B for an application of the Buchanan–Eaton–White model to the question of the power of "small" groups.)

All the foregoing preferences-based rationales for redistribution imply that when redistribution is implemented it improves economic efficiency strictly understood, just as the building of bridges, the delivery of mail, the administration of justice, and the dredging of canals do. For this reason, one should use the words *transfers* and *redistribution* sparingly. I find it useful to think of the supply of income insurance, human capital, secure property rights, and other amenities acquired by income redistribution as being nothing but the provision of goods and services. Using the words *goods* and *services* instead of transfers and redistribution is also a reminder that if we believe that governments systematically redistribute more than the nonmarket sector does or, for that matter, redistribute less, it is because we think of them in organicist, despotic, or monolithic terms (see Section 1.2). Replacing the language of transfers by that of goods and services is not mandatory, but it does help to avoid pitfalls in thinking about a difficult subject.

1.2.   Models of government

The discussion in this section is based on a classification of various models of government articulated on or organized around the captions of "doctrines" and "traditions." Because the presentation may not be as limpid as it should be, the argument at certain junctures may be difficult to follow. To help the reader, I provide a classificatory nomenclature in Table 1.1, the sole purpose of which is to serve as a guide. It can be disregarded with no loss of substance.

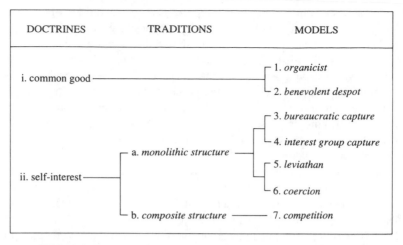

DOCTRINES	TRADITIONS	MODELS

i. common good ——————————— ⌐ 1. *organicist*
                              ⌐ 2. *benevolent despot*

                    ⌐ a. *monolithic structure* ——— ⌐ 3. *bureaucratic capture*
                                                    ⌐ 4. *interest group capture*
ii. self-interest —   ⌐ 5. *leviathan*
                                                    ⌐ 6. *coercion*
                    ⌐ b. *composite structure* ——— 7. *competition*

Table 1.1. Seven models of government.

All discussions of the place and role of governments in the affairs of human beings and of societies, whether they be directly or only tangentially concerned with the subject, rest on one of two basic presuppositions or assumptions that provide foundations to what, with only slight exaggeration, we may call "doctrines." In this chapter's presentation, the first of these is based on the presupposition, which to give it saliency I express in polar form, that governments are embodiments of the common will and that as such they pursue the common good. We may call it the *common-good doctrine.* The second and opposite doctrine says, again expressed in the form of a polar assumption, that governments are nothing but the embodiments of the interests of those who inhabit the halls of power or of those with whom they collude, or both. It could be labeled the *self-interest doctrine.*

It is easy to raise what are essentially unanswerable questions about the definition of the words *common* and *good* in the expression "common-good doctrine," but I propose that we leave these aside and, as do most of those who function under the assumption's sweep, proceed as if the two terms could be rigorously and operationally defined. If we do this, we must recognize that the common-good doctrine has nurtured two different models of government. The first, which can be called the *organicist model,* recognizes no autonomous preferences or demands of individuals different from those that are ascribed to the collectivity. Historically, the organicist model has had more sway whenever, through one mechanism or another, collectivities have refused to conceive of themselves as groupings of distinct persons but instead have defined themselves as made up of individuals of a particular creed, cranial specification, ethnicity, blood type, or language. The second model that is rooted in the common-good doctrine recognizes the preferences and demands of individual persons but proceeds on the supposition that these preferences and demands can somehow be aggregated into a collective welfare or utility function that is given expression by a body or institution – in effect, a benevolent despot – which, it is usually further assumed, maximizes the collective function.[5] We may call this model the *benevolent despot model*.

The two models are very different from each other in conception and in consequences, but they share one important element. Governments that embody the singular preferences and demands of collectivities and governments that are in the hands of benevolent despots who have aggregated every person's preferences or demands know what is "good" for "their" citizens and, essentially as a matter of definition, single-mindedly secure that common good. Why? Because, for the first, there is only one "good" – the same for all – and because that "good" is exactly the same as the one wanted by the government. And, for the second, because governments are by assumption benevolent.

Turning our attention to the self-interest doctrine, we note that this doctrine has nourished two traditions of discourse: one based on the proposition that governments are *monolithic* structures and another on the proposition that they are *composite* structures.

The first of these traditions sustains four kinds of models of government. It is useful to divide them into two subsets, each containing two groups of models. In the first group of the first subset, the candidates and parties that represent the successful electoral coalition (or, for that matter, the dictator who has seized power) are captured by the bureaucratic agents that have been employed to implement the winning platform (or the dictator's program). These agents do not, however, produce and supply the bundle of goods and services catalogued in the platform or in the program or, more exactly, do not produce them in the desired volume, but, as good captors are wont to do, produce and supply what they want for themselves. For those who choose to use these *bureaucratic capture models,* governments are monoliths in the hands of bureaucrats, and although elections are part of the landscape, they are in effect mirages and illusions with no real significance.

In the second group of models of the first subset, the representatives of the electorally successful coalition (or, again, the dictator) are not captured by their bureaucratic agents. Instead, both representatives and bureaucrats (or dictator and bureaucrats) are shanghaied by rent-seeking interest groups. In these *interest-group capture models,* governments are, in effect, conceived as

<hr/>

5. I do not have in mind a collective welfare function such as the one that preoccupied Kenneth Arrow (1951), but one like that found in conventional Welfare Economics. For the distinction between the two, see Samuelson (1967).

producers and suppliers of rents. When governments appear to be supplying "ordinary" goods and services – building hydroelectric dams, constructing roads, broadcasting television programs, or collecting statistics – they are, these models assert, engaged in creating rents for the purpose of redistributing them. One should add that scholars [see, for example, Landes and Posner (1975)] who cultivate these models have displayed considerable ingenuity in developing arguments that purport to show that what looks like competition among politicians, bureaucrats, and others (for example, judges) who work in governments is, when properly conceived, like elections, nothing but mirage and illusion. Governments, they argue, are really monoliths, notwithstanding the appearances. (For a critical assessment of Landes and Posner's analysis, see Appendix C.) Finally, when it is assumed that monolithic governments are efficient, their efficiency is entirely for the benefit of those who control them and is therefore an unqualified calamity for other citizens whose preferences and demands, if they are attended to at all, are satisfied only by accident.

It is intriguing that though they are diametrically opposed in conception and though they are derived from very different methodologies, the organicist and the capture models that derive from the governments-as-monoliths tradition predict that those who are not organically incarnated in the apparatus of state for the first and those who cannot collude with the governing coterie for the second will be abused and exploited. That being said, observation reveals that organicist (in our times typically nationalist) governments are often intolerant vis-à-vis their "minorities" – those who are not of the "proper" creed, blood, ethnic background, or language – and that they sometimes act to suppress them. Governments-as-monoliths of the capture variety, however, being able to extract larger rents when their citizenry is more numerous and wealthy, are generally more supportive of economic growth and therefore more tolerant of behaviors that are economically productive.

In the second subset of models that grow in the governments-as-monoliths soil, the notion of monopoly is not associated with that of capture by non-elected agents; it is simply assumed that governments are monopolies. It is useful to distinguish again between two groups of models in this second subset. In one, governments are treated as leviathans maximizing their own surplus. An important part of the analysis of these models seeks to convince that the assumption of monopoly is reasonable even though some features of governmental organization appear to be inconsistent with the assumption. In *leviathan models,* it is possible to assume that the governing coterie is forced to cater to the preferences and demands of citizens during a short period preceding elections, but in the most famous version of these models – that of Brennan and Buchanan (1980, pp. 6–8) – elections are denied even that capacity.

In the second group of models in the second subset, monopoly is over coercion or, in the words of Joseph Stiglitz (1989), over compulsion and not over surplus or rent. Those who ply the leviathan models have devoted considerable effort, as I have just noted, trying to convince us that governments are really surplus-maximizing monopolies. Those who work what we may call the *coercion model* have basically taken the assumption of monopoly over coercion to be more or less obvious. Thomas Borcherding (1983) simply takes it as fact. Stiglitz (1989) argues that we all have the basic freedom to exit organizations that inflict on us demands that we find unacceptable but that we do not have the freedom to exit the state. That it is not possible, in some basic sense, to exit the state is easily granted, but to have power the coercion model also needs the first part of the foregoing proposition: namely, that exit from other coercive organizations is possible at reasonable cost. The evidence points in the other direction. Families coerce (think of abused children and battered wives who do not exit), churches coerce (think of the large number of Jews who at different periods of history well understood that their life and property were more secure if they converted to Christianity; and do not forget the Inquisition), labor unions coerce gently when helped by governments and violently when not; guilds coerce by forcing excessively long apprenticeships on sons to whom fathers and associates do not grant the freedom to choose crafts other than their own; corporate bodies, including universities, coerce by demanding that their employees kowtow to their "cultures." The list could be extended. On the assumption of monopoly over coercion, Stiglitz (1989) adroitly explains many organizational features of democratic governments – features that I will later associate with composite structures and with competition – which, he reasons, are there to soften the blow of compulsion. If governments do not have a monopoly over coercion, as I have just argued they do not, it must be that one can explain the existence of divided powers and of competition on other grounds. And so it is. In concluding this brief discussion of coercion models, I mention the recent work of Matthew Palmer (1992) who builds on the assumption that because citizens have an incentive to falsify their preferences for the (Samuelsonian) public goods they really want, they will have a demand for coercion that guarantees that the public goods are effectively provided. The approach has the virtue of providing a "democratic" rationale for coercion and as such is a contribution to coercion models. But the assumption of monopoly combined with the demand assumption leads to the conclusion that there is less coercion than would obtain under competition – a most undesirable but inevitable conclusion that Palmer, however, does not draw.

We can now turn our attention to the last group of models, which have roots in the doctrine that governments are inhabited by self-interested individuals. In these models, governments are not conceived to be monolithic but composite structures in which powers are divided between a multiplicity of autonomous and quasi-autonomous centers of power. It is because of that feature that, in labeling the whole of Part I, I have made use of *The Federalist's* (Hamilton, Jay, and Madison, 1787–8) felicitous description of federal states as "compound republics" and have called the governments analyzed in *competition models, compound governments.*

In these competition models, powers are not only separate – a notion I discuss in some detail in Chapter 3, Section 3.1 – but the centers of power of which compound governments are constituted are assumed to be "balanced" one vis-à-vis the other and to "check" one another.[6] As we shall discover, checks and balances are not the only form competition can take, though it is most certainly an important and all-pervasive one.

There is a school of thought, with roots and branches almost everywhere, that derives from Walter Bagehot's classic *The English Constitution* (1867) and that associates the notions of the separation (or division) of powers and of checks and balances with the American congressional system of government. As I will mention again (in Chapter 3, Section 3.5), Bagehot and the school of thought he inspired and inspires are simply wrong on this point.[7] First, the idea of a separation of powers has occupied the minds of some of the best political philosophers and political scientists for more than two millennia, as the superb monograph by Epaminondas Panagopoulos (1985) abundantly documents. The ancients and many others closer to us were concerned with an optimum separation and balance between the organs or branches of government that often, though not always, were the monarchy, the aristocracy, and the democracy (eventually called the "citizenry"); and they worked hard at formulating principles that would guide them in designing "good" governments.[8] The American Constitution mechanically borrows from these principles: For monarchy read unelected President, for aristocracy read unelected Senate, and for democracy read elected House of Representatives to obtain the *exact* design of the government contained in the 1787 Constitution. The notions of a separation of powers and of a balance among them and the derived notion of checks and balances are, therefore, not exclusively Ameri-

---

6. I do no more than mention, and only in this footnote, a separation of powers that in democracies is nowadays so widely accepted that it is no longer mentioned, namely, that between church and state – a separation inaugurated by the American and French revolutions – which eliminated "the use of religion by the state to reinforce and extend its authority . . . and the use of the state by the clergy to impose their doctrines and rules on others" (Lewis, 1992, p. 52).

7. Mount (1992, Chapter 2) provides an excellent review and analysis of the work of two (besides Bagehot) of the greatest pillars of that school of thought whom he calls "the simplifiers"; namely, Albert V. Dicey and Ivor Jennings.

8. I refer those who believe that the word "branch" should be restricted to the American Congressional system of government to its use by Mount (1992 at, for example, p. 113), who is solely concerned with the British Parliamentary system.

can. What is borrowed and has been experienced before (Renaissance Venice – a celebrated case among many – immediately comes to mind) cannot be exclusively one's own.

Bagehot and his school are wrong for another reason. In the Westminster model of parliamentary government as it exists today in Canada, say, there may not be much of a *formal* separation of powers and possibly not much balance between the Executive (the Cabinet) and the governing party. But who will deny that genuine separation exists between the judicial branch and the other branches of government? Who will deny that, properly empowered by a Charter of Rights and Freedoms, the judiciary is capable of checking the executive and the legislative branches, and that it does? And who will deny that opposition parties, during "Question Periods" in the House of Commons, are capable of checking the governing party and do so? I conclude that it is unproductive to forgo the use of empirically apposite concepts for the pretense of defending a model of parliamentary government that was already obsolete when Bagehot published his monograph.[9]

In a remarkable and immensely useful book, Ferdinand Mount (1992) shows that Bagehot and those who followed him promoted views of the British Constitution that were essentially reflections of the *zeitgeist* of the epoch in which they lived and of their class and, as such, misrepresented some of the more fundamental features of that Constitution. Mount forcefully argues that "the simplifiers" (see footnote 7) not only prevented the development of a model that would have permitted a better understanding of the British Constitution and of the parliamentary government on which it rests but had a crippling influence on the actual functioning of that system by restraining its natural evolution.

Pointing out that the British Constitution is not so much unwritten as unassembled in one place, Mount marshals a large amount of evidence related to constitutional, legal, parliamentary, and administrative practices to establish that the British Constitution and parliamentary system have been for centuries and remain based on the principles of the separation of powers and checks and balances. It is impossible to summarize that evidence here. Let me, to illustrate, mention two small points. Mount documents that it is absolutely contrary to the facts of history to suppose that the Cabinet can act as if the backbenchers of the governing party are passive. He shows that an informal separation of powers between the two centers of power exists and that it has consequences. With much appropriateness, Mount (1992, p. 101) insists that for England, which is typically assumed not to have any charter or bill of

9. *"The English Constitution* [was] first composed as a series of essays for *The Fortnightly* [and] published in book form in 1867 – the very year of Disraeli's Reform Act which abruptly and finally ended the period of classical parliamentary government it describes" (Crossman, "Introduction," *The English Constitution,* 1963, p. 1).

rights, "the Magna Carta of John, the Magna Carta of Edward I, the Petition of Right, the Bill of Rights, the Act of Settlement, and so on . . . were intended as a permanent record and entrenchment" of rights.

Many more studies of the quality and power of Mount's would be welcome as evidence of the pervasiveness of intragovernmental competition. Sometimes, however, the evidence is almost more commanding because the author does not intend to make a point. In three brief but riveting pages, in a book that purports to be no more than a narrative, seasoned with comments and anecdotes, of Michel Rocard's three-year tenure as France's Prime Minister (1988–91), Jean-Paul Huchon (1993, pp. 47–9) makes the point, without using the language, that following de Gaulle's presidency, the Executive Branch of the French government, with or without "cohabitation" – one party controls the President's *Palais de l'Elysée* and another the Prime Minister's *Hôtel de Matignon* – was characterized by checking. As Huchon notes, competitive behavior of that sort cannot be inferred from a reading of the Constitution of the Fifth Republic, but it is nonetheless a product of that Constitution. The absence of appropriate concepts notwithstanding, much of Huchon's excellent book focuses on the operations of checks in the French parliamentary government's bicephalic Executive Branch between 1988 and 1991.

Having said all this, I wish to defend myself against the accusation too easily made that what I have just argued denies any genuine differences between parliamentary and congressional governments. The problem is one of the level of abstraction selected to analyze a particular problem. An example may help clarify what I have in mind. The theory of supply and demand and the derived theory of markets that economists have developed can be applied, giving proper attention to market structure, to virtually all traded goods and services. At the level of theory an apparatus exists that is fairly general and is capable of application to a broad range of institutional contexts. If, however, an economist wants to study the market for baseball players or the market for pollinating bees, he or she will have to do what Simon Rottenberg (1956) and Steven Cheung (1973) did and sift through a great amount of descriptive and institutional material. These two studies – and others – show first that the same theory of markets can be used to organize and to guide the analysis and, second, that the market for baseball players and that for pollinating bees are completely different from each other. If, therefore, at some level of abstraction it is possible to analyze all governments with a general conceptual apparatus, that does not deny the possibility of genuine fundamental differences between types of governments.

One of the reasons so many students of politics and of governmental systems are unable to detect any separation of powers and any checks and balances in parliamentary governments is that they have locked themselves

not the case, the remainder of this section identifies four concepts
cy that can be found in the literature of Public Choice, Public
s, and Welfare Economics and offers a brief sketch of their content
ugh to facilitate identification and a selection.[10]

gh the four concepts do differ from one another, it is important not to
e the differences. In some cases, the differences have their origin in
s that are emphasized: For example, one concept of efficiency em-
ransactions costs, and another neglects these costs altogether. Rec-
n is then easily effected. If differences should not be exaggerated,
ould they be dismissed. They can and have played an important role
y the public sector has historically been conceived and analyzed.

t prejudice as to its relative importance, let me begin with a notion
cy that can be called "welfare-economics" efficiency, a conception
es from theories of public goods and optimal taxation. According to
f these theories, public goods are efficiently supplied when, for each
m, the sum over persons of the marginal rate of substitution between
goods and some preselected *numéraire* is equal to the marginal rate
rmation between the goods and the *numéraire* – to the real produc-
f the goods. That efficient supply condition is not, however, attain-
use, in the context of the voluntary provision that is postulated, all
ave an incentive to falsify their preferences. The "pseudo" prices
on, 1969) or taxprices implicit in the efficient provision conditions
ore not feasible either. Under these circumstances, efficiency on the
requires that the revenues needed to pay for the public goods be
in the most neutral way possible – that is, in such a way as to
the excess burden of taxation. In the Welfare Economics *weltan-*
, income redistribution is exogenous – it is founded on a preference,
m, or precept vested in an ethical observer or planner and embodied
welfare function (SWF). Optimal tax theory's ambition is to be able
planner what should be done to obtain a more equal distribution of
while minimizing the total burden of taxation. The theory builds on
nptions: First, that a more equal distribution calls for higher margin-
s and therefore for heavier excess burdens of taxation – a cost; and
hat a more equal distribution, when the marginal utility of income is
g for everyone, improves the welfare of the less-well-off more than
s that of the better-off – a benefit. By choosing negative and positive

no claim to completeness and, consequently, the conceptions of efficiency embodied
ssions like deficit reduction, duplication of functions, devolution of responsibilities,
vatization – currently popular in political, financial, and media circles – are not
ed. In any case, these conceptions have received little systematic attention in the
e.

into a legal-constitutional frame of mir
standing arrangements and behaviors
precedent. The legal-constitutional
quence: It induces those so gifted to th
that governments do or do not possess.
nearly continuous variable – points on
take virtually any value between zero

How are we to choose among these
answer to this question is that the selec
of congruence that the models have wit
than done. Indeed, as I have emphasize
polar types and as such are neglectful
Second, in some instances, the origina
and some of their components recombi
real world. For example, an organicist-n
or another, may be a composite structu
though with less intensity and less persi
structure. These considerations and oth
mit and will defend in the chapters tha
embodied in the tradition of government
the *self-interest doctrine* provides the be
ment appropriate for an understanding
mocracies of the world – the mature,
democracies of Canada, India, Israel, Jap
tries of Western Europe; the chronically
and Mexico; and the budding democracie
Europe and Russia. It also provides the
recommendations that would make gov
more efficient, in a sense to be determin

In a nutshell, this book defends the ide
cies just listed are compound governmen
mous and quasi-autonomous centers of
ministries, divisions, authorities, corpora
that these centers compete with one anotl
the goods and services demanded by citiz

1.3.   Concepts of efficiency

The words *efficiency* and especially *ineffi*
sions of governmental policies – in partic
embody the public finances of jurisdiction
thinking that the concepts these words ide

that this
of effici
Economi
– just er
   Altho
exaggera
the factc
phasizes
onciliati
neither s
in the w
   With
of effici
that der
the first
one of t
the pub
of trans
tion cos
able be
citizens
(Samue
are the
tax sid
collect
minim
schau
moral
in a so
to tell
incom
two as
al tax
secon
decrea
it wor

10. I m
    in
    an
    dis
    lite

income tax rates that balance costs and benefits at the margin, an optimal rate schedule is obtained that is equitable and also efficient because it makes the total burden of taxation as small as possible. The problem is more complex, however, than the foregoing discussion seems to make it because, among other complications, the earning capacities of people and the distribution of these capacities vary and are not easy to ascertain, because the responses of people to taxation vary and are difficult to observe, and not least because a choice must be made from a variety of specific parameterizations of the SWF.

From the perspective of this study, two features of welfare-economics efficiency in respect of the public finances are important. The first is the assumption that at the level of individual citizens and per force at the level of the organization of governments, there are no *behavioral* links or connections between the volume and the quality of goods and services (including redistribution) provided by governments and the taxes they collect to pay for them, beyond the necessary accounting equality of outlays and revenues plus debt. The assumption is most clearly and succinctly stated by Stiglitz (1989, p. 22), who is not discussing welfare-economics efficiency, however. Citizens, he writes, "do not assess the value of the services provided to them by the government, and pay a commensurate amount." The assumption could be easily rationalized to be a consequence that in the presence of public goods people will misrepresent their preferences; the assumption is, however, much more ancient than the discovery of this voluntary provision failure theorem. It is assumed and is reflected in academic curricula and in the organization of textbooks that decisions by governments in respect of revenues and expenditures are made completely separately. The recommendation that neutrality be one of the most – and for a group of Public Finance economists, *the* most – important criterion of tax reform derives from that conception of efficiency.

The second feature of welfare-economics efficiency that from the viewpoint of this study must be noted is that efficiency must be exogenously imposed. With one notable but only partial exception that I mention immediately, there does not appear to exist any natural forces at work in the politico-economic universe that prompt governments to become welfare-economics efficient, that is, to supply goods and services and to tax efficiently from a welfare-economics perspective. On the contrary, economists of the Welfare Economics persuasion generally trust governments to deal efficiently with market failures, but see politics – the activities of politicians, bureaucrats, judges, lobbies, electorates, and so on – as an impediment to "good" economic policy.

The exception to which I have just alluded is Becker's (1983, 1985) theory of pressure groups in which competition between groups leads to an efficient tax system, namely, to one that minimizes the excess burden of taxation and is therefore welfare-economics efficient.[11] In Becker's model, however, the interests of those participating in politics are and must be antithetical. In the simplest version with only two groups – one that is taxed, called t and another that is subsidized, labeled s – if the government provides, let us say, \$X of defense, it must be that s benefits from the service and t pays for it. That, I believe, is too limited a domain of application to salvage welfare-economics efficiency from exogenous enforcement.

The second concept of efficiency to be considered can be called "transaction-costs" efficiency. In most applications it pays little attention to public finance problems, although it is preoccupied with questions of logrolling over expenditure projects, pork-barrel politics, and the like. It is for the most part only indirectly concerned with the efficient supply of public goods and the efficient collection of taxes. Like much of the rest of Transaction Costs Economics, it is basically preoccupied with what appears to be the failure of certain mechanisms – in Public Choice theory with failures associated with voting, logrolling, contracting, information requirements, and others – and with the efficiency of the institutional responses to these failures – responses such as reputation, trust, agenda structures, committee systems, seniority, and so on. In an important paper, Donald Wittman (1989) has argued that "democratic political markets are organized to promote wealth-maximizing outcomes" and that "the arguments claiming that economic markets are efficient apply equally well to political markets" (pp. 1395–6). In fact, Wittman has applied to standard arguments for political market failure the logic of Transaction Cost Economics and on the basis of that logic has argued for a presumption that institutional responses to failures of one sort or the other are efficient in the sense of being welfare-maximizing.[12]

Unlike welfare-economics efficiency, which is erected on bodies of theory that except for tax laws, tax codes, and the coefficient of some basic behavioral relationships, has limited use for models of government and of other institutions, transaction-cost efficiency is rich in institutional analysis. It is based on the premise that efficiency is generated by "natural" forces – that it is the product of institutions, arrangements, and understandings that result from self-interest, or competition, or both. Whether, net of the cost of operating these institutions, arrangements, and understandings, it replicates welfare-

---

11. Becker is not a practitioner of Welfare Economics. However, in view of his successful attempt, in particular in his 1985 *Journal of Public Economics* paper, to reconcile his model of politics with some historically important components of Welfare Economics, I feel entitled to place him, at least transitorily, in that tradition.

12. After this study had gone through a final revision, I received from Wittman a manuscript entitled *The Myth of Democratic Failure: Why Political Institutions Are Efficient* (University of Chicago Press, 1995), which extends the argument of the 1989 paper in many interesting dimensions. I regret not having had the manuscript earlier.

economics efficiency is not known. To my knowledge, the problem has not been studied.

A third notion of efficiency in respect of government and of public policies is appropriately called "constitutional" efficiency. Born of Buchanan and Tullock's (1962) distinction between a constitutional or rule-making stage and a policy-making stage as basic elements in the political "calculus of consent," this view states that outcomes will be efficient if unanimity or near-unanimity governs decisions at the constitution-making stage, because under this requirement the rules that will be selected will be the best possible for the individuals who have agreed to them.[13] According to this notion of efficiency, attempts to evaluate the decisions and outcomes of the policy-making stage on the basis of exogenous criteria such as those of welfare-economics efficiency, for example, are fundamentally meaningless if the decisions and outcomes are governed by unanimously or quasi-unanimously agreed-on rules at the constitution-making stage. This does not mean that it is not possible to formulate tax laws and tax codes as well as spending laws and spending codes. In a notable contribution to tax theory, Brennan and Buchanan (1980) have derived a number of propositions about the structure of a constitutionally efficient tax system made up of "in-period" tax laws generated by constitutional rules that had been unanimously agreed on "out-of-period" by the individual members of the jurisdiction.

In his Nobel lecture, Buchanan (1987) argued that this notion of efficiency can be traced back to the work of Knut Wicksell (1896). Wicksell, as Buchanan recognizes, was making the case for unanimity or near-unanimity and for simultaneity of expenditure and revenue decisions at the policy-making stage. But Buchanan argues, given that unanimity or even quasi-unanimity and simultaneity are not achievable in practice at that stage, it is possible to salvage Wicksell's insight that social welfare will be at a maximum only if all individuals are allowed to participate in political decisions, if as it were we transfer the requirement of unanimity or near-unanimity from the policy-making to the constitution- or rule-making stage. I do not take issue with Buchanan's position or deny the validity, in its own frame of reference, of Buchanan and Tullock's notion of constitutional efficiency in government and in politics, but I note, in anticipation of the discussion of the fourth concept of efficiency, that the empirical impossibility of in-period unanimity or quasi-unanimity, which led to the reinterpretation of Wicksell, is only a presumption or at most an observation of the world made without the benefit

13. The distinction was anticipated by Jean-Jacques Rousseau, as the following quotation, taken from Robert Dahl (1956, p. 35), documents: "There is but one law which, from its nature, needs *unanimous* consent. This is the social contract. . . . Apart from this *primitive* contract, the vote of the majority always binds the rest" (my italics). The word *primitive* has many meanings. One of them − surely appropriate in the context − is *original* or *primary*.

of a hypothesis or empirically relevant theory. Indeed, Wicksell himself, Wicksellians, and non-Wicksellians all appear to have understood Wicksell's *A New Principle of Just Taxation* (1896) as a plea for the *reorganization* of governments that would insure unanimity or approximate unanimity as well as simultaneity in respect of expenditure and revenue decisions. The idea that real-world governments may to a degree already be organized to mimic these requirements of efficiency does not appear to have retained much of the attention of scholars. I have already suggested and will later suggest anew that the original Wicksellian model, *with one major amendment related to the presence of competition,* can be used to understand the organization and operation of real-world governments. It is therefore important to look at the conception of efficiency that underlies the original Wicksell model.

Before doing so I must insist, as Buchanan and Tullock (1962) already have, that for constitutional efficiency to obtain, rules devised at the constitution-making stage will demand more than unanimity. They will also have to be designed in a context in which "the individual is *uncertain* as to what his own precise role will be in any one of the whole chain of later collective choices that will actually have to be made" (Buchanan and Tullock, 1962, p. 78, italics in the original) or, put differently, they will have to be made "behind a veil of ignorance" (Rawls, 1971, p. 136). Buchanan and Tullock (1962, pp. 78–9) argue that uncertainty is likely to exist at the constitution-making stage. That may well be the case. For my part, I could give more credence to the presumption if it could be demonstrated that the rules designed at the constitution-making stage were to always *precede* and be *independent* of in-period policies. If constitutions adjust to events that are the product of policymaking or if their evolution is governed by in-period incidents, the presumption of uncertainty or of a veil of ignorance has to be abandoned and with it the presumption of constitutional efficiency even in the presence of near-unanimity. There is a further problem. To be useful constitutional rules must have some degree of permanency, which history tells us is acquired at the cost of some degree of generality and, therefore, imprecision in the formulation and drafting. This makes it possible to apply the rules in circumstances that resemble but are not completely identical to the original ones. The generality and imprecision also call for doctrines of interpretation and for the development of a body of jurisprudence, all of which complicate the problem of enforcement. If because of this, out-of-period rules are not strictly binding on in-period decisions, it becomes difficult to know whether outcomes are constitutionally efficient or not.

Constitutional efficiency is often described by reference to a game such as, let us say, hockey. Given that the rules that govern how hockey is played are, to a rough approximation, set out-of-period and are to all evidence unanimously accepted by players, referees, coaches, and club owners, we have to conclude that hockey is constitutionally efficient. That in turn obliges us to conclude that self-interest constrained by competition produces (approximately) constitutionally efficient outcomes or, to put it differently, that natural forces exist that operate in such a way as to generate constitutional efficiency. However, it is not obvious that politics and hockey are games of the same genus. This is a question that begs for much more attention.

The fourth and last notion of efficiency in government to be considered can be called "Wicksell–Lindahl," or simply "Wicksellian," efficiency. It pertains to the connection between the costs and the benefits of publicly supplied goods and services or, to put it differently, to the link between the taxprices citizens pay for the goods and services provided by governments and the valuation these same citizens place on these goods and services. The connection is assumed to exist at the level of individual citizens and to take the form of well-behaved neoclassical demand functions derived in standard fashion by the maximization of individual utility functions subject to linear budget constraints (see Chapter 2). The question of efficiency then is resolved into a question about the ability of governments – and of other institutions (see Chapter 12) – to provide goods and services in quantities (and qualities) that, given their taxprices, locate individuals *on* their demand curves. If governments can do this for all citizens, the supply of goods and services is Pareto-efficient or, equivalently, the utility loss suffered by citizens is zero. If the quantities and the qualities of the goods and services supplied exceed or fall short of the volumes and qualities desired at the given taxprices – citizens are off their demand curves – the utility loss endured by citizens is positive.[14]

Knut Wicksell (1896) was the first to recognize – and a long line of economists after him [for example, Lindahl (1919), Musgrave (1938, 1959), Johansen (1965), Buchanan (1967), and Kolm (1968)] have concurred – that if collective decisions about expenditures *and* revenues are made *simultaneously* and *unanimously,* a connection or link between costs and benefits (i.e., between taxprices and valuations) will be forged and the resulting collective decisions will be Pareto-efficient and utility losses will be equal to zero. The reason for this is simple: If a marginal project is approved by all participants and its cost attached to the participants in proportion to the marginal benefit they will derive from it, no other choice can dominate that one. [Among an assortment of proofs, see Johansen (1965, pp. 129–40) for a good one].

Wicksell was concerned with the design of legislative assemblies (parliaments and congresses) and assumed that those elected to these assemblies would have perfect information about the preferences of all their constituents. The Pareto-optimal character of legislative decisions would therefore auto-

14. If citizens find themselves *off* their demand curves because of some irreducible transaction costs, such as a lack of information caused by large information costs, the outcome will be efficient if utility losses are otherwise minimized.

matically extend to all persons forming the collectivities. As noted earlier, Wicksell and his followers never managed to convince themselves that their analysis had much actual empirical content, hence its normative use by Wicksellians. An important stumbling ground in applying the construction to the real world has always been that simultaneity would seem to preclude unanimity. In Paul Samuelson's (1969, p. 501) words: "Why should one man not refuse to go to a particular Pareto-optimal point in the hope of being able to better himself by refusing to make the vote unanimous?" The Wicksellian connection, it would seem, disintegrates in the face of a Prisoners' Dilemma problem.

This logical challenge notwithstanding, it is meaningful to inquire which of the four concepts of efficiency we should select, and it is appropriate to answer that it should be the one most congruent with the model of government imposed on us by the facts. For example, if the model of government that has most power in describing real-world governments and in offering a rationale for their behavior is the model of competitive compound governments and if the concept of efficiency most congruent with that model is that of Wicksell–Lindahl efficiency, then that is the concept we should adopt.

I have already said that I will show that the model of competitive compound government is the one most capable of describing what governments actually do. I will also opt for Wicksell–Lindahl efficiency. It would, therefore, appear that I should at this juncture begin to describe how competition in compound governments generates outcomes that are Wicksell–Lindahl-efficient. Such a description would have to be based on the assumption that intragovernmental competition *alone* induces governments to automatically cater to the preferences and demands of citizens – that intragovernmental competition *alone* begets democracy. Such an assumption is untenable. Before undertaking the analysis of how intragovernmental competition leads to Wicksell–Lindahl efficiency – to the creation or molding of what I call the *Wicksellian Connection* – I must therefore pause to argue that competition can generate Wicksell–Lindahl efficiency only if a further condition is simultaneously satisfied. These two conditions or requisites will insure the existence of democracy.

1.4.   Requisites of democracy

In his well-known *A Preface to Democratic Theory* (1956), Robert Dahl suggests that democratic theory ". . . is concerned with processes by which citizens exert a relatively high degree of control over leaders" (p. 3). This statement is imprecise, but it does capture something that seems to be absolutely fundamental to what we sense constitutes a democratic order and it can therefore serve as an introduction to the discussion of the two conditions or, as the title to this section labels them, of the two requisites of that kind of order.[15] I begin by accepting Dahl's criticism of what he calls "Madisonian democracy" – a criticism based on an exegesis of Madison's and his contemporaries' writings that centers on the concept of "tyranny" in the Madisonian construction and that shows the concept to be flawed and not appropriate to the subject matter. I propose to replace that concept and, through this substitution, rescue the Madisonian paradigm from the fate to which Dahl's criticism has condemned it. Because of that substitution, I refer to the new model as one of neo-Madisonian democracy.[16]

In *The Federalist* (1787–8) and elsewhere (see Dahl, 1956, Chapter 1, for references), James Madison was in all likelihood not the first, but he was arguably the most influential person to propose that at a minimum two conditions or requisites had to be simultaneously satisfied to insure the existence of democratic order. The first of these, which has been embraced by conventional wisdom, by Public Choice Theory – the logo on *Public Choice,* the journal, is a stylized ballot – and by a significant volume of scholarship, is that some fraction of the population must be able to signal its preferences, needs, demands, frustrations, or what not at a ballot box. For Madison, that fraction was very small; for John Stuart Mill and other nineteenth-century writers, it was larger; and for most of us today who look at the matter from the perspective of universal suffrage, all these fractions seem to be small indeed. The question of the size of the franchise is important, but from a Madisonian perspective it is dominated by the question of the simple *existence* of a capacity on the part of some citizens, at points in time that are not too far apart, to cast a meaningful vote.

In the Madisonian *weltanschauung,* whatever the electoral rule, elections will beget "factions" or clusters of interests that inevitably seek to dominate the political process. There can be majority and minority factions, and their domination of the political process is identified by Madison with tyranny. To control minority factions, Madison recommends using the "republican principle," which is in effect nothing more than majority rule. To control and, at the limit, to suppress majority tyranny, the exercise of political power must be divided – something that calls for the introduction of composite structures and

---

15. What the virtues of democracy are and where they are to be found are broad and complicated questions that continue to receive considerable attention. This section is not unrelated to these debates, but its purpose is to state and examine two conditions that must necessarily be met if Wicksellian Connections (or Wicksell–Lindahl efficiency) are to exist.

16. Those interested in textual exegesis know that the meaning placed on words like *democracy* and *republicanism* by Madison and his contemporaries differ, often greatly, from that given them in contemporary discourse. I follow Dahl in using these words in today's acceptation.

of checks and balances inside these structures and, better still, inside governmental systems.[17]

From a logical point of view, the main problem with the model of Madisonian democracy is to be found in the notion of tyranny. As Dahl has shown, the concept is intractable and must be jettisoned. If the Madisonian "vision" – to use a Schumpeterian expression – is to be salvaged and given form, the concept must be replaced. The question, then, is: What can we put in its place? There are in principle many alternatives open to us, but one of these begs for special attention, especially in an exercise that, like this one, wants to be preeminently positive or descriptive. That alternative is *the supply of goods and services* as these are defined in Section 1.1. Madison argued for elections combined with divided powers (and checks and balances) to control and, at the limit, expunge tyranny; I will argue for the very same combination as the way to obtain an efficient supply of goods and services, where efficiency is defined on Wicksell–Lindahl lines.

Why insist on the need for competitive electoral contests on the one hand *and* divided powers with the accompanying checks and balances and other forms of competition on the other, with both in place and operating at the same time? Would not electoral contests *or* checks and balances be sufficient? To answer these questions, we must examine the implications for a theory of democracy of the assumptions that the essentials of politics are fully encapsulated in electoral contests or, alternatively, that these essentials are completely captured by checks and balances or intragovernmental competition. I look at each in turn.

Assume, then, that two, three, or even four centers of power are elected by a fraction of the citizenry but that by construction there are no checks and balances – no competition – governing the interaction of these elected centers.[18] The implicit assumption of Public Choice and of other bodies of theory that under these circumstances one must do as if there were only one center of power called "the" government is almost mandatory. If, furthermore, we assume, as is done in standard theory in response, one supposes, to the beckonings of the real world, that elections take place at intervals measured in

17. I use the expression "governmental systems" to refer to the set of all governments that one finds in every society. The expression is an analog to the word *industry*, which is used in microeconomics to encompass all firms that produce a commodity and its substitutes. It is also analogous to the word *industry* in being, like it, imprecise. (See Chapter 7 for a more elaborate discussion of the concept.)

18. It makes no difference for the argument of this section whether voting is assumed to be deterministic or probabilistic, or in the last analysis, whether the voting equilibrium is exogenously enforced (structure induced) or endogenously determined. As will become clear in the next chapter, I have opted for the probability voting model for the theory of Politics and Public Finance suggested in this volume. The reason for that choice will become apparent in that chapter.

years, we are led to the conclusion that electoral platforms – electoral promises – are not only central to but are the quintessence of politics.

In that frame of reference, the electoral promises embodied in platforms are
what politics is all about simply because the platform that is successful in the
electoral contest is the one that will be implemented. It becomes of central
importance therefore, to focus, to the exclusion of almost everything else, on
whether the electoral rules in place are efficient and stable, on whether the
electoral platforms of political parties converge, on whether different electoral
rules lead to different platforms, on whether votes are efficiently and fairly
converted into seats, and so on. A theory of politics based on the assumption
of a single center of power elected on a given electoral platform cannot,
however, have a meaningful supply side because, by construction and to
remain internally consistent, it has to hold that nothing of significance takes
place between elections except the diligent implementation of the electoral
platform marred only by mistakes and fortuitous exogenous disturbances.

Before considering the problem posed by the fact that citizens may be
uninformed about electoral platforms or that electoral promises may lack
credibility, let me note that a theory of democracy erected on a premise of
politics as electoral contests and nothing more sometimes has important things
to say about what goes on in the real world simply because elections are
important. It also inevitably misses so much that it becomes a fertile breeding
ground for models of bureaucratic capture and rent-seeking that often, sometimes explicitly [see Becker (1983)], do away with elections altogether.

It has been recognized for some time [see Downs, 1957; Key, 1966;
Fiorina, 1981; and Collier, McKelvey, Ordeshook, and Williams (1987)] that
because citizens rationally lack information about electoral promises or because promises are seldom if ever completely credible, it is best to shift the
focus from promises and platforms to the past performance of governing
parties – to shift from an assumption of prospective to one of retrospective
voting. My concern here is not with whether concentrating on performance
improves the capacity of voting models or with whether it provides a more
solid foundation to the "yardstick" or "tournament" competition models of the
sort proposed by Pierre Salmon (1987a; 1987b). I am instead solely concerned
with whether shifting from an assumption of prospective to one of retrospective voting provides us with a theory capable of tracking on a more or less
continuous basis the level, composition, and growth of government-supplied
goods and services (including regulation and redistribution) and the level,
structure, and growth of taxation (including debt). My concern is not whether
performance can explain voting but the much more consequential question of
whether voting can explain performance and, therefore, supply. To this last
question, the answer must without doubt be "no" for the same reason that
models of demand in standard neoclassical microeconomic theory, though

they tell us about the composition of the bundle of goods and services that firms will want to produce, do not tell us anything about supply per se and about the forces operating on that side of the market. In addition to a theory of demand, neoclassical theory has rightly developed a theory of supply. Hence, the necessity of a neo-Madisonian theory of democracy in which elections are important but in which at the minimum competition, in the form of checks and balances and in other forms also, plays a central role on the supply side.

In conclusion, for a number of reasons (not least their preoccupation with factions) Madisonians, at least in the early days of the American Republic, were very suspicious of political parties. They seriously toyed with the idea of elections undertaken in a context in which parties did not exist. They did not conceive of political parties in the way suggested by Galeotti and Breton (1986), Wittman (1989, pp. 1397–99), and others as institutions through which the "contractual enforcement" problems characterizing the relationship of citizens (the principals) to politicians (the agents) are resolved, at least in part. Neither did they think of political parties as organizations more capable than individuals acting on their own of amassing large sums of money and of mobilizing the energies of many persons and, therefore, more capable of giving to electoral contests a vitality and drive that in their absence would be altogether lacking. Therefore, even if we opt for a neo-Madisonian approach to democracy, it is imperative that we not deny to political parties the capacity to increase the intensity of competition in electoral contests.

To examine the implications of a theory of democracy based on checks and balances alone, assume that the citizenry of a jurisdiction can be partitioned into x groups and that within each group preferences are homogeneous. Assume also, to make things simple, that the government of that jurisdiction is constituted of $n (= x)$ autonomous centers of power that are well balanced and therefore in a position to check one another and that they do so. Assume also that all centers of power, severally or in coordination, are engaged in the production and delivery of goods and services. Given that centers of power are, by construction, not elected – they are, let us say, self-appointed (e.g., a military junta) or hereditary – should we, even in this simple case in which the number of groups and the number of centers are equal and potentially easily mapped into each other, expect the supply of goods and services to be Wicksell–Lindahl efficient? The answer must be negative. Why? Because in such a system, only very weak incentives exist to respond to the preferences of citizens, technically, to seek information about the own- and cross-substitution terms of the whole set of demand functions for goods and services (see Chapter 2 for a demonstration that this information is needed for achieving Wicksell–Lindahl efficiency and for a discussion of how the information is acquired) and to act on this information.

It is true that by construction the centers of power of the preceding paragraph are autonomous so that powers are necessarily divided among them and that their relations are governed by checks and balances, other forms of competition, or both. But checking in these circumstances can be used primarily not to improve the supply of goods and services but to protect personal privileges and immunities, to enhance one's status or that of one's center of power, to defend one's turf, to humiliate an opponent, to rebuff a rival's success, to feather one's bed, or to enjoy Hicks's (1935) "quiet life."

If, however, some centers of power are elected and therefore forced to turn their attention to the idiosyncrasies of the demand functions of citizens, an incentive is created not only for the elected centers but for all centers to do the same thing. The reason for this is that nonelected centers of power compete with the elected ones; if the latter have to cater to the preferences of citizens to be reelected they will in effect "drag" the nonelected centers into doing the same thing. Nonelected centers by definition do not seek the electoral support of citizens, but they are compelled by the centers that must seek such support to search for what we could call the consent of citizens. Their refusal to do so would mean that they would always lose out in their competitive struggles with the elected centers.

The mechanism I am describing is different but has a strong family resemblance to the one to which Amartya Sen (1983, 1984, 1990) refers in explaining why there are no famines in democratic countries. Sen (1990, p. 50) notes that "the Bengal famine of 1943 took place without the supply of available food in Bengal being exceptionally low" (and that "[s]ome famines have in fact occurred when the amount of food has been at a "peak" level." Sen has documented the fact that it is not the shortage of foodstuffs that causes famines but the unwillingness of the authorities to make what there is available to the starving population. However, "[w]ith a relatively free press, with periodic elections, and with active opposition parties, no government can escape severe penalty if it delays preventive measures and permits a real famine to occur." The centers of power that are structurally connected to the citizenry pull the whole apparatus of government toward the needs of the population.

We must be careful, however, not to go to extremes. Autocratic and despotic regimes must pay some attention to some of the preferences of their citizens (see Chapter 5). The evidence is that these regimes are less responsive and use more force than democratic governments do, which is *prima facie* evidence that they are less Wicksell–Lindahl efficient. The point of the foregoing, therefore, is not that nonelected centers of power are always inattentive to their citizens but only that checks and balances are in their hands not as assiduously used for calibrating expenditure and taxation decisions to the benefit of citizens.

1.5.   Competition

For many persons the concept of competition has a bad reputation. The realities it evokes are to them unsavory. In the minds of many laypersons, competition is incompatible with and even antithetical to cooperation – that is, to the execution of actions leading to coordination. With this as background, the idea that governmental centers of power – and in a broader frame of reference, other sources of supply such as families, churches, cooperatives, unions, clubs, and so on (see Chapter 12) – compete among themselves is often thought to be impertinent and cynical. It is, as a consequence, useful to examine briefly the senses in which we can say that these sources of supply compete with one another.

Early economists such as Adam Smith (1776) borrowed the concept of competition from everyday usage. Over the years, however, refinement in economic thought has transformed the concept into something that bears virtually no relationship to its original meaning. In the main corpus of neoclassical economic theory, the concept is more or less devoid of any identifiable behaviors. The state it purports to describe is associated with the concept of perfect markets, that is, with markets in which buyers and sellers are numerous and have complete and accurate knowledge of all supply and demand prices and in which products traded are homogeneous and divisible (see Stigler, 1957a). Under these four conditions, all market participants are pricetakers. Such a concept is productive – it is one that practicing economists use daily – especially when it is recognized that in applying theoretical notions, as distinguished from developing and refining them, all that is needed are approximations to the foregoing four conditions. A comparably disembodied notion of competition is also sometimes applied to the analysis of imperfect markets by making use of the so-called Cournot–Nash assumption that in reaching a decision – any decision – an entrepreneur, say, takes the behavior of other market participants as given.

On the other hand, even within the confines of neoclassical economics certain types of activities – attestations of competitive behaviors – are acknowledged. These have traditionally been treated as imperfections in competition. Among these activities, one may find the promotion by an enterprise of its goods and services through advertising, marketing, and other means; the differentiation by a firm of its goods and services from those of other suppliers through design, packaging, and innumerable genuine and artificial contrivances; and the location by entrepreneurs of their businesses on advantageously positioned sites.

Economic models of perfect and imperfect competition have for many years been applied with success to politics. In the perfect competition tradition, Charles Tiebout (1956) assumed the existence of numerous local governments that supplied goods and services for which a demand existed and that were compelled by the competition of other local governments to supply these goods and services efficiently at taxprices equal to their marginal costs. Competition in this context is between local governments (the counterpart of firms) for the patronage of mobile citizens (the analog of consuming households). Competition insures that both local governments and citizens behave, at least if the costs of mobility are low, as price-takers. In the imperfect competition tradition, Anthony Downs (1957) modeled the rivalry of political parties along the lines of the locational or spatial competition theory suggested by Harold Hotelling (1929). Both the Tiebout and the Downs models have spawned an enormous literature.

To gain insight into the kinds of behaviors associated with competition and competitiveness, it is helpful to complement the models of perfect and imperfect competition that I have just identified with the model of competition proposed by Joseph Schumpeter (1911, 1942) and other Austrian economists (Carl Menger, Friedrich Hayek, and Ludwig Mises) – hence, the label of "Austrian" sometimes applied to it (Kirzner, 1973). I call the Austrian model the *entrepreneurial competition* model. It is consistent with – is a complement to – the models of perfect and imperfect competition, a point about which Schumpeter seems to have been uncertain but which Paul Samuelson (1943, 1982) has clarified.[19] I repeat Samuelson's logic in the next paragraphs.

To model Schumpeterian entrepreneurial competition, one must distinguish between two central components that already occupy a prominent place in the original 1911 discussion. There is first a steady-state "circular flow" equilibrium in which the marginal equalities on the supply side (Samuelson, 1982, pp. 10–11), those on the demand side, and the equality of supply and demand over all markets are satisfied. The steady-state circular flow can be characterized as "a stationary solution to a dynamical process" (Samuelson, 1943, p. 61) in which "the same things" keep repeating themselves. The circular flow equilibrium, therefore, is a long-run neoclassical equilibrium, and the competitive behavior that obtains in that equilibrium is that of neoclassical theory.

The second component is associated with innovation and entrepreneurship on the one hand and with imitation on the other. In his later work, Schumpeter identified innovative behavior with "Creative Destruction" (capitals in the original) which, through "the introduction of a new good," "the introduction of a new method of production," "the opening of a new market," "the conquest of a new source of supply," and "the carrying out of the new organization of any industry" (Schumpeter, 1911, p. 66), brings forth new "things"

---

19. In *The Theory of Economic Development* (1911/1961), the two are seen as complements but in *Capitalism, Socialism, and Democracy* (1942/1975), the two are opposed.

and eliminates others. Creative Destruction derives from and defines entrepreneurship. When it is successful and therefore profitable, innovation induces others covetous of the innovational rents to imitate the actions of entrepreneurs, either by simple duplication or by producing substitutes. In the process, the imitators increase the demand for labor, capital, and other factors of production, thus pushing up their prices and the entire schedule of average costs. By increasing the supply of goods and services, they push down their prices. The increase in unit costs and the fall in supply prices eventually eliminate the rents of entrepreneurship and bring forth the circular flow equilibrium of neoclassical theory.

The innovators or entrepreneurs of Schumpeter's model are, in Samuelson's words (1982, p. 13), "temporary monopolists"; their actions cause "changes in the *quality* of market structure and entrepreneurial power" (Samuelson, 1982, p. 14, italics in original). The notion that entrepreneurs out of circular flow are temporary monopolists is not an exclusive characteristic of a Schumpeterian economy subjected to innovational shocks. As Arrow (1959) has shown, to model how relative prices adjust to an exogenous disturbance in markets that are by assumption perfectly competitive, it is also necessary to assume that market actors are temporary monopolists. In his words, "perfect competition can really prevail only at equilibrium" (p. 41); it is, therefore, a characteristic of the circular flow equilibrium.

The Schumpeterian model of entrepreneurial competition and the existence of temporary monopolists can help us to understand the place of leaders and leadership in economic life. For Schumpeter, leaders are not the individuals who "create new possibilities"; they are those who do "the thing without which possibilities are dead" (Schumpeter, 1911, p. 88). The leaders are the innovative entrepreneurs; they break out of the circular flow equilibrium. There is no place for leadership in standard neoclassical theory. In that framework, changes in technology are responses to benefit-cost calculations, so that the origin of whoever ushers them in is a matter of indifference. Utility functions can be made dynamic and the effects of advertising and persuasion can be modeled, but although one recognizes the importance and usefulness of these exercises, it must be acknowledged that they are in fact a requirement of the circular flow equilibrium in which demand guides supply and hence precedes it. There is no reason to believe that advertising and persuasion would not exist in circular flow equilibrium.

It has long been recognized, at least since the days of Marshall (1890), that in dynamics – in the movement from one circular flow equilibrium to another – entrepreneurs play a leadership role by, for example, offering new products that consumers are then coaxed into buying. Notwithstanding its venerable age, the idea that new supply usually precedes demand encounters resistance. To a degree, the resistance derives from a perception that an aspect of the normative value of the neoclassical paradigm is considerably reduced, if not fully impaired, when the preferences being served are to an extent the result of actions engaged in by the very actors who serve them (Knight, 1935). An ethical preference is not, however, a very sure guide to positive analysis.

It is time to recognize that the entrepreneurial innovation that sets the competitive process in motion, the imitation that follows, and the Creative Destruction that they generate are not inconsistent with cooperative behavior and the coordination of activities. It would, however, be a mistake to focus on these acts of cooperation and coordination and conceive of Creative Destruction as the outcome of a cooperative process. In looking for new technologies, supply sources, organizational forms, products, methods of finance, labor-management relations, and other new ways of solving supply problems, entrepreneurs consult with other people, collaborate with them on certain projects, harmonize various activities, and even integrate some operations. All these actions describe what is generally meant by cooperation and coordination. If these activities serve to bring forth new innovations, they serve only to foster competition. To the extent that cooperation and coordination make it possible for innovations to come on stream more rapidly than they would otherwise, they become a force in the process of Creative Destruction. As a general rule, we can say that in the absence of collusion, cooperation and competition can and do generally coexist and also that the presence of one is not proof of the absence of the other. In particular, we can say that the observation of cooperation and coordination does not deny that the underlying determining force is competition.

The stationary element (the neoclassical circular flow) and the dynamic process (the innovational-imitational mechanics) both apply to political life as much as they do to economic life. There are politicians and other public sector actors who, like some of their counterparts in the business world, are entrepreneurs and who therefore innovate by creating new goods and services, introducing new techniques of production, exploring for new sources of supply, devising new methods of financing their operations, designing and instating new organizational forms, inaugurating new promotion methods, discovering new ways of obtaining information about the preferences of their constituents, and originating new ways of achieving a better match between the volume and the quality of goods and services provided and the volume and quality desired by citizens.

These political entrepreneurs often achieve their ends by forming a new consensus, by introducing symbols capable of producing solidarity, by galvanizing popular energies in the face of an emergency and, last but not least, by creating, adapting, and cultivating "ideologies" that, following Downs (1957, p. 96), we can define as "verbal image[s] of the good society and of the chief means of constructing such a society," or following Joseph Kalt and

Mark Zupan (1984, p. 281) as the "more or less consistent sets of normative statements as to best or preferred states of the world." [For an appreciation of the role of ideology in politics, see Frey and Schneider (1978), Kau and Rubin (1979), Kalt and Zupan (1984), and Peltzman (1984).]

One does not have to be a keen observer of the real world or possess great imagination to see entrepreneurial competition in action in politics. In that area, the *innovative* manifestations of competition are sometimes given a name such as New Deal (Roosevelt), Fair Deal (Truman), New Frontier (Kennedy), Great Society (Johnson), Just Society (Trudeau), Nouvelle Société (Chaban-Delmas), War on Poverty (Johnson, Pearson), New World Order (Bush), Ouverture (Mitterrand), Back to Basics (Major) or Contract with America (Gingrich). Sometimes they are associated with a theme such as full employment, social insurance, deregulation, privatization, free trade, productivity, downsizing, family values, change, and many others. When successful, these innovations serve to channel rents toward the innovative entrepreneurs, who then attract a bevy of *imitators*. We can easily document that some innovations are unsuccessful. It suffices to name the New World Order and the Charlottetown Consensus as examples of recent failures in the United States and Canada.

1.6.   Assembling the building blocks

In the chapters of Part I, I focus for the most part on democratic governments and on their efficiency as suppliers of goods and services. I assume periodic electoral contests between political parties as the vehicle through which one party or a coalition of them captures, not, as Anthony Downs (1957, p. 34) puts it, "the governing apparatus," but one or a few of the multiplicity of *centers of power* that make up modern governments. I provide evidence in Chapter 3 that modern governments are constituted of many elected and nonelected centers of power – that they are really compound governments. I assume that all centers of power, severally or in coordination, are engaged in the provision of goods and services as these were defined earlier. I recognize the possibility of collusion between the units of compound governments and even examine the conditions that lead to its emergence, but I devote most of my attention to the analysis of the nature and character of intragovernmental competition.

More precisely, in Chapter 2, I begin by reformulating the accepted theory of demand for government-supplied goods and services, because that theory rests on the (sometimes tacit) assumption that demand is revealed only through the ballot box and that as a consequence there is no demand for the goods and services produced and supplied by nonelected centers of power. That chapter also discusses the role of interest and pressure groups – which I call *demand lobbies* – in the demand revelation process. I do not reject the hypothesis that lobbies are sometimes motivated by rents, but I dismiss the assumption, central to the canonical rent-seeking model, that all lobbying is rent dissipation. Instead, I assume and provide evidence in support of the hypothesis that demand lobbies offer among other things information to centers of power in exchange for a better match between the quantities and qualities of goods and services these centers plan to provide and those desired by lobby membership. These trades can contain elements of rent, but they are bona fide trades that, like all trades, generate private and social surpluses.

The idea that the centers of power that make up governmental bodies compete with one another is not new. It suffuses the centuries-old literature on checks and balances and permeates the more institutionally anchored literature on budgetary decision-making. Chapters 3 and 4 focus on these two forms of intragovernmental competition. The first offers a formal model of checks and balances that is general enough to apply to a wide range of institutional contexts – including parliamentary as well as congressional governments – and circumstances. Checking behavior is illustrated. It is then shown that decisionmakers in governmental centers of power often adopt these behaviors and that when they do the interaction generates a Cournot–Nash equilibrium. When that equilibrium is displaced following an exogenous disturbance, a number of testable implications follow that appear to be consistent with the world of experience. The chapter also shows how checking behavior in well-balanced compound governments forges Wicksellian Connections between quantities and taxprices and that checks and balances are conducive to Wicksell–Lindahl efficiency.

Chapter 4 proposes models of budgetary processes in congressional and parliamentary systems that are based on a stylized reconstruction of these processes in the American and Canadian governments. The chapter documents that, even though the underlying form of competition in the two systems is bargaining, competition is organized in sufficiently different ways in them, that in equilibrium the Wicksellian Connections forged in the two are different and not equally efficient. The budgetary equilibria are stable, but to understand where the stability comes from, a number of institutional features of the two kinds of government have to be incorporated in the analysis.

Chapter 5 provides a more standard analysis of competition applied to the market for consent. It helps us to gain a deeper understanding of the workings of competition in politics as well as of the nature and properties of consent. It also analyzes how the equilibrium in the market for consent changes when voting is introduced and the franchise enlarged and when support – money and time – is recognized. The chapter explains the place of force in politics and shows why it will be present even in a perfectly competitive equilibrium. Finally, it analyzes how the Wicksellian Connection behaves when the structure of the market is altered.

The sixth and final chapter of Part I is on bureaucracy. In conventional

Public Choice theory, bureaucracy is a source of inefficiency sufficiently powerful in some approaches to completely obliterate outcomes that would otherwise have been efficient. The underlying *weltanschauung* is that an organizational hierarchy of some sort is needed to resolve problems of management and that the one selected by principals leads to inefficiency. Chapter 6 identifies the source of this *weltanschauung* and argues that because of competition the (relatively) efficient outcomes produced by checks and balances, by bargaining, and by standard competition will not be expunged.

CHAPTER 2

Demand and its revelation

It is now conventional to conceive of the quantities of government-supplied goods and services *desired* by a consuming household as generated by the maximization of a well-behaved ordinal utility function subject to a linear budget constraint defined by predetermined (marginal) taxprices and the household's income.[1] The optimization procedure is identical, in other words, to the one employed to derive the quantities of market-provided goods and services desired by the same household. It is also standard practice to analyze the two sets of demand functions separately in recognition, one presumes, of the fact that the goods and services offered in the marketplace are purchased by consuming households severally, whereas those supplied by governmental bodies are "purchased" by the same households collectively.

To put it differently, the basis of the aforementioned distinction is to be found, one again presumes, in the everyday observation that the volumes of goods and services that households desire are not *revealed* in the same way for the two classes of demand functions. As regards the goods and services supplied in the marketplace, some consumers in collaboration with others may amass, weigh, and collate information, but however much interaction may actually take place among them, demand is ultimately revealed by the act of purchase itself. As a consequence, the theory of demand for these goods and services rightly accords only scant attention to the mechanisms through which these demand functions are revealed.

The situation is different regarding collective choices. For the demand functions to which these decisions apply, the nature, role, and properties of the revelation mechanisms must occupy center stage. It is no doubt for this reason that so many mechanisms have been proposed, and it is for this reason that a new one will be suggested in the pages and chapters that follow. Among the revelation mechanisms that have been put forward, some have been used in empirical work and are in some instances essentially empirically based

---

1. I argue in Part III that one should not restrict the supply side to market and governmental institutions. Families, churches, clubs, charitable organizations, and cooperatives are among the other bodies that participate in the provision of goods and services. In the remainder of this chapter, because I am principally concerned with demand, I will follow convention and limit the supply side to public and market sources. It is easy to extend the analysis of demand to any number of suppliers.

constructions, whereas others have remained theoretical exercises. Prominent in the first group are estimations of demand functions revealed at ballot boxes in general elections involving large populations. These empirical studies have followed two paths. On one path, firmly based on the assumption of the median voter model, bona fide partial equilibrium demand functions defined over taxprices and incomes (as well as other variables) have been estimated for a number of nonfederal – namely, state and local – goods and services. See, for example, Borcherding and Deacon (1972), Bergstrom and Goodman (1973), and Deacon (1977, 1978). Though explicitly neoclassical in design (Deacon, 1978; Rubinfeld, 1987) and therefore estimated on the expectation that the propositions related to substitution and income terms would be satisfied, none of the statistical demand functions has been concerned with the cross-substitution terms between market- and government-supplied goods and services. It is for this reason that I asserted earlier that they were partial equilibrium estimations. They have further entrenched, as a consequence, at least implicitly and with no apparent rationale, the view that the demand functions for market goods and services are always and everywhere strictly separable from those for government goods and services.

On the other path, analysis of revelation mechanisms has focused on so-called political business and political budget cycles. See, among a very large literature, Nordhaus (1975), Frey (1978), Frey and Schneider (1978), Hibbs (1977, 1987, 1992), Paldam (1981, 1989), Galeotti and Forcina (1989), Alesina (1988, 1989), Alesina and Roubini (1990), and Lewis-Beck and Rice (1992). The underlying assumption of this approach is that what is revealed at the ballot box is a demand for economic growth, price stability, low unemployment, and other macroeconomic variables. The truncation of demand into a component made up of macroeconomic variables and another component that is usually but not always disregarded, made up of all the other goods and services supplied by governments together with the assumption that the first completely dominates the second at the ballot box are, no doubt, a reflection of two facts: first, that these macroeconomic variables are of concern to all or to virtually all voters and that readily available quantitative indexes for all of them exist that make comparisons with past performance and with performance in other jurisdictions relatively easy (for a development of this line of analysis, see Salmon, 1987a, 1993); and, second, that these policy variables change over the short run relatively more than others. Yet, in view of the unresolved debate on which has more power – the strictly economic or the politico-economic approach to election forecasting and postcasting – it is too early to conclude that goods and services such as war, civil strife, scandals, abortion, racial violence, gun control, the death penalty, school prayers, and even more mundane goods and services (e.g., street cleaning, road maintenance, sewage and drainage, subway and bus transportation, and police protection, not to mention old-age pensions and unemployment insurance) should be removed from the agenda of political analysis.[2]

Referendum voting is another mechanism that can reveal underlying demand relationships and that has often been used in empirical research with that objective. Referendum voting is a particularly powerful mechanism to capture the demand for goods and services that are provided under circumstances that mimic direct democracy, and as such it fulfills to a high degree the restrictive conditions required for a licit use of such mechanisms. See, for example, Birdsall (1965), Wilson and Banfield (1965), Deacon and Shapiro (1975), Pommerehne and Frey (1976), Rubinfeld (1977), and Pommerehne (1978). Recently, Bruno Frey (1994) has argued that when the formal referendum voting rules are analyzed within "the *institutions* of direct democracy" (p. 338, italics in original) in which they are in force, referendum mechanisms have even more power than is usually granted them.

Among the demand revelation mechanisms that have remained at the level of theoretical exercises, two deserve to be briefly noted: logrolling and, adapting Edward Clarke's (1971) label, two-part pricing models. The driving force in logrolling, or vote trading, is the difference in the intensity of preferences among traders for particular goods and services. It is, therefore, a mechanism that could be more effective at revealing underlying demand relationships than ordinary voting is. By the very nature of what is required for vote trading over time, logrolling must be restricted to small populations.[3] That alone limits the value of the mechanism for the analysis of demand in all but the smallest jurisdictions. The two-part pricing model suggested by Clarke (1971), Theodore Groves (1973), and Nicolaus Tideman and Gordon Tullock (1976) reveals true demand functions for goods and services if, in addition to an initially assigned share of the cost of a given (indivisible) good, pivotal voters (those whose votes change the outcome) are required to pay the costs that their choices impose on other voters – hence, the two-part pricing nature of the scheme. The mechanism not only leads to a revelation of true demands for goods and services but these will also be intimately related to the relevant taxprices just as they are in the Wicksell–Lindahl model. It is difficult to conceive of an institutional framework in which the mechanism could be embodied. To my knowledge, none has ever been outlined.

There can be no doubt that all the analysis and research discussed in the foregoing paragraphs have shed much light on collective choices and on

2. For a recent and quite stunning vindication of the politico-economic approach, see Jean-Dominique Lafay's (1993) region-by-region forecast (two days prior to the ballot) of the 1993 French legislative elections.
3. Dennis Mueller (1967), in his "Comment" on James Coleman's (1966) attempt to extend the logrolling mechanism to the citizenry as a whole, has, I believe correctly, argued the impossibility of such a generalization.

political behavior. That being said, I must stress one limitation that is shared by all these mechanisms. I do not have in mind the vulnerability of voting mechanisms to inconsistent aggregation (Arrow, 1951), to cycling and instability (Black, 1958, Chapter 16; Plott, 1967; Mueller, 1989, Chapter 5) and to other such phenomena.[4] The limitation I underline pertains to the fact that when the demand responses of consuming households to changes in taxprices and incomes are assumed to be revealed through voting – and, in the last analysis, all the mechanisms we have noted are voting mechanisms – the model of government one is led to espouse treats governmental organizations as organic structures, benevolent despots, or monoliths (see Chapter 1, Section 1.2).

The matter can be put differently. Consider, for the sake of concreteness, a numerically small subset of the large set of all autonomous and quasi-autonomous centers of power that constitute the Canadian government, namely, the House of Commons, the Senate, and the Supreme Court.[5] Of these three, only the first is elected. A model of demand restricted to voting must, therefore, assume that the Senate and the Supreme Court do not produce and supply any good or service demanded by households and do not even play an independent role in the production and delivery of the goods and services provided by the House of Commons. In general, when by construction, consuming citizens do not directly or indirectly reveal a demand for the goods and services produced by the nonelected centers of power, these centers cannot play an independent role in providing them with goods and services. The implicit assumption is that nonelected centers of power play no role in the supply of such services as racial integration, abortion, censorship, inflation, and the Cuban missile crisis – services for which a demand must be presumed to exist and for which nonelected centers of power have in fact been prominent suppliers.

Against this conception of politics, I suggest that all the centers of power that have a significant degree of autonomy and that are constitutive components of governmental organizations are involved in supply decisions.[6] Because of their involvement, they are suppliers of some goods or services – more exactly of Lancasterian (1966) characteristics of goods and services. In that capacity, they compete with one another on a continuous basis, and each

4. For an excellent analysis of some important limitations of voting mechanisms, see Pierre Salmon and Alain Wolfelsperger (1990).
5. In Canada, the House of Commons has been made up, for many decades preceding the 1993 election, of three autonomous centers of power (three political parties) that were continuously competing with one another. For an explanation of why this was not a disequilibrium state of affairs, even if one of the three parties had never formed the government, see Gianluigi Galeotti and Breton (1986). I disregard the intra-House competition in the text.
6. For a definition of autonomy and for an illustrative list of centers of power, see Chapter 3, Section 3.1.

one is linked to citizens or to a subset of citizens by a bond that I call *consent* or *expected consent*. I analyze that bond in Sections 2.2 and 2.3, where I also describe how it can be combined with the electoral relationship underlying the revelation mechanism embodied in voting.[7]

I must stress that if nonelected centers of power are not actual or potential suppliers of some of the goods and services demanded by citizens, the checks and balances that are a feature of all political systems and that since antiquity have been regarded as guarantors of political freedom, stability, and well-being (Panagopoulos, 1985; Gordon, 1986) have no theoretical foundations except hubris, megalomania, or other similar attributes of political actors. It is difficult to imagine that checks and balances nurtured by forces of that kind would produce the beneficial results just noted. Hubris, or megalomania, or both would also drive all other forms of competition – bargaining, logrolling, innovating, takeovers – if principals in what are in the end principal–agent relationships, are by assumption refused any role vis-à-vis agents.

Without denying that hubris and megalomania do sometimes play a role in politics and possibly even in economic life [see Roll (1986) for a forceful argument to the effect that hostile takeovers in markets are often motivated by hubris], it is more consistent with economic theory and with the available evidence (refer to the literature on statistical demand functions and on political cycles noted earlier) to assume that the game of politics is not habitually played without reference to citizens. Accordingly, I suggest a theory of demand for government-supplied goods and services in which demand is channeled or directed by a politically active citizenry to nonelected as well as to elected centers of power that in turn have a very important role to play in the demand revelation mechanism that I propose.

I began this chapter by noting that nominal or optimal demand functions for all goods and services could be obtained by maximizing constrained utility functions. Notwithstanding the routine application of maximization procedures, such a proposition is more transparent for market-supplied than for government-supplied goods and services. Consequently, I devote the next section to three issues closely related to the maximization problem as it applies to government-provided goods and services. The first pertains to the definition of taxprices, the second to the role of free-riding in the analysis of demand, and the third to the substitutability of government- and market-provided goods and services. In Section 2.2, I describe how demand is revealed through a consent mechanism and suggest a way of reconciling this mechanism with voting. Section 2.3 examines the role of what I call *demand lobbies* in the demand revelation process. Section 2.4 introduces the first ingredient in the set of ingredients that will provide us at the end of the study

---

7. For a different look at the relation between consent and voting, see Chapter 5.

with genuine empirically relevant Wicksellian Connections or, to put it differently, with true empirically meaningful revealed demand functions. Section 2.5 concludes the chapter.

2.1. Utility maximization

The demand functions on which I focus in this section are individual and nominal functions. They are individual in that they pertain to single consuming units and not to aggregations of units.[8] They are nominal in that, until they are revealed through one mechanism or another, they can have no effective impact on the movement of the political system toward an equilibrium. However, because they are the microfoundations of Wicksellian Connections and of the revelation mechanism that permits a description and an understanding of the political behavior of citizens and of competitive governments, it is important to be clear about the nature of these demand functions.

Following the procedure to which I have alluded, I assume that an individual consuming citizen j ($= 1, \ldots, J$) can be characterized by a smooth concave utility function defined over a basket of market-supplied goods and services X_i ($i = 1, \ldots, I$) and a basket of government-provided goods and services G_k ($k = 1, \ldots, K$). Therefore:

$$U^j = U^j(X_i, G_k) \ \forall \ j, i, k \tag{2.1}$$

which are maximized subject to linear budget constraints (assuming, for simplicity, exogenously given incomes, M^j):

$$M^j = \sum_{i=1}^{I} p_i X_i + \sum_{k=1}^{K} t_k G_k \ \ \forall j \tag{2.2}$$

with the p_i's and the t_k's denoting market prices and (marginal) taxprices, respectively. From the maximization's first-order conditions, we can derive demand functions such as:

$$X_i^j = X_i^j(p_i, t_k, M^j) \ \forall \ j, i, k \tag{2.3}$$

and

$$G_k^j = G_k^j(p_i, t_k, M^j) \ \forall \ j, i, k \tag{2.4}$$

Three problems, already noted, beg for attention. To repeat, they are: (1) how are the taxprices (the t_k's) defined?; (2) how does free-riding affect the maximization procedure?; and (3) what is the meaning of the substitution between X_i and G_k (the $\partial G_k / \partial X_i$'s that maximization generates)? I look at each in turn.

---

8. They could obviously be aggregates of consuming households if these had the same preferences. On aggregation, see Section 2.3, Subsection i.

i.   *Taxprices*

The centers of power that constitute modern governments supply a large array of goods and services (G_k). (For a list that illustrates this variety, see Chapter 1, Section 1.1.) Without exception, the production of these goods and services uses up real resources. That is, their production absorbs human capital (such as time, energy, health, psychological well-being), physical capital, land, natural resources, and intermediate goods and services. These resources can be garnered by using the proceeds of taxation, of debt (including the printing of money), and of intergovernmental grants, by requiring that consuming citizens themselves pay for the goods and services (as is the case with most regulations) and/or by directly commandeering factors of production.

An increase in the volume of any one good or service produced uses up more resources; as a consequence, the volume of some other good or service will of necessity be smaller.[9] I call the increment in the amount of a good that a given consuming citizen forgoes (following an increase in, let us say, a sales or a property tax) to pay for a unit increase in the supply of any one good or service, the *marginal taxprice* of that good or service to that citizen.[10] Marginal taxprices may exceed or fall short of average taxprices. However, because it simplifies the analysis (and economizes on data requirements), it is generally assumed that marginal and average taxprices are equal. That assumption also correctly describes the behavior of marginal taxprices – always the relevant variable – when perfect competition obtains.

Tax systems are usually made up of many tax bases and rates. Consequently, as Buchanan (1967, Chapter 2) stressed years ago, the position and slope of the demand curve for any good or service depends, *ceteris paribus*, on the tax bases and/or rates that are varied simply because the burden of taxes differs. This makes it more difficult to obtain well-specified measures of taxprices, but as Arthur Denzau and Robert Mackay (1985) have shown, a theoretically tractable concept of marginal taxprices can be devised whatever the complexities of the tax system.

When goods and services are paid for by issuing debt, especially long-term debt, the taxprices that enter the demand functions must incorporate one or a series of discount factors that will relate the future to the present. The size of these discount factors will depend significantly on the attitudes and dispositions of the present generation – the one that is consuming the goods and services – vis-à-vis future generations; for example, whether the living care

---

9. I am, therefore, without impairing generality, assuming full employment and zero growth.
10. I could alternatively have called them Lindahl prices, benefit prices, or user prices. These expressions are all synonyms.

much, little, or not at all about the well-being of those who will come after them. Debt finance does, as a consequence, further complicate the concept and especially the measurement of taxprices, but in principle it remains a theoretically well-defined and tractable notion.[11]

ii.   Free-riding

It is often alleged that the taxprices paid by a given citizen depend on the person's ability, as well as on that of others, to free-ride. The argument goes as follows. For any government, the total of expenditures must be equal to the total of receipts. If there is any free-riding, expenditures will have to be curtailed, taxes increased, or a combination of both implemented. As a consequence, the demand functions of any citizen will be unstable or at the very least the outcome of a complicated process involving all consuming citizens in strategic interaction.

In the Public Economics literature, free-riding occurs in the presence of, let us say, public goods provided through voluntary institutional arrangements such as clubs. A balanced budget at which these clubs break even requires that the taxprice paid by each demander be equal to the (compensated) marginal value the demander places on the volume of the good supplied and that the sum of the taxprices over all demanders be equal to the (constant or increasing) marginal cost of production. However, because public goods are by definition available to all in equal, or more or less equal, quantities, each demander has an incentive to misrepresent his or her preferences and thus be charged a lower price. A balanced budget, except for small groups (Olson, 1965), cannot be achieved. As a result, demand functions are unstable.

A number of schemes that would at once preserve the voluntary character of the supply of public goods while removing the incentive to free-ride through falsification of preferences have been proposed (see Inman, 1987, for a survey of that literature), but all have problems of their own. Whether for that reason or for some other, none of these incentive schemes has ever been adopted anywhere, which would appear to throw us back to square one in the matter of the free-rider problem.

This is not the case, however. To deal with the problem, we must turn our attention away from the incentive schemes of Welfare Economics toward the political institutions of the real world. To begin, recall Buchanan's (1967) argument that when taxprices are given – have to be paid – the incentive of demanders to free-ride by misrepresenting their preferences vanishes. That argument is correct. As I have just stated it, it does, however, neglect the fact

11. If one is willing to assume that the Ricardian Equivalence Theorem (see, for example, Barro, 1974) applies, then debt finance poses no additional problem.

that when taxprices are "listed" or "posted," free-riding ceases to take the form of preference falsification – Buchanan's point – and takes instead that of tax avoidance and evasion.[12] To be convinced of the truth of this proposition, the reader need only answer the question of whether a person who habitually avoids or evades taxes would or would not continue to do so if, instead of a public good, a pure private good such as orange juice was government-supplied, as was the case in the United Kingdom for more than twenty years following World War II.

Real-world technologies to deal with the misrepresentation of preferences may never be available, but technologies to monitor compliance to tax codes and to enforce tax laws exist. Monitoring and enforcement impose costs on avoiders and evaders; the expected value of those costs can be estimated. Given that the expected utility of the sums garnered through avoidance and evasion can in principle also be calculated, equating expected marginal costs with expected marginal benefits will determine a *ceteris paribus* equilibrium volume of free-riding or, more precisely, an equilibrium volume of tax avoidance and evasion. It is only in terms of this equilibrium that the marginal taxprices that enter the demand functions (2.3) and (2.4) are defined. The problem is not different from the one encountered in regard to the demand functions for market-provided goods and services. These functions are stable only as regards free-riding on market prices if an equilibrium volume of fraud can be assumed. If, for example, some consumers could at zero expected cost make use of a gun to force other consumers to pay for the goods and services they themselves are purchasing, demand functions for market-supplied goods and services would likewise be unstable.

Before moving on, I note that the technologies used to control the free-riding that manifests itself in tax avoidance and evasion are made up of more than monitoring and inspection routines and enforcement through indictments and prosecutions. If we interpret Walter Hettich and Stanley Winer's (1988) results on tax structure in the framework of this subsection, we could conclude, as they suggest we should (p. 710), that the number of rate brackets, the size of bases, as well as the anatomy of exemptions, deductions, and credits are all components of the technologies designed to control avoidance and evasion. In Hettich and Winer's model, these elements of the tax structure

12. In a world in which governments are not completely exogenous, it is virtually impossible to distinguish between tax avoidance and tax evasion. Years ago, Musgrave (1969, p. 128) distinguished between taxpayer and "tax collector compliance" and Carl Shoup (1969, pp. 427–32) wrote about "unilateral" and "bilateral evasion" to account for the fact that at the level of tax collection, if not at that of tax legislation, both payers and collectors may collaborate to "evade" taxes. Rod Cross and Keith Shaw (1981) have offered a suggestive discussion of the adjustments or behaviors that are possible when evasion and avoidance are treated as substitutes and complements.

are determined in part by administration costs that include "the cost of monitoring compliance and enforcing tax codes" (p. 706, n. 11). Recently, Kimberley Scharf (1994) has suggested a model in which tax credits constrain the tax evasion often associated with international capital flows.

Given an equilibrium volume of tax avoidance and evasion and, therefore, well-defined (marginal) taxprices, the demand functions (2.3) and (2.4) are neoclassical demand functions and can be expected to satisfy the properties that these functions display whenever they are derived from a constrained maximization of utility exercise. In other words:

1. The demand functions will be homogeneous of degree zero in market prices, taxprices, and incomes.
2. The weighted average of income elasticities will add up to unity (with the weights given by the relative share of each good and service in total expenditure).
3. Compensated own-substitution terms will be negative.
4. Compensated cross-substitution terms will be symmetric.

The last property (like the others) holds for all goods and services irrespective of whether they are provided by governmental centers of power or by market organizations. As a consequence, we not only have:

$$\left(\frac{\partial G_r}{\partial t_s} \right)_{U^j} = \left(\frac{\partial G_s}{\partial t_r} \right)_{U^j} \quad \forall j,\, r,\, s \tag{2.5}$$

but also

$$\left(\frac{\partial G_r}{\partial p_s} \right)_{U^j} = \left(\frac{\partial X_s}{\partial t_r} \right)_{U^j} \quad \forall j,\, r,\, s \tag{2.6}$$

It follows that market-provided goods and services can be substitutes for or complements of government-supplied goods and services. This conclusion has important consequences for the operation of the demand revelation mechanism proposed in this volume and must be analyzed in more detail.

iii.   Substitution

There are no demand functions for government-supplied goods and services in standard Taxation Economics. Instead, these goods and services are imposed on populations by governments (that are in effect benevolent despots) to correct market failures, to rectify less-than-optimal income distributions, or to achieve other ends. These objectives can be pursued, however, only if resources are available. Hence, the need for taxation. Except for lump-sum taxes, which do not exist save as mental constructions, all taxes in standard theory are distortive. They "force" citizens to adjust their consumption of market-supplied goods and services, their labor supply, savings, risk taking, location, family size, and so on, but they have no effect on the margin of substitution between market-provided and government-provided goods and services. Taxes influence individual but not collective choices pertaining to government-supplied goods and services.

Let me illustrate the matter with an example. Imagine a situation in which there are only two market-supplied goods (X_1 and X_2), which are substitutes for each other, so that $\partial X_1/\partial X_2 < 0$; and there is only one government-provided good (G). However, as in standard analysis, I assume that $\partial G/\partial X_1 = \partial G/\partial X_2 = 0$. (To simplify, I also suppose that the supplies of labor, savings, risk taking, and so on are fixed.) Now, suppose that the government decides to increase by one unit the quantity of G provided. This decision will require additional revenues, which, I assume, are collected by increasing the sales tax on X_1. This higher tax will force a further substitution away from X_1 toward X_2 and will increase the distortion in consumption patterns. The marginal cost of funds to pay for the unit increase in G is, in that framework, equal to the additional amount of revenue levied plus the increment in excess-burden or welfare costs (Browning, 1976).

If, however, we assume that for citizen j, X_1 and G are substitutes for each other, so that $\partial G/\partial X_1 < 0$ and if, to simplify calculations, we let $\partial X_2/\partial X_1 = \partial G/\partial X_2 = 0$, the marginal cost of the increased tax on X_1 is only the amount of X_1 forgone to pay for the additional unit of G. The larger the value of the additional quantity of X_1 that must be given up (through the instrumentality of a higher sales tax, say), the greater the marginal opportunity cost of G and the smaller the size of the increment demanded.

Imputing excess burdens to taxes is, therefore, a consequence of the assumption that consuming citizens do not substitute between market- and government-supplied goods and services. It is a consequence of the assumption that to satisfy his or her desire for one more unit of G, an individual must sacrifice some amount of X_1. As a result of that reduction in the quantity available for consumption, the individual is better off than he or she would have been had no taxes been levied and G not provided.[13] Though this assumption pervades the literature and, reflecting that fact, though demand functions defined over both classes of goods have not to my knowledge been estimated, I suggest that the assumption is untenable. As evidence for that view, I take the fact that virtually all the goods and services governments currently supply are or have been provided in one society or another by nongovernmental organizations (see Chapter 12). It could be argued that the implied substitutions were not in response to relative price changes. Such an

---

13. Even if taxes do not have an excess burden, public supply of goods and services, as I argue later, will almost always have.

argument, if put forward, could be addressed only by a reference to the facts. An assumption poses no such challenge – it can simply be dismissed.

The existence of substitutability between government- and market-supplied goods and services implies that separability of demand functions on the basis of supply sources cannot be accepted even though the underlying revelation mechanisms are completely different for the two types of goods and services. Such a conclusion should come as no surprise to anyone who recalls that substitutability is an attribute of preference functions and not of revelation mechanisms.

2.2.   Demand revelation

Some of the autonomous and quasi-autonomous centers of power that make up democratic governments attempt to build more than one kind of relationship with consuming citizens; centers may seek electoral support, consent, money, affection, connections, status, and many other things. To proceed, it is necessary to simplify this complex reality. As a preface to achieving that end, it is well to remind ourselves that politics (that is, the governance and management of collective undertakings) though not exclusively about power, is largely ruled by it. Voting models based on the assumption that the bodies I am here calling *elected centers of power* maximize expected votes, implicitly but correctly presume that effective political power is for these centers a *ceteris paribus* positive monotone function of the probability of securing the electoral support of citizens. The point was underlined by George Stigler (1972) some two decades ago, more or less at the same time that under his (1971) very influence the school of thought now labeled Chicago Political Economy (Stigler, 1989) decided to veer away from voting and power to concentrate on interest groups and pressure politics. Because they are also implicated in the governance and management of collective undertakings, nonelected centers of power, like the elected ones, deal in political power. They do not by definition, however, maximize expected votes. I assume that they maximize expected consent. As a consequence, I disregard money, social connections, hubris, and other variables that at certain times may be important for a detailed understanding of political behavior.[14]

The main difference between the probability that a vote will be granted to a given center of power and the probability that consent will be accorded to that or to another center – two variables that are elusive and difficult to measure with any accuracy – is, I suggest, to be found in the way these probabilities are externalized. The probability of electoral support is externalized from time

14. In Chapter 5, I examine how the search for money and other amenities can affect the character of the political equilibrium.

to time by the act of voting for a candidate, party, or office, but it is just as real between elections and is then externalized through polls. The probability of consent, on the other hand, is externalized by signals such as approval ratings, mail, telephone, and telefax campaigns, letters to newspapers, midterm and by-election voting, public demonstrations, civil disobedience, and at the limit, insubordination, mutiny, and sedition. Few measures of consent are available. Pollsters seldom provide us with indexes of the consent citizens grant to supreme courts, nonelected senates, central banks, and other autonomous and quasi-autonomous nonelected centers of power, though it would be a relatively simple matter to do so.[15]

Taking the foregoing remarks about the externalization of probabilities as granted, I simply assume that all centers of power – whether elected or nonelected – maximize expected consent on the presupposition that for elected centers the number of expected votes is proportional to the volume of expected consent granted them or, alternatively, that the correlation between expected votes and expected consent is positive and highly significant.[16] One can rationalize the assumption that centers of power maximize consent by arguing that consent is a measure of endorsement or of approval given by citizens to centers of power for what they are or are not doing. In the absence of endorsement or approval, the centers of power would lose some legitimacy and, therefore, some capacity to compete with other centers of power. The demand functions for the goods and services (or for the characteristics of goods and services) provided by elected and nonelected centers of power will, as a consequence, be revealed through a consent mechanism. Two questions pertain to that mechanism. The first, addressed in Subsection i, relates to the motivation of citizens to use the mechanism, and the second, examined in Subsection ii, concerns the mode of operation of the mechanism.

i.   Motivation

For the goods and services provided through the marketplace, demand is revealed, as I have already noted, by the purchases of consumers. To put it differently, given market prices (and incomes), the quantities bought are the result of consumers' initiatives reflecting their preferences for market-supplied goods and services. Things are different in the public sector. In that

15. It is sometimes possible to squeeze information out of data that were not initially collected to measure the consent granted to nonelected centers of power. For a masterful study that makes this possible, see Richard Johnston (1986).
16. I am extremely grateful to Gianluigi Galeotti for the many hours of discussion on this and related matters. These, providentially, came at a time when I was coming to the conclusion that the problems with which I was grappling were intractable. He cannot, however, be held responsible for the outcome of these discussions as reflected in this and the next chapters.

arena, given taxprices (and incomes), quantities are not purchased by citizens: Quantities are made available to them by governmental centers of power. How, then, are demand functions revealed? It would be disingenuous, to say the least, in an exercise whose object is to discover how demand is revealed, to assume that, *ex ante,* centers of power know the preferences of consuming households. We must then begin our analysis of the forces that motivate citizens to reveal their preferences by focusing on a fundamental information problem.[17] I therefore assume that as a consequence of imperfect information concerning the preferences of citizens, centers of power will provide, except by accident, goods and services in quantities that will be either larger or smaller than the quantities desired by consuming households at the taxprices they confront, and I show that these departures from optimality inflict utility losses on these households.[18]

To better appreciate the significance of this information problem, consider Figure 2.1, which depicts three levels of utility ($U_0 > U_1 > U_2$) that citizen j could derive from one market good (X) and one government good (G). Given the market price of X, the taxprice of G, and j's income, the budget constraint is xx*. Maximization of utility subject to this constraint tells us that the amount of G desired by j is G*. When the quantity made available to j is, let us say, G' ($< G*$), j suffers a utility loss, which in Figure 2.1 is equal to xy ($= \lambda$) – a compensating variation measure (in units of the numéraire X) of the consuming household's reduction in utility.

An alternative partial equilibrium measure of utility losses – also useful – can be derived by using the compensated demand curve of consumer j for good G. That demand curve is shown as D^j in Figure 2.2. If the predetermined tax price is t*, the quantity desired of G is G*. If the quantity provided, because of imperfect information concerning D^j, is G'' ($> G*$), j suffers a utility loss equal to abc ($= \lambda''$). To see this, it suffices to note that at G'', j pays a total of 0t*bG″ but derives utility equal to 0t*acG″, which is smaller than 0t*bG″ by abc. Similarly, it is easy to see that if j is provided with G' ($< G*$), he or she suffers a utility loss of ab′c′ ($= \lambda'$). By paying G′c′aG* more than he or she is currently charged, j would gain in utility a sum equal to G′b′aG*, which exceeds G′c′aG* by ab′c′. It should be noted that the more inelastic the

17. The information problem, as will become clear, is exactly the same whether public bodies supply Samuelson-type (1954) public goods and services or simply private goods and services. In other words, the presence of public goods raises no particular difficulties, as will become readily apparent (see Section 2.4).
18. In Chapters 3 and 4, we shall discover that even if information about the preferences of citizens is perfect, the quantities of goods and services provided to citizens by governmental centers of power can differ from those desired because of certain institutional characteristics. I neglect these sources of utility loss in the remainder of this chapter.

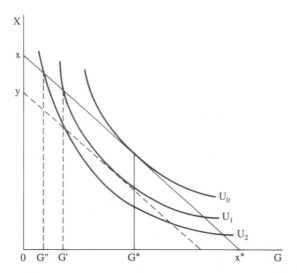

Figure 2.1. A "compensating variation" measure of utility loss.

demand curve at the predetermined t*, the larger will be the utility loss resulting from a difference between actual and desired volumes of G.

Utility losses are not sufficient by themselves to motivate j to reveal his or her preferences. The incentive is provided by the expectation entertained by j and by other consuming households that by granting (or withholding) more or less consent to centers of power, they can induce the centers to alter the quantities provided. Economic theory tells us that the most powerful force justifying such an expectation is the existence of competition between centers of power. Even though it is possible to conceive of a monolithic center of power searching for the preferences of citizens by, as it were, competing against itself over time, the inducement to acquire information about the demands of consuming households is incomparably stronger – and only then reliable – when nurtured by the competitive drive of other centers of power.

To understand how competition operates, suppose that one center (call it "a") pledges G' of G (less than G* in both Figures 2.1 and 2.2), and that a second center ("b") promises G" (less than G' and G* in Figure 2.1 and greater than G* in Figure 2.2). This will induce j to grant his or her consent to "a" simply because the utility loss associated with G' (equal to λ in Figure 2.1 and to λ' in Figure 2.2) is smaller than the loss linked to G" (equal to λ'', which is shown only in Figure 2.2). It seems reasonable to assume that the stronger the competition between centers of power, the more will the demand for goods and services by citizens be revealed. Competition between centers

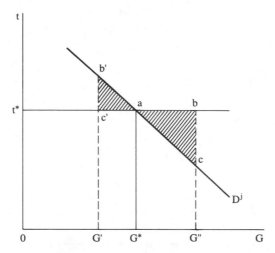

Figure 2.2. A partial equilibrium measure of utility loss.

of power is, therefore, the essential driving force of the revelation mechanism that leads citizens to reveal their demand functions for goods and services, and I will focus on competition throughout the remainder of this volume. As will also become clear, the underlying demand curves that are revealed are the long-sought-after Wicksellian Connections.

ii.   Mechanism

I have earlier introduced the assumption that centers of power maximize expected consent. Formally, for a given center – call it "a" again – expected consent (EC_a) is:

$$EC_a = \sum_{j=1}^{J} \phi_a^j \qquad 1 \geq \phi_a^j \geq 0 \tag{2.7}$$

in which ϕ_a^j is "a"'s subjective probability that j will grant it his or her consent. The assumption, also introduced earlier, that expected electoral support (votes) (EV_b) is proportional to expected consent, implies that the probability that j will vote for an elected center of power – call it "b" – is $\pi_b^j = k\phi_b^j$, for $k \neq 0$ with $1 \geq \pi_b^j \geq 0$, so that

$$EV_b = \sum_{j=1}^{J} \pi_b^j = k \sum_{j=1}^{J} \phi_b^j, \quad k \neq 0 \tag{2.8}$$

I now borrow from the probabilistic voting literature the notion that the probabilities of consent (ϕ_a^j) – and the probabilities of voting (π_b^j) – are continuous and twice differentiable functions of the policies or actions of centers of power, which in the present context means that they are functions of utility losses. (See Mueller, 1989, and Lafay, 1992, for reviews of and references to that literature.) To be specific, I assume that there are N centers of power, indexed n (= 1 , . . . , N) and that the probability that citizen j will grant his or her consent to one of them, let us say to center "a", is a function of the utility losses (λ) – defined earlier with the help of Figures 2.1 and 2.2 – which that center and the others impose on j. We then have:

$$\phi_a^j = \phi_a^j(\lambda_a^j,\lambda_n^j) \; \forall \; j, n \neq a \tag{2.9}$$

with $\partial\phi_a^j/\partial\lambda_a^j < 0$ for all j's and $\partial\phi_a^j/\partial\lambda_n^j > 0$ for all j's and all n $\neq$ a. Granted that for an elected center of power (let us say "b") $\pi_b^j = k\phi_b^j$, k $\neq$ 0, it follows that

$$\pi_b^j = \pi_b^j(\lambda_b^j,\lambda_n^j) \; \forall \; j, n \neq b \tag{2.10}$$

with as earlier, $\partial\pi_a^j/\partial\lambda_a^j < 0$ for all j's and $\partial\pi_a^j/\partial\lambda_n^j > 0$ for all j's and all n $\neq$ a. I also borrow from the theory of probabilistic voting the assumptions that the ϕ_n^j (and π_n^j) functions are strictly concave in λ_a (and λ_b) and strictly convex in λ_n (with n $\neq$ a for the first, and $\neq$ b for the second), properties that I use in the next section.

We have seen (Subsection i) that the ϕ_a^j function – and, by the assumption of proportionality, the π_b^j function also – presupposes competition between centers of power. We can now see that equations 2.9 and 2.10 also formalize the idea that the electoral success of an elected center of power – center "b", for example – depends on the actions of other centers of power, including nonelected ones. To put it differently, the expected vote of an elected governing party can be adversely affected not only by the actions of opposition parties but also by, among others, those of a supreme court, a nonelected senate, a central bank, or an intelligence service. In view of the fact that political science, history, and journalism are replete with case studies and anecdotes suggesting that in a number of instances elected governing parties were defeated by nonelected bodies, it is useful to have a model capable of integrating these facts. The standard voting models cannot do this.

If we had "perfect" measures of ϕ^j for all centers of power, we could, by simply tracking their time paths and relating these to the quantities of the goods and services provided to j or to a group of j's – a standard multiple regression exercise – obtain theoretically correct estimates of j's demand functions for all government-supplied goods and services. But, as we have seen, the ϕ^j's depend on the λ^j's – the utility losses – which in turn are defined for given taxprices. Is it appropriate, even with an equilibrium volume of free-riding, to assume that taxprices are given? Can we, to put it differently, assume that an analysis conducted in a partial equilibrium context in which taxprices are parametrically given will be valid in a general equilibrium framework in which taxprices are endogenous and variable? As we shall see immediately, the answer is "yes," with one minor additional assumption.

No doubt there are governmental centers of power that harbor the belief that they can and do have a significant and enduring effect on the level of the (marginal) taxprices of the goods and services they supply. They are not on that account different from a host of business entrepreneurs operating in competitive environments who are convinced that the prices at which they sell the goods and services they produce reflect decisions that they themselves make. If queried, these entrepreneurs would affirm in near unanimity that taxes, say, are fully shifted forward to consumers or backward to factors of production.

These beliefs may not be completely illusory even for the suppliers who operate in perfectly competitive environments. Kenneth Arrow (1959), more than thirty years ago, made the point that economics lacks a theory of price formation and adjustment. Even though some work on the question has been done in the intervening years, there is still little definite on the matter that elicits general agreement. Arrow argued that in the short term prices have to be the outcome of rational hands-on decisions of market agents, even if in the longer run these prices reflect the impersonal forces of supply and demand. Because neoclassical economics allows only monopolists (oligopolists) and monopsonists (oligopsonists) to have price policies, Arrow suggested that the market agents who take decisions about prices have to be seen, even in perfectly competitive markets, as transitory monopolists or monopsonists. Jevons's Law of Indifference, that only one price will rule in a competitive market, therefore holds only in equilibrium. On the path to equilibrium, we will observe distributions of prices influenced by sellers, buyers, or both, even in markets that are perfectly competitive in terms of the usual conditions related to product homogeneity and divisibility, number of suppliers, entry conditions, and information.

Nevertheless, the assumption that in competitive environments neither suppliers nor demanders can have a noticeable influence on prices remains a useful and productive assumption for many problems. In that spirit, we could assume that the changes we often observe in (marginal) taxprices are not the result of actions undertaken by centers of power but system-wide responses to changes in the sum of individual demand and supply functions reflecting variations in technologies (including the technologies used to control tax avoidance and evasion), preferences (including the subjective moral inhibitions to escape taxes), endowments, and the ability of governmental centers of power to compete with alternative sources of supply such as families, churches, charitable organizations, clubs, and labor unions (see Chapter 12).

If we make that assumption, which is associated with the paradigm of perfect competition in prices, centers of power must be seen as taking marginal taxprices as given and, as portrayed in Figures 2.1 and 2.2, as competing with one another by varying quantities. Theirs is a world of quantity competition. Exogenous or system-wide adjustments in taxprices, perceived or known by citizens to be such, cannot have any effect on the volume of consent granted to centers of power by citizens. If, however, because of information problems, citizens do not perceive the changes in taxprices to be exogenous or if centers of power have some power over taxprices because price competition is less than perfect, variations in taxprices will affect the expected consent granted to centers of power.

To appreciate what happens when there is a change in taxprices (quantities provided remaining constant), we can no longer limit the analysis to the utility losses associated with differences in quantities desired and supplied but must include in the analysis the direct burden of tax payments. It is useful to temporarily abandon the language of utility loss that I have been using so far and to replace it with the equivalent language of excess burden, which is more in harmony with that of direct burden. Consider then what happens to citizen j when the taxprice of good G increases from t^* to t'. We must distinguish between two cases, namely, that which obtains when the quantity of G provided is greater than the amount desired and that which obtains when the amount supplied is smaller than the volume desired. These two cases are shown in Figure 2.3(a) and 2.3(b).

When the quantity actually supplied (G') is greater than the quantity desired (G^*) at the initial taxprice t^*, the excess burden of public provision is equal to abc. A rise in the taxprice from t^* to t' with the supply remaining at G' increases j's expenditures on G from Ot^*aG' to $Ot'a'G'$, and the direct burden of these expenditures rises by the difference or by $t^*t'a'a$. Excess burden grows from abc to $a'b'c$. The total burden of the taxprice increase is, therefore, $t^*t'a'a + a'b'c > abc$ always.

When G'' is smaller than G^* at the initial taxprice, the excess burden of public provision is def. If the taxprice increases to t' with supply remaining at G'', total expenditures on G will rise from Ot^*fG'' to $Ot'f'G''$ and the direct burden of these expenditures will, as in the first case, increase by the difference or by $t^*t'f'f$. The excess burden, however, shrinks from def to $d'ef'$ and will shrink as long as the taxprice is lower than $\hat{t}$, after which it will necessarily increase. The total burden of the taxprice increase is $t^*t'f'f + d'ef'$, which may be greater or smaller than def when but only when $t' < \hat{t}$. If $dd'f'f > t^*t'f'f + d'ef'$, the total burden of a taxprice increase will be negative – it

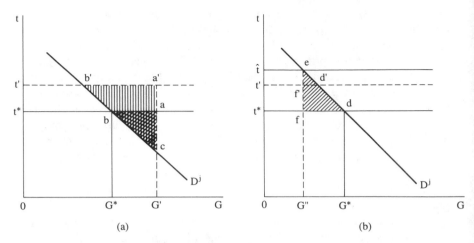

Figure 2.3. Measuring the utility loss of an increase of the tax price of a good.

will make j better off. For this to happen, the direct burden of the taxprice increase must be small relative to the reduction in the initial excess burden. The first part of this proposition is more likely the smaller the increase in taxprice is (for increments below t̂) and the smaller in *absolute* terms the volume of G supplied; the likelihood of the second part is greater the smaller, *relative* to the volume desired, the amount of G provided, and the larger j's elasticity of demand for G at t*.

Put differently, if we assume that the initial (pretaxprice increase) excess burden (def) is small because quantity competition between centers of power is vigorous and has therefore made the difference between G* and G″ small, a taxprice increase will in general make j worse off. This is the assumption I mentioned earlier as being needed to guarantee the validity of the partial equilibrium analysis in a general equilibrium context. In what follows, being almost exclusively concerned with the different *modi operandi* of quantity competition among centers of power, I will suppose that this assumption holds and as a consequence I will disregard the minor possibility that a taxprice increase could make j better off. I will, in other words, proceed on the assumption that a taxprice increase will always reduce the consent that a center of power can expect if it is itself responsible for the higher taxprice and will raise consent if the higher taxprice originates with other centers of power.

The reader can verify that, on the same logic, reductions in tax prices will make j better off and that as a consequence their effects on expected consent will be the exact opposite of those associated with increases in taxprices.

The onus of the foregoing is that when price competition is perfect and taxprices change as a consequence of system-wide adjustments in supply or demand functions to exogenous disturbances but that, because of information problems, citizens believe the changes were caused by one or more centers of power, the effect of these price changes on the welfare of j will affect the volume of consent that j will grant to centers of power. The outcome will be identical when price competition is imperfect and the changes in taxprices are effectively caused by one or more centers of power. We must be aware, however, that the domain over which j's welfare can change when quantities change is different from that over which welfare can vary when prices change. It will be recalled that the λ's – associated with quantity changes – are always positive or, at the limit, equal to zero. That is, they can take values between zero and $+\infty$, whereas the measure of welfare change associated with price variations, which we may label θ, can be positive or negative and can therefore take any value between $-\infty$ and $+\infty$. Because I am mostly concerned with understanding the behavior of political systems under quantity competition, I will continue, with little loss in generality, to work with the λ's and therefore with the expected consent and expected vote functions – equations (2.9) and (2.10) – defined earlier, referring to the θ's only when necessary.

2.3. Demand lobbies

The discussion in the preceding section should have made clear that one of the most, if not *the* most, serious problems confronting all centers of power attempting to become or to remain competitive is a need for adequate information about the ϕ^j's (and the π^j's) of equations (2.9) and (2.10). More precisely, centers of power need information on three types of variables: first, on the magnitude of the changes in all λ's (and θ's) when the quantities and qualities (and the taxprices) of the goods and services they themselves supply change – on the inverse of the own-elasticity of demand functions at ruling taxprices; second, on the size of the changes in these λ's (and θ's) when the quantities and qualities (and the taxprices and market prices) of the goods and services supplied by other centers of power and by the market (recall equations 2.6 of Section 2.1) change – on the inverse of the cross-elasticities of demand functions. Chapter 3 emphasizes that goods and services are, for the great bulk of them, bundles of (Lancasterian) characteristics. Third, in view of that fact, centers of power also need information on how the goods and services they are planning to supply should be designed because, for most goods and services, the characteristics can be combined in a large, sometimes very large, number of ways.

Vote intention data, available publicly, are proxies for the $\sum_j \pi^j$'s. These intentions do not as a rule pertain to the supply of a particular good or service but to a whole vector of these, so that it is usually impossible for centers of power to form even a crude idea of the $\partial \pi^j / \partial \lambda^j$'s that are relevant to themselves. Pollsters, furthermore, do not provide much public data on the $\sum_j \phi^j$'s. In addition, centers of power can and do seek information privately on the λ's (and θ's) by purchasing confidential data from pollsters. (Many centers of power have a continuous association with one or more polling firms.) Because public information is by definition common knowledge, private information is particularly valuable for those centers that can obtain it in competing with centers that cannot.

However, poll and survey data, even of the private variety and even when very detailed, cannot illuminate all the relevant dimensions of demand functions – the inverse own- and cross-elasticities – or reveal all the characteristics that citizens want the goods and services supplied to possess. Furthermore, polling is by construction totally incapable of conveying information from centers of power to citizens about the rationale for the design of many goods and services supplied. An important complement to poll and survey data is the information obtained from groups that are identified in the literature as interest or pressure groups or as lobbies and that I call *demand lobbies.* However, given that the groups are as a rule organized around a particular interest, it would not be inappropriate to call them *interest groups,* and given that they do exert pressure on centers of power, the term *pressure group* would also not be inappropriate. It is to emphasize the central role these groups play in the demand revelation process that I have chosen to call them demand lobbies.

Jan Potters and Frans van Winden (1990, 1992, 1993) and Potters (1992) have stressed that if the transmission of information is not given a central role in the analysis of lobbying, it is often difficult or even impossible to understand how groups exert pressure and how they influence the behavior of centers of power. (On a relationship between information and pressure different from that stressed by van Winden and Potters, see Appendix D.) Sometimes, of course, monetary contributions are the conduits through which pressure is applied. Potters and van Winden's point should not be dismissed, however. Some evidence, discussed later, indicates that many groups – possibly a majority – make no monetary or any other sorts of contributions to the election campaigns of elected centers of power or to nonelected centers. That should not be surprising. Other organizations – for example, churches, charities, foundations, committees of inquiry – are incessantly lobbied by groups that favor one policy orientation over another without being the beneficiaries of monetary or other in-kind contributions. Pressure is exercised through the transmission of information.

In addition, political scientists [see, for example, Smith (1975), Pross (1986), Finkle, Webb, Stanbury, and Pross (1991) and Young (1991)] have documented that demand lobbies do convey information to elected and non-elected centers of power. I assume therefore that one of the important activities of demand lobbies is to transmit information to centers of power on the utility loss suffered by their members and on the preferences and demands of these members as well as on the volume and characteristics (see Chapter 3) that goods and services should possess if they are to match these preferences and demands. In addition, demand lobbies transmit information from centers of power to their membership on certain properties of the goods and services these centers have provided. This aspect of information transmission is particularly important when the goods and services supplied are complex, a feature that may itself be the outcome of compromises forced on centers of power by competition (for a development of this idea, see Subsection iii of this chapter and Chapter 3, Section 3.4).

To understand how demand lobbies operate, it is important to know something about their composition and about how, severally but *in toto,* they interact in equilibrium with the set of all centers of power. That problem is discussed in Subsection ii of this chapter. It is also essential to appreciate how the lobbies deal with what are in effect agency problems – namely, the problem of shirking by lobby members and that of reverse shirking by lobby managers. These two problems are discussed in Subsections ii and iii, respectively, of this chapter. Cheating and reverse cheating are problems that concern the internal organization of lobbies. A quite different problem pertains to the relations of lobby managers with centers of power. It arises when these relations are collusive and the collusion leads to information falsification and, through that medium, to rent-seeking. I discuss that problem in Subsection iv of this chapter.

i. *Aggregation and the interaction of demand lobbies with centers of power*

If the information that demand lobbies convey is to be correctly interpreted by centers of power, it must be as limpid and transparent as possible. In other words, if the necessarily imprecise and informal qualitative information from demand lobbies is to provide accurate measures of the interval on which the own-elasticities and the cross-elasticities of the demand functions of lobby members are located and of the range over which the desired characteristics of the goods and services supplied are to be found, lobbies must be constituted of persons who, in regard to a particular good or service, confront essentially the same marginal taxprice and therefore desire to be provided with the same quantity and quality of that good or service. In other words, lobbies will be constituted of persons who, at a given taxprice, have essentially the same own- and cross-elasticity of demand and the same preferences for goods and services and their characteristics. Demand lobbies are, in respect of particular goods and services and their ruling taxprices, aggregations of individual demand functions having the same properties. We must, therefore, agree with Wittman (1989, p. 1,400) that citizens choose their lobbies.

As a consequence, we should expect demand lobbies to be organized around single issues or single interests or around closely related issues or interests, which does not mean that citizens (or firms) are single-issue persons (or bodies). They can be and often are members of many demand lobbies. We should also expect – a point already noted by Stigler (1974, p. 363) – that every broad interest and concern will be represented by many demand lobbies. The exact number of these lobbies will be determined by the significant differences in the relevant populations in respect of own- and cross-elasticities of demand and in respect of the preferences for the characteristics of goods and services. For example, on issues such as feminism and the environment, which involve large numbers of persons and on which opinions range widely from radical to moderate – from low to high own-price elasticities of demand for particular goods and service – we expect the number of demand lobbies to be large and so it is [see Phillips (1991) and Trzyna (1989)].

What is true for women's issues and the environment is also true for broad concerns pertaining to trade, commerce, industry, finance, labor, education, health, the arts, culture, youth, sports, civil rights, housing, zoning, old-age pensions, delinquency, the professions (for example, lawyers, architects, physicians, engineers, chiropractors, plumbers, and electricians) and the interests of minorities (for example, disabled persons, aboriginals, visible minorities, and ethnic groups). In respect of every one of these, the number of demand lobbies is large.

In the last analysis, the information transmitted by demand lobbies to elected and nonelected centers of power pertains to the probabilities of consent (and the probabilities of vote) of lobby members and on how these probabilities vary – that is, on the sign and size of the $\partial \phi^1 / \partial \lambda_n^1$'s for all l (= 1, . . . , L) demand lobbies and all n (= 1, . . . , N) centers of power. Lobbies transmit information about these variables to insure that the utility losses that would otherwise be inflicted on lobby members are minimized.

As a result of this transmission of information, demand lobbies and centers of power are linked. These links or avenues of interaction can be represented by a N × L matrix – that is, a matrix of N columns for the N centers of power and of L rows for the L demand lobbies. If we assume, as I have done earlier (Section 2.2), that the ϕ_n^1 functions – the cell entries of the N × L matrix – are continuous and strictly concave in the λ's "controlled" by a lobby's "own" centers of power, and strictly convex in all the other λ's, it can be shown, as

Wittman (1984) has done, that a noncooperative Nash equilibrium exists.[19] It can be shown that if each center of power acts on the assumption that the actions of all other centers are given, each center, in seeking to maximize expected consent, will make the λ's as small as possible. It is an important conclusion that under the assumption of probabilistic voting, which I have borrowed, all citizens and hence all lobbies – not just the median or some other unique individual – count. All centers of power seek the consent of all citizens and of all lobbies.

The $N \times L$ center–lobby matrix also implies that citizens and demand lobbies are capable of recognizing the singular contribution of each center of power to increases and decreases in utility losses – to the λ's and the θ's. Two studies bear directly on this question. The first, from Arthur Schram and Frans van Winden (1989), makes use of the latter's (1983, 1987) "interest function" approach to politics – an approach that, incidentally, marries snugly with the theory of probabilistic voting and therefore with the model I have adopted. The approach is based on a voting model in which the various political parties that constitute the governing coalition are not "held equally responsible for government policies . . . by the voters" (Schram and van Winden, 1989, p. 266). Their empirical investigations, though based on ad-mittedly weak data, support the conclusion that voters differentially perceive the contribution of coalition members to the supply of goods and services. This conclusion means that these parties – these centers of power – compete with one another on a continuous basis. We owe the second study to Lafay (1989–90) who, making use of a different formalization of electoral competi-tion, is able to show at the conceptual and at the empirical level – though also on the basis of noisy data – that opposition parties compete continuously with the ruling party for the support of citizens. This competition would not happen unless citizens were aware of the contribution of opposition parties to their welfare.

ii.   Shirking by lobby members

As noted, demand lobbies have to resolve two agency problems. The first, the object of this subsection, originates in the fact that the members of all lobbies (the principals in a principal–agent relationship) seek a common goal and have as a consequence an incentive to shirk (free-ride). That problem has received enormous attention [Moore (1961), Olson (1965), Stigler (1974), and

---

19. Lafay (1992) has noted that Wittman's demonstration need not be restricted, as it is in the 1984 paper, to pairwise comparisons and selection of candidates or, in the present frame-work, to pairwise comparisons of centers of power by citizens or lobbies.

Salmon (1987a, 1987b) are important contributions]. The second, the object of the next subsection, derives from the fact that group "leaders" – Pierre Salmon's expression – or group managers (the agents) have an incentive to cheat or shirk and have the capacity to do so. To my knowledge, Salmon is the only writer to have stressed the importance of this second problem.[20]

It would serve no purpose to review the literature on the various instruments that group or lobby managers can in principle use to control shirking by members. That has already very competently been done [for example, Salmon (1987a)]. I concentrate instead on what governmental centers of power themselves contribute to the solution of this problem. It is not surprising that the managers of lobbies would want to deal with cheating because if they did not and lobbies were to vanish, members would be worse off and management out of a job. It needs to be emphasized that if lobbies were to disappear, the capacity of centers of power to compete with one another would also be adversely affected. Centers, therefore, have an interest in the existence and in the effectiveness of lobbies.

Rochelle Stanfield (1981), Jack Walker (1983), James Bennett and Thomas DiLorenzo (1985), Paul Pross (1986), Finkle et al. (1991) on the basis of primary evidence and James Wilson (1973) and Salmon (1987a) on the basis of secondary evidence have independently documented that governmental centers of power actually sponsor the creation of demand lobbies (interest and pressure groups) and subsequently finance their activities. Many, possibly all, lobbies receive direct or indirect financial support from centers of power to conduct purely lobbying activities. Many lobbies are tax exempt. For others, the lobbying expenses of group members can be charged against the revenue of the business concerns to which the members belong. In still other cases, donations received from the public, which are in part used for lobbying, can be charged, according to one formula or another, against the taxable income of donors. Finkle et al. (1991, Table 7.3), on the basis of noisy data, calculate that during the fiscal year 1986–87, eighteen departments (ministries) of the Canadian government paid a total of $185 million to 462 different groups or lobbies. Young (1991, p. 139) reports that his "survey data [of a New Brunswick sample of interest groups] reveal that . . . 19.7% of all associations received funding from local governments, 27.9% from the central government, and 39.3% from the provincial government." Susan Phillips (1991) notes that a large number of women's organizations in Canada are funded by the federal government and by some provincial governments. Bennett and

20. Though ignored in the literature, this second agency problem also plagues Buchanan's (1965) clubs, Olson's (1965) interest groups, and Becker's (1983) pressure groups as well as other rent-seeking bodies. Clubs directly provide their members with goods and services. In all relevant cases, they will have a management so that the club will be presented with a reverse shirking problem.

DiLorenzo (1985) provide a large volume of quantitative data on the financial resources granted by the United States government to groups that surely constitute a sizeable subset of all demand lobbies in the United States. Their sources are diverse and not strictly comparable and, as a consequence, aggregation over the whole is not permissible, but the numbers they report, especially in their Appendix, point to enormous sums. Stanfield (1981) and Walker (1983) also provide evidence for the United States, and Margot Breton (1991) documents that social services lobbies in France have benefited from public funds.

Sometimes the support is indirect. Pross (1986) reports that at the end of the 1970s, the Canadian government appointed an interest group to act as a "middleman" between the sellers and the buyers of a commodity, thus allowing the middle man to collect a percentage of the sales price as a commission (p. 196). He also reports that government support "can take the form of special subsidies for publication, consulting fees, subventions for hospitality at conferences, aid for specific projects, travel grants, and so on" as well as "payment for specific services (such as research services, commissions on the sale of hunting licenses, and so on)" and "secondment of personnel to specific groups," a practice, Pross claims, which is "more common in Europe than in Canada" (pp. 196–7).

In Walker's (1983, p. 397) words "group leaders [have] learned how to cope with the public goods [free-riding] dilemma not by inducing large numbers of new members to join their groups through the manipulation of selective benefits, but by locating important new sources of funds outside the immediate membership." The point of the foregoing is that governmental funding is an important contribution to the solution of the shirking problem diagnosed by Olson (1965). We cannot proceed without attempting an answer to the question of why governmental centers of power make that kind of contribution. The answer must be, at least as long as we hold to the assumption of rational behavior, that centers of power find it in their interest to do so. That interest, I have been suggesting, is the *quid pro quo* that lobbies provide to the contributing centers – namely, information about the properties of the demand functions of lobby members and, therefore, about the factors that help to determine the probabilities of consent.

Demand lobbies, in other words, transmit information on variables that becomes the basis that centers of power use to design, produce, and supply goods and services in quantities and qualities that match those desired by citizens. Lobbies know that in respect of the supply of virtually all goods and services, many centers of power and, therefore, many demand lobbies are involved. They also know that in designing and producing goods and services, many centers of power have to coordinate their activities and, hence, work together. They know, third, that all centers of power seek to maximize expected consent. Finally, they know that the outcome of the competitive struggle between the centers of power will be a Nash equilibrium like the one, noted earlier, derived by Wittman (1984) or like the ones derived in the next two chapters. There can be no reason, therefore, why they would try to falsify the information about preferences and about utility losses that they are transmitting to centers of power to influence supply outcomes. Falsification in any direction would only make lobby members worse off. As a consequence, it is rational for centers of power to sponsor the creation of demand lobbies and to fund a volume of their activities large enough to ensure their survival, since the centers can expect truthful and unbiased information from demand lobbies.

iii.   *Reverse shirking by lobby managers*

I have so far limited the discussion to the question of whether lobby members have an incentive to falsify information about the properties of their preference and demand functions and about the size of utility losses. I have argued that they do not. We must now ask whether lobby managers have an incentive to shirk in the transmittal of that information to centers of power. The answer to that question is that they do on the only assumption that transmission is costly in time and effort. Lobby members no doubt adopt a variety of measures to reduce the volume of this sort of reverse shirking from which they are the ultimate victims. Some of these measures may mimic those recommended by optimal contract theory. But – and that is what I wish to emphasize in this discussion of the benefits of demand lobbies to governmental centers of power – we should also expect these centers of power, because they maximize expected consent and therefore wish to do their best for their constituencies, to take steps aimed at reducing the gravity of the agency problem of cheating by management.

   And they do. Demand lobbies are often legally required to be invested with letters patent or with a written constitution registered with one government department or the other. They must also file annual reports of their activities, including an income statement and a balance sheet; and they are exposed to periodic detailed audits. The activities of management are in turn often circumscribed by law [see Weisbrod (1988, pp. 119–20 and Appendix DE)]. One of the accepted avenues of redress in cases of serious managerial abuse is reference to the courts. Governmental centers of power do not undertake to control managerial shirking because of the satisfaction they derive from honest behavior – they do it to obtain truthful and unbiased information about the preference and demand functions of citizens and about the size of utility losses inflicted on them so as to be able to compete more effectively with other centers of power.

iv.   *Collusion and rent-seeking*

The discussion has to date been mostly focused on only one of the information transmission activities of demand lobbies, namely, that which pertains to information related to the properties of the lobby members' demand functions for goods and services. Demand lobbies do, however, perform another important information transmission task: They convey information to their members on the performance of centers of power as suppliers of goods and services, on the attributes of especially complex goods or services, and on the reasons supply does not match demand as well as was initially imagined. This is a particularly important activity in a world in which states of nature are uncertain and in which, as a consequence, it may be difficult to impute responsibility for favorable and unfavorable supply outcomes, and in a world, furthermore, where supply outcomes are the product of a sometimes fierce competitive struggle between centers of power that can force compromises in original positions and modifications in promises made or intimated.

Because the management of demand lobbies is relatively close to the actual processes of politics, it will be able to a degree to disentangle the part of a particular supply outcome caused by a benevolent or malevolent state of nature from the part caused by centers of power. It will be able to identify the alterations in original positions that are the result of a genuine need for compromise. Demand lobby managers, as a consequence, possess information superior to that which lobby members dispose of. The asymmetry in the distribution of, let me call it, supply information – to be distinguished from the demand information discussed in Subsections ii and iii – between managers and members of demand lobbies creates an opportunity for collusion between centers of power and lobby managers capable of generating rents that can be shared between them.

Asymmetric information provides an opportunity for collusion and rent-seeking. That opportunity may not be exploitable, however. To be able to exploit it, lobby managers must be able to convince their members that a particular supply outcome from which they (the managers) and the personnel of the relevant centers of power personally benefit was generated by a particular state of nature or by the necessity of compromising on original positions and promises in the competition with other centers of power, or both, even though none was the case. Collusion between centers of power and lobby managers will be more likely, the easier it is for the second to falsify information about the performance of the first.

Without making any claim about priority or about necessity and sufficiency, I suggest some of the conditions which, if they are present, will increase the incidence of collusion and of rent-seeking. First, if the state of nature that is alleged to be responsible for an outcome is difficult to ascertain and its relation to the outcome in the best circumstances controversial, it will be easier for lobby managers to misinform their members about a particular supply outcome. Second, the more asymmetric the distribution of information, the easier it will be to misinform members. This condition is more likely to obtain whenever lobby managers are friendly with some centers of power, either because of day-by-day involvement in supply decisions or because of previous employment by a center of power. To put it differently, the distribution of information between lobby managers and lobby members will be more asymmetric the greater the volume of "repeat business" between lobby managers and centers of power. Third, the incidence of collusion and of misinformation will be greater, the more difficult it is for lobby members to detect the rents that are accruing to lobby managers and to centers of power. Fourth, the more they are trusted by lobby members, the more likely lobby managers are to falsify information. Fifth, collusion is easier when numbers are small. If the design, production, and supply of a good or service can be effected with a few centers of power and a few demand lobbies, collusion will be more likely because it will be easier to construct a coherent story – a coherent falsehood – and to live by it. Sixth, collusion will be easier, the greater the difficulty of entry into the production process. One of the permanent problems of politics concerns who should and who should not be involved in the supply process. In the case of certain goods and services, it is relatively easy to erect barriers to entry; for most goods and services, however, entry is free and collusion more difficult. Seventh and last, collusion is easier if information falsification does not adversely affect third parties. If, for example, a competing center of power is disadvantaged by the false information or by the rents that are created, one should expect reprisal, which could possibly dissolve the collusion.

It should be clear that in a competitive frame of reference, the creation of rents and their seizure by individuals must be the consequence of collusion or of other obstacles to competition. In such a frame of reference, as the discussion of redistribution and transfers in Chapter 1 (Section 1.1) made clear, it is not easy to distinguish between genuine rents and the goods and services provided by governmental centers of power to citizens and lobbies. The situation is not very different from that which obtains in the marketplace where the stream of genuine rents and the stream of other amenities (including, of course, the returns to specific qualities, location, etc.) cannot be easily disentangled either.

2.4.   The Wicksellian Connection

A discussion of how competition between centers of power forges or builds a behavioral connection between the quantity and quality of the goods and services supplied by these centers of power and the taxprices citizens must pay for them, which minimizes utility losses, can only be broached in this chapter. It is necessary to know more about the forms that competition can take and about the *modus operandi* of these forms to be able to appreciate how utility losses are minimized and how the Wicksellian Connection is constructed.

It is possible at this early stage, however, disregarding the complications that are inherent in the *modi operandi* of political competition, to appreciate the place of information in the edification of the Wicksellian Connection. (For a discussion of an alternative informational conduit that appears to generate something like a Wicksellian Connection, see Appendix E.) To proceed, assume that there are only two centers of power – "a" and "b" – and two homogeneous demand lobbies – 1 and 2 – with "a" representing Lobby 1 and "b" Lobby 2. Assume, to make things as simple as possible, that Lobby 1 has a demand for only one good, namely G, which is supplied by the centers of power in amount G_0 at a fixed taxprice t*. Lobby 1's demand curve is portrayed in Figure 2.4 by D_G^1. Lobby 2, in addition to a demand for G (depicted as D_G^2), also has a demand for a market-provided good X, which is shown as D_X^2 in Figure 2.4. Lobby 2, therefore, is the entire market for X.

In the initial situation, it is easy to verify that Lobby 1 suffers a utility loss equal to efg, and that Lobby 2's utility loss is equal to e'fg'. In addition, Lobby 2 consumes X_0 of X at market price P_{x0}. Now assume that center of power "a" becomes perfectly informed about efg and that for one reason or another it is able to have the production and delivery of G reduced from G_0 to G_1. As a consequence, the utility loss of Lobby 1 falls to zero and the expected consent granted "a" by 1 rises. Lobby 2, however, is much worse off – its utility loss is now equal to eg'h, which reduces the expected consent that 2 grants to "b." What can "b" do to alter that state of affairs? As the problem is set up, "b" cannot change G_1 (it is the outcome of, let us say, a game that "b" has lost) or t*, which is exogenously given. If the problem had allowed for goods and services produced and designed by "a" and "b" that were either complements to or substitutes for G, "b" might have turned its attention toward these goods and services. However, the way things are, "b" can do nothing else but turn its attention to the market for X in the hope of improving its fortune.

If we assume that "b" is fully informed about eg'h and if, to simplify the presentation, we also assume that G and X are substitutes made legitimate by the optimization exercise of Section 2.1, "b" could pursue a number of avenues to reduce eg'h to zero. It could (1) subsidize the consumption of X, (2) subsidize its production directly or through programs like accelerated depreciation or funded R and D, (3) tax domestic and/or foreign market substitutes of X, or (4) it could itself purchase some X all in magnitudes that would induce a

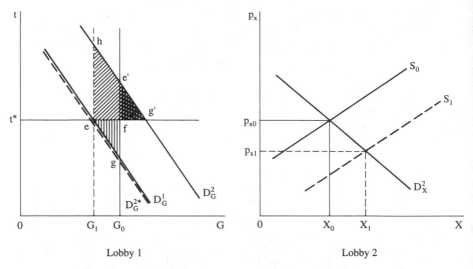

Figure 2.4. A "primitive" pareto efficient Wicksellian Connection.

shift in D_G^2 to D_G^{2*}, which in Figure 2.4 is drawn as a broken line that fully overlaps D_G^1. In Figure 2.4, I assume a policy that shifts the supply curve of X from S_0 to S_1, which is assumed sufficient to move D_G^2 to D_G^{2*}.

It is worth noting that the final outcome would be the same whether G was a conventional Samuelsonian public good or an ordinary private good. Preference orders and demand functions are perfectly revealed in both cases. In addition, it should be observed that the final outcome is Pareto-efficient, that the reduction in the production of G and the shift of the S-curve have moved the politico-economic system from a second-best to a first-best equilibrium as these notions are defined in the standard theory of second-best. (For a definition of these equilibria and for discussions of the policy problems that pertain to second-best environments, see, for example, Lipsey and Lancaster, 1956; Davis and Whinston, 1965; McManus, 1967; and Mougeot, 1989, especially pp. 201–12.) It is not necessary to insist that if "a" and "b" are in possession of information about the utility losses – the λ's and the θ's – that is less than perfect and that if they act on this imperfect information, they could move the system toward its first-best position but stop short of reaching it; they could also worsen the initial second-best equilibrium.

One point needs to be emphasized. The process of competition that leads to the revelation of demand functions and to Pareto-optimal Wicksellian Connections relies in an essential way on the ability of centers of power to supply private goods as well as on the centers' capacity to alter the prices of these goods. It should come as no surprise, therefore, that governments are in fact heavily involved in providing all sorts of private goods. Such provision is not an aberration but a requirement of efficiency.

The theory of second-best and the model suggested in this section have one more thing in common: Neither contains a mechanism that would move the system from a second-best to a first-best position. The policymakers in the theory of second-best, as elsewhere in Welfare Economics, are "do-gooders," whereas those in the discussion centered on Figure 2.4 pursue their own interest. Motivations alone, however, are not equilibrium-inducing mechanisms, as we know from standard microeconomic theory in which all entrepreneurs are self-interested profit maximizers who nevertheless produce very different equilibrium outcomes, depending on whether competition has been suppressed, is imperfect, or is perfect. I return to this issue in Section 3.4 of the next chapter.

2.5.   Conclusion

The theory of demand adumbrated in the preceding pages has taken seriously the facts that there are numerous centers of power in all governments and that few of them are elected. Rejecting the idea that the competition that exists between these centers of power is solely motivated by hubris or megalomania, I have argued that the incitation to compete is furnished by the need of centers of power for the consent of citizens. Citizens in turn grant more of their consent if, at given taxprices, centers of power provide them with goods and services in quantities that more closely approach the quantities they desire. I have also argued that it is intragovernmental competition that activates the mechanisms that lead citizens to reveal their nominal demands for government-supplied goods and services. It is the same competition, I have further argued, that explains why governmental centers of power not only sponsor the creation of demand lobbies but also contribute to the solution of the problem of shirking by lobby members and of that of reverse shirking by lobby managers. I acknowledge the possibility of collusion and of rent creation and seizure by lobby managers and centers of power, and I list some of the conditions that make collusion more likely. Finally, I begin the analysis of the Wicksellian Connection by showing that when information about utility losses is perfect, it is possible to generate first-best Pareto-efficient equilibrium outcomes that are located directly on the demand curves of citizens. Whether such equilibrium results are in fact produced is the object of the next three chapters.

CHAPTER 3

Checks and balances

The preceding chapter was almost entirely devoted to matters that pertain to demand. This chapter and those that follow do not neglect demand (see Section 3.3), but they focus on supply. I propose a model of checks and balances that I believe can illuminate the behavior of governments as unalike as those of, let us say, Canada, France, Italy, and the United States. To execute that assignment, my first task is to argue that the governments of the countries I have just named and no doubt those of many others must be conceived as aggregations of centers of power – as compound governments. My second task – undertaken in Sections 3.2 and 3.3 – consists in showing that the supply of goods and services by governmental centers of power is achieved through concessions, compromises, and accommodations but also, and just as critically, through the expression of what in Chapter 1 (Section 1.5) I called Schumpeterian entrepreneurship. All these achievements are caused or brought about by checks and balances that are in turn a particular form or manifestation of competition. The view put forward in this chapter is, therefore, that the collaboration between centers of power and the harmonization and coordination of their activities that can be observed is not the result of spontaneous cooperation between them but the product of competitive checking that elicits concessions, compromises, accommodations, and entrepreneurship – behaviors that if they are cooperative, are nevertheless a response to competition. In Section 3.4, I indicate how checks and balances serve to build Wicksellian Connections or Links between quantities supplied and the taxprices that have to be levied to pay for them and how, therefore, demand functions for government-supplied goods and services are revealed by the operation of that form of competition. I have already noted that the model of checks and balances I am proposing is general enough to embrace the supply behavior of all modern democratic governments. I must, therefore, return in Section 3.5 to the widely accepted view that checks and balances are an exclusive feature of the American system of government and, as a consequence, are absent from parliamentary governments.

If competition is not to degenerate in strife and warfare – if it is to be beneficial – it must be governed by rules in politics as in economics. My third task, the subject matter of Section 3.6, is to examine some of the rules that are essential for the efficient operation of a democratic order of government. This is an exceedingly difficult task. I must give immediate warning, therefore, that Section 3.6 will do no more than lay some preliminary groundwork. Section 3.7 concludes the chapter.

3.1.   Compound governments

The centers of power relevant for the analysis of governmental production and supply are those that possess some degree of autonomy, namely, those that are under the management of persons who have the capacity to make decisions and the ability to implement these decisions, which, as I endeavor to show, implies a capability to use one or more of the checking instruments I describe below. Some of these centers have their origin in constitutional law, some in statute law, others in organizational design, and others still in time-sanctioned conventions. That fact, as we shall immediately discover, is central to an understanding of compound governments as well as to an understanding of how those who are ultimately accountable for the decisions and activities of centers of power become capable of using checking instruments.

The literature on centers of power and on checks and balances has historically been focused, most appropriately, on the question of the separation of powers or on that of the structure of so-called mixed governments. In deference to that tradition, whose life now exceeds 2,500 years, I begin by looking briefly at the concept of the separation of powers before proceeding with the analysis of the organization of compound governments.

Expressions such as "separation" or "division" of powers must be used with care. A failure to do so has been and remains a major cause of the sometimes profound misunderstanding regarding the nature of compound governments and of checks and balances regularly encountered. Based on some literal acceptation of the word *separation* or the word *division,* some discussions proceed on the generally implicit supposition that checks and balances require that centers of power be isolated, even insulated, from one another and that their activities not overlap. Casual observation then reveals that governmental centers of power are not isolated and that their activities overlap, from which it is concluded that powers are not separated and that checks and balances must, therefore, be absent.

Separation of powers is not an expression that pertains to the separation of centers of power. It refers to the separate, singular, and distinctive authority (power in the singular) possessed by these centers of power. The authority is separate, singular, and distinctive because it has its source – its foundation – in a separate, singular, and distinctive base. For some centers that base is constitutional law, for others it is statute law, for others still it is organizational design, or honored customs, conventions, or traditions, some of which may be the result of historical accidents. Separation of powers, therefore, means that the authority of a center of power cannot easily be taken away from it and abolished. Some bases are not easily assailable, and they are therefore more secure than others. Still, observation tells us that even very vulnerable centers of power will resist, sometimes fiercely, attempts to erode their authority.

In the discussion that follows, I seldom make reference to the separation of powers. Instead, I continue to describe centers of power – those, in any case, that are relevant for the analysis of checks and balances – as autonomous or quasi-autonomous. The autonomy or quasi-autonomy I will then be referring to is given to these centers by the separation of powers.

The literature on the separation of powers distinguishes between three branches – also called departments or organs – of government, to wit, the legislature, the executive, and the judiciary. The division of the legislative branch into two chambers – into, let us say, a House and a Senate – is sometimes acknowledged, but the significance of that fact for checking behavior is rarely recognized. Moreover, the opposition parties of parliamentary governments are seldom perceived to be genuine centers of power, a neglect that is doubly serious in bicameral systems. In view of all this, I must stress that to understand governmental production and supply, one cannot in general treat legislatures as if they were monolithic, but for reasons that should become clear one must make explicit that they are often constituted of a number of genuine autonomous centers of power. Let me illustrate by reference to Canada. The executive and legislative branches at the national level in Canada are constituted of four autonomous centers of power (at least if we consolidate, as we probably should not, the executive and the governing party into one single unit).[1] They are the Cabinet, the two opposition parties in the House, and the opposition party in the Senate. Furthermore, the widespread habit of treating the Cabinet as a single center of power – no doubt nurtured by the doctrine and practice of cabinet solidarity – is acceptable in some context, but in many others – such as in that of budget-making (see Chapter 4) – it simply runs counter to reality.[2]

When we turn our attention to the judiciary, the literature on the separation of powers and on mixed governments projects again the image of a branch made up of a single center of power. The existence of a hierarchy of courts and of a multiplicity of more or less specialized tribunals is, in effect, as-

1. The reason for the "probably" is that we know little about what goes on in the governing caucus – in the meetings that bring the parliamentary governing party and the cabinet together. It is not impossible, nay, it is highly probable, that the publicly displayed common front of the two groups reflects background bargaining and negotiation. In that case, the governing party and the cabinet would be best conceived as two separate centers of power, the view I adopt in Chapter 4.
2. See also the reference to the bicephalic nature of the Executive Branch of the French Government in Chapter 1, Section 1.2.

sumed not to matter. Still, courts higher in the structure decide on whether cases coming from below will stand, and some courts can and do invalidate the decisions of other courts in matters that pertain to the delivery of goods and services. In addition, courts and tribunals of all sorts often interpret the decisions of cabinets, legislatures, and centers of power that are not recognized as formal organs of government; they sometimes nullify these decisions; and in some cases even force these bodies to legislate in regard to the supply of some particular good or service.[3]

The literature that I have been considering will take us no further on the matter of identifying autonomous centers of power. We must, however, acknowledge that in addition to the widely recognized formal branches, compound governments are constituted of sometimes many other autonomous or quasi-autonomous centers of power which, for convenience, I will temporarily call *arm's length agencies*.[4] Their number is large and their variety great, so much so that it would be difficult to list them all and virtually impossible to describe them in detail. Simply to illustrate, let me mention central banks, intelligence services (at the national level in the United States there are, for example, five such services: the Federal Bureau of Investigation, the Central Intelligence Agency, the Defense Intelligence Agency, the National Security Agency, and the National Reconnaissance Office), diplomatic corps, and military establishments. In addition, there are advisory councils, police forces, parole boards, granting bodies, regulatory, human rights, language, and other commissions, auditing and inspection offices as well as welfare, cultural, and other agencies. That list can be easily expanded.

I can do no better in concluding a discussion that seeks to establish that modern governments are compound structures than quote from Nelson Polsby's (1986, p. 3) basic political science text:

> [I]nstead of three branches of government, each with its clearly defined sphere of competence and activity, there may be five branches of govern-

3. One should note at this point that the whole of the so-called *mani pulite* (clean hands) operation in Italy dedicated to the investigation of corruption in government and in other sections of society was initiated and conducted by the Judicial Branch of the Italian government – a branch that is neither elected nor appointed by the Executive and Legislative branches and that is, as a consequence, very independent or, in the language I have adopted for this study, very autonomous.

4. In his description of governments, Scott Gordon (1986) refuses, as I do, to restrict the notion of centers of power to the "formal organs of government." His list of additional centers includes "political parties, the press, business firms, labor unions, churches, educational institutions, public interest groups, etc." (p. I.2). A number of these bodies have an influence on political equilibria, but from the demand side. They do, indeed, constrain suppliers but only as demanders do. I am exclusively concerned with centers of power internal to governments. Political parties are therefore on my list as they are on Gordon's, but, as *additional* or new centers of power, I include only opposition parties because governing parties are already accounted for in the formal branches of government.

ment in any particular issue area, or seven, or twenty, or only one. The number of "branches" varies from time to time and from issue to issue.

Such a view is not only descriptively accurate. As Polsby implies and I intend to show, it is also the only one that correctly mirrors the actual processes of production and supply in compound governments.

As a preliminary to the analysis of these processes, let me introduce the distinction, basic to Chapter 2's argument but so far awkwardly absent from this chapter's discussion, between elected and nonelected centers of power. The management of arm's length agencies is generally not elected, though in a few cases constituency members may have an input in their selection. In democratic societies, there is always at least one and usually two, three, or more elected centers of power in what, out of respect for tradition, I continue to call the formal branches of government, though nonelected centers are also present in these organs. In the United States, for example, the head of the executive – the President – the House of Representatives and the Senate are elected, whereas the executive itself (excluding, of course, the President) and an important fraction of the judiciary are not. In Canada, on the other hand, the whole executive (the Cabinet) is, as a rule, elected as is the House of Commons, whereas the Senate and the entire judiciary are not.[5]

To proceed, I continue to use the hypothesis, introduced in Chapter 2, that all centers of power – whether elected or nonelected – maximize expected consent. The question that must now be considered pertains to the ways and means centers of power use to achieve that end. Among these, I select and, for the remainder of this chapter, focus on the use of checks (or checking instruments) by centers of power and on the responses, actions, and behaviors which that use elicits. I reserve the analysis of other forms of competition for the next two chapters.

3.2.   Definitions and assumptions

I begin the study of governmental production and supply and of the place and role of checks in these activities by addressing two topics that are preliminary to my main interest but that have to be dealt with before I can address that interest. The first, the concern of Subsection i, pertains to the relationship between checking and balancing and the second, the object of Subsection ii, relates to the nature of checking instruments and to some attributes of governmental production and supply processes.

---

5. Sometimes, usually in extraordinary circumstances, one or more nonelected Senators are appointed to the Cabinet. All in all, these are rare events.

i.   Checking and balancing

Knowledge of the vast literature on checks and balances which, as I have
already noted, has its origin in antiquity, can be claimed by only a small group
of specialists to which I do not belong. We are all extremely fortunate,
however, in being able to use two superb monographs – one by Epaminondas
Panagopoulos (1985) and the other by Scott Gordon (1986) – which provide a
detailed and fascinating history of the evolution of the concepts and of the
doctrines to which they are related.[6]

Three interconnected ideas central to the history of this evolution are particularly important for the present discussion. All three relate to the relationship
between checks and balances. The first idea is that to have the capacity to
check it is necessary that the centers of power that constitute compound
governments be balanced or equipoised vis-à-vis one another – hence,
the concentration of that literature on the separation and distribution of
powers and responsibilities and on the division and dispersion of political
power among the centers that make up compound governments. Over the
years, the institutions that provided the background to the reflection, first of
the Greeks, then of the Romans, followed by the Venetians, the Florentines,
the British, the French, and the Americans, kept changing, but the preoccupation throughout remained focused on the necessity of guaranteeing balance
between ever new constellations of centers of power, on the means of achieving that balance, and on the consequences of moving away from it. I return
briefly to this matter in Section 3.6 of this chapter. The position I take there is
that one should identify the notion of balance with that of autonomy of quasi-
autonomy, which as argued earlier, derives from a properly understood idea of
separation of powers.

The second idea – in fact, an implicit assumption – central to the history of
the debates on checks and balances is that if centers of power are balanced,
they will necessarily check each other. The burden of this implicit assumption
is that if the *institutions* are balanced or equipoised, the *behavior* adopted by
participants in the political process will of necessity be characterized by the
use of checks. Checking behavior, in other words, derives from balance. The
assumption found its way into the discussions naturally and unobtrusively, no
doubt because the analysts were primarily concerned with the problem of
balance – that is, with the problem of institutional design – and also, one
surmises, because they were observing that equipoised and, hence, autonomous centers of power in fact checked one another. It is an unfortunate

---

6. There are two editions of the Gordon manuscript. The first is dated 1985; I use a "revised"
   version dated 1986.

assumption for at least two reasons. First, it easily leads one to the view that the capacity to check derives from institutional arrangements and from legal and constitutional dispositions alone and not also from the productivity of the resources allocated to the use of checking instruments and from the responses of citizens to the use of these instruments. Second, it induces one to disregard the possibility of collusion between subsets of centers once a separation of powers and, hence, balance is achieved.

The third idea that drove many of the protagonists engaged in the millennial debates on checks and balances follows from the first two. It is that balancing is a substitute of sorts for checking and that as a consequence one need be concerned with only one of the two, especially if one's primary preoccupation is the design of a "good" compound government. This, too, helps us to understand why that literature is largely focused on balances. It will transpire, as I proceed, that checks and balances are related, but it should also become clear that the relationship between the two realities is a complicated one that is not well described by a word like substitution.

ii.   Checking instruments illustrated

One of the main difficulties, one soon discovers, in understanding checks and balances and in modelling their purpose and use is a lack of knowledge concerning the instruments that centers of power use to check one another. Though some checking instruments have their origin in constitutional and legal arrangements, many more are the product of conventions, circumstances, shrewdness, resourcefulness, or simply gall. For that reason, a complete list of all of them will, in all likelihood, always be beyond our reach. It is possible, however, to come to appreciate their nature by considering a few specimens from among those that are more often used.

Without prejudice as to significance and effectiveness and, certainly without claiming to be exhaustive but to stress their ubiquitousness, I list twelve prototypes that are more or less generic:

1. The formal power of veto and the more informal capacity to annul or disregard decisions and to shelve reports, notices, and other documents.
2. The formal power of judicial review and the less formal power, exercised by specialized tribunals and countless other authorities, to rescind and revise the decisions of other centers of power.[7]

7. For example, in 1985 the Canadian Government's Auditor General sued the Minister of Finance and the Minister of Energy, Mines and Resources as well as the Deputy Ministers of these two departments in the Federal Court of Canada. The Canadian Human Rights Commissioner sues government agencies on a more or less continuous basis. These actions take place while scholars keep arguing that checking is not a feature of parliamentary governments.

3. The power to obstruct, including the power to filibuster, to control debate through agenda manipulation, to introduce meaningless amendments, to force a division through a formal recorded vote, and to refuse to vote.[8]

4. The power, during formal question periods, to obtain information from cabinet ministers about matters related to the management of their departments, about their motives in pursuing certain objectives, and about their personal conduct.

5. The power to make appointments to committees, legislatures, courts, and other centers of power – including what is colloquially known as "packing" – and the power to dissolve committees, to force resignations, and to fire incumbents.

6. The formal power to introduce amendments and the less formal power to obtain *sub rosa* the abrogation of legal prerequisites.

7. The power to create commissions of inquiry, to force the creation of such commissions, or to prevent their creation.

8. The power to mobilize, at public expense, ad hoc constituencies, such as chambers of commerce, artists, and women's groups to support or to oppose specific policies.

9. The power to plant information where it will harm other centers of power and benefit one's own.

10. The power to refuse to implement all or part of legislated policies and the power to require the enforcement of such policies.

11. In the preparation of official documents (including speeches), the writing of committee decisions, and the drafting of legislation, the power to slant policies in particular directions.

12. The power to cover up and the power to bring litigable matters before the courts.

Checking instruments such as these and others more or less like them are used by centers of power to extract concessions from other centers and to force them to compromise on initial positions. To put it differently, a center of power undertakes to check another center in order to oblige the latter to compromise. The often repeated dictum that "politics is the art of compromise" is a backhanded endorsement of the view that politics is competitive and that a primary means of competition is the use of checks, for no one would compromise unless forced to do so. Concessions and compromises

8. On May 8, 1993, the French newspaper *Le Monde* (p. 24) reported that Mrs. Simone Veil's office had released a document "hostile" to certain recommendations contained in a draft law prepared by the office of Mr. Charles Pasqua. What is remarkable about the news item is that Veil and Pasqua were both ministers in the Cabinet of Mr. Edouard Balladur, the French Prime Minister. Veil was checking Pasqua before the very eyes of a consensus adamant that checking is not a feature of the French political system.

cannot be conceived as pertaining *exclusively* to the negative actions of giving up on, backing down from, or renouncing an initial position; they must also and, I suggest, principally be thought of as belonging to the class of positive activities associated with innovative Schumpeterian entrepreneurship. To compromise is to come up with something else, with an alternative that meets the objection of the center of power that made use of the check as well as the preferences of one's own constituency.

To understand the nature of these concessions and compromises in more detail, it is indispensable to have some appreciation of the nature of governmental production and supply processes. To understand these processes it is necessary first to recognize three attributes they possess. A first one derives from the fact that all or virtually all the goods and services designed and produced by governmental centers of power are decomposable into elementary characteristics not unlike those that Kelvin Lancaster (1966) took to be the basic elements of consumption technologies, though the discussion here is focused on production technologies. Put differently, all the goods and services G_k ($k = 1, \ldots, K$) that were introduced in Chapter 2 can be described by a vector of characteristics Z_w ($w = 1, \ldots, W$), such that

$$G_k = (Z_{kw}) \; \forall \; k,w \tag{3.1}$$

Any tractable assumption can be made about the relationships linking the G_k's to the Z_{kw}'s if it is consistent with the facts that the characteristics are objective and, in principle, measurable and that they can take a wide range of values, including zero.

A second attribute of governmental production and delivery processes – one that derives from the very nature of compound governments – is that a number, sometimes large, of centers of power are directly or indirectly involved in designing and combining the characteristics that once gathered in one whole, become identified as goods and services. It is possible that not one of the characteristics of a given good or service will be of interest to a particular center of power, whereas all or a subset of them will be of interest to another. More precisely, it is possible that the constituency of citizens and of demand lobbies represented by a particular center of power will have no preferences for the characteristics of a given good or service, whereas the constituency of another center may have preferences for all or for a subset of them. A third attribute of production and supply processes, therefore, is the existence of formal and informal jurisdictions over characteristics reflecting the preferences of the constituencies of the various centers of power.[9]

---

9. The language of constituencies, jurisdictions, and representation is obviously borrowed from a different domain of realities and is not strictly apposite in the present context. It does, however, sufficiently simplify the presentation without, it seems to me, generating any significant confusion to warrant its adoption for the remainder of the chapter.

Given these three attributes, it is possible to offer a stylized chronology of the sequence of decisions and actions of the various centers of power that are or could be involved in the production and supply of goods and services. A chronology more or less like it buttresses the formal model of the next section. Let me then suppose that initially a center of power announces its intention to provide a particular good or service. I assume that this announcement takes the form of a document that lists the quantity of the set of characteristics that center of power proposes as the constitutive elements of the good or service in question.

As a second step, all the other centers of power with jurisdiction over one or more of the announced characteristics – including those centers that reckon that the characteristics over which they have jurisdiction have been unjustifiably left out – will calculate the size of the difference between the volume of the proposed characteristics and that preferred by their constituencies. They will then make a decision about whether to use the checking instruments at their command by weighing the expected benefits and the expected costs of employing them to reduce the size of the estimated differences. Finally, in what can be treated as a third and last step, each center of power will recognize that all the other centers are making decisions about using the checking instruments at their disposal. As a consequence, they will incorporate into their own calculus the fact that in the absence of collusion success by a given center of power will reduce the difference between the initially announced volume of characteristics and the volume preferred by that center's constituency but will necessarily widen that difference for the constituencies of the unsuccessful centers.

3.3.   A formal model and some implications

It is time to develop a model of when, how, and with what effect checking instruments are used by governmental centers of power engaged in the production and supply of goods and services and to use that model to derive some implications and corollaries that are in principle testable. To do so, I must first rejoin the assumptions, introduced in Chapter 2, that all centers of power act to maximize expected consent (EC) and supplement it with the additional assumption that they do so by employing the checking instruments at their command. To simplify the presentation, let me also assume, at least temporarily, that there are only two centers of power, which I will call "a" and "b". That simplification in reality requires the further assumption that centers of power compete with one another; permitting collusion would void any effort at understanding the use of checking instruments. I look at the problem of collusion later, but for the moment I rule it out.

To insure dimensional homogeneity, I assume in this section only that a monetary equivalent ($E\Omega_i$, i = a,b) for expected consent exists. The assumption can be rationalized on the basis of the observation that the approval ratings of politicians who are discovered to be "on the take" generally falls, implying that expected consent can, as it were, be sold in a surrogate market and, through that device, converted into cash. Let me also suppose that the size of $E\Omega_a$ (and equivalently for $E\Omega_b$) depends on the monetary value of resources – time, energy, effort, and matériel – allocated to checking instruments. Let the value of these resources be e_a and e_b for centers "a" and "b" respectively. It would, of course, be possible to work with a disaggregated model in which each checking instrument was individually identified; that would permit a recognition that some instruments are complements to, whereas others are either substitutes for, or independent of other instruments. Such disaggregation would add to our understanding but at the cost of considerably complicating the presentation.

Given these assumptions, the monetary equivalent of the consent that center of power "a" will expect to gain is given by

$$E\Omega_a(e_a, e_b)$$

with $\partial E\Omega_a / \partial e_a > 0$ and $\partial E\Omega_a / \partial e_b < 0$ as measures of the marginal productivity of checking instruments for each center of power. The monetary equivalent of the costs to center "a" of using checking instruments must be set against the monetary equivalent of the expected gains in expected consent. We therefore have:

$$E\Omega_a(e_a, e_b) - e_a \tag{3.2}$$

For center of power "b," the monetary equivalent of the expected loss in expected consent, including the monetary equivalent costs of making use of checking instruments, is given by

$$E\Omega_b(e_a, e_b) + e_b \tag{3.3}$$

with $\partial E\Omega_b / \partial e_a < 0$ and $\partial E\Omega_b / \partial e_b > 0$.

Variable e_a will be chosen by center of power "a" to maximize its expected gains, and e_b will be chosen by "b" to minimize its expected loss. The first-order condition for a maximum of (3.2) – center of power "a" objective function – is:

$$\frac{\partial E\Omega_a}{\partial e_a} + \frac{\partial E\Omega_a}{\partial e_b} \cdot \frac{de_b}{de_a} - 1 = 0 \tag{3.4}$$

A similar condition can be obtained for center of power "b". If we assume that centers "a" and "b", acting in Cournot–Nash fashion, take each other's use of checking instruments as given, the conjectural variation term de_b/de_a in (3.4) is equal to zero and that expression becomes:

$$\frac{\partial E\Omega_a}{\partial e_a} = 1 \tag{3.5}$$

For center of power "b," the corresponding expression is:

$$\frac{\partial E\Omega_b}{\partial e_b} = -1 \tag{3.6}$$

It is natural to define expected consent (or its monetary equivalent), as I have done in Chapter 2, as

$$EC_i = \sum_{j=1}^{J} \phi_i^j \quad i = a, b \tag{3.7}$$

in which ϕ_i^j is the probability that citizen j will grant his or her consent to center of power i. If, without loss of generality, we restrict our attention to a single good or service made up of m characteristics over which "a" and "b" have complete or partial jurisdiction, we can, by extending the analysis of Chapter 2, define a variable λ_i^j – the utility loss inflicted on citizen j by center of power i,i = a,b – which makes it possible to relate variations in the volume of the m charcteristics to ϕ_i^j. To that effect, let λ_i^j be equal to the sum, over the m characteristics, of the difference between the volume of characteristic Z_w which, at its predetermined marginal taxprice, citizen j desires, that is $Z_{wi}^j{}^*$, and the volume initially announced, namely Z_{wi}^j, or

$$\lambda_i^j = \sum_{w=1}^{m} \alpha_{wi}^j (Z_{wi}^j{}^* - Z_{wi}^j) \quad \forall j \quad i = a, b \tag{3.8}$$

in which α_{wi}^j is equal to the difference between the predetermined marginal taxprice and the marginal valuation placed on the volume of Z_{wi}^j initially announced, a number that depends on the size of the elasticity of demand for Z_{wi}^j at the predetermined taxprice (refer to Figure 2.2 in Chapter 2 and to the discussion of that figure to, *mutatis mutandis,* verify that relationship). It follows that $\alpha_{wi}^j \gtrless 0$ depending on whether $Z_{wi}^j{}^* \lessgtr Z_{wi}^j$, in such a way that $\lambda_i^j > 0$ as long as $Z_{wi}^j{}^* \neq Z_{wi}^j$.

Given this definition of the utility loss from governmental supply of a bundle of characteristics, it becomes possible to use the expected consent function (2.9) of Chapter 2, which I repeat here, for center of power "a" as

$$\phi_a^j = \phi_a^j(\lambda_a^j, \lambda_b^j) \tag{3.9}$$

with $\partial\phi_a^j/\partial\lambda_a^j < 0$ and $\partial\phi_a^j/\partial\lambda_b^j > 0$; and for center of power "b" as

$$\phi_b^j = \phi_b^j(\lambda_a^j, \lambda_b^j) \tag{3.10}$$

with $\partial\phi_b^j/\partial\lambda_a^j > 0$ and $\partial\phi_b^j/\partial\lambda_b^j < 0$.

In the absence of exogenous disturbances, the marginal taxprices facing citizens will, given perfect price competition, remain constant as will, as a consequence, $Z_{wi}^j{}^*$. Under these circumstances, λ_i^j will vary only when Z_{wi}^j varies (again refer to the discussion of Figure 2.2 in Chapter 2). If we now assume that this last variable is a function of the use of checking instruments, we then have for center "a"

$$Z^j_{wa} = f_a(e_a, e_b) \quad \forall\, j, w \tag{3.11}$$

and for center "b"

$$Z^j_{wb} = f_b(e_a, e_b) \quad \forall\, j, w \tag{3.12}$$

The *ceteris paribus* effect of a change in the use of checking instruments on expected consent for centers of power "a" and "b" can be calculated with the help of equations (3.7) to (3.12). Incorporated into the first-order conditions for a maximum – equation (3.5) – we obtain for center of power "a"

$$\frac{\partial E\Omega_a}{\partial e_a} = \sum_{j=1}^{J} \left(\frac{\partial \phi^j_a}{\partial \lambda^j_a} \cdot \frac{\partial \lambda^j_a}{\partial f_a} \cdot \frac{\partial f_a}{\partial e_a} \right) = 1 \tag{3.13}$$

and, referring to equation (3.6), for center of power "b"

$$\frac{\partial E\Omega_b}{\partial e_b} = \sum_{j=1}^{J} \left(\frac{\partial \phi^j_b}{\partial \lambda^j_b} \cdot \frac{\partial \lambda^j_b}{\partial f_b} \cdot \frac{\partial f_b}{\partial e_b} \right) = -1 \tag{3.14}$$

In reading equations (3.13) and (3.14), it is important to keep in mind that $\partial f_i / \partial e_i$ ($i = a, b$) can be either positive or negative: Checking instruments can be used to increase or reduce the volume of any characteristic. These changes will, however, always reduce utility losses.

The first-order conditions (3.13) and (3.14) tell us, for example, that for a given constituency of like individuals (see the discussion of the composition of demand lobbies in Chapter 2, Section 2.3, Subsection i), if the marginal productivity of resources is greater for center of power "a" than for center of power "b," the first will spend, other things being equal, more on checking than the second will. If we assume that second-order conditions guarantee stability, equations (3.13) and (3.14) can be solved to obtain standard Cournot–Nash reaction functions that can be used to determine an equilibrium employment of checking instruments by the two centers of power. Comparative statical changes in these reaction functions brought about by exogenous shocks would then provide us with implications which, in principle at least, should be testable. I offer six such implications, together with a few corollaries and some casual applications to real-world phenomena.

A first implication, a direct consequence of the Cournot–Nash assumption, is that an exogenous increase in the productivity of the resources allocated to checking instruments that affected centers "a" and "b" equally would leave their relative checking efficiency or capacity unchanged. In other words, only the relative – not the absolute – productivity of checking instruments matters. For the same reason, it follows that an increase in the productivity of the resources absorbed in checking that affected only one center would improve its chance of success relative to that of the other center. Examples of exogenous events that could affect the relative efficiency of checking instruments are the introduction of a Charter of Rights and Freedom, triumph in war, the death or resignation of a committee chair, or the public disclosure of a "scandal."

An interesting corollary of this first implication relates to the relationship between checks and balances. If it were possible by the continuous and judicious alteration of institutional structures to maintain a strictly equiproportional distribution of power and, therefore, a balance among all centers of power, as the Pythagorean supporters of checks and balances advocated (Panagopoulos, 1985), these alterations could undo any exogenous changes in the efficiency of resources allocated to checking instruments. Checks and balances would then be related to each other, making the widespread habit of using the two words together always correct. However, as we have seen and will emphasize anew in Section 3.6, because balance is a prerequisite for checking, that relationship is not in general a very close one.

A second implication of the proposed model of checks is that centers of power with jurisdiction over characteristics that are in inelastic demand at ruling taxprices will use checking instruments more vigorously than those that have jurisdiction over characteristics whose demand is elastic, whenever announced and preferred characteristics differ. Why? Simply because an inelastic demand implies a larger utility loss for provisions that depart, even a little, from the ones desired and, therefore, means large gains in expected consent from an even small use of checking instruments. In other words, inelastic demand implies large α's in equations (3.8) and, therefore, large λ's even for small differences in desired and actual volumes of characteristics. A small change in the volume of any one of these characteristics will consequently generate a large reduction in λ and a large gain in EC. This may explain why "passionate" minorities – constituencies with strong preferences (large marginal rates of substitution) for particular characteristics – when they are represented by a center of power, often obtain the bundle of characteristics they desire.

A first corollary of this second implication is that the production and supply of goods and services in compound governments will, *ceteris paribus,* be efficient in the sense of generating equilibrium vectors of characteristics for goods and services that reflect the preference intensities of all constituencies of citizens that are represented by centers of power if these are able to alter, even marginally, the vector of characteristics in the direction desired by their constituents. It is a standard platitude that electoral contests do not allow for differences in the intensity of preference of citizens. It should be clear that in a neo-Madisonian democracy (Chapter 1, Section 1.4) in which both elections and competition obtain, differences in the intensity of preferences affect supply outcomes. This can explain why some citizens vote for political parties that never form the executive but that can still use checking instruments effectively, and why constituencies lobby to be represented by a center of power that is an integral part of the structure of a compound government.

A second corollary closely related to the first is that even if the checking game, as I have modeled it, is zero-sum for centers of power, it is positive-sum for citizens. Competition, in politics as in economics, is beneficial in the sense of generating a surplus for citizens.

If the constituency of a center of power is more sensitive to changes in λ – in the utility loss from governmental supply – than is the constituency of the other center, a third implication of the theory of checks I am proposing is that, *ceteris paribus,* the first center will employ checking instruments more forcefully than the second simply because their use by the first will lead to larger increments in expected consent than their employment by the second. A differential sensitivity or responsiveness to variations in utility losses from public production and supply will depend, to a degree at least, on the sense of obligation that constituencies have vis-à-vis centers of power. One should, then, expect that centers with strongly committed constituencies would make a less insistent usage of checking instruments than those whose constituencies are more capricious. "Ideological" constituencies are likely to be less sensitive to changes in utility losses than "pragmatic" ones and, *ceteris paribus,* are likely to lose out in the competitive use of checking instruments. This could help to explain why the ideological extremes of the political spectrum do not often have their preferences reflected in legislation.

It must be remembered, however, that the ϕ's – the probabilities that citizens will grant their consent to centers of power – are subjective variables. There are, to be sure, ways and means that can serve to externalize these probabilities, that is, to make them public (see Chapter 2, Section 2.2), but although all are imperfect modes of externalization, some are more effective than others. A corollary of the third implication is that the constituencies with access to means of externalization that are less costly per unit of externalization will appear to be more responsive to changes in utility losses, so that centers of power that represent them will make a more vigorous use of checking instruments than will centers whose constituencies can access only poor externalizing vehicles.

The next three implications of the model are more easily appreciated if we move from a context of two to one of many centers of power. Let me then assume that there are N autonomous or quasi-autonomous centers of power. This extension allows us to recognize that any good or service made up of many characteristics will be produced and supplied, if not by all N centers of power, very often by a substantial subset of them. A fourth implication of the theory of checks that I am suggesting, then, is that whenever a good or service is announced to citizens by a center of power, the announcement must be obscure or ambiguous, because the center making the announcement is in general incapable of knowing *ex ante* the force that other centers of power will apply in using the checking instruments at their command to alter the configuration of characteristics of the announced good or service. To put the matter differently, the center of power making the announcement generally has itself but a vague idea of the equilibrium vector of characteristics that will in the end constitute the good or service it is announcing.

A first corollary of this fourth implication is that announcements made by centers of power that are relatively more efficient in using checking instruments will be more specific than those of centers that are relatively less efficient. For example, very unpopular governing parties should be expected to make very obscure and ambiguous announcements, whereas more popular ones should be more specific. A second corollary is that announcements relating to goods and services that, from a technical point of view, are made up of few characteristics will be more specific than the announcements pertaining to goods and services that are inherently made up of many characteristics, because fewer centers of power will be involved in the production and supply of the former than of the latter. One would, therefore, expect the announcements of central banks and of specialized regulatory bodies to be less obscure and ambiguous than those of welfare and cultural agencies.

To derive the fifth implication, it is necessary to distinguish between elected and nonelected centers of power. If elected centers announce bundles of characteristics or make use of checking instruments to obtain volumes of them that guarantee large utility losses to certain constituencies, the members of these constituencies may grant all their consent to nonelected centers of power and none to the elected ones, which is another way of saying that they may abstain from voting. Put differently, because one acquires consent by reducing the utility losses inflicted on citizens by making use of the resources at one's command, if these resources are not used for that purpose by centers that have jurisdiction over the pertinent characteristics, consent will not be forthcoming and for elected centers of power that means no votes. This can help us to understand why many minority groups vote less often than majority groups do. It can also explain why minorities often choose to obtain what they want outside governments – through the market, for example.

The sixth and last implication to be derived from the model outlined earlier pertains to collusion and to its incidence.[10] I assume that two or more centers of power collude when, given the productivity of the resources at their dispos-

10. In analyzing a different form of intragovernmental competition, I provide a more detailed discussion of collusion in Chapter 5, Section 5.3.

al, their constituencies' demand for the characteristics of goods and services, and the responsiveness of these same constituencies to changes in utility losses, the centers choose to employ the checking instruments over which they have command at levels of intensity that are lower than those that would maximize their respective expected consent. Given the opportunity to collude, why would centers of power do so? In a word, because what can be secured through collusion – Hicks's (1935) "quiet life", monetary and/or material perquisites, Richard Roll's (1986) hubris, or whatever – is of more value to them than expected consent.

It is important not to confuse collusion and capture. Capture may be easier to realize if centers of power are colluded, but if they are not, it will require that captors inveigle two, three, or more centers of power to obtain the vector of characteristics they desire. From casual observation, it seems that the Canadian broadcasting industry, the American gun lobby, the Neapolitan Camora, and the Calabrian N'drangheta have all captured a multiplicity of centers. Collusion, on the other hand, is an attribute of the internal organization of compound governments.

Some factors are more conducive to collusion than others. For example, small numbers, a main concern of oligopoly theory, is surely important. Proportional representation, when it fosters certain types of coalition governments, may be significant [Breton and Galeotti (1985) and especially Galeotti (1991)]. The manner of nominating and appointing the heads of centers of power may favor collusion, as can certain restrictions on the autonomy of centers. These factors are all components of balance. I leave them aside here by assuming optimal balance. Under these circumstances, the incidence of collusion between centers of power will depend on two interrelated phenomena: (1) the extent to which constituencies are properly informed about the effect of the use of checking instruments by particular centers of power to reduce the utility losses of public production and supply – on the size of $\partial\lambda^j/\partial f_n$ and of $\partial f_n/\partial e_n$ ($n = 1, \ldots, N$) in generalizations of equations (3.13) and (3.14); and (2) the extent to which centers of power are correctly informed about the effect of changes in utility losses on their constituencies' subjective probability of granting them their consent – on the size of $\sum_j \partial\phi^j/\partial\lambda^j$.[11]

A corollary of this sixth implication is that there should be less collusion the more public the debates and dealings surrounding the production and supply of goods and services are, the better the quality of the political media is, the more easily political information can be accessed by journalists and by others

---

11. Note the resemblance between the first of these two conditions relating to collusion among centers of power and the condition, discussed in Chapter 2 (Section 2.3, Subsection iv), pertaining to collusion between the managers of lobbies (constituencies) and centers of power.

– the more effective, that is, are freedom of information laws – and the more active the demand lobbies supported by governments for that purpose are (see Chapter 2, Section 2.3). We should, therefore, expect some degree of collusion (and some corruption) in all compound governments. Its incidence should, however, vary among them. The implication and its corollary lead us to expect that the incidence of collusion will probably be greater, having corrected for scale, in local than in national governments, in the governments of less developed than in those of more advanced countries, and in the governments of dictatorships than in those of democracies, because the informational problems of constituencies and of centers of power are more severe in the first than in the second type of governments. The evidence, such as it is, appears consistent with the three predictions.

3.4.   The Wicksellian Connection anew

The discussion in Sections 3.1 and 3.2 and the model in Section 3.3, as well as the model's implications and corollaries, have made clear, I hope, that the use of checking instruments by autonomous and quasi-autonomous centers of power to maximize their expected consent (or monetary equivalent) leads to the provision of goods and services – of bundles of characteristics – that minimize the utility losses inflicted on citizens and demand lobbies. That discussion and model contain in implicit form a Wicksellian Connection. If it turned out that in equilibrium the minimum of utility losses for all citizens was zero, all would be on their demand curves and a first-best Pareto-efficient Wicksellian Connection achieved. If the minimum of utility losses is positive, but because of irreducible constraints cannot be made smaller, citizens are off their demand curves but by the smallest amount possible and the Wicksellian Connection obtained would still be Pareto-efficient but second best.

We can gain a deeper understanding of checking behavior, of the uses to which checking instruments can be put, of the meaning of concessions and compromises, and of the notion of unanimity that plays such an important role in Wicksell's (1896) own discussion of the Wicksellian Connection, by performing a few simple exercises to give graphic representation to these abstract concepts. For that purpose, assume, as in Chapter 2's discussion of the Wicksellian Connection, that there are only two centers of power – "a" and "b" – and two demand lobbies 1 and 2 with again "a" representing Lobby 1 and "b" Lobby 2. Assume also, solely to simplify, that when "a" and "b" acquire information about 1 and 2's utility losses, that information is perfect. Imperfect information would affect the results in the way indicated in Chapter 2, Section 2.4.

Let us now assume that initially the situation is as portrayed in Figure 3.1. There, the exogenously given taxprice is t* and the volume of characteristic

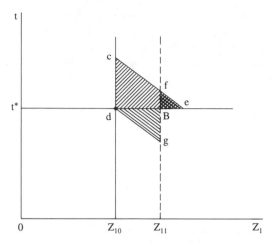

Figure 3.1. Fixing a point on the Wicksellian Connection.

Z_1, which center of power "b" proposes to produce, is Z_{10}. At point d – given by the coordinates t* and Z_{10} – Lobby 2 experiences zero utility loss and is, therefore, on its demand curve (assumed to go through that point), whereas Lobby 1 is off its demand curve (a section of which is shown as ce) and suffers a utility loss equal to cde. Lobby 2 then supports the production of Z_{10}, but Lobby 1 does not or, to put it differently, ϕ_b^2 is "large" and ϕ_a^1 "small." As a consequence, "a" will check "b" in an effort to oblige it to make a concession. If the check "a" makes is successful, the output of Z_1 may or may not change. It will not change if the concession "b" makes leads to a compromise that could cause a change in the design and production of one or more other characteristics of the good or service to which Z_1 belongs, a change in the design and production of characteristics of other goods and services, or a change in the position of supply and demand curves for market goods and services through changes in the appropriate taxes and subsidies – changes that would, if of the "right" magnitude, shift Lobby 1's demand curve inward to go through point d, without in any way altering the position of Lobby 2's demand curve for Z_1, which also goes through that point. With Lobby 1's demand curve going through point d, that lobby's utility loss is reduced to zero. In view of what is required, the checking by "a" can be successful only if it is accompanied by compromises on one or more other fronts, all of which are manifestations of creative Schumpeterian entrepreneurship. For that reason, concession and compromises – the inevitable complements to the use of checking instruments – are manifestations of entrepreneurial competition and innovation.

At point d, both lobbies unanimously support the production of Z_{10} of Z_1 at taxprice t* *and* of the substitutes or complements that hold the demand curve of Lobby 1 in a position such that it passes through point d. In addition, at d the marginal valuation of Z_{10} by Lobbies 1 and 2 is equal to t*, and as a consequence, the decision is not only unanimous but also reflects a simultaneous balancing of benefits and costs. Wicksell's two requirements – unanimity and simultaneity – are satisfied.

It may not, however, be possible to find substitutes or complements to Z_1 or, if found, to produce them in the quantities and qualities necessary to move Lobby 1's demand curve to point d. That possibility is more likely when cde is large at the initial proposal (t*,Z_{10}). In turn, cde is more likely to be large if the demand for Z_1 by Lobby 1 is, at t*, very inelastic, that is, if Lobby 1's preference for a larger volume of Z_1 than the initial Z_{10} is very intense. However that may be, in that case checking by "a" will be successful only if it first leads to a concession whereby "b" accepts an increase in Z_1 to, let us say, Z_{11}. Lobby 2 now endures a positive utility loss equal to dBg, and Lobby 1's utility loss has fallen from cde to fBe. From the analysis in Section 3.3, we know that dBg can be greater, smaller, or equal to fBe. What is important is that whereas Lobby 2 was on its demand curve in the initial situation, neither lobby is in that position after the concession by "b": point B is on neither 1's nor 2's demand curve.

Notice, however, that the range of alternatives over which compromises are possible has been considerably broadened. Instead of being limited to varying substitutes and complements aimed at shifting Lobby 1's demand curve, compromises are now possible on substitutes and complements directed at shifting Lobby 2's demand curve as well. Assuming that there are no information problems and no barriers to creative entrepreneurial give and take, both lobbies will support compromises that will lead to shifts in their respective demand curves that in the end will have them both going through point B, a point that reflects unanimous consent between the two lobbies. If we choose to interpret the concession made by "b" following the check made by "a" as an adjustment under duress, point B will reflect only quasi-unanimous consent, giving to that expression a meaning different from that bestowed on it by Wicksell (1896), but one that is, I believe, consistent with his view.

If, from that B equilibrium point – given by the (t*, Z_{11}) coordinates – we now exogenously increase the taxprice from t* to t', the amount of Z_1 desired by Lobby 1 will be equal, as can be verified by reference to Figure 3.2, to Z_1^1 and the quantity desired by Lobby 2 will be Z_1^2 on the assumption, first, that 1's and 2's responses to a price rise are different and, second, that both reduce the quantity of Z_1 demanded when its price is increased. The utility loss experienced by Lobby 1 is t*t'A'v + A'vB and that suffered by Lobby 2 is t*t'A''w + A''wB. These losses will give rise to a process of checking, concessions, and compromises like the one described earlier in the discus-

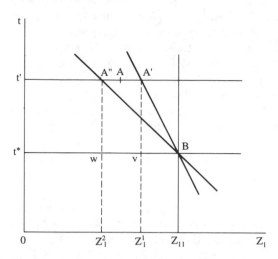

Figure 3.2. Deriving the whole of the Wicksellian Connection.

sion of Figure 3.1 and will lead to an equilibrium on the interval A'A″ in Figure 3.2 at, say, A. By repeating this exercise for different values of t, a locus A,B,C,D,E, . . . (C,D,E, . . . not shown) will be traced, revealing a genuine Wicksellian Connection. This Connection or long-run (allowing for the effects of checking instruments) demand curve is both different and not different from standard neoclassical market demand curves. It is *not* different in that it is derived on the assumption that when taxprices vary quantities of substitutes and complements also vary, and the prices of other goods and services are constant. It *is* different in that the underlying revelation mechanisms are of an altogether different kind, being strictly individual for market demand curves and collective – that is, driven by competition between centers of power – for the demand curves of government-provided goods and services.

3.5.   A digression on American exceptionalism

With the discussion of the preceding sections as background, I can now turn my attention to the widespread claim, forcefully expounded by Bagehot (1867) and incessantly repeated since [for recent reaffirmations, see Vincent Ostrom (1987), William Riker (1987) and James Wilson (1987)], that checks and balances are not to be found in parliamentary systems of government.[12]

12. It is true that before Benjamin Disraeli's Reform Act of 1867, when Bagehot was writing, there were few noncolluded centers of power and therefore little checking in the governmental structure of the United Kingdom. It is a sad fact that Bagehot's snapshot of the British

These systems differ considerably from one another and have all changed enormously over time, but they do partake of a common genius or character and can therefore for some purposes be lumped together in one class as I, following the authors whom I have just referred, shall do.

While expatiating on the virtues of the separation of branches (powers) in the United States government, Wilson (1987, p. 50) writes that ". . . a congressional system has some advantages over a parliamentary one; for one thing, the former permits investigation of executive misconduct that the latter does not." It is hard for one who has seen Cabinet Ministers – and over the years, quite a few of them – be the objects of public enquiries, forced to resign their portfolios, and even jailed to make sense of such a statement. There is a misreading of the facts in Wilson's assertion, but there is more. There is also an ingrained belief, rooted in an untested doctrine of American exceptionalism, shared by many non-Americans, that simply declares that checks and balances are a feature of the American system of government and of none other.

The investigations of executive misconduct in the Canadian parliamentary system to which I have just alluded did not happen because the Ministers or their colleagues suddenly became remorseful and repentant but in most cases because of the power granted to opposition parties to obtain information during question periods in the House of Commons. The question period of parliamentary systems can be such an effective checking instrument that in the matter raised by Wilson I would conjecture, on the basis of admittedly casual evidence, that there is little difference between congressional and parliamentary systems. In fact, I incline to the view that checking is sometimes more effective in the latter than in the former, not only in apprehending miscreants but also in a multitude of other endeavors.

I would suggest to those who insist that checks and balances are a feature of the American congressional system alone that they consider the following facts. The formal centers of power that the delegates to the Philadelphia Convention engineered in the 1787 Constitution were the following: (1) a President, chosen by an Electoral College appointed by state legislatures, who would, as a consequence, be more "pre-eminent for ability and virtue," for "wisdom and integrity," and for "merit and talent" than if elected by the people and who was, because of that, given the right of veto; (2) Senators, appointed by the same legislatures, who, the delegates said, "ought to come from, & represent the Wealth of the nation" and thus "establish a balance that will check the Democracy"; (3) a Supreme Court, appointed by the nonelected

Government in the mid-1860s came to be identified as the Westminster model of parliamentary government. It is as if the government over which John Quincy Adams presided (1825–9) had been branded *the* model of congressional government.

President and ratified by the nonelected Senators to guarantee that it be truly independent; and (4) an elected House of Representatives (all quotations are from Panagopoulos, 1985, p. xi).[13] That particular organization of the formal organs has always been assumed to constitute balance. The older writers had sought balance between monarchy, aristocracy and democracy and the American Founding Fathers followed their recipe to balance presidency, senate, and democracy more or less obsequiously as the quotations I have just given indicate.[14] Balance, it was assumed, would induce checking and, though the Supreme Court, which had been given short shrift in the Constitution, did not check until the justly famous 1803 case of *Marbury* v. *Madison,* Chief Justice John Marshall's articulation on that occasion of the doctrine of judicial review and the surrounding circumstances of the case indicate that the Court felt that it had become "balanced" enough to check the Executive, so that the assumption would seem to be warranted.

Two things stand out from the foregoing discussion. The first is that if one refers to today's actual constitutional arrangements in the United States, one must acknowledge that they have little resemblance to the original. But the formal organs, everyone seems to agree, are still balanced and, no doubt, check one another. That should make clear that a fixation on the formal organization to the neglect of the actual workings of systems can be very misleading. The second is that the constitutionally prescribed organization of the U.S. government in the early days of the Republic uncannily resembles the organization of the formal organs in a number of modern-day parliamentary systems. In these, the chief executive is elected but only as member of Parliament. *Qua* chief executive, that is, as Prime Minister, he or she is selected in party conventions or in caucuses whose procedures and machinations cannot be much less transparent than those governing the selection of Presidents in the earlier Electoral Colleges in the United States. The Prime Minister does not have a right of veto, though it is not an exaggeration to say that few if any government bills are tabled in the House that he or she opposes. Those who are named to the Upper Chamber are often appointed by

13. Before 1913, U.S. Senators were appointed for six-year terms by state legislatures. Presumably because they were intended to "represent the Wealth of the nation," the Constitution is silent on the so-called "doctrine of instructions" according to which the states instructed their senators as to how they should vote on every piece of legislation coming before them. Under strict construction and effective enforcement, the doctrine says that senators are simple agents – or, in William Riker's (1955, p. 463) words, "servants" – of state legislatures. As it turned out, the senators did not abide by the doctrine of instructions and the Senate, as a consequence, acted as an autonomous center of power. (See also Chapter 5, Section 5.2.)
14. The American Founding Fathers' contribution to politics was, therefore, not related to the separation of powers and to checks and balances. Their justly deserved fame as political innovators derives from their invention of genuine federalism.

the Prime Minister, and for life, to provide "sober second thought." If they do not "represent the Wealth of the nation" – and who will say that they do not – they certainly cannot represent, in the same way, the interests of those who elect the Lower Chamber. The higher court, also appointed, is distinct from the other branches. Balance is, therefore, present, and checking should be presumed to take place.

3.6.   Balanced governments

Sections 3.1, 3.2, 3.3, and 3.4 have proposed a positive or descriptive model of checks. It would have been possible in principle to adhere to the same strategy in analyzing balances. The current state of our knowledge makes it difficult, however, to formulate general models that are descriptive of the structure and of the evolution of rules and other constitutional arrangements. As a consequence, the discussion that follows is largely normative and aimed at giving meaning to the concept of balance in the checks and balances expression.

The foregoing analysis has recognized the existence of elected and non-elected centers of power in compound governments, but it has not made much of the distinction. This is as it should be when one is investigating how the checks component of checks and balances works. When attention turns to the balances component, the distinction does, however, become central to the analysis. To understand why this is so, think of a compound government as if it were a stationary carousel. The hub of that carousel is made up of the executive and legislative branches; at the end of the spokes radiating from that hub are the various quasi-autonomous and autonomous, largely nonelected, centers of power. The carousel, however, is not symmetric: Some spokes are longer than others because their length is proportional to the degree of autonomy the centers of power possess in such a way that the longer the length of the spoke, the greater the autonomy and the greater, *ceteris paribus*, the capacity to make effective use of checking instruments.

To a significant degree, the hub controls and regulates, first, the number of centers of power attached to the carousel; second, the length of each spoke and, hence, the degree of autonomy of each center; and, third, the division of intragovernmental powers and responsibilities among centers. There are restrictions on the capacity of the hub to create and dismantle centers of power, some of which are constitutional whereas others are political, but its latitude is in general considerable. That latitude is even greater regarding the degree of autonomy of centers – the length of the spokes. Indeed, the senior personnel – that is, those who are responsible for decision-making – is very often appointed by the executive at the hub and will as a consequence often have or adopt a coloration that is not much different from that of the appointor. Finally, the hub, again usually the executive and again with considerable latitude, decides on the powers that will be assigned to each center of power. This assignment problem is different from that analyzed in the theory of federalism, but it has this resemblance to it that, as in federal states, there are assignments that reduce the degree of competition among units to near zero. Kenneth Wheare's (1963) "classical federalism" is of that variety. The hub can, therefore, choose a division of powers that will reduce checking behavior among centers of power to the neighborhood of zero.

As regards the balances component of checks and balances, the first problem that a theory of these phenomena must resolve is that of the design of "optimal" constraints on the capacity of the hub to decide on the number, the autonomy, and the responsibilities of the centers of power so as to guarantee that checking and, therefore, competition among centers is not rendered trivial or, at the limit, entirely suppressed. If we take a casual look at compound governments around us, it appears that the number of centers of power is generally large. In some instances, the assignment of powers to these centers could be altered to increase checking, but that seems to me to be a fairly limited problem. What is more serious in my view is the matter of autonomy and, in particular, the matter of appointments. There could be fewer appointments. I see no obvious reason why, for example, the heads of, let us say, central banks, security and police services, cultural agencies, regulatory bodies, and even judges should be appointed. Other modes of selection besides appointment and election not only exist but are in use; these would make for more autonomy and independence and, hence, for more balance.

In designing the constraints on the capacity of the hub to determine the number of centers of power, their autonomy and their responsibilities, it is crucially important if the hub is elected that its capacity to act as a hub – in, for example, breaking deadlocks or in managing important change – be great enough to forestall the desire that some nonelected centers of power may entertain to capture the elected hub and impose their will. The problem is particularly serious regarding military and constabulary centers which, having dominion over force, can be tempted to initiate such hostile takeovers. This problem of capture or of hostile takeovers is important because elections are the most basic instrument that democratic societies possess to measure consent or the lack of it. Elections provide opportunities to bankrupt some centers of power to which sufficient consent is no longer granted. Nondemocratic regimes lack such a powerful mechanism of entry and exit and are as a consequence more prone to collusion. An optimally designed system of balances is, therefore, needed to ensure an optimal use of checks. It is thus that checks and balances are joined with each other and linked to democracy.

3.7.   Conclusion

I have provided a framework to analyze checks and balances and have proposed a theory of the use of checking instruments from which six implications
and a number of corollaries that possess empirical content have been derived.
To achieve that end, I have demonstrated that all modern governments are
compound governments, that is, institutions constituted of many autonomous
or quasi-autonomous centers of power. I have made and illustrated the point
that autonomous centers of power, by virtue of their very autonomy, have
command over checking instruments. I have then assumed that all or virtually
all goods and services produced and supplied by compound governments are
made up of characteristics over which the centers of power have jurisdiction.

Because centers of power seek the consent of constituencies of citizens,
because these grant consent in amounts that vary with the volume of characteristics offered, and because that volume is obtained by making use of checking instruments, centers of power compete with one another to produce and
deliver, through concessions and compromises, a vector of characteristics that
meets the preferences of citizens and, through that channel, forge Wicksellian
links between taxprices and the valuations of goods and services provided.
These links or connections are Pareto-optimal and are either first or second
best; they are, in effect, long-run demand curves revealed through the use of
checking instruments by competing centers of power.

CHAPTER 4

Budgetary processes

Competition can take the form of checks and balances as described in the preceding chapter, but it can also take other forms in the same way that competition in the market for, let us say, theatrical productions takes a form different from that which characterizes the market for corporate control. The analysis in this chapter focuses on the competitive behavior of participants engaged in budget making in two different types of governmental structures, namely, congressional and parliamentary governments – more precisely the American congressional and the Canadian parliamentary governments. The budgetary process is only one among many loci of activity – the regulatory process is another important one – that characterize the spectrum of governmental decision making. All these loci could (and should) be studied. I have chosen to focus on the budget because the outcome of budget making brings us into intimate contact with the Wicksellian Connection that joins the tax-prices charged and the quantities of goods and services demanded by citizens and supplied by governments. In addition, budget making has been carefully and extensively examined and described by students of both congressional and parliamentary governments.

I argue first, that even though the morphology or organization of competition in congressional and parliamentary systems is different, the budgetary processes are competitive in both and, second, that the existence and stability of budgetary equilibria are shaped by institutions that are particular to each form of government. More precisely, I argue that institutions such as caucus, budget secrecy, prime ministerial power, and a permanent, nonpartisan, senior bureaucracy – all idiosyncratic institutions of parliamentary governments – are needed for the existence and stability of competitive decision making in that type of structure, and that the same result is obtained in congressional governments by other institutions, among which are the control of party leadership over agendas, the system of standing committees, and the presidency, which are all institutions peculiar to that form of government. I note immediately that the foregoing does not imply that these institutions as they exist today are essential to their particular forms of government. They can change. However, the weight of the argument is that if their ability to sustain equilibrium outcomes is impaired or suppressed, other institutions will be needed to perform these tasks if the systems are to survive.

96

As already stated, I focus on budgetary processes at the federal (national) level in Canada and in the United States more or less in the form these processes have taken in the past decade. Two points need to be made about this research strategy. First, it is necessary to focus on particular governmental structures because neither congressional nor parliamentary systems exist in pure form. The two are living organisms and, as a consequence, not only evolve but evolve along different trajectories. Canada's parliamentary system, for example, though of the same "genotype" as those of Australia and Great Britain, is a distinct "phenotype." Second, because they evolve, governmental forms must be analyzed at one moment in time. The present is neither better nor worse than any other period for that purpose, though it is undoubtedly more relevant. Still, I must warn that if I had chosen to examine, say, the pre-1965 Canadian parliamentary system or the U.S. congressional system circa 1900 or even that system prior to the Congressional Budget Reform Act of 1974, though I am confident that the same general conclusions would have emerged, the analysis would have been different in a number of respects. Because of this confidence that the models apply, *mutatis mutandis,* to all congressional and parliamentary systems, I will continue to refer to them in the plural.

Budgetary processes are extremely complex and are completely described only by what amounts to an enormous mass of detail whose sheer volume can impede formal analysis. It is surely because of the attention lavished on these details that we possess excellent descriptive studies of budgetary processes but no theory. To model, it is essential to do away with many details. In that spirit, I will propose stylized versions of budget making in congressional and parliamentary systems that retain only those elements necessary for a particular rationalization of the processes, more or less as is done in the formulation of a theory of household budgets when the multiplicity of details that enter a consuming unit's actual spending actions are disregarded.

It is important to keep in mind that the meaning of the common parlance and media expression "the budget" is different in Canada from its meaning in the United States and that both meanings are different from the usage in this chapter. In Canada, what is called "the budget" is "related only loosely to the implementation of expenditure policy. Rather, the principal role of the budget speech is to bring together aggregate revenues and expenditures in conjunction with setting out stabilization policy and to initiate tax changes" (Musgrave, Musgrave, and Bird, 1987, p. 37). In the United States what is referred to as "the budget" is "mainly a plan or program for government expenditure, not for government revenue raising" (Buchanan and Flowers, 1987, p. 153). In this chapter, the expression covers both expenditures and revenues; when necessary, I distinguish between the expenditure and the revenue budgets.

The chapter is organized as follows: The next two sections provide models of the budgetary process, first in parliamentary and then in congressional governments. Section 4.3 examines the nature of the Wicksellian Connection in the two forms of government. Section 4.4 concludes the chapter.

4.1.   The budgetary process of parliamentary governments

As argued in the preceding chapter, compound governments are made up of a multiplicity of centers of power, but for the purpose of modeling budgetary processes, I disregard many of these centers. In fact, in the case of parliamentary systems, I retain only the centers of power that are directly associated with Parliament – more precisely with the House of Commons – and those directly related to the operation of Cabinet, and in the case of congressional systems only those directly associated with the Congress and the President. I retain only those centers that are strictly required by the logic of the models I adopt to rationalize budgetary processes.[1] There are also bodies and institutions that are traditionally not associated with budgetary processes but that play an important role in the models of this chapter. I introduce them as the logic of the models calls them on stage.

i.   Stylized structure

Though it was not always the case, modern parliamentary governments incorporate the principles of responsible government according to which ministers one by one and Cabinet as a whole are answerable to Parliament.[2] Furthermore, because each of the various departments, councils, agencies, and crown corporations that constitute the administrative part of government – all the bureaus that make up the bureaucracy – is headed by a minister, the entire administrative machinery of government is answerable to Parliament.

Parliamentary governments are also called Cabinet governments and for good reason. First, though private member bills are allowed and some are enacted, the overwhelming majority of policy proposals and all money bills that come before Parliament originate with ministers and their bureaus. Because of that, in the stylized structure I disregard private member bills. Second, though Parliament and parliamentary committees generally amend

1. For example, though the Canadian Office of the Auditor General and the American General Accounting Office play a role in budgetary processes, they are not part of the models of this chapter, nor are the central banks that may be important in some circumstances. Two points can be made about the absence of these and other centers of power from the models proposed in this chapter. First, increasing the number of autonomous centers of power would reinforce the logic of the models. Second, introducing the absent centers of power in the argument is, in general, easy.

2. I am grateful to Stéfan Dupré for helping me clarify the difference between parliamentary and responsible government and, thus, allowing me to remove an error from an earlier draft.

bills brought forward by ministers, party discipline insures that bills are enacted in a form acceptable to Cabinet. I neglect the problems that arise when Cabinet is in a minority position in the House of Commons because of the complications that this poses. Though they are important for electoral competition, these problems have only minor influence on the organization and effects of interministry competition in Cabinet governments. Minority status, if it does anything, increases the degree of competition, so that ruling it out does not weaken the point this chapter advances.

Dominating Cabinet and the bureaucracy is the Prime Minister, who appoints all ministers, deputy ministers, parliamentary secretaries, heads of agencies, and others, and can terminate any of these appointments at will.[3] The Prime Minister shuffles the Cabinet whenever he or she decides to do so and does so at a moment of his or her choosing. The Prime Minister only indirectly participates in the revenue and expenditure budgetary processes. In fact the Prime Minister is directly active in only one cabinet committee – Priorities and Planning – which "is an inner Cabinet in all but name" (Van Loon, 1983, p. 95). I assume that Cabinet (or the "inner Cabinet") approves or disapproves of budgetary decisions but is not formally engaged in the budgetary process. This is a derogation from reality. But because the Prime Minister in fact manages and directs both Cabinet and the Priorities and Planning Committee, the very critical and central role he or she plays in the model discussed in Subsection ii makes the assumption less restrictive than it would appear at first sight.

All line ministers and their departments are involved in the expenditure budgetary process; the revenue budget is, however, the responsibility of the Minister of Finance alone.[4] As a matter of actual practice, there are minor consultations between the Prime Minister and the Minister of Finance on the revenue budget, but line ministers are not formally (the meaning of "formally" will become clear in the following subsection) consulted and are informed of the content of the budget only a few days before it is presented to Parliament in the much touted budget speech. If one reflects on the effect of changes in taxation on the electoral fortunes of ministers and of governing parties, it seems anomalous that the Prime Minister would give so much power to one minister and that the line ministers should accept that the minister be given that power. The conventional explanation for that state of affairs is budget secrecy [see, for example, Hartle (1982) and Maslove, Prince, and Doern

---

3. There are exceptions to this statement. Some appointments – for example, the Governor of the Bank of Canada and the Auditor General – can be dismissed only after a joint address of the House of Commons and the Senate.
4. Some ministers – for example, the Minister of Justice and the Minister of Consumer and Corporate Affairs – are only incidentally involved in that process. Their role would undoubtedly be greater in a model of the regulatory process.

(1986)]. However, unless one knows why budget secrecy exists, one is left without an explanation for the enormous power wielded by the Minister of Finance. An explanation follows.

The expenditure budgetary process unfolds at two levels.[5] The first pertains to policies and the second to the programs to which the policies that have been approved at the first level give rise. Policy discussions at the first level begin in interdepartmental committees – of which, according to Colin Campbell and George Szablowski (1979), there were at the time of their study nearly 100 – and then go to cabinet committees before reaching Priorities and Planning, the Cabinet, or both – a three-tier structure. At the second level, program discussions take place in one-on-one encounters between the Secretariat of Treasury Board and line departments.

For the purpose of modeling, I simplify that reality. I disregard interdepartmental committees altogether. I further assume that when Priorities and Planning or Cabinet does not approve of a decision made by a cabinet committee, the decision is sent back to that committee (or to the department) for further discussion. I therefore focus exclusively on cabinet committees and, perforce, neglect the three-tier decision-making structure. The Minister of Finance and the President of Treasury Board are in fact members of all cabinet committees. Because of the necessary bookkeeping relationship that total expenditures bear to total revenues plus borrowing or minus debt repayments, Finance and Treasury Board tend in fact to work as a team. I assume that this is the case [for evidence that this is a not an unrealistic assumption, see Hartle (1982)]. I call the team the Minister of Finance.

The stylized structure just described can then be summarized by the following six propositions (in slightly different order from the foregoing):

1. Every one of the bureaus (departments, agencies, councils, crown corporations, etc.) that constitute the administrative side of government is a responsibility of a minister.
2. All expenditure bills originate with line ministers, are sanctioned by cabinet committees, and are tabled before Parliament by Cabinet.
3. The Minister of Finance alone is responsible for the revenue budget and for choosing the date for tabling that budget before the House of Commons.
4. In dealing with line ministers and therefore with expenditure items of the expenditure budget, Finance and Treasury Board act as a team, which I call the Minister of Finance.
5. The Prime Minister appoints all ministers and shuffles Cabinet at a time of his or her choosing.

5. For evidence that this is the case, see Hartle's (1988) masterful depiction of the expenditure budgetary process and its historical evolution.

6. Cabinet is in a majority in the House of Commons and enforces party discipline.

ii.   The model

The stylized structure of government just outlined correctly underlines the critical position of cabinet ministers in parliamentary systems. Because of that status, cabinet ministers, the senior bureaucracy under them, or both are the primary and principal targets for the pressures of citizens and demand lobbies. To put it differently, if the information related to the demand functions of citizens and to the utility losses associated with the goods and services currently or prospectively supplied to these citizens (see Chapter 2) is not revealed at the ministerial level, it will simply not enter the budgetary decision-making process. Elected politicians who are not in the Cabinet (backbenchers) – whether of the ruling party or of the opposition – are also subjected to the pressures of citizens and demand lobbies. But unless these pressures influence ministers, senior bureaucrats, or both, their effect on the budgetary process will be negligible.

Sometimes backbenchers are privy to information about the preferences of citizens and demand lobbies and about the size of the utility losses inflicted on these same citizens and lobbies. That information can be communicated to the ministerial level through two principal channels: parliamentary debates and meetings of the governing party's parliamentary caucus. To understand some aspects of the behavior of political parties, Galeotti and Breton (1986) have argued, following a line of reasoning initiated by John Stuart Mill (1863), that the function of parliamentary debates is to give representation to the "opinions" of citizens and lobbies. These debates, conducted in a forum that Mill called a "Congress of Opinions," are part, in other words, of a process through which information related to what citizens and lobbies want is collated and communicated to governmental ministries.

Little is known about parliamentary caucuses and about their role in the political process. We know that the governing party's parliamentary caucus[6] brings together with ministers, the backbenchers and the senators[7] who belong to that party. The caucus is chaired by the Prime Minister, and its deliberations are conducted under a rule of secrecy. The justification for such

---

6. There are many caucuses. Nongoverning, or opposition, parties have them. There are also subcaucuses: for example, regional caucuses, such as the Ontario and Quebec caucuses of the Liberal Party. I neglect all of these in the text.
7. In Canada, senators are appointed, not elected. Still, most of them have constituencies and hence bring information about the preferences and utility losses of some citizens to caucus and seek to influence legislation. Their presence in the caucus is indirect evidence of the importance of caucuses in the political process.

a rule is easily understood, as are the reasons for the breaches to which it is sometimes subjected. I suggest that it is in caucus that certain information about the views of citizens and lobbies to which backbenchers are privy is conveyed to ministers. Caucus, according to that view, provides an opportunity to backbenchers to support, oppose, and seek changes in the measures that are being debated or contemplated by Cabinet.

I suggest also that a continuous lack of success in influencing ministerial positions would be an incentive to breach secrecy as a way of putting indirect pressure on Cabinet via the media, opposition parties, or outside lobbies. Accordingly, if caucus deliberations never allowed backbenchers to influence Cabinet and policies about the goods and services supplied, it would be more difficult to enforce party discipline. Caucus, in other words, is a complement to party discipline. Caucus as a forum that permits backbenchers sometimes to influence ministers and Cabinet is a feature of parliamentary, not of congressional, governments. In the next section, I note that in the second of these governmental forms, information about the preferences and the utility losses suffered or anticipated by citizens is primarily targeted on members of Congress. It is for this reason that in congressional systems caucuses (now more often called conferences) serve to decide on the day-to-day business of the House and of the Senate, to choose congressional leaders, to organize House and Senate committees and to select their membership (Polsby, 1986) but not to influence the Executive.

Not all the preferences of the public for goods and services that are conveyed to cabinet ministers and to ministries can be incorporated into the equilibrium budget: Some will have to be traded off against others and some will have to be jettisoned. I embrace Hartle's (1982, 1988) view, based on a careful examination and analysis of the evidence, that the process which leads to equilibrium outcomes is one of bargaining. I do not, however, make use of Hartle's implicit model of bargaining but instead adopt – and adapt – the model of "Bargaining in the Shadow of the Law" developed by Robert Cooter and Stephen Marks with Robert Mnookin (1982) to rationalize the process. Following these authors, who borrowed with acknowledgment the title of their paper from Mnookin and Lewis Kornhauser (1979), I propose a model of cabinet government that I call "bargaining in the shadow of the Prime Minister."

The Cooter–Marks–Mnookin bargaining model is the only model I know that makes it possible to give formal recognition to prime ministerial power while allowing for the fact that the prime minister is not directly involved in the bargaining process itself. As will become clear shortly, the power of the prime minister is essential for the existence and stability of equilibrium budgetary outcomes.

In the stylized structure of Subsection i, discussions are assumed to take place between groups of line ministers and the Minister of Finance in cabinet committees. I, however, begin the discussion by assuming that bargaining is on a one-on-one basis involving the Minister of Finance (F) and one line minister (M) only. Having described that process, I bring the committee dimension into the analysis.

The bargaining context is the following. F and M formulate bargaining strategies – contingency plans – that are time sequences of offers and counter-offers. The strategies are derived from the maximization of expected utility functions defined over sums of money – the sums demanded by M and those offered by F for the provision of goods and services – on the assumption that each participant has expectations about what the other will do. Bargaining strategies can be "hard" or "soft." A strategy is harder than another if it leads its owner to demand more than, or at least as much as, what that owner would have demanded had the other strategy been followed. A harder strategy is, therefore, less likely to lead to an early agreement (equilibrium outcome) than a softer one. M and F's expectations about each other will influence the degree of hardness of the bargaining strategies. Expectations are rational – that is, they are unbiased relative to objective reality. Any bias is eliminated through learning, so that in equilibrium subjective and objective probabilities correspond to each other. The equilibrium resulting from the process to which these assumptions give rise has been called a Bayesian–Nash equilibrium. In the words of Cooter, Marks, and Mnookin (1982, p. 233): "[i]t is Bayesian in the sense that each player's optimal strategy is derived from a subjective probability distribution over his opponent's move, and it is Nash in the sense that no one cares to revise his strategy given the strategies of others."

To give concreteness to the bargaining process, assume that a given line minister (M_j) opens the process by formulating a demand for, let us say, X_0 to provide a particular good or service. The Minister of Finance (F) counters by offering Z_0 which, to make sense, must be assumed to be less than X_0. Figure 4.1 – adapted from Cooter, Marks, and Mnookin (1982, p. 231) – shows M_j's demands and F's offers (in dollars) on the vertical axis as a function of time measured on the horizontal axis. The strategies or patterns of concessions over time that correspond to these functions are shown as curves M and F, respectively. The Nash equilibrium bargaining outcome is shown as t_0 which, referring to the vertical axis, also indicates a particular allocation of funds to M_j.

The positions of the M and F curves are a function of the expectations that the bargaining parties entertain about each other. For example, an increase in F's resources over what was initially expected would shift the M curve to, say, M'. M_j would adopt a harder bargaining strategy. To appreciate the significance of such shifts in strategy, we must allow for the shadow of the Prime Minister. There are two possible outcomes to bargaining conducted in that

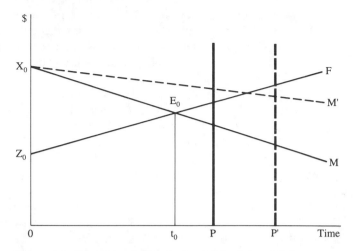

Figure 4.1. Bargaining in the shadow of the Prime Minister.

shadow: one – t_0 in Figure 4.1 – arrived at by the parties alone and another, signaling a breakdown in negotiations, which happens when the M and F curves intersect to the right of the vertical line drawn above point P. That point indicates the moment of prime ministerial intervention in the bargaining process. Its location is at the discretion of the Prime Minister but is a function of the power he or she commands: The smaller that power, the farther out to the right will P be located. A theory of prime ministerial power is beyond the scope of this chapter; as a consequence, I treat it here as an exogenous variable.

The Prime Minister can intervene in the bargaining process in a number of ways. The chosen forms of disciplinary action will depend on a host of variables, including the Prime Minister's personality. For the sake of concreteness and without loss of generality I assume, however, that the only mode of intervention is a cabinet shuffle. The use of that instrument is a measure of the power of the Prime Minister and also, therefore, of the limits of that power. Ministers, who I assume to be averse to risk, do not like shuffles because of the attendant risk of demotion, giving to that word the broadest sense possible – this gives force to the use of the instrument. But the Prime Minister cannot continuously reshuffle the cabinet because of the aura of incompetence, not to mention the chaos that repeated shuffles would inevitably create – this points to the limits of prime ministerial power.[8]

8. Cabinet shuffles are not always or even generally on a grand scale. One minister can be "promoted" to the Senate, to an ambassadorship, or to some other position. Such appointments require reshufflings that do not, as a rule, signal incompetence or produce chaos but that can still achieve the desired objective.

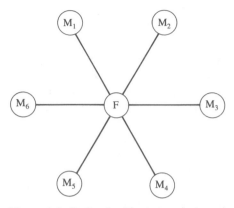

Figure 4.2. Stylized cabinet committee structure.

As Figure 4.1 is constructed, a shift in bargaining strategy on the part of M_j, from M to M′, will lead to a breakdown in bargaining. Should we expect the outcomes of bargaining to be mostly equilibrium points to the left of P, or should we instead anticipate numerous breakdowns? There are a number of institutional features of parliamentary governments that bear on that question. Though all are subject to change, two are in a sense almost intrinsic to that type of government: budget secrecy and prime ministerial power itself. Both are related to other structural characteristics of the bargaining context that need to be looked at independently. I do this immediately after the analysis of secrecy and power.

To introduce the bargaining model, I assumed that only one line minister (M_j) and the Minister of Finance (F) were engaged in bargaining. It is time to modify this assumption. Instead of one line minister, assume that n (>1) line ministers are involved. However, continue to assume that line ministers do not bargain directly with each other but only with F on a one-on-one basis, according to a pattern such as the one shown in Figure 4.2. This assumption can be justified on the following grounds. First, reductions in the appropriations of a particular line portfolio are available to another portfolio only via F. That matches actual practice [see Hartle's (1988) analysis of A, B, X, and Z budgets]. Second, new policies and new programs require new funds, which can come only from F and therefore require bargaining with F.

But if bargaining is assumed to be on a one-on-one basis with F, why also assume that it is conducted in cabinet committees with the participation of many line ministers? Essentially, because that is an effective way to forestall collusion between one or more line ministers and F to the exclusion of other ministers. Bargaining takes place in cabinet committees because these committees allow line ministers to police budget secrecy – the secrecy pertaining to the revenue budget to which the Minister of Finance (F) is bound vis-à-vis his or her cabinet colleagues (what is sometimes called "internal" secrecy).

The question, then, is why budget secrecy? The answer is that in the absence of secrecy bargaining would be unstable. Why? Because any concession accorded by F to M_j would be an occasion for all n M_i's ($i \neq j$) to revise their own strategies. Budget secrecy, then, allows F to keep his or her bargaining strategies with different line ministers independent of each other, while making it rational for line ministers not to revise their own strategies when concessions are made by F to one or another particular line minister. The point is that in the absence of budget secrecy, F's contingency plans would be easily estimated, inducing line ministers to adopt harder bargaining strategies. This would not only increase the frequency of bargaining breakdowns and the consequent need for prime ministerial intervention but would also destroy the possibility of stable Nash equilibrium outcomes. An interesting by-product of budget secrecy, then, is that it legitimizes the assumption of a Nash process according to which one's strategy is not altered if others persist in their existing strategies.

Four other points deserve to be emphasized. First, even though line ministers are not bargaining directly with one another, the scarcity of the resources at F's command necessarily implies that there is (indirect) competition between them. Second, because it increases the incidence of Nash equilibrium outcomes, budget secrecy economizes on prime ministerial power. The implication is that secrecy is wanted by the Prime Minister, who purchases it by giving to the Minister of Finance the enormous power described in Subsection i. Third, budget secrecy reduces the expected gains from collusion among line ministers and, therefore, the incidence of collusive agreements. Widespread collusion would lead to more bargaining breakdowns and, therefore, would beg for prime ministerial intervention. In that way also, budget secrecy economizes on prime ministerial power. Fourth, if budget secrecy were replaced by budget openness, one or more alternative institutions that would in effect be substitutes for secrecy would have to be invented or would spontaneously evolve.

Traditional explanations of budget secrecy focus on external secrecy – that maintained vis-à-vis the general public – and are based on the idea that without it insiders could benefit from a change in tax legislation at the expense of others. As Allan Maslove, Michael Prince, and Bruce Doern (1986) have already noted, that rationale rests on the view that information can be accessed by some people and not by others. For, as they correctly point out, "[i]f everyone were to receive a preview of a budgetary item at the same time, no unfair advantage would exist" (p. 76). Maslove, Prince, and Doern's explanation for internal secrecy – that affirmed by the Minister of Finance vis-à-vis cabinet colleagues, often including the Prime Minister – rests on an announcement effect. In their words, the unveiling of a hitherto secret budget provides "an opportunity [to the government] to demonstrate effective economic management by announcing policy initiatives to respond to economic problems and to take advantage of positive developments" (p. 76). Given the debacles that followed the December 1979[9] and the November 1981[10] budgets, one is not surprised at the diffidence with which they suggest that hypothesis.

Neither the traditional nor the Maslove–Prince–Doern explanations can account for the "excess" power "given" to the Minister of Finance – an excess over that accorded other ministers – which would simply vanish if budget secrecy were jettisoned.[11] Neither can these explanations account for the absence of budget secrecy in congressional government systems. More important, they do not recognize that what principally needs to be explained, a point underlined by Hartle (1982), is the "exclusion of other ministers from the [revenue] budgetary process" (p. 2), not the exclusion of the public. The rationale suggested here explains all these phenomena.[12]

As we have just seen, budget secrecy induces line ministers to adopt softer bargaining strategies in regard to expenditures than they would if the revenue budget process were wide open; this increases the incidence of Nash equilibrium outcomes. The possibility of a cabinet shuffle has a similar effect, except that it uses up some prime ministerial power. In principle, however, that possibility affects all ministers alike, including the Minister of Finance. As a consequence, if the incidence of Nash equilibrium outcomes is to increase – a

9. The government fell on a budgetary confidence motion. For a good, though incomplete, account of that episode see Robert Bothwell, Ian Drummond, and John English (1981, pp. 364–5).
10. Immediately after the Budget Speech, which announced all sorts of changes in tax legislation, the Minister – the Honourable Allan MacEachen – was berated in the House of Commons and in the media and judged to be incompetent, a number of the measures that had been proposed were withdrawn or modified, and the deputy minister – Ian Stewart – was put in a doghouse that he inhabited to the end of his career in the government.
11. One of Hartle's (1982) explanations for secrecy is similar to the one I have just suggested. However, he did not incorporate it into his model.
12. It has sometimes been said that line ministers support and would even promote (revenue) budget secrecy either because the contents of revenue budgets are generally not popular or because the responsibilities of Ministers of Finance and the decisions they are called upon to make are such as to be a barrier to their political career and to that of all those who are too close to the portfolio. It is difficult to appraise such a view. It is true that in Canada, Ministers of Finance have seldom become leaders of their party and, therefore, Prime Ministers, though the current Prime Minister – the Right Honourable Jean Chrétien – was once Minister of Finance. Furthermore, the situation is different in France, the United Kingdom, and in other parliamentary systems. Second, the portfolio confers enormous power, which would seem attractive in itself and can be put to good use in the future. Finally, revenue budgets need not be and are not always unpopular.

result desired by the Prime Minister – the expectation entertained by the Minister of Finance of being shuffled must be smaller than that held by line ministers. But the Prime Minister cannot communicate that overtly to the Minister of Finance – a guarantee of tenure would completely undermine prime ministerial power. However, because expectations are rational, subjective and objective probabilities must eventually coincide. The Minister of Finance (and other ministers), albeit without being certain, can therefore assume by reference to history that he or she is less likely to be shuffled than line ministers are. A testable implication of the theory of parliamentary government suggested in this chapter, then, is that the average tenure in office of ministers of finance is greater, *ceteris paribus,* than is that of line ministers.[13]

The power of the Minister of Finance, as measured by the capacity to adopt harder bargaining strategies, is directly related to that of the Prime Minister, increasing as that power increases. Figure 4.1 can help make that point. A shift in P to P′, reflecting a reduction in the volume of prime ministerial power, makes it possible for line ministers to adopt harder strategies without increasing the incidence of intervention. Popular wisdom, which blames the Prime Minister for excessive increases in the size of the government, is therefore, *ceteris paribus* (see Chapter 12 for an explanation of this *ceteris paribus*), correct. What it usually misses, however, is that the cause of that phenomenon is a deficiency in the power of the Prime Minister.[14]

In 1979, the Canadian government reformed the expenditure budgetary process by introducing what came to be called the Policy and Expenditure Management System (PEMS), also known as the envelop system.[15] The new system is more complex than the older one and in addition has been modified a number of times since its inception.[16] It can, however, be given a simplified representation. This is done in Figure 4.3. Contrasted with the pattern of Figure 4.2, line ministers (M) in Figure 4.3 do not bargain with the Minister of Finance (F). Instead, there are now envelops or Superministers (S) who bargain with F. The M's bargain with S over money for ongoing programs and over policy reserves, that is, money for new programs.

The new system reorganizes competition in two major ways. First, it allows for more Nash equilibrium outcomes, essentially because the S's will follow softer bargaining strategies because they are not bargaining for themselves but

13. The *ceteris paribus* is to account for deaths, scandals, resignations for genuine health reasons, and other sources of prompt exits, in addition to the point made in the next paragraph.
14. I do not deal here with the possibility that the Prime Minister may want more expenditures on some or on all policies, because the question of the appointment of ministers to particular portfolios is outside the purview of the chapter. It is through the composition of the Cabinet that the Prime Minister implements his or her expenditure programs.
15. For excellent descriptions of the new system see Hartle (1988) and Richard Van Loon (1983).
16. Canada had seven Prime Ministers between 1979 and the time this chapter was being revised (November, 1994), and most of these fine-tuned the system to some extent.

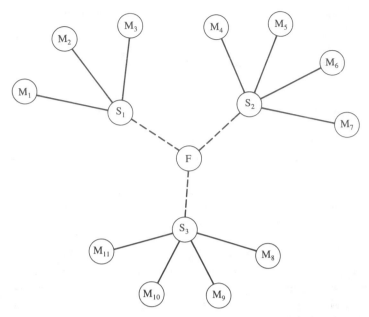

Figure 4.3. Stylized cabinet committee structure after PEMs.

for others – the standard agency problem. Second, it intensifies the competition between the M's, because of the consequent reduced quantum of available resources in each envelop.

I have mentioned the 1979 reform for one reason only: to underline the fact that structural changes, by altering the organization of competition, can have important effects on the allocation of resources. There can be little doubt that PEMS has produced what was expected of it – a reduction in the rate of growth of public expenditures. That, I suggest, was because PEMS changed the organization of competition to achieve that end.

One more issue must be examined before concluding this already long discussion. The analysis so far has been concerned exclusively with the structural and other forces that produce equilibrium allocations of resources among ministries and other agencies of government – allocations that reflect the preferences of citizens and demand lobbies. These equilibrium allocations must, however, be enforced. In the market sector of economies, equilibrium allocations are for the most part enforced by judicatures, but these cannot enforce allocations inside governments.

It has been suggested [for example, by Weingast and Marshall (1988)] that in parliamentary, as distinguished from congressional, systems, equilibrium allocations are enforced by political parties. They do this, according to Barry

Weingast and William Marshall, by controlling "entry into the competition for individual seats and the positions of power within the legislature (e.g., the ministerial positions in Britain), and [because] they wield considerable influence over the distribution of legislative (read: electorally useful) benefits" (p. 159).

Political parties in parliamentary systems do not and cannot enforce equilibrium allocation, not because they do not control positions of power within the legislature – they have nothing to do with ministerial appointments in Canada, as distinguished from, say, New Zealand – but simply because they can be and are periodically defeated in electoral contests. By the rules of the game, a defeat implies a totally new cabinet, that is, a new Prime Minister, a new Minister of Finance, and new line ministers. It also means a completely new majority in the House of Commons. The predefeat nexus between citizens and demand lobbies on the one hand and government on the other is in political terms entirely destroyed.

If political parties cannot enforce the equilibrium allocations determined in bargaining, who can and who does? I suggest that it is the senior bureaucracy – arbitrarily defined to include those bureaucrats who have legitimate access to cabinet documents – that performs that function. That is why in parliamentary as contrasted with congressional systems that bureaucracy is permanent and nonpartisan.[17] In the next section, following Weingast and Marshall (1988), I argue that in congressional governments, equilibrium allocations are enforced by standing committees. For reasons discussed in that section, I add to these committees the control that party leaders exercise over agendas. As a consequence, there is no need for the senior bureaucracy to be permanent and nonpartisan, and it is neither.[18]

We must now enquire, first, into how the senior bureaucracy achieves that end, and second, into why it wants that result. I look at these questions in sequence. Breton and Ronald Wintrobe (1982, Chapter 3) have shown that senior bureaucrats as well as other bureaucrats can sabotage and block proposals put forward by line ministers if they choose to do so (see also Chapter 6, this text). But senior bureaucrats can also make clear to their ministers that other goods and services that are good substitutes for the ones they favor exist and that these could be supplied without upsetting the senior bureaucracy as a constituency. This helps to explain why cabinet ministers in a new government often find relations with their senior bureaucrats difficult (see, for exam-

---

17. Senior bureaucrats, however, are sometimes dismissed, either because they are deemed to have been too partisan or for other less obvious reasons. For an illustration, see Bothwell, Drummond and English (1981, p. 360). The fact that almost all dismissals find a place in historical narratives is, I would think, proof that the senior bureaucracy really is nonpartisan.
18. For a good discussion of the place of the senior bureaucracy in the U.S. federal government, see Hugh Heclo (1977).

ple, Crossman, 1975, and Newman, 1973). This is sometimes interpreted as bureaucratic partisanship toward the old government. I suggest that on the contrary it reflects a commitment of the senior bureaucracy as a constituency to existing equilibrium allocations.

This brings me to the question of why bureaucrats want to preserve extant equilibrium allocations. The bureaucracy of any organization and per force its senior bureaucracy is a network (or a set of interlocking networks) of trust relationships. The network mediates trades in which informal services are exchanged for informal payments. As Breton and Wintrobe have argued, some of the informal payments take the form of characteristics – à la Kelvin Lancaster (1966) – that are integral components of the goods and services provided. Because of that very fact, the senior bureaucracy has a vested interest in the existing bundle of goods and services. It is to protect what has been and remains their "pay" that senior bureaucrats enforce equilibrium allocations.

That poses a problem, however. According to Breton and Wintrobe, the efficiency of bureaus in promoting the policy objectives of ministers depends on the volume of trust between them and the senior bureaucrats. But if these bureaucrats are committed to existing allocations that the new ministers may want to change, how can trust accumulate between the two? While recognizing that such a situation poses a challenge, the difficulty is reduced by the tradition, enforced from within, of a nonpartisan bureaucracy. Why? Because a politically neutral and uncommitted bureaucracy will more willingly engage in trades with cabinet ministers whose political persuasion they neither commend nor condemn. Informal trades, as Breton and Wintrobe (1982, Chapter 4) have shown, eventually lead to the accumulation of trust.

4.2. The budgetary process of congressional governments

It is often taken for granted that the budgetary process is more elaborate and complicated in the American congressional than in the Canadian parliamentary form of government. The paramount importance given to budget secrecy in Canada as contrasted to an outwardly more transparent process in the United States and the fact that revenue budgeting is less detailed than expenditure budgeting, are no doubt responsible for that view.[19] However that may be, the presumed greater complexity of Congressional budget making is not apparent in the stylized structures of the two processes. Let me then suggest a stylized version of the budgetary process at the federal level in the United States that supports that point.

19. Tax codes are extremely detailed. In Canada, however, spelling out the details is not part of the budgetary process but is left to the Department of National Revenue, which is responsible for implementing the revenue policies formulated by the Department of Finance.

i.   Stylized structure

At the heart of the American budgetary process is Congress's "power of the purse," which derives from Article I, Section 9, Clause 7 of the Constitution and states in part that "No Money shall be drawn from the Treasury, but in Consequence of Appropriations made by Law." The process, however, does not begin in Congress but in the Executive branch. There, after the setting of generally loose and informal ceilings by the President (Polsby 1986, pp. 165–9) based on agreed upon forecasts that bring together the Council of Economic Advisors, the Office of Management and Budget (OMB), and the Treasury, budget estimates that take these ceilings into account are received from departments, bureaus, and agencies. These estimates are then examined and adjusted by the OMB to reflect presidential priorities – so-called presidential oversight – before being sent as a recommendation to Congress. That document is received by the Congressional Budget Committee. That Committee, with the corresponding House of Representatives and Senate Committees, within a short time after receiving the budget, must agree on and pass a concurrent budget resolution, which sets overall limits on spending (and on revenue) for the fiscal year. The limits are designed to constrain the subcommittees to which the budget will be transmitted. The first committee to receive the budget after the budget resolution is the House Appropriations Committee, which divides it into segments and distributes them to thirteen functional subcommittees.[20] The subcommittees hold hearings, then review, revise, and rewrite whatever they wish of their portion of the budget and forward it to the full committee, which can but seldom does introduce further changes before sending the document to the House. After it is passed by the House, the House budget is sent to the Senate where, except for the possibility of more extensive floor deliberations, the process is virtually the same as in the House. A penultimate version – the product of compromises between the House and Senate budgets – is then reviewed in the light of the earlier concurrent budget resolution. If the limits contained in that resolution have not been met, adjustments must be made in expenditures, revenues, or both, or in the limits themselves. A second concurrent budget resolution that sets new spending ceilings and revenue floors is then passed. Actual appropriations and (sometimes) taxes are thereupon adjusted to the limits contained in the second resolution. The final version of the budget is thereafter sent to the President. (What happens then is discussed in Subsection iii.)

Revenue budgets or tax messages from the President are not yearly events but happen, in the words of Richard Musgrave and Peggy Musgrave (1984),

---

20. In practice the President's budget goes to the House Appropriations Committee before the budget resolution as a way of economizing on legislative time.

"when political and other circumstances are ripe for 'reform'" (p. 41). A presidential tax message is first sent to the House Ways and Means Committee, where it is subjected to very much the same process as the one just described for the expenditure budget. It is then forwarded to the Senate Finance Committee for a repetition of that process. After reconciliation of House and Senate versions in conference committees, the final draft is sent to the President.

The revenue and expenditure budgetary processes are further complicated by the ability of members of the House and of the Senate to introduce private bills and to add spending or tax riders to any bills that come before them. In all cases, however, these are referred to committees for discussion.

The foregoing stylized structure of the budgetary process in congressional systems makes clear that little of it can be properly understood without some knowledge of the committee system. That system is not only complicated but is also permeated with informal arrangements that make its description difficult. The outline that follows, though enormously simplified, captures all that is needed for the model of the next subsection.

The procedures used to appoint members to the various legislative committees and subcommittees (henceforth committees) vary between House and Senate and between political parties. I will tone down or disregard these differences, except when they are essential for an understanding of the system. All committees are bipartisan. Appointments to them are controlled by party conferences or caucuses – one for each party. The party conferences are managed by the party leaderships.[21] The party ratios – the relative numbers of members from each party – are agreed upon in deliberations between party leaders but tend to reflect ratios in the House and in the Senate.

Appointments to chairs are made on the basis of seniority, where seniority is measured by committee service, not by time spent in Congress.[22] In the Senate, the principle of seniority is more or less absolute, whereas in the House it is relative, since chairs go to the most senior members of the majority party. Chairs, in consultation with party leaders, set committee agendas, hire and fire committee staffs, define the tasks and allocate the time of these staffs, create subcommittees to which they appoint chairpersons and members, decide which part of a bill goes to one subcommittee instead of another, deter-

---

21. For the House of Representatives, the leadership includes the Speaker (from the majority party), Majority and Minority Leaders, Whips and Conference chairs as well as the chairs of all committees. In the Senate, the leadership is made up of the corresponding persons, except that there is, of course, no Speaker.

22. There have been many revolts against the seniority rule. As a consequence, accession to chairs is now effected through voting in party conferences. However, those elected by ballot have often been the same as those that the seniority rule would have chosen (White, 1987, pp. 108–9; Polsby, 1986, p. 120).

mine the policy domain or jurisdiction of their subcommittees, and, last but not least, decide when a bill is ready to proceed to the floor of the House or Senate, whichever applies. As a consequence, chairs not only influence the shape of bills but can also decide to push some of them forward rapidly or simply let them die on the order paper.[23]

The power of committees and of committee chairs is enormous. Each committee is more or less an island, even though some coordination may result from the actions of the majority party leadership. The capacity of committee chairs, each within its respective jurisdiction, to maneuver for what they want is so great that it is best to assume that they obtain what they set out to get.

Once a bill reaches the floor of the House or that of the Senate, voting is usually along party lines (Polsby, 1986, p. 128). The real business has been done before, not unlike what goes on in parliamentary systems!

It may help understanding to summarize again the stylized structure with the following seven propositions:

1. The President prepares a (revenue or expenditure) budget and sends it to Congress.
2. A concurrent budget resolution is passed by House and Senate Budget Committees.
3. Congress segments the budget and distributes the parts to functional committees.
4. After hearings, the committees review and rewrite the budget segment by segment in generally uncoordinated fashion.
5. The sum of the segments, after a compromise conference of the House and Senate, is approved by Congress.
6. If the negotiated sums exceed those in the concurrent budget resolution (see item 2), a new resolution is passed.
7. The final version of the budget is sent to the President.

ii.   The model

Not all demands brought to bear on Congress can be satisfied. The decision-making process through which rationing and adjustments are made cannot be rationalized by a bargaining-in-the-shadow-of-the-law or by a bargaining-in-the-shadow-of-the-President model because competition is not structurally organized in that way. Competition in committees is not regulated by the Executive or by a Minister of Finance or anyone who controls or has custody

---

23. Before reaching the floor of the House, bills must clear a Rules Committee whose task it is to control the flow of legislation. An equivalent committee operates in the Senate. These committees have enormous power, because they control the agendas of the House and Senate. I neglect them in what follows.

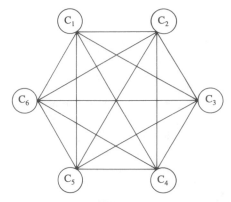

Figure 4.4. Stylized congressional committee structure.

of revenues. As a consequence, the organization of competition does not resemble that depicted in Figures 4.2 and 4.3 but is more akin to that portrayed in Figure 4.4. According to that pattern, in each committee all members (C_i) deal and negotiate with one another. The most appropriate model to formalize that kind of situation is that of logrolling, introduced in the theoretical economics of politics literature by Anthony Downs (1957) and further refined by, among others, James Buchanan and Gordon Tullock (1962), by James Coleman (1966), by Tullock (1970), and by Dirk-Jan Kraan (1990). In their presentation of the model, Buchanan and Tullock suggested that it was applicable to "many of the institutions of political choice-making in Western democracies" characterized by "representative assemblies" (p. 134). The model, however, seems inconsistent with the use of party discipline in the legislatures of parliamentary systems and, as I have implicitly argued, also with the organization of competition and bargaining in cabinet committees. (It may, however, be apposite as a way of rationalizing what goes on in parliamentary caucuses.) But the model applies, without doubt, quite well to the operation of congressional committees and subcommittees.

It has long been known that logrolling, like majority voting, is unstable. The instability is, at the theoretical level, so dominant that substantial effort has been deployed to explain what appears to be a considerable real-world stability of outcomes. In the discussion that follows, except for a minor (though I believe significant) codicil, I borrow from the important work of Kenneth Shepsle and Barry Weingast (1981) and that of Weingast and William Marshall (1988) to suggest that the existence of stable equilibrium logrolling outcomes is the result of two unique institutions of congressional governments: the control by party leaders of committee agendas and the standing committee system.

It is not inappropriate to say that the logrolling, which goes on within the confines of any particular committee, is controlled by the party leadership. Each party's leadership is responsible for the implementation of its legislative program. The power of the majority party's leadership is considerable: It includes the power to determine the number, composition, and jurisdiction of subcommittees, to appoint committee members and their staffs, to decide on the legislative fate of private bills, and a roster of other things. It is through these instrumentalities that agendas are controlled and restricted.

Shepsle and Weingast (1981) have shown that restrictions on the domain or set of items that can be placed on an agenda contribute to the stabilization of logrolling. The restrictions have this effect because they reduce and potentially even eliminate the temptation committee members would otherwise face of reneging on one agreement by joining in another, which a more extensive and variegated agenda makes possible. The control over agendas and the greater difficulty of reneging on agreements it induces in turn reinforce the stability necessarily engendered by the trust that long-term trading between logrollers generates (Breton and Wintrobe, 1982, Chapter 4). Coleman (1983) has stressed the importance of trustworthiness as a stabilizing agent in logrolling without mentioning that it is, in part at least, a correlate of the agenda control emphasized by Shepsle and Weingast.

However that may be, it seems clear that the majority party's leadership is capable of controlling and restricting agendas and in doing so makes a contribution to the stability of logrolling. There is, therefore, a real sense according to which the role of political parties is just as critical in congressional as it is in parliamentary systems. The habit of calling only the latter "party governments," which is so pervasive in the Political Science literature, should consequently be renounced.

Arleen Leibowitz and Robert Tollison (1980) have shown that a committee system increases the probability that the political program of the majority party will be enacted, because committees reduce the incidence of adverse coalitions in the House and Senate as a whole. What is missing from their model, however, is an explanation of why committees are not ad hoc. Weingast and Marshall (1988) have shown that committees can perform the Leibowitz–Tollison task efficiently only if they are permanent institutions, that is, standing committees.

The Weingast–Marshall model is ingenious. It assumes that committees have veto power over policy changes because they completely control the flow of legislation to House and Senate floors. It also assumes that chairmanship of and membership on committees are on the basis of seniority or of bids by new members and by members who wish to transfer from one committee to another. As a consequence, there is only restricted logrolling among the committees. Adjustments to exogenous shocks are effected by members trading their position on one committee against that on another.

Let me illustrate the mechanism by using one of Weingast and Marshall's own examples. There are two committees. One has jurisdiction over dams and bridges, the other over certain types of regulations. Through a process not described – which I identified earlier as restricted logrolling – a decision is made to build a dam and to enact certain regulations. Once the dam is built, those who supported the regulations just to get the dam have an incentive to renege on the deal – that is, to form a new coalition against the regulation in order to get a bridge, say. But because they cannot bring antiregulation legislation to the floor of the House or of the Senate, the deal is secured – enforcement is guaranteed. The only way to undo the agreement is for members of dams and bridges committee to transfer to the committee that controls regulations.

The Weingast–Marshall mechanism alone would appear to be robust enough to stabilize logrolling, so that the party leadership's control over agendas that I discussed earlier would seem superfluous. If one accepts the institutional assumptions of their model, that is no doubt the case. But if their Condition 2 (1988, p. 143), which describes the seniority system, is an acceptable stylized rendition of the Senate, it will not do for the House of Representatives. Indeed, following an election that changed the majority from, say, Democrats to Republicans, the whole configuration of House committees would be changed. Not only would the speaker, majority leader, and majority whip be changed, but the chairs of all committees as well as the party ratios would change (Shepsle 1975). The fact that between the mid-1950s and the November 1994 elections, the Democrats had a continuous majority in the House hides this structural element, but it is no less real for that.[24]

True, the Senate could act as a stabilizing element, but a change in majorities there, though it leaves committee chairs unaltered, produces a number of other important changes. For these reasons, the role I have imputed to party leadership's control of agendas is important; it is a complement to the committee system because that system cannot alone carry the full burden assigned to it by Weingast and Marshall, a point with which the Weingast of Shepsle and Weingast (1981) would presumably agree!

In the foregoing discussion, the role of the presidency is very limited. In practice, that is not the case, as even a cursory look at recent budgetary history will show (see Lammers, 1982). The Executive not only initiates the

24. It is noteworthy that virtually all the empirical evidence that Weingast and Marshall bring forward in support of their hypothesis relates to the House, not to the Senate, and pertains to a period of uninterrupted Democratic Party majority, which guarantees that seniority alone will operate.

budgetary process, but it is also responsible for implementing the congressionally approved budget. That is the source of many problems. Indeed, because of the significant dissociation between expenditure and revenue decisions in Congress (see Section 4.3), the sums appropriated for expenditure not only very often exceed expected revenues, but they also very often exceed the sums requested by the Executive. The President can then, if he finds the excesses unacceptable, use the veto power that Congress can and not infrequently overrides. The veto is, however, such an indiscriminating instrument that it can be used only sparingly. The President can also rely on impoundments – a procedure used by presidents to control the expenditures of congressionally appropriated funds through deferrals and rescissions. Impoundments are now effectively part of the budgetary process, but they have been and remain a source of acrimony.[25] The problem is that to a considerable extent the burden of connecting revenues with expenditures is placed on the Executive, which possesses machinery that is either too powerful or not powerful enough for an effective job. The problem is not caused by the "inherently arbitrary nature of government accounting" (Auerback and Kotlikoff, 1987, p. 104) or by a failure of the Ricardian equivalence between debt and tax finance, but by the way competition is organized in congressional governments. The discussion in Section 4.3 should help to clarify this point.

4.3.   The Wicksellian Connection once again

If the characterization of the budgetary processes in congressional and parliamentary governments suggested in the last two sections at all approximates the reality of budget making in these two forms of government, a very important implication of that characterization for the Wicksellian Connection needs to be emphasized.

To see that the *modus operandi* of parliamentary governments, as modeled in Section 4.1, forges a genuine Wicksellian Connection between costs and benefits, assume that the bargaining between the Minister of Finance (F) and every one of the line ministers (M_j) resolves itself in (Pareto-optimal) Bayesian-Nash equilibria. Assume further that the volume of resources over which F has command is given and that the sum, over all line ministers, of the expenditures resulting from the bargaining equilibria exactly matches F's resources in such a way that a balanced budget obtains. Then, disregarding information problems, it is easy to see that the budgetary process of parlia-

---

25. "The dispute [over impoundments] embittered Nixon's relations with Congress and probably contributed to congressional support for 1974 impeachment proceedings that forced the president to resign in the wake of the Watergate scandal" (Lammers, ed., 1982, p. 53).

mentary governments will mold a tight Wicksellian Connection between the costs and benefits associated with the public supply of goods and services. It does so, first, by having line ministers bargain in cabinet committees one-on-one with the Minister of Finance, thus building a connection between expenditures and revenues on a item-by-item basis, and, second, by making use of a prime ministerial shadow to prevent participants from holding out in the hope of being able to better themselves. The first of these attributes insures simultaneity in the valuation of costs and benefits. The second guarantees unanimity, which in this context is known as "cabinet solidarity." A line minister who would publicly denounce a bargaining equilibrium would in all likelihood entice the Prime Minister out of the shadow and be the likely target of his or her power and wrath. Hence, solidarity.

When prime ministerial power is weaker – the P-line is farther right in Figure 4.1 – cabinet solidarity will be less and so will unanimity. Wicksell's (1896) notion of a "workable" or "approximate unanimity" of $(100 - x)\%$ can be rationalized as an empirical judgment to the effect that prime ministerial power is on the average generally less than the amount required to guarantee full unanimity or full cabinet solidarity. The percentage of line ministers holding out – x – is in that perspective a measure of the tightness (or looseness) of the Wicksellian Connection and a measure of the degree of efficiency in supplying goods and services.[26]

If in addition bargaining breaks down between the Minister of Finance and one or other line minister, so that the latter's budgets are the product of prime ministerial intervention or if total expenditures exceed or fall short of total revenues – situations that can arise even if the bargaining for all line ministers generates Nash equilibria and, *a fortiori,* if bargaining breaks down – then the Wicksellian Connection will not be as tight as in the ideal situation analyzed earlier. The actual degree of tightness of that connection is an empirical matter. My own view – the product of nothing more than casual observation – is that when the power of the Prime Minister is significant, tightness is considerable as long as *operating* expenditures match revenues.

When we turn our attention from parliamentary to congressional governments – as modeled earlier – the situation changes dramatically. In the latter form of government, simultaneity in the valuation of costs and benefits, to the limited extent that it exists, is the product of the force of the concurrent budget resolutions and in any case operates only at the level of *aggregate* spending and revenue. In other words, the House Ways and Means Committee and the Senate Finance Committee conduct their business separately and indepen-

26. The foregoing argument is not inconsistent with Serge-Christophe Kolm's (1968) rationalization and technical defense of Wicksell's "approximate unanimity," which rests on the difficulties (costs) of achieving unanimity through finite exchanges and transfers among members of a given population.

dently from the House and Senate Appropriations Committees.[27] Without simultaneity, the question of unanimity is meaningless.

The near absence of simultaneity alone helps to explain the chronic obsession in congressional government societies with devices such as the Gramm–Rudman–Hollings automatic expenditure-cutting legislation, with impoundments, with spending limits, and with constitutionally prescribed balanced budgets – all measures that have little currency in the debates of parliamentary government societies, except at the fringe where knowledge of how parliamentary governments function appears to be minimal.

The same fact of the separation of expenditure and revenue decisions and the search for ways and means to connect the two would lead one to predict that the incidence of earmarked taxes, trust funds, and special accounts would be much higher in congressional systems than in parliamentary systems in which virtually all revenues have to be vested in a consolidated revenue account under the Minister of Finance as a result of the way competition is organized. The simultaneity of decision that earmarking engenders reduces the weight that must be borne by the concurrent budget resolutions and by other devices such as impoundments, ceilings, and automatic cuts, which are all always very divisive and destabilizing.[28] It also builds partial Wicksellian Connections.

I insist that the lack of Wicksellian simultaneity, the consequent meaninglessness of unanimity, and the partial nature of Wicksellian Connections in congressional governments do not derive from logrolling per se but from the context in which logrolling takes place. I am not adopting here the strictures leveled at logrolling by Tullock (1959), William Riker and Steven Brams (1973), Thomas Schwartz (1975), and others who argue that logrolling leads to governmental expenditures that are too large. Instead, I focus on the fact that logrolling in congressional governments is centered on expenditure programs and is only tenuously related to available revenues. The point is better appreciated if we take note that even if desired aggregate expenditures could be made to match expected aggregate revenues – through a forceful use of the concurrent budget resolutions, some Gramm–Rudman provision, or other measures – the simultaneity of decisions on costs and benefits and the derived Wicksellian Connection between expenditures and revenues would still be loose and certainly much looser than in parliamentary governments, where bargaining is conducted on an item-by-item basis or, at worse, on limited bundles of goods and services.

27. This separation and independence are the basis of the Weingast-Marshall mechanism. Genuine, even if limited, simultaneity of expenditure and revenue decisions would void that mechanism by reconnecting all agreements via the budget constraint.
28. This rationale for the origin of earmarking, though different in details from that suggested by Buchanan (1963), can without difficulty be reconciled with the logic he puts forward.

In concluding this section, note that if we disregard the utility losses caused by the less than perfect information regarding the demand functions of citizens, the tighter Wicksellian Connection between expenditures and revenues in parliamentary than in congressional governments implies that utility losses from public supply of goods and services are smaller in the first than in the second. Anticipating on the analysis in Part III, we would have to conclude that parliamentary governments are more capable than congressional governments of competing against alternative suppliers of goods and services – families, churches, clubs, cooperatives, and others. They would, other things being equal, as a consequence be larger relative to some benchmark such as gross national product. (See also Appendix D.)

4.4.   Conclusion

The budgetary process of parliamentary governments, as modeled in Section 4.1, is an obvious extension of the model of checks and balances proposed in Chapter 3. I have imposed more institutional structure on the checks and balances model, and I have been preoccupied with a different sort of problem – one more central to the traditional concerns of public economics – but the family lineage is clear. In the case of the budgetary process of congressional governments, the family resemblance may not be as transparent, but the competition that necessarily regulates the exchanges rationalized in the logrolling model as well as the onus that often befalls on the presidency to bring aggregate expenditure in line with aggregate revenues and, to do so, to confront the Congress – all are clear manifestations of checks and balances.

I have also argued that the organization of intragovernmental competition leads to the construction of Wicksellian Connections tighter in parliamentary than in congressional governments and that, as a consequence, *ceteris paribus* utility losses inflicted on citizens by a less than optimal provision of goods and services will be larger in the second than in the first. I conclude by repeating a point made in Chapter 3 but that has received ample support in this one, namely, that an understanding of checks and balances and of their consequences cannot focus on a few formal features of governmental structures but must delve into the institutional make up of the public sector.

CHAPTER 5

Consent, suffrage, and support

Consent, more precisely expected consent, has played an important but fairly formal role in the previous three chapters. It will be useful to look at the concept in more detail, to examine on what it is founded, to analyze how it is connected to the use of repression or force, which is a dimension of all political systems, and to investigate how it relates to other concepts such as suffrage (voting) and support (money, time, and other types of allocations).

In politics, as in every other area of human activity, the motives that govern decision making and behavior are enormously complex. That fact must occupy center stage when one's analysis concentrates on the motivations themselves. If, however, one is focusing on the workings of competition and on the role of suppliers and demanders in that process, it is not only legitimate but essential to simplify. Accordingly, I assume that decisionmakers in the various centers of power that constitute compound governments are solely interested in political power and that they act to maximize the value of that variable. There is no accepted general definition of political power or for that matter of any other kind of power. To proceed, I conceive of power as a form of capital used to produce two different streams of services, the sum of whose present values is a measure of its worth. The first kind of service takes the form of benefits or amenities peculiar to each center of power and to the individual decisionmakers who inhabit them. The second is manifested in repression, which, I later argue, is necessary to insure governability. What repression or the use of force produces, is, therefore, a source of utility to decisionmakers.

Following Samuel Bacharach and Edward Lawler (1981), I further assume that power (P) is accumulated or produced by securing the consent (c) of people, by gaining their support (s), and by winning their suffrage (v). Consent, support, and suffrage are, then, three factors of production used to produce power.[1] Given the power function $P = f(c, s, v)$, I also assume that $f_i > 0$ and that $f_{ii} < 0$ (with f_i and f_{ii}, the first and second partial derivatives of

1. I am grateful to Janet Landa for pointing out that by expending resources on propaganda and indoctrination through, among other things, the development and diffusion of overarching doctrines, and the promotion of certain symbols (flags, anthems, insignias, and emblems), centers of power can increase the marginal product of the three factors of production. I will make use of that fact in the next section.

122

the arguments of the power function). I postpone until Section 5.2 a discussion of the sign of the cross-derivatives.

Variation in the volume of each of the three factors of production can take place at two margins: (1) widening of consent, support, and suffrage when the number of persons who offer them increases (an extensive margin), and (2) deepening of consent, support and suffrage when their intensity or the volume offered by any one person expands (an intensive margin). Maximization by centers of power implies that per allocated dollar the two margins will be equalized. I assume that such an equality holds at all times and therefore neglect extensive and intensive margins in what follows.

It would be unduly repetitive to develop a model of the market for consent followed by one on the market for support and then a third on the market for suffrage. There is enough similarity in the fundamentals to justify a decision to limit the chapter to the presentation of a model of consent and to introduce support and suffrage as variables that make the analysis more general. The next section, therefore, suggests a partial equilibrium theory of political consent; then in Section 5.2 I introduce support and suffrage in the model. Section 5.3 extends the analysis by looking at two important problems, namely, collusion and the breakdown of competition. Section 5.4 brings the chapter's conclusion to bear on the nature of the Wicksellian Connection, and Section 5.5 concludes the exercise.

5.1.   A model of political consent

It is often said that people "give" their consent to persons or institutions. I begin the discussion of the market for consent by noting that from an economic perspective people never "give" their consent, because if they did political power would not be a valuable capital asset. It would be a free good of which everyone could have as much as he or she wanted, and as a consequence politics would be unstable or anarchical. We must recognize that consent will be forthcoming only – will be supplied only – if it is "paid" for. In the market for consent, some individuals (the people, the citizens) will "sell" consent, and others (centers of power) will "buy" it. A market for consent therefore, cannot exist unless there is a "price," or *quid pro quo,* against which consent is traded. What is that price?

On the basis of the analysis in Chapter 2, it is straightforward to assume that the supply price of consent (P_s) is inversely related to the marginal utility loss associated with the provision of government-supplied goods and services, that is, $P_s = 1/\Delta\lambda$ (where $\Delta\lambda$ is a measure of marginal utility loss under the assumption that taxprices are exogenously given). The smaller the utility loss inflicted on citizens, the larger, *ceteris paribus,* will be the volume of consent offered by these citizens.[2] The amount of consent demanded by centers of power or by those who are active in them is, I assume, negatively related to its demand price, which reflects the behavior of the marginal productivity of consent ($f_c > 0$ and $f_{cc} < 0$ of the political power function introduced earlier).

These preliminaries behind us, we can turn our attention to the analysis of the market for consent. It will simplify the presentation and the comparative static analysis if I work with particular specifications of supply and demand. I will call the supply specifications *dispensations* and the demand specifications *rules*.

On the supply side of the consent market – in recognition that the foundations of political legitimacy (to be defined shortly) have varied over time and from society to society – I examine two polar models: one that assumes that the foundation of legitimacy is divine will (a *Vox Dei* dispensation) and another that supposes that its basis is popular will (a *Vox Populi* dispensation). I insist that these are polar specifications of supply that are heuristically helpful but are imprecise images of the real world. However, as the discussion that follows should make evident, mixed dispensations are easy to handle.

On the demand side of the consent market, again to simplify, I restrict myself once more to two polar specifications. I begin by assuming that political power is either *individually* or *collectively* owned.[3] It is probable that the polar extreme of individual ownership of political power has never existed, although it seems likely that when power was held by the Roman Caesars or by families (houses) such as the Bourbons, the Hapsburgs, the Hohenzollerns, and the Stuarts and, in our days, the Batistas, the Duvaliers, the Marcoses, and the Somozas, the polar limit is approximated. Recent and ongoing communist regimes also depart from the extreme and are probably best characterized as oligarchies, though that term was devised to characterize different types of rule. However that may be, I limit my discussion in this section to the stylized polar extreme. Collective ownership of political power corresponds to the situation that obtains when, in the words of Richard Auster and Morris Silver (1979), power is "widely held," that is, when governments are constituted of a large number of centers of power. To analyze how the equilibrium price of consent is determined and the changes that take place in the volume of political power accumulated as market structures change, I analyze the cases

2. This is the same assumption, in a different context, as the one made about equations (2.9) and (2.10) in Chapter 2.
3. The idea that political power (or the apparatus of the state) can be either individually or collectively owned ("widely held") was, to my knowledge, first used by Richard Auster and Morris Silver (1979). In addition, these authors argue, as I do, that when political power is very widely held, rents to political actors are zero (p. 73). It is their opinion that this state of affairs, however, never exists. That is, of course, a question about facts which can be resolved only through careful empirical work.

of individual and collective ownership, first under a *Vox Dei* and then under a *Vox Populi* dispensation. It is a simple matter to move from these polar cases to the more realistic ones.

i.   A Vox Dei *dispensation model*

In *The English Constitution,* Bagehot (1867) argued that a "[g]overnment [is] entitled to be called legitimate" if it is "capable of creating in the mind of [people] a feeling of moral obligation to obey it" (p. 83). If one recognizes, as one must, that "a feeling of moral obligation" is not a state but a variable, legitimacy is also a variable quantity. I define a *Vox Dei* dispensation as one in which the "feeling of moral obligation to obey" rulers and governments is "creat[ed] in the mind" of people by reference to doctrines that assert that all authority comes from God. Legitimacy, under a *Vox Dei* dispensation, is as a consequence rooted in a belief that rulers govern by divine right. That belief – like all opinions, convictions, and feelings to which human beings hold when sufficient ground for verifiable knowledge does not exist – is never absolute.[4]

As a consequence, the "feeling of moral obligation to obey" governments is not only variable; it is also limited. It is hardly surprising, therefore, that historians often disagree about the nature of the dispensation that exists in a society at a moment of time. It has been said that "[i]n the early seventeenth century nearly all English people saw the king as an absolute ruler governing a nation of Christians by divine right" (Wootton, 1986, p. 18) and that by the end of the century that state of affairs had largely passed. Others have pointed to the French Revolution as marking the definitive end of *Vox Dei* dispensations in Europe. The problem is further complicated by the fact that analysts generally do not distinguish between dispensations and orders – between supply and demand. For example, it is not always clear whether the laments in England and on the Continent that followed the deposition and beheading of Louis XVI, the King of France, were concerned with the passing of the dispensation or with the demise of the individual ownership of political power, because both, temporarily, went out at the same time. That identification problem is inherent because, as I will repeatedly emphasize, both supply (the dispensation) and demand (the rule) – like Marshall's scissors – are needed to determine the nature of political regimes and of political equilibria.[5]

4. I am in effect assuming that throughout history human beings have faced (at least) two different types of propositions: one that could be verified by reference to the real world (or to experience) and another that could not. I am also assuming that they gave, at the existential level at least, more credence or weight to the first than to the second.
5. In 1933, shortly after the Nazi takeover of Germany, Joseph Goebbels in a radio address declared that "the year 1789 is hereby eradicated from history." The French campaign and the fall of France in 1940 were celebrated in the same spirit "as a victory over 'discarded ideals'

To proceed, assume that the cost of accumulating political power through the purchase of consent is lower, the greater is the legitimacy of a ruler. In other words, assume that the greater the legitimacy – the greater the "feeling of moral obligation to obey" – the lower is the supply price of consent at all volumes of consent. However, because beliefs or feelings by their very nature are never absolute, it must be that under a polar *Vox Dei* dispensation, though the supply price of consent is the lowest possible, it is never zero. The schedule depicting this minimum minimorum supply price of consent over all volumes of consent is labeled S(D) in Figure 5.1. Why should it be positively sloped? Why, in other words, should the price asked by those who supply consent rise as the amount of it offered increases? To answer this question, it suffices to recall that the supply price of consent is the inverse of the marginal utility loss inflicted on citizens by a provision of goods and services which, at given taxprices, differs from the one desired, that is $P_s = 1/\Delta\lambda$. The supply price of consent must rise, therefore, on the elementary supposition that if $\Delta\lambda$ is constant – the size of the utility loss does not change – citizens will have no incentive to offer more consent. To be induced to offer more, $\Delta\lambda$ must fall and P_s, consequently, rise.

If it is also the case when a *Vox Dei* dispensation obtains that political power is individually owned – the center of power and therefore the government is, in the language of economics, a monopsonist in the consent market – then the equilibrium price of consent will be OR in Figure 5.1, the equilibrium quantity transacted will be OC'_m, and the surplus accruing to the autocrat will be RSTU determined by d(M) and MC(D) – the marginal to the supply curve S(D).[6]

To be in a position to describe a first property of this monopsony equilibrium, we must recognize that when the center of power purchases OC'_m of consent there will still exist in the population an amount of "nonconsent" – an amount of dissent – not shown in Figure 5.1. The reason for the existence of dissent is that in the presence of positive information costs it is never possible to eliminate all utility losses. To deal with the dissent that persists when the

---

and the 'subhuman revolution' of 1789" (Bracher, 1970, p. 10). It is not clear in this case whether Goebbels thought that the dispensation had been repealed – a sort of *völkisch* dispensation introduced – or whether a rule of individual ownership of power would henceforth constitute the form of government. As Minister of Propaganda, he did not have to be careful in distinguishing between supply and demand!

6. I use the word *monopsonist* and not *leviathan* as do, among others, Brennan and Buchanan (1980), because as the number of separate centers of power grows and one goes from monopsony to competition, the standard language of economics is not only more evocative but more appropriate than that of leviathan. However that may be, my autocrat and the Brennan–Buchanan leviathan (pp. 26–30) have much in common.

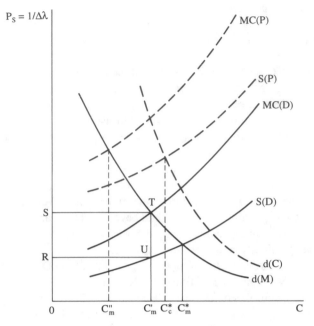

Figure 5.1. Competitive and monopsonistic equilibria in the market for consent (C) under *Vox Dei* and *Vox Populi* dispensations.

consent market is in equilibrium, the center of power will resort to force or to what I call *repression*.

In the present partial equilibrium framework, I assume that the governability of society – the ability of governments to govern – is a product of consent and repression alone. I noted earlier that in addition to yielding a stream of benefits to its owners, political power was also needed to guarantee governability. We can now see what that means: Power, which derives from consent, makes the use of repression possible. There is a paradox in that fact: The larger the volume of consent that has been secured, the greater the ability to use repression, but the less of it that is needed for governability. In this narrow sense, it is possible to say that consent and repression are substitutes for each other *in the production of governability*.

If we now assume that the demand and supply schedules are the same under competition and monopsony and if we adopt the convention that under competition – when, given the dispensation, the price paid for consent is at its highest – the amount of repression used is at a minimum, a first property of the OC'_m equilibrium is that more repression is used under monopsony than under competition because, as Figure 5.1 indicates, $C'_m < C^*_m$ always. That seems a reasonable property. A second is that at C'_m we observe the coexistence of some consent and the "exploitation" [to use Joan Robinson's (1933) expression] of his or her subjects by the autocrat, that is, both OC'_m and RSTU are positive.[7]

A third characteristic of equilibrium is that the *demand price* for consent is positive. Autocratic rulers under *Vox Dei* dispensations have sometimes been described as benevolent because they made gifts to their subjects. These gifts should not be seen as signs of benevolence but as the price of consent – as compensation for the utility losses attributable to war, unemployment, and other goods and services supplied by rulers.

Such is the meaning of the triumphal arches, public baths, amphitheaters, temples, and of the legendary *panis et circenses* of ancient Rome. It is also the appropriate rationale for the carnivals that flourished in Venice, Florence, and Turin and then spread to all Europe and beyond. These carnivals were the occasion for spectacular pageants, popular theater, singing, folk dancing, feasts, and sexual liberty and were not only tolerated by the Church and by civil rulers but were financially supported by the latter [see Darnton (1985)]. Similarly, the great cathedrals of Europe – Noyon, Laon, Paris, Canterbury, Chartres, Saint Ouen, Trier, Marburg, Toledo, and Utrecht, to name only a few of the most famous – though in the possession of the Church, were often built at the request of civil rulers and were the recipients of financial largess from these rulers. These cathedrals were built for religious celebrations, but they also served as what we would now call community centers. There the troubadours read their poetry and their ballads, and there medieval theater flourished. Gifts by rulers to their subjects for the purpose of eliciting consent was, as the Bible tells us, also practised in ancient Israel. It is reported that after he had officially entered the city of Jerusalem, which he had just conquered from the Jebusites with a view to making it the capital city of the country he was trying to unify, King David "distributed among all the people, among the whole multitude of Israelites, men and women, a roll of bread to each, a portion of dates, and a raisin cake" (2 Samuel 6, 19). A reading of his life indicates that David was a generous, even a magnanimous man, but that does not stand in the way of interpreting his gifts as the price paid for the consent of "the whole multitude of Israelites." After all, his main problem was to govern, and his generosity and magnanimity were ways of not putting too much reliance on repression.

Finally, if for one (exogenous) reason or another, belief in the divine right of rulers erodes, the supply price of consent rises in the direction of S(P) in Figure 5.1. And because the autocrat's demand function will not have

---

7. The autocrat could obviously be a price-discriminating monopsonist and make the surplus even larger.

changed – nothing has happened to the autocrat on the demand side – the stage is set for the use of more repression to protect private ownership of political power. Consent purchased at C''_m is necessarily smaller than the amount bought at C'_m. The increment of repression will be large or small depending on whether the erosion of belief in divine right is extensive or limited, as well as on the slopes of the supply and demand curves.

The case of collectively owned political power under a *Vox Dei* dispensation does not appear to have any corresponding referent in the real world, nor should we expect anything else. A full collective ownership of political power exists when there are many centers of power and therefore when the apparatus of the state is competitive. As one approaches the polar extreme of collective ownership, one also approaches perfect competition, because the bidding for consent by a large number of centers of power pushes the price of consent upward and dissipates monopsony or oligopsony surpluses.

However, under a *Vox Dei* dispensation, it is relatively easy for the various centers of power to collude or to merge. Indeed, the conviction that all authority derives from above is easy to reconcile – and historically was reconciled (Wootton 1986, pp. 23 and ff) – with the view that power should be vested in a single repository. So if the dispensation is *Vox Dei,* the incentive on the part of the people to oppose collusion, merger, and therefore a higher concentration of power is effectively nonexistent.

The only incentives at work in the system are those that push the centers of power to collect the monopsony rents by colluding, by merging, or by the forceful suppression and annihilation of one or more centers (see Section 5.3). If as a result of a fortuitous exogenous event a *Vox Dei* society found itself with a multiplicity of competing centers of power, such an equilibrium would be unstable; within a short time the demand side of the consent market would become a monopsony.

Such instability would appear to characterize a number of Third World countries, which are not by any means polar *Vox Dei* dispensations but in which a significant fraction of the population appears unwilling or incapable of accepting that it is the source of political legitimacy. In these circumstances, the dispensation can be described as a surrogate *Vox Dei* dispensation whose instability calls for autocratic rule. One is led to conclude that only individual ownership of political power is stable under a *Vox Dei* dispensation or one like it.

ii.   *A* Vox Populi *dispensation model*

A *Vox Populi* dispensation, at the other end of the spectrum, is based on a belief on the part of the people that political legitimacy derives from themselves. At the polar extreme, it implies a belief that all and not only a subset of the people are the source of legitimacy. Historically, *Vox Populi* dispensations have often been restricted to special groups: the landed gentry, the bourgeoisie, the moneyed and propertied classes, and so on. That notwithstanding, this section is concerned with the polar case only.

Under a polar *Vox Populi* dispensation the supply price of consent for all possible quantities is at its maximum maximorum and is shown as S(P) in Figure 5.1. If political power is collectively owned in such a way that competition is perfect, the demand curve will be d(C) and equilibrium determined where supply and demand are equal, that is, where d(C) = S(P), with OC^*_c the amount of consent traded.

Will the demand curve for consent under competition, namely d(C), always be above and to the right of the demand curve for consent under monopsony, or d(M), as the two curves are drawn in Figure 5.1? Demand curves for factors of production – in this case for consent to produce political power – are derived on the assumption that the prices of substitutes are given. In the partial equilibrium analysis of the consent market on which this section focuses and holding the volume of repression used temporarily constant, the only substitutes for consent are propaganda, indoctrination, overarching ideologies, symbols, and other factors of that kind (see footnote 1). It seems reasonable to assume that the cost of using these substitutes will be lower in autocratic regimes simply because centralization will guarantee that there is no dissonance in the transmission of messages. To put the matter differently, if we assume that there are economies of scale and economies of scope in the use of the listed substitutes, it would follow that the more autocratic the regime, the greater the exploitation of economies of scale and of scope and, therefore, the lower the unit price of indoctrination, ideologies, and of similar control devices. Autocrats would, as a consequence, make greater use of the substitutes so that the marginal productivity of consent curve under monopsony would always be below and to the left of the equivalent curve under competition. Under pure autocracy the distance between the two curves could be "substantial."

Furthermore, if the greater need for repression under autocratic rule is translated in the proposition that, in producing governability, repression and consent are better substitutes (see foregoing for a discussion of the sense in which repression and consent are substitutes) under monopsony than under competition, then d(M) will be more elastic than d(C). This proposition is portrayed in Figure 5.2. The two isoquants G_c and G_m are isogovernability curves for alternative amounts of consent and repression under competition and monopsony, respectively. The degree of substitution between consent and repression is greater along G_m. A fall in the price of repression relative to that of consent, from AA′ to $B_cB'_c$ and $B_mB'_m$, increases the demand for repres-

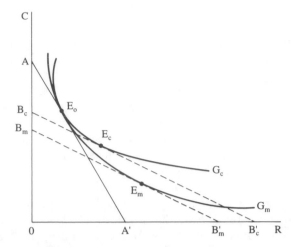

Figure 5.2. Substituting consent (C) for repression (R) under competitive and monopsonistic conditions.

sion along G_m more than along G_c and therefore increases the demand for consent less.

Two interesting properties of equilibrium under a *Vox Populi* dispensation and collective ownership of political power can be noted. The first is simply that the amount of repression used to produce governability is, under this dispensation and rule, at an absolute minimum. This can be seen in Figure 5.1 where $C^*_c > C'_m > C''_m$, inequalities which hold as long as economies of scale and of scope in using indoctrination, propaganda, and ideologies are "substantial" and are exploited by autocrats, guaranteeing that C''_m and $C'_m < C^*_m$.[8] The second property of equilibrium is that C^*_c describes a situation in which the rents accruing to public sector decisionmakers are zero.[9]

Modern dictatorships as a general rule do not operate under polar *Vox Populi* dispensations. It is true that the rhetoric used by many of these regimes seeks to convey the impression that they approximate such polar dispensations. It is even true that many of their institutions have been designed with an outside veneer of democracy, which is intended to project the same image. Let me, then, temporarily accept these regimes' rhetoric and institutional posturing and proceed to examine one important difference, in equilibrium, between

8. In Figure 5.1, $C^*_m > C^*_c$ which would seem to deny that repression is least at C^*_c. However, as I have argued earlier, C^*_m is not a stable equilibrium and will not be observed in the real world, except transitorily.

9. It is possible to have rents in a perfectly competitive market simply by assuming the presence of specificity in some or all factors of production. I do not do this here because to do so would add nothing to the discussion that is not already well known.

autocratic rules under the polar extremes of *Vox Dei* and *Vox Populi* dispensations.

The equilibrium volume of consent under a polar *Vox Populi* dispensation is C''_m in Figure 5.1. It is always less than C'_m, the equilibrium amount under a *Vox Dei* dispensation. Using C^*_c and (neglecting its instability) C^*_m as benchmarks of minimal repression under the two dispensations, Figure 5.1 tells us that $(C^*_c - C''_m) > (C^*_m - C'_m)$ and, therefore, that the amount of repression used by autocrats is greater under *Vox Populi* than under *Vox Dei* dispensations. This may help us understand why Napoléon Bonaparte, who made a formal show of the fact that unlike previous autocrats who had been *Roi de France* he would not be *Empereur de France* but *Empereur des Français* – thus signaling, at least to the still powerful revolutionary elements with whom he had previously flirted, that he was aware that the dispensation was changing from *Vox Dei* to *Vox Populi* – had to create upon assuming this new autocratic role a police force under Joseph Fouché. Even if by modern standards this force was quite restrained, it was still a decidedly ferocious apparatus and one that by any reckoning was more implacable than what had been in place before. It may also shed light on a point made by Aleksandr Solzhenitsyn (1973) that in czarist Russia repression was less than it was under Lenin and Stalin in the Soviet Union. In a word, autocratic rule under *Vox Populi* would appear to be more brutal and sanguinary than under *Vox Dei* dispensations.

Modern dictatorships, however, are neither polar *Vox Dei* nor polar *Vox Populi* dispensations but somewhere between these two extremes. If the supply price of consent is depicted by S(D) and S(P) under *Vox Dei* and *Vox Populi* dispensations, respectively, then the supply price under modern dictatorships would be something like S(M) in Figure 5.3. These modern regimes differ in one other respect from the stylized autocratic regimes I have so far been analyzing: Though they have fewer and less effective centers of power than democratic governments do, they are not constituted of only one of these centers and, as a consequence, they are not devoid of internal competition. To deal with this fact I make two assumptions: first, that dictatorial regimes can usefully be classified into two categories, and second, that what distinguishes these two classes of dictatorships most is the number of centers of power on the demand side and the ability of these centers to compete with one another.[10] I call those regimes in which the centers of power are fewer and

---

10. The assumption that dictatorial regimes can be usefully dichotomized is common. See, for example, Kirkpatrick (1979) and Wintrobe (1990). No one to my knowledge has used the degree of competition on the demand side of the consent market to distinguish between the two groups. As the following quotation indicates, Jeane Kirkpatrick may have been groping for something of that kind. She writes: "Authority in traditional autocracies is transmitted through personal relations: from the ruler to his close associates (relatives, household mem-

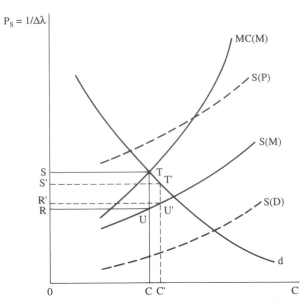

Figure 5.3. Comparing equilibrium consent in personal and impersonal dictatorships.

less competitive *personal* dictatorships and those in which the centers are more numerous and more competitive *impersonal* dictatorships.[11]

By definition, there is more competition on the demand side in impersonal than in personal dictatorships, so that the price paid for consent is higher and the volume of consent transacted is greater in the former than in the latter. Referring to Figure 5.3, the price paid for consent in personal dictatorships would be OR, whereas it would be OR' in impersonal regimes and the volume of consent traded in the latter would be OC', whereas it would be OC in the former (OR' and OC' have been arbitrarily located, but because under perfect competition, assuming that the demand and supply curves remain unchanged, the price would be OR* (not indicated) where d = S(M), OR' must be above OR and OC' larger than OC).

Note also that the size of the rents or surpluses that accrue to dictators is larger in personal than in impersonal regimes – that RSTU > R'S'T'U'. As

bers, personal friends) and from them to people to whom the associates are related by personal ties resembling their own relation to the ruler. The fabric of authority unravels quickly when the power and status of the man at the top are undermined or eliminated. The longer the autocrat has held power, and the more pervasive his personal influence, the more dependent a nation's institutions will be on him. Without him, the organized life of the society will collapse" (p. 38).

11. Kirkpatrick's (1979) labels are traditional or right-wing and socialist, revolutionary or left-wing; whereas Wintrobe (1990) refers to tinpot and totalitarian dictatorships.

such, impersonal autocrats are less likely targets for what Harold Demsetz (1968) has called "competition for the field" or for what William Baumol, John Panzar, and Robert Willig (1982) call "contestation." The presence of competing centers of power provides more anonymous avenues through which citizens can access the apparatus of state in impersonal dictatorships, whereas the only effective avenue to that apparatus in personal regimes is the autocrat and his or her camarilla. It is important to keep matters in perspective: Dictatorships are dictatorships. Repression is an important instrument of governability in these regimes. The point of the foregoing is simply that impersonal tyrants pay a higher price for consent and therefore obtain more of it than do personal autocrats. As a consequence, the impersonal tyrants use less repression than the personal autocrats. They may also be more stable.[12]

If we compare personal and impersonal autocratic regimes with one another and with democratic regimes, the foregoing analysis suggests a number of testable propositions. A first is that governments have more consent in democracies than in dictatorships but also that governments of impersonal tyrannies have more than those of personal autocracies. A corollary of this is that repression will be smallest in democracies, be greater in impersonal despotisms, and be the largest in personal autocracies. A second implication is that the surplus accumulated in office will be smallest in democracies and smaller in impersonal than in personal regimes. As the ownership of political power becomes more collective, the surplus accruing to public sector decisionmakers tends to zero. As a consequence, as long as the marginal utility of wealth declines, one expects the number of wealthy people entering politics to be larger in democracies than in dictatorships, since in the latter regimes surpluses are garnered in politics. Finally, one expects the decisionmakers of personal autocracies to leave office having accumulated more wealth for their own use than officials of impersonal tyrannies, holding, of course, the length of tenure as well as other relevant variables constant.

5.2.   Introducing suffrage and support

It is time to acknowledge that decisionmakers in *some* centers of power, though they may seek the consent of people, will also want to win their vote because the constitutional rules specify that to be a member of these centers, one must be elected. As a consequence, governmental structures will now be made up of two types of centers of power: In one the occupants will seek only the consent of people, whereas in the other they will want their consent and their suffrage. We must enquire into whether this structural change will have an effect on the outcome of competition among centers of power.

12. I examine the problem of stability in Section 5.3. For an enlightening analysis of this
    problem, which ascribes a central role to economic as well as to political conditions, see
    Wintrobe (1990).

To give concreteness to the analysis, consider the previously described (see Chapter 3, Section 3.5) political structure of the early American Republic, which Alexis de Tocqueville (1835, 1840, p. 156) hailed as "one of the great discoveries of political science in our age." Recall that the following were the basic building blocks of that structure: a President elected by a College whose members were appointed by state legislatures; a Senate whose members were appointed by the same state legislators; a House of Representatives elected by the people; and a Supreme Court appointed by the President.[13]

As Tocqueville recognized and as Chapter 3 acknowledged, that structure was conducive to competition. However, there is an aspect of it that is easy to neglect but that must be explicitly taken into account if the workings of competition are to be correctly understood. I am referring to the fact that the House of Representatives, and only the House, was elected by the people. We can therefore assume that members of that body sought consent but that they also acted to obtain the suffrage of voters, and that all the other centers of power would have limited themselves to competing in the consent market.

To appreciate the meaning of that fact, I consider the behavior of the House of Representatives (henceforth, House) in its relations with the general public and then in relations with the other centers of power constituting the government. I proceed as follows: I first lay down the general principles governing these relationships and then to illustrate the principles bring a few selected facts, taken from the history of the early days of the American Republic.

To deal with the first question, I divide the public into two mutually exclusive groups: one that has the right to vote and another that does not. Before enfranchisement, assuming that that state existed, the House, to maximize its political power, would have acquired consent from the two groups in such a way as to equalize the marginal contribution of consent per unit of effort. The amounts purchased from each group when the marginal value of consent per unit of effort is m_0 are shown as OC_0 and OC'_0 in Figure 5.4(a) and 5.4(b).

Suppose now that one of the two groups is given the right to vote and the other is not. The present discounted value of that right is difficult to estimate in any particular instance, but as a general proposition, it must be presumed to be as large as the value of resources – money, time, energy, and, in some cases, lives – allocated by hitherto nonenfranchised groups to obtain it. As a matter of history, it is a fact that the value of resources allocated to that end has been positive and, as a consequence, it must be assumed that the present value of the right is positive. Securing that right will shift the supply curve of consent *and* suffrage of those just enfranchised in a rightward direction – from V_0 to V_1 in Figure 5.4(a).

13. Even if it was true that "Washington and his successor John Adams refused to appoint Republicans to any of the judicial offices under their control," and even if "[p]ositions on the federal branch went only to men who were strong partisans of administration policies" (Ellis, 1971, p. 14), after *Marbury* v. *Madison* in 1803, the Court became competitive.

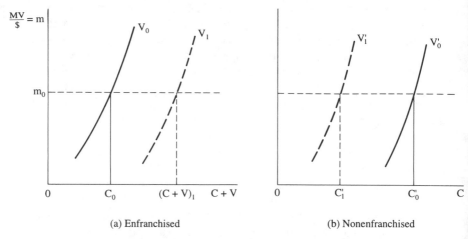

(a) Enfranchised   (b) Nonenfranchised

Figure 5.4. The effect of changing endowments on political equilibria.

Earlier I made the assumption that when the quantity of consent changes, intensive and extensive margins are always kept equal: If the supply price of consent is exogenously pushed up, say, the volume of consent forthcoming increases, that is, both the *intensity,* or depth of consent, and the *number* of persons offering it increase. The same thing holds for suffrage: The *probability* of a favorable vote and the *number* of approving voters increase. As a consequence, it is not only legitimate but appropriate to add (horizontally) the supply schedule of consent with that of suffrage, as I have done, to show the extension of the franchise. The resulting displacement of the V-curve in Figure 5.4(a) causes the equilibrium quantities purchased to shift from OC_0 to $O(C + V)_1$. If the total volume of resources that the House can expend is given, the amount of consent purchased from the nonenfranchised will fall from OC'_0 to OC'_1 as the supply schedule shifts from V'_0 to V'_1 in Figure 5.4(b) as a result of the operation of that resource constraint. The overall effect of partial enfranchisement is a worsening of the relative position of the nonenfranchised. It would be a relatively simple matter, beginning with this proposition, to develop a dynamic model of the extension of the franchise. Indeed, if giving the right to vote to one group makes other groups worse off, we should expect these latter groups to mobilize and to expend resources to acquire such a valuable asset.

The effect of awarding the right to vote on the relative position of the House vis-à-vis the other governmental centers of power is the obverse of what has just been described for citizens. Indeed, before the right to vote is given, all centers of power compete in a homogeneous market, but the introduction of that right transforms that market into a differentiated one. The degree of differentiation will depend on the extent to which consent and suffrage are substitutes for each other. If we assume that they are imperfect substitutes, we would be led to conclude that the competitive status of the House vis-à-vis the other centers of power would be enhanced as a result of the differentiation provoked by the introduction of the franchise. On the other hand, if the fraction of the population that obtained the franchise was an unbiased representative sample of the whole population, the differentiation of the market would have no observable consequences, because the nonenfranchised would in effect be free-riders.[14]

The fraction of the population that in fact had the right to vote was very small in the early years of the American Republic. At the close of the Revolution, excluding Indians who were not enumerated, the population was equal to approximately 3,250,000 people. Subtracting females and children, blacks, indentured servants, convicts, and others who did not have the right (because of educational qualifications, literacy tests, residency or property requirements, and poll taxes) or the physical ability to vote because many citizens were "on the move to distant and isolated places, [such as] the northern frontiers of Vermont and Maine, . . . the Mohawk Valley of New York, the Monongahela Valley of Pennsylvania, the wilds of Kentucky and Tennessee . . ." left "perhaps 120,000 Americans [who] could meet the property, religious, or other qualifications to vote" (Miller, 1969, pp. 112–13) – just slightly over 3.5 percent of the total.[15] The franchise was not only limited. In addition, as Jackson Main (1961) has carefully documented, the interests of the citizens who were enfranchised and those of the population who were not were far from the same. As a consequence, the subset of people who voted was not an unbiased sample of the whole population.

It seems reasonable to conclude that the relationship of the central government of the young Republic with its citizens is tolerably well captured by the foregoing analysis centered on Figure 5.4. Before proceeding, note that this analysis can also shed some light on the hypothesis first advanced by Orin

14. There would be no free-riding, but the same result would obtain if elected representatives, in Burkian fashion, chose not to represent their constituents but instead spoke for "the whole" or for "the nation." In his 1780 "Speech to the Electors of Bristol," Edmund Burke argued: "Parliament is not a congress of ambassadors from different and hostile interests, which interests each must maintain, as an agent and advocate, against other agents and advocates; but Parliament is a deliberative assembly of one nation, with one interest, that of the whole – where not local prejudices ought to guide, but the general good, resulting from the general reason of the whole. You choose a member, indeed; but when you have chosen him he is not a member of Bristol, but he is a member of Parliament" (Burke, 1949, p. 116). Except for one quick reference, I do not further consider the Burkian view and, on the basis of the results of the election in Bristol, feel justified in doing so.
15. Forrest McDonald (1982, p. 118) estimates that for the selection of delegates to state ratifying conventions only about one in twenty-five Americans – or 4 percent – could vote.

Libby (1894) and given prominence by Charles Beard (1913) to the effect that the American Constitution was designed by its authors to further, if not their own interests, those of their class. The hypothesis was sharply criticized by Robert Brown (1956) and by Forrest McDonald (1958) but recently in part rehabilitated by Main (1960).

Even if the foregoing analysis supports the Libby–Beard–Main position, it does not do so by invoking some failure or distortion imputable to competition but by reference to the effects of the distribution of endowments or entitlements among citizens. It is instructive in this connection to consider the case of Renaissance Venice, which though called a republic was an aristocracy and not by any stretch of the imagination a democracy, even in the limited sense in which that word can be used to describe the political system of late eighteenth-century America. Renaissance Venice was a city of approximately 100,000 inhabitants, of which 2,000 men who belonged to 136 patrician families – or 2 percent of the population – had the right to vote (Gilbert, 1987). Gordon (1986) makes the case that on what I call the demand side of the market there were many centers of powers competing with one another.

It would appear, then, that the political equilibrium in Renaissance Venice would have been very much like that of late eighteenth- and early nineteenth-century America. That seems not to have been the case and Gordon tells us why. He notes (Chapter 3, pp. 25–26) that in sixteenth-century Venice "[n]obles and commoners lived in the same districts, often in the same buildings and attended the same churches. There was more daily contact between them than now exists, in democracies, between elected representatives and electors," adding, "members of the Great Council were familiar with the views of the general citizenry, and gave them expression, albeit filtered, in the organs of the state." The fact that the noblemen were a more or less unbiased sample of the whole population would have prevented a Libby–Beard–Main situation from arising. Indeed, the Venetian government probably mirrored the preferences of the population during that period, more or less as a democratic government does today.

In the relations of the House to the other governmental centers of power, there are at least two historical facts that seem to indicate that the differentiation of the market consequent on the limited franchise did enhance the relative competitive position of the House. The first of these is the 1798 Sedition Act, which empowered "the President at his discretion . . . [to expose] to fines and imprisonment American citizens acting openly 'with intent to defame . . . or bring into contempt or disrepute the President or other parts of the government'" (Miller, 1969, p. 141). It is difficult to interpret the use of such strong medicine except in a context in which the ability of the President to compete is somehow impaired. I limit the foregoing to the Presidency, because it appears that the Act was effectively applied only to sedition against that office. In the shorter run, the Act was attacked by many, including James Madison and Thomas Jefferson, and led to various adjustments. One of these, I suggest, is that it provided an impetus for a presidency based on popular suffrage that could more effectively compete with the House.

The second historical fact pertains to the disregard of appointed senators for the "doctrine of instruction," according to which senators were to take directives (instructions) from those who appointed them.[16] William Riker (1955) imputes the disregard to two factors: (1) the absence of an enforcement mechanism, like the power to recall senators under Article V of the Articles of Confederation, combined with the weakness of a threat not to reappoint, given that the terms of office of state legislators were shorter than those of senators; and (2) the spread of public canvassing after 1830 to ascertain the will of voters as to who should be appointed to the Senate. Riker's analysis is enlightening, though it does not in my opinion give enough emphasis to the fact that by canvassing the electorate, prospective senators were not only able to force the hand of state legislators regarding their appointments but were also forced to compete against the House. Canvassing meant that senators were not only competing against representatives for consent but also for suffrage. As a result, the market for consent and suffrage became *less* differentiated, and as a consequence the doctrine of instruction became obsolete.

In concluding the analysis of the effect of the franchise on the distribution of entitlements and of the effects of the latter on the characteristics of political equilibrium, it should now be clear that there are two directions along which the franchise can be extended: (1) increases in the number of centers of power that seek suffrage; and (2) increases in the fraction of the population that has the right to vote for each center. The second of these is obviously multidimensional in that the increase in the number of the enfranchised need not be the same for all centers. We look at the effect of each of these in turn.

A *ceteris paribus* increase in the number of centers seeking the suffrage of an electorate that constitutes only a fraction of the total eligible population will increase the effectiveness of competition between these centers and will, as a consequence, force them to be even more diligent in catering to the preferences of the enfranchised. But the lot of the nonenfranchised will at best be only marginally improved in absolute terms and will worsen in relative terms (relative to the situation that would obtain if no one was enfranchised). Competition, given the distribution of entitlements in late eighteenth-century America, did not serve to bring governments closer to all the people. The Fathers of the U.S. Constitution and the authors of *The Federalist* (1787–8),

---

16. For a more elaborate discussion of the doctrine, see Chapter 3, footnote 13.

who were mistrustful of the people and wanted to keep them at bay, were successful in designing a political structure that in the early years did exactly that.

To put it differently, the political structure *The Federalist* defended was one in which there would be competition on the demand side but in which the distribution of entitlements conferred by the limited and nonrepresentative character of the franchise would insure that the nonenfranchised were worse off than if there had been less competition but a more equal distribution of entitlements. For a system that is so structured, Edmund Burke was right to insist that good representatives should be spokespersons for the nation as a whole!

Let me now hold constant the number of centers of power that seek suffrage and examine the effect of the extension of the franchise to the whole of the eligible population. The consequences of doing this are straightforward: The equilibrium points are again depicted by the solid curves in Figure 5.4, namely OC_0 and OC'_0. The introduction of a universal franchise produces a political equilibrium that is the same as the one that would obtain if competition were over consent alone. Under these circumstances, suffrage is really only an instrument – albeit a very important one – to guarantee orderly entry into and exit from politics (see Chapter 3, Section 3.6).

The situation will change once again if support is introduced into the system. To offer support, it will be recalled, is to offer money, time, and effort. Acknowledging the fact that money can buy the last two items, I identify the supply of support with the supply of money and assume that there are only two relevant margins: (1) an intensive margin along which we measure the amount of money or support offered by any one person; and (2) an extensive margin that measures the number of persons supplying money or support. If we assume again that the two margins are equalized by rational political actors, then the supply of support schedule can be added to that for consent and suffrage.

But here also we must acknowledge that endowments vary. To simplify, let me again assume that there are only two groups: the bourgeoisie and the proletariat. I further assume that the second of these groups is not capable of offering any support whatsoever. These assumptions will generate a political equilibrium very much like the one depicted by the broken curves in Figure 5.4 if we simply identify Figure 5.4(a) with the bourgeoisie and 5.4(b) with the proletariat and if we assume the existence of a universal franchise. The effect of the introduction of support and of the assumed distribution of endowments is to effectively disenfranchise the proletariat.

An implicit recognition of that fact may be what guides many governments when they decide to equalize the distribution of endowments by making direct and indirect contributions to groups falling within what I have called the proletariat. (This rationale for governmental contributions to special interest groups is different but complementary to that suggested in Chapter 2, Section 2.3.) The effect of these contributions is to equalize endowments somewhat and thus push the political equilibrium to what it would have been under universal suffrage when the demand and the supply of consent effectively determined the outcome.

The equilibrium produced by the V_1 and V'_1 curves of Figure 5.4 must be given a different meaning depending on whether the demand side is competitive or not, but qualitatively the equilibrium is as represented in the diagram.[17] In that equilibrium, the proletariat is effectively reduced to transact with those centers of power that for whatever reason can only seek consent. It is often noted that the courts, which as a rule do not seek suffrage and on the whole stay away from support, often adjudicate to the advantage of those whom I call the proletariat and whom Landes and Posner (1975, p. 876) call "the least politically influential segments of society." That is not because the courts are constructed to behave that way but because in the competition in which they are engaged with other centers of power the distribution of endowments leads them in that direction.

The transactions between the bourgeoisie and the centers of power that accept support give rise to what may be called special-interest legislation – to what Stigler (1971) has analyzed under the heading of "regulation." If the analysis in this section is at all correct, these transactions could not be curtailed or eliminated by tinkering with the machinery of government. Their control requires, as has just been emphasized, either that the supply of support be disallowed or that the endowments of support be equalized.

5.3.   Collusion and breakdown

In Chapter 3, Section 3.3, I commented on the factors that could lead to collusion that were essentially derived from the model of checks and balances suggested in that chapter. I review these here and add a few more inspired by the more general model of the present chapter. I do not claim completeness on the matter, but in view of the importance of the phenomenon a broader discussion seems warranted.

In the theory of ordinary markets, it is generally agreed that collusion is more difficult, the larger number of firms because when there are many firms, cheating by any one firm imposes smaller damages on the others and also

17. In the case of competition, it is the marginal values of whatever is purchased (MV) to their price (P) that are equated. Under collusive monopsony, it is MV to their marginal costs (MC) < P that are brought into equality; and under price discrimination it is still MV/MC that are equated, but the MC's vary between groups, depending on the elasticity of the supply schedule of each group.

because policing would-be cheaters is more difficult (Stigler, 1964). Inside governments, collusion between centers of power is also easier when numbers are small and for the same reasons. There is no logical necessity for centers of power to increase in number as governments grow in size – a government may become large because one or two centers of power (for example, the police and the armed forces) expand. At the same time, it is difficult to imagine that very small state machineries would possess many centers of power. As Adam Smith (1776, Chapter 3) knew very well, the same is true of markets (see also Stigler, 1951). This fact would help to explain why competition appears to have been so weak in the small governments of nineteenth-century Europe and North America.

The procedure used to select those who will be responsible for the governance of centers of powers can also influence the ease of collusion among centers. There are many possible methods of selection, but it is sufficient for the purpose at hand to focus on only two: appointment and election. If individuals are directly elected or if their nomination is publicly scrutinized by "members opposite," they are less likely to collude with individuals in other centers of power who are similarly selected. On the other hand, individuals who are appointed, especially by members of their own political party or of their own interest group, more easily collude because their interests are likely to be the same. Dominance of a single party in political systems in which selection is predominantly by appointment is, therefore, conducive to collusion.

A third factor that can lead to collusion is secrecy, especially if secrecy finds its justification in national security or other similar *raisons d'Etat*. It is not only collusion among centers engaged in intelligence and counterintelligence activities or in defense planning and similar work that secrecy encourages but also collusion among centers of power such as the Executive and some arm's length agencies on matters that are only remotely related to national security and defense. For this reason, a large military establishment reduces the overall extent of intragovernmental competition simply by making it easier to hide under the cloak of the military things that would otherwise be in the open.

Fourth, collusion among centers of power is easier when the political order is dominated by machine politics. Vincent Ostrom (1987, p. 183), who emphasized this factor in a different context, bears to be quoted at length because of the cogency of his analysis:

> When [machine politics is] carried through to its full potential, political organizers have incentives to slate candidates for all the numerous legislative, executive, and judicial offices in their relevant political jurisdictions; to procure positions on public payrolls for those assisting in organized efforts to conduct campaigns, canvass votes, and deliver voters to the polls; to control

the decisions made by public officials elected as a part of the organization's slate; and to receive contributions from those who benefit from the decisions taken. The successful organizer becomes a "boss" in control of the different offices where his candidates have been successful. . . . By virtue of his control over legislative, executive, and judicial offices, the boss manages the diverse centers of authority as though his were a fully integrated system of command.

Not much need be added, except possibly to emphasize that the influence of machine politics on collusive behavior operates principally through the ability of bosses to select and control candidates for office. It is not necessary, therefore, that machine politics be as organized as it was at the end of the past century and at the beginning of the present one in the United States for the forces of collusion to be operative; more quiet coteries, such as the Family Compact, so influential in the Upper Canada of the 1840s, will do as well.

To conclude, modern governments are so large that in the absence of detailed knowledge about their internal structures and the features of the interactions and practices in them it is very difficult, if not impossible, to form a judgment about the extent of collusion in them. There is an impressive amount of nonsystematic information pointing to the existence of strong internal competition. I am convinced that when the assumption that governments are constitutionally or inherently monolithic is abandoned, research will reveal myriads of forms hitherto unimagined of competitive behaviors and, no doubt, of collusive practices as well.

Collusion is only one of the pathologies that can cripple competition and affect the operations of governments. The breakdown of intragovernmental competition is another. A typical, though extreme, instance of breakdown is the takeover of a significant subset of the totality of autonomous or quasi-autonomous centers of power by one of them, as happens with the establishment of a military dictatorship. Less extreme forms of breakdown do happen. However, to economize on space and because military takeovers are so widespread, I limit myself to these in the discussion that follows.

There are essentially three different types of military takeovers, or *coups d'état:* takeovers from democratically elected rulers, from autocratic civilian rulers, and from rival military juntas. I will assume that competition has already been curtailed in the latter two types of regimes prior to a takeover and, therefore, will concern myself mainly with the first, although some of the things I will have to say on that type of takeover will apply to the last two also.

The evidence as reviewed and summarized by Wintrobe (1990) is that military regimes are unstable in that takeovers often end by a re-transfer of the apparatus of state to democratically elected civilian rulers. Two questions must, therefore, be addressed: First, why are problems sometimes "solved" by military takeovers – why are they not left to competitive forces? And, second, why are takeovers unstable?

Military decisionmakers, like their counterparts in other governmental centers of power, seek to maximize their political power. Not being elected, they have no derived demand for suffrage but only for consent and support. At the risk of oversimplifying a reality that is not only complex but that varies from time to time and from place to place, let me suggest that the military pay for consent and support in one or more of the following ways: (1) a credible defense posture against possible aggressors that, when there are military encounters, must manifest itself in victory and thus buttress national pride; (2) successful peacekeeping missions abroad that enhance the international stature and prestige of the country; (3) disbursements for military hardware, research projects, and other military undertakings that are sufficiently above the real costs of production to permit patronage; (4) the protection of some vested interests, such as those of land owners; and (5) the provision of help and assistance to civilian populations that are victims of natural or other conflagrations.[18]

If the volume of consent and support (which can take the form of kickbacks from defense procurements or of more or less explicit promises of good jobs following retirement) supplied is sufficiently large to insure that the net yield to political power is as large as what it would be in the next best alternative, and therefore more or less in equality with net yields elsewhere in the system, a competitive equilibrium will prevail. If for any of a multiplicity of reasons the military are not able to offer the same defense posture, peacekeeping operations, patronage, protection of special interests, and the same assistance to afflicted civilians that they had hitherto provided, the amount of consent and support forthcoming will diminish. Partial demobilization of military centers of power or a degree of collusion with other centers of power may maintain the net yield on the political power of military decisionmakers and, therefore, something like a competitive equilibrium.

If, however, following a sharp permanent reduction in the supply of consent and support, even partial demobilization is not possible because, say, a military career is a very high status occupation in that society and if collusion is not workable, then the stage is set for a military takeover of the apparatus of state.

The restrictions on demobilization are the most important factor leading to takeovers. The inability to pay for consent and support is also essential, but if in the face of this inability demobilization was not too difficult to carry out, a competitive equilibrium with equal net rates of return to political power in

18. It is with these that they seek to reduce the utility losses of public provision of goods and services for which they are responsible.

every use could be sustained. It is tempting to assume that military takeovers are the only kinds of takeovers that are possible because the military have, if not a monopoly over repression, at least a comparative advantage in its use. That temptation must be resisted: It is the difficulty to demobilize, not the capacity to use repression, that causes the disequilibria that lead to takeovers.

The military in some societies find it difficult to demobilize because they in effect conceive of themselves as a caste or a priesthood. Any priesthood, even without control over repression, would seek to break the impasse created by a sharp reduction in the flow of consent and support in the same way – the ayatollahs and the mullahs of present day Iran are an example of this. This also explains why in some societies the threat of takeovers by the military or by other priesthoods does not exist. Effective competition and the sustainability of competitive equilibrium in political marketplaces, as in economic marketplaces, require free entry *and* exit.

Why are military and other like takeovers unstable? To answer this question, we must recognize that one of the reasons a takeover is capable of raising the yield on the political power of the military is that it changes the distribution of endowments. Put simply, it suppresses the centers of power that maximize their political power by trying to win suffrage and thus it disenfranchises the citizenry. If prior to the takeover the franchise has been universal, one of the consequences of the takeover, even if the military are efficient at securing the consent of the population, is to favor those groups that are capable of supplying more support in exchange for policies, as the analysis of Figure 5.4 has emphasized. The evidence we possess is that the rich participate in politics more actively than do the poor [see, for example Frey (1971)]. If the distribution of resources is skewed toward the higher-income members of society, a military takeover will generate a flow of special-interest legislation for the benefit of these individuals.

A military takeover, then, will often produce a flow of goods and services favorable to the rich, but it will also lead to an increase in the amount of repression used. The reduction in the number of centers of power implies less intragovernmental competition and therefore an equilibrium in the consent (and support) market to the left of the competitive equilibrium (see Figure 5.1). Much of that repression will be directed at the newly disenfranchised. We should therefore expect these individuals to organize and to seek to return to the *status quo ante*. These efforts not only provide an explanation for the instability of military takeovers; they also tell us that military dictatorships established after the overthrow of civilian dictators will be less unstable than those following the removal of democratically elected rulers, because the drive to organize and to gain the franchise is likely to be weaker in the first than in the second case.

5.4.   The Wicksellian Connection once more

What the present chapter has to say about the Wicksellian Connection is straightforward, given that the price of consent in the market for that reality is defined for all market structures to be the change in utility loss inflicted on citizens by a change in the quantity (and/or quality) of a good or service provided by a center of power. Tracking the equilibrium price of consent, therefore, tracks the strength of the Wicksellian Connection – the tightness of the link between quantities supplied and quantities desired at given taxprices for these goods and services.

This being so, it follows that the Wicksellian Connection will be weaker under *Vox Dei* than under *Vox Populi* dispensations and that under the second – under the first, recall, there is only one stable equilibrium – it will be stronger when competitive conditions prevail on the demand side than when autocracy obtains. Under autocratic rule, the Wicksellian Connection will be weaker when the dictatorship is personal and stronger when it is impersonal. Finally, the Wicksellian Connection will be stronger when endowments – defined either in terms of the franchise or in terms of disposable resources – are distributed more equally. These conclusions are not only consistent with those derived in the earlier analysis of checks and balances and of budgetary processes; they are also consonant with what are generally taken to be the virtues of democracy and the evils of autocracy, though I have no difficulty in granting that these virtues and evils are, when the whole of reality is considered, much greater than depicted in this study. This being said, I believe that the virtues and evils analyzed in this chapter are very important. I also believe that Wicksell's intuition that economics can be brought to bear on the efficiency of alternative political organizational forms is supported.

5.5.   Conclusion

This chapter has proposed a model of a market for political consent that permits the analysis of the effects of various market structures: monopsony (autocracy), oligopsony (oligarchy), and competition (democracy) on alternative specifications of the demand for and the supply of consent.

The basic model, interestingly, is amenable to the analysis of variations in the volume of suffrage (voting) and of support (monetary and other allocations) in that these factors alter the basic endowments or entitlements of political actors and in this way have an influence on the pattern of equilibrium outcomes. The model is also used to shed light on the nature and forms of collusion between governmental centers of power and on some characteristics of the breakdown of competition, as happens when there are military takeovers. Finally, we have seen that the analysis is consistent with our earlier probings of the Wicksellian Connection – that intragovernmental competition serves as a revelation mechanism for government-supplied goods and services.

CHAPTER 6

Hierarchy and bureaucracy

In older treatises and monographs – those written prior to Tullock's (1965) and to Niskanen's (1971) books – it would have been acceptable to end an exercise on competitive compound governments with Chapter 5. In the 1990s that is no longer possible. The work of these two authors, that of many others laboring in the tradition they have inaugurated, and the more recent work of scholars whose roots are in a different tradition require that we consider what the presence of bureaucracy and hierarchy does to results established when bureaucracy and hierarchy are absent. Why? Because in all these writings, hierarchy and bureaucracy are a subversive force, one that prevents or undoes beneficial and therefore desirable results.

As a consequence, we must ask whether hierarchy and bureaucracy are in reality as disruptive as the literature I have just mentioned makes them out to be. If we give an affirmative answer, we would have to conclude two related things: first, that the study of compound governments like that in the preceding chapters – and, incidentally, that of elections, interest groups, constitutions, and other like phenomena – is worse than a waste of time, it is a gross alienation. And, second, that to understand the supply of goods and services by governments – by business firms? – we should focus to the virtual exclusion of everything else on hierarchy and bureaucracy. If our answer to the question is negative, we must be able to identify the assumption or assumptions that generate models of subversive hierarchies and bureaucracies and to demonstrate that the assumption or assumptions need not be granted our allegiance.

To proceed with the enquiry – to attempt an answer to the question of the preceding paragraph – we must first define with some care the exact nature of the problem of hierarchy and bureaucracy. That is done in Section 6.1. Then, in Section 6.2 I sketch a few important and influential models of subversive, or inefficient, bureaus. In the third section, I look at models in which hierarchies and bureaucracies are efficient and show that the difference between the two kinds of models can be found in the different assumptions that are made about the role of principals and about competition. Section 6.4 concludes the chapter.

6.1. The problem defined

As a first step in circumscribing the object of our analysis, it is useful, without in any way committing oneself to the model of hierarchy and bureaucracy that has been derived from agency theory (see Section 6.2, Subsection i), to borrow from that tradition the notion that an agency problem will appear whenever the preferences of principals (such as owners, sponsors, managers, employers, or heads in centers of power) and those of agents (such as administrators, employees, or subordinates) differ and whenever information essential to their relationship is distributed asymmetrically among them. An agency problem arises because agents, in addition to an incentive, have a capacity or ability to pursue objectives that are not those of their principals but their own.

From that perspective, three basic agency problems are attributes of centers of power and of other organizations. If we consider corporate enterprises, a first agency problem is that which Adolf Berle and Gardiner Means (1932) ascribed to "the separation of ownership and control," which is deemed to color the relationship of stockholders (owners) and administrators. If we think not of business corporations but of governmental centers of power of which the owners are citizens, the agency problem is a characteristic of the link between citizens and center heads, whereas for nondemocratic governments such as communist dictatorships the problem pertains to the relationship of party and nomenclature.

A second agency problem governs the relationship of politicians (managers) and civil servants (workers) inside centers of power (and other organizations). This problem is complicated by the fact that bureaucracies are generally constituted of a large number of bureaus horizontally or vertically situated vis-à-vis one another in such a way that the management–worker problem is replicated in each bureau as well as among the bureaus that are hierarchically positioned in respect of one another. A third agency problem arises in the relationship of bureaucracies and those who consume the goods and services they produce. This problem has received considerable attention following George Akerlof's (1970) pathbreaking analysis of the market for used cars (lemons). For example, public regulation and quality standards as proposed by Hayne Leland (1979), or reputation as suggested by Benjamin Klein and Keith Leffler (1981) and by Carl Shapiro (1983) are possible remedies for this agency problem.

Though recognizing that the three agency problems are related to one another, we will be preoccupied in this chapter with only the second one – that pertaining to intraorganizational matters. Our problem is the agency problem that encompasses the internal relationships of centers of power and how these relationships affect the capacity of the various centers to perform and to compete with one another.

To delimit the boundaries of the investigation, I have borrowed some language from the theory of agency and made use of the concept of agency problem that arises when information is distributed asymmetrically between principals and agents and when these persons pursue different goals. The first of these elements is an attribute of what is often called information structures and the second, of decision structures. These two concepts play an important role in this chapter.

Information structures subsume and summarize some of the attributes of the information available to those I continue throughout to call principals and agents. These structures are sometimes assumed to be very simple to insure mathematical tractability, but fairly complex structures play an important role in some models. Some of the characteristics of information structures that have retained the attention of scholars are whether information is complete or incomplete, whether it is verifiable or unverifiable (by a third party), and very important, whether it is distributed symmetrically or asymmetrically between principals and agents. It is a common but not universal practice to take an information structure as given and to study its implications for bureaucratic behavior. However, as Kenneth Arrow (1985a) has stressed, information structures must be assumed to reflect a desire on the part of some organizational actors to minimize costs so that a tolerably complete theory of bureaucracy must be able to state what constitutes an equilibrium information structure for some realistic set of constraints.

Decision structures embody the choices and strategies adopted by principals and agents in their relations with each other and among themselves. Choices and strategies must be credible or time consistent. It is not permissible, for example, to suppose that a principal or an agent has the complete freedom to alter an initially adopted strategy if, over time, it turned out to be in his or her interest to do so, because such a supposition would imply an absence of commitment. Such a strategy would, therefore, not be credible. It is also important that information and decision structures be compatible with each other.

To understand how, in different circumstances, the information and decision structures interact with one another, we need to take account of three basic features of the internal organization of centers of power that the literature of sociology, political science, organization theory, and management science – which, to abbreviate, I will henceforth call the sociological literature – has shown to be essential. They pertain (1) to the existence, nature, and character of formal and informal structures; (2) to authority and power in centers of power; and (3) to the routine or nonroutine character of any center's activities.

All hierarchical and bureaucratic organizations have a *formal* as well as an *informal* structure. Two things about this proposition must be noted. The first is that formal and informal structures are real and their existence well documented. The second is that one must be careful not to assume that the two structures work in opposition to, or in isolation of, each other. In fact, as I will have occasion to emphasize later, the two structures are, to use Henry Mintzberg's (1979, p. 11) expression "intertwined" and that for two reasons: first, because the formal authority structure is "seldom completely specified" (Jackson, 1982, p. 31) – there is space for an informal structure; and, second, because the "formal structure often reflects official recognition of naturally occurring behavior patterns" (Mintzberg, 1979, p. 11) – there are dimensions or components of the informal structure present.

The scientific study of bureaucracy began in 1925 with Max Weber (1946 and 1947), who had earlier developed the concept of "ideal type," by which he meant the constellation of abstract characteristics that, though not necessarily descriptive, are supposed to capture the essence of a given reality. The characteristics he identified for bureaucracy – the lines of communication embodied in organizational charts, the official system of authority reflected in job descriptions, and so on – all pertain to the formal authority structure.

Because Weber's characterization of bureaucracies fitted so snugly with Frederick Taylor's (1911) increasingly applied authoritarian management principles (based on the standardization of tasks) and with those, also increasingly employed, of Henri Fayol (1917) (based on direct supervision), it took a long time to recognize the existence and role of informal structures in the working of organizations. When it came, the recognition was ushered in on two fronts at the same time. On one front, sociologists, including among the pioneers Robert Merton (1936 and especially 1940), Philip Selznick (1949), Alvin Gouldner (1954), and Michel Crozier (1963), showed on the basis of empirical evidence, first, that formal structures are often inefficient (dysfunctional) and, second, that informal structures exist that sometimes improve and at other times worsen the performance of formal structures. On the other front, the interpretation that industrial psychologists – among them Fritz Roethlisberger and William Dickson (1939) and Elton Mayo (1945) – placed on the data accumulated in the series of studies and experiments carried out at Western Electric's Hawthorne plant outside Chicago during the late 1920s and early 1930s, initially to confirm Taylor's and Fayol's management principles, showed, to the contrary, that "social interaction" and "human relations" have an important role to play in the determination of work effort and output levels.

What then are informal structures? Briefly, they are the coalitions or networks of unofficial relationships that play a continuous role, sometimes positive and sometimes negative, in the collection and communication of information and in the coordination of tasks inside and, at times, beyond the confines of organizations (centers of power). One of the reasons informal structures do not always countervail and negate the intent of the impersonal formal structures is that self-interested principals will adjust the latter to the former whenever doing so contributes to the objectives they are pursuing and is feasible. [For evidence that principals behave in that way, see Galbraith (1973) and Section 6.3.]. In addition, there are forces – technology and other situational factors, such as size – that have an impact on the formal and the informal structures simultaneously and move them in the same direction (Perrow 1967).

The relationships that define the networks or coalitions that constitute the informal structures are of two basic types, which sociologists have called vertical and horizontal (or lateral) relationships. The earlier research focused almost exclusively on the informal vertical relationships between principals and agents. Eventually, attention was given to informal horizontal relationships, but the first studies were confined to the relationships among rank and file.[1] The later work of Dalton (1959), Elliot Chapple and Leonard Sayles (1961), Henry Landsberger (1961), and George Strauss (1962) showed that informal lateral relationships were also important among management. To focus on one type of network to the exclusion of the other does, therefore, necessarily disregard an important aspect of organizational realities.

The relationships that define principal–principal, principal–agent, and agent–agent networks are not only unofficial but are also bilateral and even multilateral. Gouldner (1960) used the word "reciprocity" to describe that feature.[2] The relationships are based on exchanges which, given that they take place in informal networks, can be called *informal transactions*. The research of sociologists who have paid special attention to these transactions makes clear that they have two features in common: (1) They are seldom simultaneous or spot transactions but instead are intertemporal; and (2) the currencies or quid pro quos used to clear "markets" are as variegated and heterogeneous as they are in barter transactions, which they tend to mimic. To illustrate, these market-clearing quid pro quos include use of company cars and airplanes, signing privileges in restaurants and bars, accelerated promo-

1. "In the early studies exploring informal structures, it was presumed that they characterized only the lower strata of the organization: managers and executives were immune to such developments. But empirical studies by [Melville] Dalton (1959) and others dispelled such notions" (Scott, 1981, p. 83). I will return to this fact shortly.
2. Gouldner's analysis of the "norm of reciprocity" moves easily from the normative to the positive and, in the process, appears to use the concept of norms in two quite different senses. According to one of these, the norm of reciprocity, complemented more than a decade later by the "norm of beneficence" (Gouldner, 1973), are universal phenomena that are essential for the stability of all systems of social interaction. According to the second acceptation, norms are specific prescriptions regulating exchange, and they vary from culture to culture. As I will argue in Section 6.3, both meanings conceal the basic question of what sustains time-dependent reciprocity or exchange. Norms exist, but they are not given by nature and are therefore the outcome of some kind of human activity or interaction.

tions, public recognition manifested in decorations and awards, long-distance calls chargeable to the company, well-decorated offices, especially laudatory recommendations, travel, leaves of absence, abstentions from agitation or unrest, and so on almost ad infinitum.

The formal structure of organizations varies, not only across types of organizations, such as business corporations, government departments, universities, hospitals, charities, and so on, but also within each type. The reasons for this variety are numerous and not fully understood. The sociologists who are sometimes identified as "contingency theorists" have underlined the role of age, size, technology, and internal power relations as determinants of organizational forms. For a good summary of the contingency literature, see Mintzberg (1979, pp. 215–97). Oliver Williamson (1975), building on the work of Herbert Simon (1957), has stressed the importance of "bounded rationality" and shown that the phenomenon can be used to rationalize the emergence of unitary or U-form organizations and their transformation along the lines documented by Alfred Chandler (1962) into multidivisional or M-form bureaucracies.

If we use the word *authority* to describe the jurisdiction, dominion, and control that principals have over agents, we can use the word *power* – as sociologists often do [see, among many, Crozier (1963), Pfeffer (1981), and Mintzberg (1983)] – to depict the ascendancy, mastery, or sway that agents have over principals and other agents.[3] The existence of authority does not have to be established. It is obvious. What sociologists have abundantly documented is the presence of power in organizations, how it is acquired, and the uses to which it is put.

Authority is an attribute of formal structures, whereas power is a characteristic of informal structures. In a basic sense, then, the second internal feature of organizations is a complement of the first, but it is an important one. As the sociological literature of the past thirty years has emphasized, it is not possible to appreciate how organizations function without understanding the relation of authority to power. We will discover the truth of this proposition as we proceed.

A fraction of all the activities performed by the principals and agents who inhabit a given organization has been described as formalized (Whyte, 1948), habitual (Bennis, 1959), programmed (Simon, 1960), mechanistic (Burns and Stalker, 1961), well defined (Frank, 1963–4), and routinized (Crozier, 1963; Perrow, 1967), and the balance has been depicted by words or expressions that refer to an opposite quality or character. David Hickson (1966), who twenty-five years ago reviewed the pertinent literature, was able to show that beyond

---

3. The concept of power in this chapter is obviously different from that used in Chapter 5; here, the discussion is about bureaucratic power, whereas Chapter 5 concerned political power.

divergent languages and terminologies, all researchers were describing and analyzing the same phenomenon, which, to simplify, I will call the *routine-nonroutine* dichotomy.

Beyond identifying the dichotomy and devising ways of measuring it (see Hickson, Pugh, and Pheysey, 1969), scholars have sought to discover the origin of the phenomenon, paying particular attention to the influence of technology [defined as operations technology, materials technology, and knowledge technology (see Perrow, 1967)].[4] They have examined its significance for variables such as the adjustment of agents and especially of organizational structures to routinization (Hage and Aiken, 1969) and the effect of nonroutinization on the level of anxiety felt by agents (Presthus, 1958). At the same time, other scholars, working in the Fayol–Taylor scientific management tradition, have explored ways and means of increasing the fraction of routine activities performed by agents so as to make authority and supervision more effective (Brown, 1960).

From the point of view of the relationships of principals and agents in organizations, one of the more important implications of the routine-nonroutine dichotomy or, more precisely, of the existence of nonroutine activities in organizations is that the supervision and monitoring of agents who are potentially fractious and recalcitrant to authority may be very difficult. In the presence of nonroutine activities, founding the relationships of principals and agents on mandates, directives, and commands will in general be much less efficient than constructing them on some other basis, such as trust and loyalty. Precise instructions related to the activities that are nonroutine cannot, almost by definition, be given. Within broad statements of goals, principals have no alternative but to rely on the initiative and enterprise of their agents. The incentive problem as regards these activities becomes one of discovering methods of stimulating this type of response from their agents.

Organizations have formal and informal structures whatever the fraction of their activities that are routinized. However, there is evidence [see, for example, Hage and Aiken (1969)] that the importance and role of both horizontal and vertical networks – the components of informal structures – may be greater in organizations in which the function of nonroutinized activities is larger. This is supported by Crozier's (1963) analysis of two bureaus (a clerical agency and a state tobacco-manufacturing monopoly) in which all activities were very highly routinized, but in which the presence of uncertainty caused by machine breakdowns allowed the maintenance personnel to

4. Wintrobe (1982) has suggested a model in which the fraction of nonroutinized activities – the level of discretion of agents – is "positively related to the average wages of employees [agents], and inversely related to the age of the firm, the age of its capital stock and industry, the extent of its division of labour, employee turnover, and to its size as measured by the number of its employees" (p. 662).

adopt nonroutine behaviors and strategies that differed from those encoded in the formal structure.

6.2. Models of inefficient bureaus

The models of this section focus on bureaus – the component parts of bureaucracies – and as a consequence have nothing to say about interbureau competition or, of great importance, about the effect of competition on the relations of principals and agents that they model. Keep in mind that the models discussed in this section use the words *bureau* and *bureaucracy* interchangeably and in full innocence. I focus first on the canonical principal–agent model and then on what I call the *discretionary power* model.[5]

i. The principal–agent model

The economic analysis of the relationship of a principal to the agent who has been hired to perform certain tasks or approached to provide certain services was not initially conceived as a model of intraorganizational behavior. The analysis was originally focused on such phenomena as insurance, law enforcement, sharecropping, physician–patient relations, and the delegation of decision-making authority. True, the development of the theory of implicit labor contracts made it clear that the model had applications to some of the internal operations of firms (and presumably of other organizations), but it was only with the formulation of models of imperfect monitoring and of imperfect, yet non-zero, information by Joseph Stiglitz (1975), James Mirrlees (1976), Milton Harris and Artur Raviv (1978), Bengt Holmström (1979), and others that it became possible to apply the principal–agent model to bureaucracies and hierarchies.

The principal–agent model of organizations, which has been primarily focused on business firms, conceives of bureaucracies as constituted of a set or nexus of contracts. The prime concern of scholars working in this tradition is the analysis of incentive contracts, that is, of contracts embodying payment or fee schedules designed to elicit from agents performance that is optimal from the point of view of principals. To put it differently, the performance of tasks and the provision of services are assumed to be irksome and therefore to cause shirking on the part of agents. The job of principals is to deal with this shirking by devising compensation schemes that will motivate agents to act in ways that are advantageous to the principals.

5. The use of the singular is no doubt premature given the abundance and variety of models that are still not fully integrated with one another. However, there appears to be enough sight-recognition and cross-referencing by those who work principal–agent models to justify the singular.

Excellent recent surveys of the agency model of organizations exist. As should be expected, each emphasizes a different facet of the central paradigm: I mention Oliver Hart and Holmström (1987), Martin Ricketts (1987), Daniel Levinthal (1988), and Holmström and Jean Tirole (1989). A new survey would serve no purpose. However, a brief sketch of the model is necessary as an introduction to some important recent contributions, in particular those of Tirole (1986) and Jean-Jacques Laffont (1988, 1990), but also to facilitate a comparison of the information and decision structures associated with that tradition and those embodied in other approaches.

Agency models possess two basic features: (1) principals and agents who pursue different goals or objectives and (2) uncertainty or incomplete information that is assumed to be paramount in their relationship. That uncertainty can take two forms according to whether, in Arrow's (1985b) words, principals are affected by "hidden action" on the part of agents or by "hidden information" at their command. The behaviors associated with these two types of uncertainty are often called moral hazard and adverse selection, respectively. The hidden action that has retained most of the attention of scholars is the effort of agents, but other actions such as vigilance and carefulness could be the object of analysis. In hidden information models, it is assumed that the agent has made an observation that he or she uses but in ways that do not allow the principal to verify if it is to the principal's advantage.[6]

In the brief sketch that follows, in conformity with the bulk of the literature, I concentrate on the hidden action model, though considerations derived from the hidden information paradigm are noted. A principal hires an agent (or a number of identical agents) to perform a certain task. The agent exerts some effort (e), which produces an outcome whose payoff (in money) is π. The problem faced by the principal is to devise a wage contract (w) that will maximize the payoff net of wages. If e is observable by both parties, the contract between them will be trivially simple: In exchange for some level of e, let us say e*, the principal will pay the agent an agreed-upon wage w*.

If the payoff, however, does not depend on e alone but also on some uncertain states of nature θ, so that $\pi(e,\theta)$, the principal's problem is only marginally more complicated than the one we have just examined as long as both parties can observe θ. Under such circumstances, the wage contract or payment schedule will depend on the observable magnitudes of π and θ, so that w = w(π,θ). If we assume that the principal receives a sum π*, which depends only on θ, the agent's wage contract will be w = π − π*(θ). The contract will stipulate that the agent should remit to the principal an amount equal to π*(θ) − that is, a sum that varies with θ − and keep the rest. This means that more

---

6. In a recent paper Robert Kaplan (1984) has argued that at the higher levels of organizational structures agents overwork; if so, the only problem is one of hidden information.

effort on the part of the agent will benefit the agent alone, so that an incentive problem does not arise. If, therefore, a risk-averse agent agrees to exert a given level of effort, a risk-neutral principal will accept bearing all the risk, that is, will extend full insurance to the agent.

A genuine principal–agent problem is considered to arise only if the postulated information structure is such that neither e nor θ is observable by the principal. If all the principal can observe is π, the wage contract will of necessity depend on that variable alone, that is, w = w[π(e,θ)]. Under these circumstances, a fundamental conflict will arise between the idea that a risk-neutral principal should offer full insurance to a risk-averse agent on the one hand and the incentives facing the latter on the other. Why? Because a promise on the part of the principal to pay a fixed sum to the agent whatever the state of nature – the extension of full insurance – would make remuneration independent of effort inasmuch as the agent could blame an adverse θ for a low π, even if such an occurrence was the result of the agent's shirking. An incentive-compatible contract, given the information structure, will require that the agent bear some of the risk even though the agent is risk-averse and the principal risk-neutral. Risk-sharing benefits have to be sacrificed for the sake of providing incentives that will elicit (nonobservable) effort. It is therefore clear that if the principal could obtain, even only somewhat noisy (Holmström, 1979), information about the effort of the agent, a contract could be designed that would be preferred by both parties. If the principal could monitor the effort of the agent through, let us say, random spot checks that were not too costly to carry out and that would produce signals that were not completely misleading, both parties would be made sufficiently better off for the agent to accept being monitored (Stiglitz, 1975). Monitoring can be viewed as a substitute for inefficient risk sharing.

There is not much in the foregoing that is conducive to a significant understanding of bureaucracies and hierarchies, except the seed idea that monitoring can be rewarding to all the parties in a principal–agent relationship. What allowed the simple paradigm I have just sketched to evolve into a model of bureaucracy and hierarchy was the retrospective surrogate re-reading in the light of the "seed idea" of Tullock's (1965) discussion of control-loss (the idea that only a fraction of a principal's instructions are implemented at each stage or level of a hierarchy) and of Williamson's (1967) demonstration that if control-loss exists and if the spans of control or of supervision are of fixed size, a profit-maximizing supervisory hierarchy will arise.

In this tradition, then, an organization is conceived as a pyramidal structure in which agents or workers at the lowest level – call it level-1 – are engaged in the production of that organization's output. Neither their level of effort nor the vicissitudes of nature under which they are working are observable by the principal; only the outcome of the production activity can be observed. If, however, these workers are monitored by level-2 supervisors, everyone can potentially be made better off. But because the quality of supervision decreases as the span of control increases, not all level-1 workers in a large organization can be monitored by a single level-2 supervisor. If many level-2 supervisors are needed, a third level and possibly higher levels of supervision will be required to monitor the supervisors directly below them.

So far the argument has been based on the assumption of identical agents. Allowing for differences in skills, abilities, expertise, and other characteristics will give rise to a hidden information or adverse selection problem whenever principals are incapable of distinguishing between those agents who are better endowed and those who are not, simply because we cannot assume that agents will truthfully reveal their real characteristics. Adding this complication does not, however, modify the nature of bureaucracies and hierarchies because supervisors, who can interpret signals and thus acquire information on the real characteristics of agents, can potentially make all participants in organizations better off.

What can principals and their supervisors do when they observe another (lower level) supervisor or an agent shirking? How can monitoring be effective? A common answer to this question is that shirkers can be dismissed. The threat of dismissal infuses monitoring with value. However, as Shapiro and Stiglitz (1984) have shown, such a punishment is not credible, at least in competitive labor markets in which a fired shirker can find immediate reemployment at the same wage rate. But if an organization is paying efficiency wages – a premium over the competitive wage to elicit performance – it would appear that a laid-off shirker would be penalized by losing the efficiency premium. That would not be the case, however, if all organizations were paying efficiency wages, because a dismissed shirker could then find reemployment at the higher wage and would not be dissuaded from shirking. But if all organizations are paying wages that are in excess of the competitive market-clearing wage, persistent natural unemployment will appear that will act as a "worker discipline device" and invest monitoring with value. Shapiro and Stiglitz (1984, p. 443) are confident that unemployment can serve as an effective disciplining device for "lower-paid, lower-skilled, blue-collar occupations." They appear to be in doubt, as I am, of its potency for other occupations.

The effectiveness of monitoring does not have to rely on unemployment. Another answer to the question that opened the preceding paragraph has been suggested by Edward Lazear (1979, 1981). If agents accept not to be compensated by a wage that is period by period equal to the value of their marginal product but instead agree to a contract that stipulates a stream of payments whose present value is equal to the present value of their marginal product, but that is at first lower than that product and in later years higher, they will have an incentive not to shirk so as not to be fired, because if they were they would lose the present value of the excess of wages over marginal product owed them.

It must be emphasized that whenever a supervisor or an agent is accused of shirking and is dismissed, the question arises of whether that person was really shirking or whether a higher-level supervisor or the principal fraudulently accused the person of doing so. The problem is particularly serious if earnings increase with the age of the supervisor or of the agent more than would be called for by on-the-job training and, therefore, more than by improvements in productivity. In that case principals will have an incentive to fire their agents as soon as the wage owed them exceeds the value of their marginal product. What reduces that incentive is the willingness on the part of principals to acquire a reputation of being good employers.

The value of such a reputation derives from the fact that interaction among principals and agents is not a once-and-for-all event but extends over time. Though there are gains to the dishonest dismissal of agents and of supervisors, there are also costs, one of which is the impossibility of long-term Lazear-type contracts. Considerable attention has been devoted to the analysis of repeated interaction and to the construction and preservation of a reputation [see, for example, Radner (1981)]. Reliance on reputation to close the canonical version of the principal–agent model of bureaucracy and hierarchy does, however, pose a problem. If principals can acquire the reputation of being good employers, why can agents and supervisors not acquire one of being good employees – that is, employees who do not shirk? Or, to put the matter differently, if agents can be persuaded to trust principals, why cannot principals be induced to trust agents (on this point, see Miller, 1992). And if they can, would that not greatly alter and simplify in the direction indicated by Arrow (1985b, pp. 48–50), the complicated fee schedules that the theory now demands – and the real world often does not provide – as inducements to exert effort or to reveal information?

As will no doubt have been noticed, the canonical principal–agent model of bureaucracy and hierarchy I have just sketched is concerned exclusively with the formal structure of organizations. Given the documented importance of informal structures in the life of all organizations (see Section 6.1), Tirole's (1986) model of collusion in hierarchies, formulated within the principal–agent framework, is a very important extension of the accepted doctrine. Tirole's model begins by postulating a three-tier hierarchy made up of a principal who is risk-neutral and of a supervisor and an agent who are both risk-averse. By construction (Axiom 1, p. 183), the principal "lacks either the time or the knowledge required to supervise the agent." That job is assigned to the supervisor, who reports to the principal. The agent is the only person engaged in the production of output. The payoff (π) from the agent's activity depends on his or her effort (e) and, additively, on an uncertain productivity parameter (θ), which can take two values only: high and low.

The information structure on which all the important results depend is as follows. The agent always privately observes θ and then chooses e. That produces some level of π, which is observed by all members of the hierarchy. For the reasons indicated earlier, there is a conflict between insurance and incentives, so that additional information beyond the commonly observed π becomes valuable. This is where the supervisor comes in. He or she is assumed to be able to observe θ in some states of nature but not in others. The supervisor, furthermore, like the principal, is never able to observe the agent's effort. Given observation of θ, the supervisor makes a report (r) to the principal, whose content is assumed to be verifiable information. The report can be truthful or it can conceal the true evidence. On the basis of π and r, the principal offers to the supervisor and to the agent a grand contract that fixes the fees each will be paid.

Tirole now allows for the possibility of collusion between the supervisor and the agent. One way of rationalizing this possibility is to imagine that the collusion takes the form of a side-contract which specifies that the agent will "pay" the supervisor a sum that is also a function of π and r, in exchange for an untruthful r on the part of the latter. Tirole (1986, p. 184ff) calls such sums "covert transfers" or simply "transfers." There is, of course, no harm in using a label of that kind. However, for reasons that will become clear shortly, I use the word *takings* instead of transfers. Musgrave (1970) used the word *taking* as a verb, to circumscribe behaviors which I believe to be very similar to those Tirole has in mind.[7]

To understand in formal terms what motivates collusion, imagine a state of nature in which the productivity parameter is high and is observed by both supervisor and agent. Under these circumstances, the supervisor is indifferent between being truthful or untruthful – a lie that takes the form of reporting to the principal that nothing has been observed – because the supervisor will receive the same payment, whatever the report. The agent, however, would prefer that the supervisor conceal the true state of nature and therefore has an incentive to offer a bribe to the supervisor that will induce the latter to lie to the principal – thence, the collusion.

At a less formal level, collusion is motivated by the takings, which can be appropriated by the colluding parties if the supervisor alone or the supervisor and the agent together manipulate the information that must be transmitted to the contract-designing principal. Tirole (1986, pp. 185–6) analyzes two types of manipulation, namely, concealment and distortion, and associates different types of takings with each.

---

7. For a qualification of this view, see the next footnote.

To model the nature and the effects of collusion, Tirole assumes that the principal offers a grand, or comprehensive, contract to the supervisor and to the agent that specifies a fee schedule consistent with exogenously determined reservation wages (the individual rationality or participation constraints) and with appropriate incitations to effort (the incentive compatibility constraints), while deterring them from colluding (a set of new coalition incentive constraints). In the formal model, collusion does not therefore actually occur, but potential collusion induces the principal to reward supervisor and agent by offering them sums that are exactly equal to those they would obtain by colluding. Tirole calls this the "equivalence principle" (p. 195) because the outcome embodied in the grand contract would be replicated if the principal did not offer that contract but allowed the supervisor and the agent to draw up a collusive side-contract (Tirole, 1986, p. 195, n. 21). The grand contract (or its equivalent "spontaneous" organizational replica) is optimal given the constraints, but the principal is worse off than if collusion was not possible.[8]

More recently, Laffont (1988, 1990), always within the principal–agent framework, has enlarged the analysis of informal structures by assuming a hierarchy in which, in addition to a principal and a supervisor, there are two agents. This hierarchy allows him to model new types of interaction that may characterize the informal relations of supervisor and agents. In particular, by assuming that information about total production – about the sum of the two agents' output – which the supervisor transmits to the principal is verifiable by the latter but that information about the individual production of each agent is not, the supervisor is either able to collude with one agent to exploit the other or alternatively can set up a prisoner's dilemma game between the two agents and extort from both benefits (takings) of one kind or the other. Laffont also shows that if these behaviors are anticipated, the principal will draw up a grand contract that will compensate the agents for the exploitation or extortion. The overall efficiency of the organization will be lower than if the supervisor had been benevolent, however.

It is not possible to exaggerate the importance of the work begun by Tirole and Laffont, which enlarges the principal–agent paradigm to account for some of the behaviors sociologists have rightly associated with the informal struc-

8. In 1988, Tirole extended the notion of "transfers" and pointed to possible applications he had briefly mentioned, but not used, in his 1986 paper (Tirole, 1986, p. 186). That extended notion of transfers includes such things as affection, respect, smiles, and other aspects of personal interaction stressed by the Human Relations school, as well as "acts of co-operation" among agents, between agents and supervisors, and even between them and principals (see the reference to managers in Tirole, 1988, p. 464). These transfers, as the Human Relations school emphasizes and Tirole recognizes, will increase output and payoffs and will, therefore, make principals better off. I find it difficult to treat smiling and other civilized and decorous behaviors as manifestations of collusion. I therefore adhere to the more restricted definition of collusion and treat all lateral transfers as takings.

ture of organizations. That said, it must also be recognized that the new models focus exclusively on lateral or horizontal relationships, that is, on relationships in which principals have no part. The exclusion of principals and the consequent impossibility of vertical networks or coalitions derives in turn from the exogenous and to a degree arbitrary character of the information structures that are assumed.[9] As a consequence, though they draw up optimal incentive contracts and cannot therefore be described as completely resigned, the principals of Tirole and Laffont cannot, either, be said to do much if anything to defend themselves against the collusive and other behaviors that adversely affect them. They are passive.

If principals were allowed to play a role in choosing information structures and in designing and redesigning organizations – activities that these writers acknowledge as important [see, for example, Tirole (1988, p. 465)] but that play no role in their models – and, through these activities, in influencing the decisions and strategies of supervisors (middle management) and agents, they would then be active members of various coalitions we would have to call *vertical networks*. The informal structure would then possess the two basic components, noted in Section 6.1, that sociologists have documented exist.

ii.   *The discretionary power model*

In much the same way that the dominant preoccupation of scholars working in the principal–agent tradition is an understanding of the business firm, students laboring in what I am here calling the discretionary power framework are concerned almost exclusively with governmental departments and ministries and with public enterprises. When the intraorganizational agency problem is defined by reference to an information structure in which the distribution of information between principals and agents is asymmetric and by reference to a decision structure in which principals and agents pursue different objectives, the distinction between these two classes of bureaus and hierarchies is empty.[10]

Though the discretionary power analysis of bureaus has its origin in Tullock's (1965) writings, it is Niskanen (1971) who elaborated the basic idea and produced the first formal model. Notwithstanding the model's exclusive preoccupation with public bureaus and the dominance of research on these bureaus by those who follow the Tullock–Niskanen approach, it is possible to argue that the real antecedent of the discretionary power model is William

---

9. Tirole (1986, Proposition b, pp. 198–9) proves, for his model, that such vertical relationships cannot exist in equilibrium.

10. This does not mean that the distinction is always empty. It may be relevant for an analysis of the owner–manager or the organization–consumers (or clients) agency problems noted in Section 6.1, but I do not discuss these problems in this chapter.

Baumol's (1959) maximization of sales theory of the business firm. In addition to the fact that the assumptions of maximization of sales and maximization of budgets have much in common, the two have been defended by reference to what are essentially the same arguments.

As is the case for the principal–agent paradigm, good surveys of the discretionary power model exist (see, among others, Orzechowski, 1977; Bénard, 1985, Chapter VII; Acheson (1988); and Mueller, 1989, Chapter 14). However, in my view, there is in some surveys and textbooks a tendency to overemphasize the derivation of formal equilibrium conditions and to dwell on the comparative static results to the detriment, if not of the information structure, at least of the decision structure, which is essential for a correct appraisal of the model. I will redress that tendency in what follows.

Niskanen was aware that organizations are generally composed of many bureaus or, in his own words, of "component units" (1971, p. 16). He was also aware that the output of these units is often very difficult, even impossible, to define operationally and to measure, so that decision making is concerned with activities and programs with scant or no attention given to the relationship between these and output levels (pp. 26–7). However, for the sake of tractability, he formulated his model for a single bureau that produced and supplied a well-defined output. In that first basic step, which to my knowledge all writers working in that tradition have also taken, the discretionary power model has nothing to distinguish it from the canonical principal–agent model.

Though the radical importance of information structures had been appreciated by only a few pioneers when Niskanen was developing his model, he clearly perceived the importance of these structures and suggested one that is essential to his results. It has the four following characteristics:

1. Principals possess no information or knowledge about the production technologies that could be used to produce the output they want, about input vectors, and about the unit prices of these inputs.
2. Principals can costlessly observe (and measure) the output produced by their agents and are able, furthermore, to place a value on all volumes of it that are produced.
3. Agents possess complete information about available technologies, input vectors, and factor prices needed to produce the output.
4. Agents know the value that principals place on all quantities of output, so that they, in fact, possess full information about the valuation or utility functions of principals.

Except for the fourth characteristic, which is, however, essential to the whole discretionary power construction, this information structure is really not very different from that underlying the canonical principal–agent model. Niskanen's agents are assumed to maximize their budgets, to which all the amenities of office – including salary, reputation, power, status, and so on – are assumed to be positively correlated. A fraction of these budgets correspond to the takings sought by the agents of the Tirole and Laffont models. Given the information structure just described and supposing that a credible equilibrium strategy exists that will allow the obtainment of the desired budgets – a matter I discuss in detail later – Niskanen is able to show that budget maximization by agents leads to levels of output and to budgets that are larger than the ones agents would be allocated if information was symmetrically distributed. In particular, by assuming that the total value and cost functions are quadratic and by requiring that total budgets not exceed total costs (the so-called budget-constrained model), Niskanen shows that output is exactly double what principals would have asked for had they been better informed.

In his review of Niskanen's (1971) monograph, Earl Thompson (1973) took issue with some of the implications of a maximand based on budgets alone. Migué and Bélanger (1974), pursuing the same line of criticism, proposed a more general objective function formulated in terms of "discretionary budgets" (the difference between the total budget and the minimum cost of producing the output) instead of total budgets. They were able to show that even if, in general, takings in the form of larger budgets are still important, they are smaller and are combined with other possible utility-yielding amenities. Niskanen (1975) was prompt to accept the amended formulation since nothing in it significantly disfigured his own model.

It would therefore appear that the discretionary power model should be understood as a contribution to the analysis of horizontal relationships that are a component of the informal structures of organizations in the same way that the Tirole (1986) and Laffont (1990) models are. We will see shortly that this is the case, but I must deal first with an important matter related to the strategy that agents are presumed to follow to achieve maximum budgets. Niskanen (1971) has been interpreted, I believe correctly, as adopting the view that to obtain the largest possible budget, agents confront their principals with take-it-or-leave-it choices.[11] We owe to Thomas Romer and Howard Rosenthal (1978, 1979) the formulation of a precise theory of take-it-or-leave-it choices, also called agenda-setting or agenda-control. Romer and Rosenthal's main preoccupation was understanding agenda-setting by budget (expenditure) maximizing agents when decisions are made by referenda, by "voting on California-style popular initiatives" (1978, p. 41), or by other methods of "direct democracy." They left open the question of whether agenda-control could correctly describe the relations of Niskanen's principals and agents, though they appeared to be skeptical that it could (1979, p. 564, n. 4).

---

11. Niskanen wrote that "[b]ureaus [agents] do not, in fact, present their sponsors [principals] with an all-or-nothing choice. But the offer of a total output for a budget, under many conditions, *gives them the same type of bargaining power*" (1971, p. 25, n. 2, my italics).

What the Romer–Rosenthal theory makes clear is that, stripped of all refinements, agenda-control requires only that agents have full knowledge of the preferences of principals – characteristic (4) of the information structure described earlier – and that agents systematically exploit that knowledge by deciding which items will appear on agendas for the "yeas" or the "nays" of principals who are thus restricted to take-it-or-leave-it decisions between the agents' own demand and no output. Jonathan Bendor, Serge Taylor, and Roland Van Gaalen (1985) have pointed out that a strategy of that sort does not rest on the postulated superior technical knowledge and expertise of agents – characteristic (3) of the information structure – but on a presumed *formal* capacity to set agendas, that is, on an authority that derives from the formal structure. Thompson (1973), Cheryl Eavey and Gary Miller (1984), in addition to Bendor et al., have, rightly in my opinion, denied that authority to agents.[12]

Thompson was the first to note that to be consistent with Niskanen's information structure and budget-maximization assumption, agents had to adopt, not a take-it-or-leave-it or an agenda-setting strategy but one that rested on the misrepresentation of the information over which by construction they have exclusive command. In Thompson's own words, misrepresentation of information "implies that: (a) [f]or outputs below that desired by the bureaucrats [agents], trustee [principal]-expected average costs *fall* with output (at a rate faster than benefits) even though actual costs do not . . . ; and (b) [f]or outputs above the desired output of the bureaucrats, trustee-expected average costs *rise* relative to benefits" (1973, p. 951, italics in original).[13] A variant of this strategy, which we may call the misrepresentation-of-costs strategy, was independently rediscovered and given a first formal garment by Breton and Ronald Wintrobe (1979). It is now widely recognized (Spencer, 1980; Moene, 1986) that a strategy of this kind is implied by Niskanen's assumptions. It follows that the discretionary power model is concerned with the informal structure of organizations, since no strategy of that kind would ever be cod-

12. It is, as a consequence, rather disconcerting to discover that, in the *Handbook of Public Economics,* both William Oakland's (1987, p. 530) and Robert Inman's (1987, p. 714) discussions of Niskanen's theory of bureaucracy uncritically accept the agenda–control take-it-or-leave-it mechanism as the one regulating the relationship of principals and agents.

13. For Migué and Bélanger's discretionary budget maximizing agents, the strategy is different. Barbara Spencer (1980) has showed and Karl Moene (1986), on the basis of a slightly different demonstration, has confirmed that in that case agents misrepresent true costs to principals by arguing that as output expands, average costs rise faster than they in fact do. Recently, after confirming that his conversion from the total budget to the discretionary budget maximizing hypothesis was now complete – the conversion was already apparent in 1975 – Niskanen (1991) unambiguously affirmed his adhesion to Romer and Rosenthal's (1978, 1979) take-it-or-leave-it mechanism without any apparent awareness of Spencer's (1980) and Moene's (1986) definitive demonstration that this is not the mechanism to marry with the discretionary budget-maximizing hypothesis.

ified in formal authority structures and official contracts. Furthermore, because principals are assumed to be passive, the only component of that structure which receives attention is, as in the principal–agent model of the Tirole–Laffont variety, the one concerned with horizontal relationships.

Thompson thought that the misrepresentation-of-costs strategy was "implausible" (1973, p. 951). Breton and Wintrobe (1982, pp. 33–37) showed that, whether plausible or not, it is not a credible equilibrium strategy, because even if principals are completely passive as required by the information structure, the misrepresentation strategy would come apart every time there was a decline in a principal's demand for output. In diagrammatic terms, the demand curve would then be completely inside the misrepresented negatively sloped cost curve so that equilibrium output would be zero. Such a strategy would obviously never be adopted by budget-maximizing agents.

If take-it-or-leave-it or misrepresentation-of-costs strategies will not do, it remains true that legions of economists and political scientists have historically been fascinated by Niskanen's discretionary power model; this must be explained, I suggest, by the fact that by focusing on informal structures and on takings – especially after the modification suggested by Migué and Bélanger – the model was dealing with something real and important. We now know, after the contributions of Tirole and Laffont, that agents can avail themselves of takings if they can collude – without doubt a feature of the informal structures of organizations.

Before proceeding, we must come to terms with some of the implications of abandoning the assumption that principals are passive. Soon after the publication of Niskanen's monograph, Breton and Wintrobe (1975) argued that active principals would adopt antidistortion and control devices such as monitoring, overlapping bureaus, duplication of procedures, and the acquisition of information from alternative sources as long as, at the margin, their cost was less than their value. They showed that the use of these and other like devices would reduce the equilibrium size of takings compared to those that would obtain in a Niskanen bureau.[14] A few years later, Barbara Spencer (1980), disregarding the possible use of antidistortion instruments, demonstrated that if principals sought and obtained the elementary information that the average cost curve for the output they desire intersects the demand curve, agents will not be able to act as perfectly discriminating monopolists the way they do in Niskanen's model and will, as a consequence, have to be satisfied with smaller takings. Subsequently, Gary Miller and Terry Moe (1983) argued that if principals conceal their preferences from agents – if characteristic (4) of the information structure is jettisoned – the latter would be forced to reveal

14. They did not make the point, as they could, that the use of almost any of these control devices would effectively scuttle all misrepresentation of information strategies of the kind needed in Niskanen's model and thus void the whole construction.

the true cost of output and forgo all takings. Finally, Bendor et al. (1985) showed that if principals require that agents announce a unit price for the output they are proposing to supply, budgets and other takings will be larger than those wanted by principals only if demand for output is inelastic, because that is the only circumstance that allows agents to announce a price that is higher than the true cost of output. The assumption that principals are passive is therefore not an innocuous one. It has to be discarded.

6.3. Models of efficient bureaus and bureaucracies

As I have already noted, the canonical principal–agent and the discretionary power models make no distinction between bureaus and bureaucracies. As a consequence, they do not allow for the possibility of competition between bureaus in bureaucracies. The absence of competition is no doubt largely responsible for the usually tacit assumption that principals are passive. The absence of competition, combined with passive principals is the reason the models conclude to pervasive takings as signs and measures of inefficiency. In these models, if principals (politicians) were for whatever reason dedicated to the construction of a Wicksellian Connection aimed at minimizing the utility losses experienced by citizens, the agents (the bureaucrats) if not purposely then at least obliquely, would act in such a way as to undo the Wicksellian Connection more or less completely.

In what follows, I travel on a different path. I present first a model of the internal arrangement within single bureaus, which builds on the assumption that principals are active. Then, in Subsection ii, I analyze the character of competition in bureaucracies and examine its consequence on the efficiency of equilibrium outcomes. In a world of active principals and of competition, bureaus and bureaucracies are no longer always and everywhere subversive.

i.   Single bureaus

Gérard Charreaux (1990) has aptly called the model of the internal organiza-tion of single bureaus first suggested by Breton and Wintrobe (1982) the *informal transactions model*.[15] That model and later extensions (see, in par-ticular, Wintrobe and Breton, 1986) have one thing in common with the Niskanen–Tirole–Laffont focus on informal structures – to wit, the impor-tance of horizontal or lateral networks – but it parts company with this view of organizations by recognizing a crucially important role to principals. To ap-preciate the similarities and the differences between the two approaches, it is

15. Charreaux (1990) also provides an excellent survey of the model, regrettably available only in French.

convenient to begin with Breton and Wintrobe's (1982, Chapter 3) notion of "selective behavior." In the last analysis, that term or more exactly the reality it seeks to encapsulate, relates to the power of agents as distinguished from the authority of principals (see Section 6.1). To understand the origin and basis of that power and, therefore, the phenomenon of selective behavior, one must start with the information structure that underlies Breton and Wintrobe's model.

That structure has much in common with those ruling in the canonical principal–agent and in the discretionary power models – for example, the idea that information is asymmetrically distributed between principals and agents. But it also differs from these structures in significant ways. The information structure is adequately described by the five following characteristics:

1. Principals are conceived as making decisions about policies related to, for example, capital equipment, financing, salaries, promotions, advertising, takeovers, product design, sources of supply, pollution levels, transportation, health insurance, pensions, defense, and a countless number of others (Breton and Wintrobe, 1982, pp. 13–22). Principals do not possess the knowledge or the information necessary to make these decisions. In general, they do not even know what information they need or how to evaluate the information that is made available to them.
2. Principals are aware of their lack of expertise and of their inability, acting alone, to evaluate and use information that is transmitted to them.
3. Principals know that they must rely on agents to make decisions and that, under certain circumstances also known to them, these agents are capable of forming collusive coalitions or networks that will be used to make them (the principals) worse off.
4. Principals are able to appraise whether they are better off or worse off as a result of any decision made in the organization.[16]
5. Agents collect, appraise, interpret, combine, and transmit information to principals, and participate in decision-making.

The information structure is not sufficient in itself to understand the nature of selective behavior or how principals deal with the phenomenon. Consideration must also be given to informal structures (and, eventually, to the relationship that these have to formal structures). Breton and Wintrobe suppose

16. This fourth characteristic is not part of the information structure in Breton and Wintrobe's (1982) model. They assume that principals monitor and supervise their agents and thus acquire information about organizational decisions and behaviors. However, to simplify and because monitoring is a subsidiary appurtenance of organizational designs in their model, I have chosen to leave it out of the present outline.

that informal structures are made up of two components that they call *vertical* and *horizontal networks*. A network is called vertical whenever the informal – that is, the noncodified and therefore nonauthority – relationships between any subset of an organization's members include principals. When principals are not involved in a network, it is said to be horizontal.[17] To illustrate, in an organization composed of a principal (P), a supervisor (S), and three agents (A_1, A_2, and A_3), a relationship comprised of A_2 and A_3 would be a horizontal network, whereas one made up of P, S, and A_1 would be a vertical network. In all real world organizations, the number of levels as well as the number of principals and agents is larger than in the foregoing illustration, and the set of networks, both horizontal and vertical, is consequently also larger.

Networks, like markets, are institutions that exist to mediate exchange among members. However, unlike as in markets, there is no law and law enforcement or any other third-party enforcement of contracts in networks. Gouldner (1960), whose work I mentioned in Section 6.1, relied on "norms" to enforce informal intertemporal exchanges (see footnote 2, this chapter). Lester Telser (1980), Klein and Leffler (1981), and Shapiro (1983) have analyzed how the prospect of future or repeat trades can serve as an enforcement mechanism. Breton and Wintrobe (1982, Chapter 4) argue that it is trust (or loyalty) that supports gainful exchanges in organizational networks and serves to enforce contracts. They devote considerable space to the formulation of a theory of the production and accumulation of trust between network participants and show that trust is a kind of human capital whose cost of accumulation is shared by the parties involved and that, as a consequence, it possesses certain attributes of a pure public good. They also show that trust can support intertemporal exchanges and that the volume of it that exists between two network members is a positive function of the number and size of transactions between them.

What are the objects – Breton and Wintrobe call them "informal services" – bought and sold in networks? Ultimately, they are all related to the accumulation, adaptation, and transmission of information that principals need to make decisions and to coordinate tasks. Breton and Wintrobe (1982, pp. 37–42) illustrate some essential features of these services by concentrating on three of them: (1) natural entropy (the nonvolitional degradation of information as it moves through organizational ladders), (2) inescapable information leakages, and (3) unavoidable red tape or slowdowns in the organization's operations. I limit the present discussion to natural entropy. It is well known (Tullock, 1965; Downs, 1967; Williamson 1967) that information from agents

---

17. This definition is slightly different from the one used by Breton and Wintrobe (1982). I have adopted it following Pierre Salmon's (1988) criticism of the original definition.

and that from principals (commands and inquiries) in the process of transmission are inevitable victims of natural entropy, if only because information must be "condensed" if principals are not to be "buried under tons of facts and opinions" (Downs, 1967, p. 117) and if agents are to receive operationally adapted instructions and queries. The entropy is inevitable and, thence, natural because it is not caused by actions inspired by the self-interest of principals and agents.[18]

Breton and Wintrobe (1982) underline two interrelated corollaries of natural entropy. First, agents can either reduce or increase entropy relative to its natural level. Second, if they opt for the second alternative, the very existence of natural entropy makes it difficult, if not impossible, for principals to detect that they have done so, because agents can generally provide supporting evidence to "demonstrate" that the observed entropy was produced by nature. This ability in general will increase with the fraction of an organization's activities that is nonroutine. The two corollaries in turn help to define selective behavior and the foundation it provides to the (bureaucratic) power of agents. It is the capacity of agents to decide either to improve the situation (utility, profits, or wealth) of principals or alternatively (at odds of being detected that are in general trivially small) to worsen the situation that gives them power, a capacity that is in turn positively related to the fraction of nonroutine activities in an organization. (Recall Section 6.1's discussion of power versus authority and of nonroutine versus routine activities in organizations.)

An important element is missing from the foregoing discussion of selective behavior and bureaucratic power. Some agent acting alone may have the capacity to increase entropy above its natural level.[19] But in general, especially if the costs of "antidistortion devices" (Downs, 1967; Breton and Wintrobe, 1975) are low, that outcome will require the collaboration of a number of individuals. These persons, Breton and Wintrobe assume, will behave as a group if the increment in entropy (relative to the natural level) to which they are a party yields to each one of them a taking that is not less than his or her marginal contribution to the total. It is the existence of trust between group members that acts as a guarantor that each will be awarded his or her expected share. Groups of agents that are thus held together by bonds of trust are called

18. At the formal level there is much in common between *natural* entropy – and the other *natural* factors in the examples of informal services in Breton and Wintrobe (1982, pp. 39–41) – and the variable representing the random states of nature in the canonical principal–agent model of hierarchies and bureaucracies.
19. Among the acts of deceit, manipulation, cheating, subversion, and sabotage that agents may undertake in an effort to increase their takings, increments in entropy may be the one act that is the most susceptible to individual action. But, as noted in the text, even for this act, the collaboration of others will often be beneficial.

horizontal networks. Two more or less obvious points follow from the foregoing. First, for horizontal networks in which trust is even only moderately strong, monitoring and supervision are not likely to be very effective responses to the malfeasance represented by the willful accentuation of entropy, which is why I have left it out of the present discussion (see footnote 16). Second, bureaucratic power is not founded on selective behavior alone but also on lateral bonds of trust among agents.

In their monograph, Breton and Wintrobe (1982) made the assumption that horizontal networks are inefficient from the point of view of principals. The networks' existence and operation were taken to reduce the utility, profits, or wealth of principals. Later (Wintrobe and Breton, 1986, pp. 532–3), to rationalize the assumption, they argued that much in the same way that the interest groups analyzed by Mancur Olson (1965, 1982), George Stigler (1971), and Sam Peltzman (1976) reduce aggregate social product, horizontal networks in organizations lessen the payoffs of principals. It is still possible to refer to that logic – especially to Olson's analysis of the reification of social systems in which interest groups acquire "inordinate" power – though we now possess in the models of Tirole (1986) and Laffont (1988, 1990) more rigorous demonstrations derived from specific information structures that lateral collusive networks are detrimental to the objectives sought by principals.

Breton and Wintrobe assume that principals are aware of the existence of horizontal networks and are able to evaluate their negative effects – characteristics (3) and (4) of the information structure. One instrument that principals could use to counter these effects is the dislocation of the horizontal networks through reorganization. But, as will become apparent later, reorganization is a two-edged sword. To understand that, consider another possible response of principals to the negative effects of horizontal networks, namely, the allocation of resources to the construction of vertical networks – that is, to the formation and development of relationships of trust in which they, the principals, are involved either directly or indirectly. (I discuss later the meaning of this qualification.)

Vertical networks of trust relationships will support trade between principals and agents. Because of vertical trust, agents will supply informal services such as more relevant and more reliable information to their decision-making principals – they will, for example, reduce entropy below its natural level – and in exchange principals will compensate agents informally. The compensations, it is important to appreciate, are not takings from principals by agents as in horizontal networks but bona fide though informal payments by principals to agents for services rendered. Exchanges in vertical networks are, then, like the ordinary exchanges that have retained so much of the attention of economists, beneficial to both parties – in this case, to principals and to agents.

If vertical networks (v) – or vertical trust – serve to make principals better off and horizontal trust (h) serves to make them worse off, the overall efficiency of organizations will depend on the distribution of trust or, to put it differently, on the relative effectiveness of the vertical and horizontal networks that constitute their informal structures. Although it seems reasonable to assume that a given individual will not participate in both horizontal and vertical networks at the same time, any organization has networks of both sorts at all times. To give more precise representation to the informal structure of organizations or, identically, to the distribution of trust between vertical and horizontal networks, we can assume that payoffs (in money) to principals (π) are a function of v and h or $\pi = \pi(v,h)$, with $\pi_1 > 0$ and $\pi_2 < 0$ and, for reasons analogous to those provided in Wintrobe and Breton (1986, pp. 533–4), $\pi_{11} < 0$ and $\pi_{22} > 0$, where $\pi_1 \equiv \partial\pi/\partial v$, $\pi_{11} \equiv \partial^2\pi/\partial v^2$, and so on.

The problems of organizational design and of the governance of organizations that confront principals are in the last analysis the problems of determining v and h, namely, the volume of vertical and horizontal trust. It would be rewarding to construct simple games in which either principals or agents or both adopted strategies with respect to v and h that maximized their respective utilities.[20] Alternatively, following Breton and Wintrobe (1982), we can assume that principals and agents accumulate v and h up to the point at which the net yields on these forms of human capital are equal to the parametrically given rate of interest. One of the virtues of this approach is that it forces analysts to look at the factors (imperfections) that prevent equalization of net yields from happening.

In small organizations, principals may be able to decide on the volume of v and of h through direct interaction and personal contacts, but in larger organizations they will be able to increase v and/or reduce h only by manipulating the formal structure.[21] In other words, principals will not be able to accumulate trust directly through personal interactions but will have to do so indirectly by adjusting and modulating the formal structure of their organization. To understand this proposition, it is essential to define formal structures differently and more broadly than has been common practice in the literature. Formal structures must still comprise the chain of command, the definition of tasks, the distribution of responsibilities, and the other attributes that have been traditionally associated with them, but in addition they must embody the features that have been emphasized in recent years in efforts to understand what is, to all evidence, the organizational superiority of the "Japanese firm"[22] [see, for exam-

---

20. I am grateful to Jean Bénard for insisting on the importance of equilibrium conditions and for suggesting possible gaming strategies applicable to this problem.
21. The same point is made and documented by Michael McKee (1988).
22. There are firms outside Japan that possess some of the organizational dimensions of "Japanese firms," hence the quotation marks.

ple, Aoki (1984, 1986, 1990) and Hashimoto and Raisian (1985)].[23] Among these features are bonus systems, lifetime employment, elongated promotion ladders, retirement gratuities (related to grade, length of service, and final salary), payment of salary while temporarily laid off, and the organization and density of supervision.

In the informal transactions model, one of the most important activities, if not the most, of principals will therefore consist in fine-tuning the formal structure – appropriately conceived – in such a way as to emphasize the attributes conducive to the growth of vertical trust while playing down those that promote horizontal trust. Given that trust is a human capital asset whose yield is the reduction in the cost of the intertemporal exchanges that it permits, principals who follow rules of rational conduct will manipulate the formal structure in such a way that at the margin the net yield on the resources expended to foster vertical trust networks is equal to the net yield on resources allocated to the destruction of horizontal trust networks (Breton and Wintrobe, 1982, pp. 78–87). This implies among other things that ruling out corner solutions, horizontal networks will be found in all organizations. The abundant documentation that horizontal networks exist is therefore not proof that vertical networks are unimportant. On the contrary, the horizontal networks that we observe in equilibrium are those that principals do not find worthwhile to remove.

We know very little about the relation of formal structures to the positive or negative accumulation of trust. Consider, for example, the widespread practice of reorganization. We should expect the use of this instrument to dislocate vertical and horizontal networks and, therefore, to reduce both vertical and horizontal trust. However, even if we assume that principals are rational, well informed, and not unduly constrained by institutional rigidities and if we consequently conclude that reorganization must reduce horizontal more than vertical trust and therefore lead to a situation in which $W^* + E > W^* + T$ (where W^* is the given formal or contractual wage, E is the efficiency payment and T is takings), tracing the effects of the practice will remain arduous and tentative until robust evidence is available.

The basic problem is that it is difficult to measure trust. Until that problem is solved, one must fall back on the strategy of exploiting the implications of its presence and of its absence. One implication, stressed by the informal

23. Breton and Wintrobe (1982, pp. 140–6) explain in some detail, in their discussion of the "Japanese firm," how these and other attributes of formal structures are related to the accumulation of trust. Much of the relevant pre-1980 literature is referenced in that section of their book. For a recent analysis of the "Japanese firm" that focuses on organization but does not use the informal transactions framework, as well as for an updated bibliography, see Masahiko Aoki (1990).

transactions model, derives from the association that is presumed to exist between takings and horizontal trust on the one hand and payments and vertical trust on the other, coupled with the argument that the volume of trust – whether v or h – is a positive function of the number and size of network exchanges.

The existence of takings has been widely documented by sociologists, but insufficient care has been given to the difficult task of sorting takings and payments. In some cases, the sorting problem is difficult to resolve. For example, academics (and many other agents) at times make personal long-distance telephone calls and have personal letters typed and mailed at their universities' expense. These actions are, in all likelihood, takings reflecting horizontal trust between them and the administrative personnel, but they could also be payments indicative of vertical trust between them and the top management (deans) of the institutions.

Some expense accounts, special office furnishings, absenteeism, and other practices of the sort are similarly difficult for outsiders to classify into takings and payments. However, large position-specific expense accounts, really plush offices, chauffeur-driven limousines, and other perquisites of that type are surely not takings. Neither are the sums and the amenities that derive from the attributes of the formal structure associated with the "Japanese firm": bonus payments, guaranteed incomes, burial lots, vacation programs, mortgages, and so on. Given that these sums and amenities are derivative of formal structures and, hence, under the authority of principals, they cannot be takings but must be payments.

In an interesting recent paper, Ronald Johnson and Gary Libecap (1989) have, without apparently being aware of it, shown that the formal structure of the United States federal civil service possesses a number of attributes that uncannily resemble those found in "Japanese firms." Their paper is primarily concerned with the role of bureaucratic rules, though they also mention such features as lifetime employment (pp. 57–8). The functions they ascribe to rules, which essentially are the protection of agents from wrongful actions of supervisors, appear to match almost perfectly the functions Masahiko Aoki (1990) assigns to the institutions that regulate labor–management relations in "Japanese firms."[24] If this reading of Johnson and Libecap is accepted, the bureaucratic rules they describe have to be seen as attributes of the civil service's formal structure that the principal (Congress) adjusts to foster the formation of vertical trust. The vertical trust supports the provision of informal services that advance the principal's goals in exchange for payments to

---

24. Not all bureaucratic rules are of the type retained by Johnson and Libecap. For a discussion of the ambiguous nature of certain kinds of rules, see Galeotti (1988), Wintrobe (1982), and Ronald Heiner (1988).

agents that are embodied in larger salaries and better working conditions and are, thus, in the nature of "efficiency wages" (Akerlof, 1982).

Principals can fine-tune the formal structure of their organization through the use of other instruments besides the sort of bureaucratic rules reported by Johnson and Libecap and besides the bonus systems, lifetime employment, elongated promotion ladders and the other formal attributes that appear to characterize the "Japanese firm." Breton and Wintrobe (1986, pp. 918–20), on the basis of evidence provided by Hannah Arendt (1973), have described how Adolf Hitler created loyalty to himself by using an organizational device that consisted in creating new, more militant, and more radical hierarchical levels, which at once increased the possibilities of promoting agents on the basis of trust almost without limit while at the same time making it easy to demote those whose loyalty was waning. Hence, the creation in 1922 of the SA (the stormtroopers), followed in 1926 by that of the SS (guard detachments), shortly thereafter by the Shock Troops, the Death Head units, the Security Service, and so on.

The existence and role of vertical trust and of vertical networks and the active role of principals in these networks can be verified in a different way. Northcote Parkinson's (1957) celebrated "law" that "work expands to fill the time available for its completion" was interpreted and formalized by Breton and Wintrobe (1979, 1982) to mean that under certain circumstances the number of principals (P) – top and middle managers – in an organization increases at the same time that the number of its agents (A) and its output decline. Are there circumstances that could generate such an outcome? A reduction in the demand for the organization's output would appear to be a necessary, but it cannot be a sufficient, condition for the law to hold. In the absence of any institutional constraints, we should expect a decline in demand to cause the number of P's and A's to be reduced more or less in the same proportion. That would not yield a workforce profile remotely resembling that called for by Parkinson's law.

Even if we assume that the skills of the P's are more specific to the activities of the organization than those of the A's, a decline in demand would cause a reduction in the number of A's more than in the number of P's, but that would still not validate Parkinson's law. If, however, we hold to the last assumption about the specificity of skills and if we further assume that some P's are indebted to some A's for informal services supplied at an earlier date, we can generate Parkinson's law. How? Simply by assuming that the P's will "pay" the A's by promoting them to a higher rank. Two things will motivate the P's to make these payments: (1) the desire to forgo a capital loss on accumulated trust; and (2) a desire to avoid the reputation of being someone who reneges on promises and who cannot, therefore, be considered a trustworthy network member. The contract enforcing virtues of vertical trust thus provide a rationale for Parkinson's law in that promotions as payment for informal services imply (1) a rise in the number of P's; (2) a fall in the number of A's; and (3) a decline in output on the only condition that the P's are more highly paid than the A's, thus causing costs to rise as the number of P's increases. McKee and Wintrobe (1993) have tested the hypothesis and found it consistent with two different sets of data – one pertaining to Ontario (Canada) schools and the other to the United States' steel industry – thus lending further empirical support to the informal transactions model.

Principals can also destroy trust and networks by manipulating the formal structure. They will want to undo not vertical, but horizontal networks. Among the instruments they can use for that purpose I have already mentioned reorganization. Aoki (1990, p. 6) notes the "rotation of personnel" as a way of "discourag[ing] the development of shop-centered interests." In a provocative analysis of the Soviet system of industrial production, Wintrobe (1988) has shown that the "Great Purge of the Party," launched by Josef Stalin in the late 1930s, was in effect a device used to destroy lateral trust networks. In my opinion, Wintrobe's application of the informal transactions model of organizations to Soviet society and his analysis within that framework of its management and evolution remains (his paper was written in 1986 but not published until 1988) with only minor modifications the best model available to understand the traumas and travails of the former Soviet Union (and of East European societies) today.

The foregoing makes clear that the inefficiencies that derive from collusion or from other behaviors of agents are not only eliminated by active principals. It also makes clear that active principals build trust relationships with their agents that insure that the latter's performance is more productive than it would be if the organization relied exclusively on the formal authority structure. In models in which agents alone are permitted to be active, the informal structure is made to operate to the disadvantage of principals and to the detriment of efficient production in that supply outcomes are worse than they would be if there were no such structure. In models in which principals are allowed to be as active as agents, however, supply outcomes can be even better than they would be in the absence of an informal structure when organizations rely on authority alone.

ii.   Bureaucracies

It is not obvious that principals would be very active if they were not operating in a competitive environment. The preceding five chapters should, however, have established that the interaction of centers of power in compound governments and in other bureaucracies is competitive. I now turn my attention to the implications for principal–agent relations of competition between centers of power. How are intraorganizational relations between principals and agents affected by competition?

We must distinguish between the competition of principals and agents for jobs – what is known in the literature as "managerial competition" (see Alchian, 1969; Jensen and Meckling, 1976; and Fama, 1980) – and the competition of principals and agents for membership in trust networks. The motivation for the models of managerial competition was Berle and Means's (1932) suggestion that, because of "the separation of ownership from control," corporate managers possessed a good measure of "discretion" – monopoly power – which made it possible for them to neglect the interests of owners in favor of their own. The basic point of the managerial competition model is that managers face competition for their jobs from lower-level managers and from managers in other firms. The market for managers, if it is competitive, will insure efficient performance on the part of managers. The degree of competition in the market for managers depends on three factors: (1) the effectiveness of techniques and the adequacy of information for evaluating the performance of managers; (2) the ease with which managers can move from one job to another; and (3) the strength of the incentive to replace inefficient managers. It follows that the question of whether the market for managers is competitive enough to eliminate managerial discretion and managerial rents and to insure efficient performance is an empirical one on which unanimity has never been achieved.

To apply the managerial competition model to bureaucracies and hierarchies, it is sufficient to postulate the existence of competition for jobs among agents and competition among principals for agents – to postulate the existence of a market in which principals and agents compete. The degree of competition in that market will be governed by the same factors that determine the extent of competition in the market for managers. The strength of that competition is therefore also an empirical matter. Even if the difficulty of evaluating performance poses the same kinds of problems in the market for principals and agents as in the market for managers, the ability of agents to access jobs – whether of other agents or of principals – and the ease with which both principals and agents can be removed from their jobs is surely quite large inside bureaucracies. That by itself is sufficient to eliminate the passivity of principals and to motivate these same principals to invest in whatever is needed to have good relations with their agents.

The ability to move from job to job and the capacity to create job opportunities by removing inefficient officeholders are conditions that pertain to competition among bureaus. Recall, however, that selective behavior – which describes the nature of the power of agents (in contrast to the authority of principals) and is the source of informal payments and informal takings – is based in trust networks. Recall also that payments and takings are not rents to be dissipated by competition but returns on the capital asset called trust.

Interbureau competition need not, therefore, eliminate all inefficiencies in bureaucratic conduct, because the inefficiencies associated with takings can remain in equilibrium. In their monograph, Breton and Wintrobe (1982, pp. 99–106) show that it is even possible under conditions of perfect competition to observe an increase in selective behavior – in the power of agents – and therefore in the provision of inefficient informal services following an exogenous disturbance. Does that mean that bureaucratic behavior will undo otherwise robust Wicksellian Connections? The answer must be that inefficient selective behavior, even under competitive conditions, can weaken Wicksellian Connections but that interbureau competition, by energizing and activating principals and inducing them to invest in vertical trust, will keep inefficient selective behavior and, therefore, damages to Wicksellian Connections at a minimum. It would be wrong to think that bureaus and bureaucracies operate to undo what competition forges by way of Wicksell–Lindahl efficiency.

6.4.   Conclusion

Much of the work of the past twenty-five years on bureaus and bureaucracies would seem to lead one to the conclusion that bureaucratic behavior is such that any forces driving governments and the centers of power of which they are constituted toward efficiency would be completely undermined by that behavior. This chapter has argued that to a large extent that position rests on the assumptions that principals are passive and that there is no competition among bureaucrats and among bureaus. Removing these assumptions does not altogether eliminate the power of agents to engage in inefficient selective behavior but is sufficient to insure the survival of strong Wicksellian Connections.

PART II

Governmental systems

CHAPTER 7

A retrospective overview

The whole of Part II focuses on *inter*governmental competition. The analysis it proposes extends that of Part I, which was exclusively concerned with *intra*governmental competition, by concentrating on the interaction of governments with one another. To simplify, the four chapters of which Part II is constituted take the relationship of centers of power within each government as given. The analysis extends that of Part I, but it also builds on it by making use of the same model of demand as that proposed in Chapter 2. It assumes that all governments maximize expected consent. All that is needed to use the model of demand is, therefore, a small change in the notation of equations (2.7) to (2.10), which the reader can easily provide.

To proceed, I must first dispose of a semantic issue. Our habit of thinking of governments as monolithic institutions is so engrained that we do not appear to possess in ordinary discourse words that would make it easy to distinguish between the entire apparatus of government on the one hand and the multiplicity of units that constitute the whole on the other. We lack a distinction such as that between industry and firms that plays such an important role in the microeconomic analysis of market supply. Among commonly used expressions, the one that corresponds most to that of industry is *public sector,* but this term contains too many elements that belong to demand to be completely satisfactory. I therefore propose to adhere throughout to the conventions of calling the apparatus of state in its entirety the *governmental system;* the component units I simply call *governments.* In addition, as already indicated, Part II and Part III disregard the various centers of power that make up individual governments. Keep in mind, however, that whenever the word *government* is used, it is as a contraction for the entire constellation of centers of power that make up governments.

Having dealt with this first problem of vocabulary, let me immediately remark that modern democratic governmental systems, even those of unitary states, are all multilevel systems. That statement continues to be true even if we insist in recognizing as jurisdictional levels only those at which political decisionmakers are popularly elected. France, Italy, and Spain, for example, which are often used to illustrate what the typical unitary state looks like, each has four levels of elected governments. Britain, outside London and its six other metropolitan conurbations,[1] also has four tiers of elected governments.[2] I have not been able to find among contemporary democracies a single example of a governmental system in which there are fewer than three jurisdictional levels (see, however, footnote 2). Furthermore, if we do not require that political decisionmakers be elected, the number of levels becomes larger mostly but not exclusively because of the importance of special authorities and special district governments – in France, *syndicats,* and in Italy, *consorzi* – that can have the responsibility for such powers or functions as schools, fire protection, police, public transportation, water, sewerage, libraries, hospitals, and cemeteries.

A theory of governmental systems that would embody a theory of federalism as a special case is still lacking. The best discussions – those that reflect at least some of the ongoing research – continue to line up, in ad hoc fashion, decentralization theorems, models of the assignment of powers, of interjurisdictional spillovers, and of intergovernmental grants, propositions related to vertical fiscal imbalance and dependence, and hypotheses about optimum jurisdictional size, fiscal mobility, and real estate markets, without, to all appearances, being wary of the fact that in the absence of a unified and complete theory it is not possible to check if these fragmentary and disparate exercises are theoretically apposite, empirically meaningful, or relevant to policy. To develop a tolerably complete and unified theory of governmental systems, it is essential to focus the analysis on the nature and attributes of intergovernmental competition.

To establish that proposition, the remainder of this chapter provides a brief overview of the literature that is concerned with the relationships that governments that are located at different jurisdictional levels on the one hand and those that inhabit the same level on the other, entertain with each other[3] – on

1. Birmingham, Leeds, Liverpool, Manchester, Newcastle, and Sheffield.
2. Prior to 1986, the year that Prime Minister Thatcher's government suppressed the Greater London Council and the six Metropolitan county governments, these seven areas had three levels of elected governments. Since 1986, London and the other six metropolitan areas have had only two.
3. I do not review early work – that by Alexis de Tocqueville (1835, 1840), James (Lord) Bryce (1888), Henry Sidgwick (1919), Johannes Popitz (1927), Harold Laski (1939), Albert Dicey (1962), and Kenneth Wheare (1963) – which, in one way or the other, is concerned mostly with vertical relationships, that is, with the assignment of powers among orders of government. (Some of that literature is examined in Breton, 1990.) I also neglect the more quantitative work of Alan Peacock and Jack Wiseman (1961), Frederic Pryor (1968), David Davies (1970), Wallace Oates (1978) and Werner Pommerehne (1977). [Much of that research has been well surveyed by my colleague Richard Bird (1979, 1986)]. I neglect all that work because I restrict my investigation to studies directly formulated in terms of, or easily converted into, the methodology of optimization and equilibrium comparative statics. I must add that for heuristic reasons, I review the literature on vertical fiscal imbalance and intergovernmental grants – a part of the writings on vertical relationships – not in this, but in the next chapter.

what I call vertical and horizontal relationships.[4] Both types of relationships have been extensively studied, though, as will become apparent, the problems to which they give rise have been satisfactorily resolved for neither. In what follows, I note some of the difficulties that scholars have encountered and have so far not been able to overcome. In the process, I sketch an approach based on intergovernmental competition that I believe must be adopted to model both vertical and horizontal relationships.

7.1.   More definitions

It is essential to make clear at the outset a few more of the semantic conventions to which I adhere throughout the discussion in Part II. The literature on vertical relationships in governmental systems has made and continues to make abundant use of the concept of *centralization* (and of decentralization). Richard Bird (1979, 1986), more forcefully than others, has warned that the concept is difficult to use and often misleading. However, in practical applications, it is sometimes possible, as recent work by Anthony Scott (1991) demonstrates, to do away with it altogether. For that reason but also because it plays such a large role in the literature I will be reviewing and because it simplifies theoretical discussions, I will use it. Later in the analysis, I also make use of the concept of *concentration* introduced in the literature by Alan Peacock and Jack Wiseman (1961). I will distinguish between expenditure concentration and revenue concentration. *Expenditure concentration* can be defined as the central government's share of total expenditures on goods and services (appropriately defined, see Chapter 1, Section 1.1) incurred by all the governments of a given governmental system. This index (or metric) may sometimes be biased. For example, if the expenditures of central and local governments fall and those of provincial or state governments rise, the expenditure concentration index could decline, but the "real" degree of concentration could easily have risen. For that reason, it may be necessary in certain circumstances to use a definition based on a vector of the ratios of the expenditures of governments located at each of all the jurisdictional levels of the governmental system to the total expenditures of all the governments of the system. *Revenue concentration* is defined in a similar way. In what follows, I use the simpler scalar definitions of expenditure and revenue concentration.

I also distinguish between powers and functions. The first is a constitutional or legal concept that I use in conjunction with the notion of centralization. The second is associated with the activities, tasks, and processes that lead to

4. Jack Walker (1969) was the first, to my knowledge, to distinguish *analytically* between horizontal and vertical intergovernmental relations. As I note in Chapter 9, he was also the first to identify these relations as competitive – he used the word "emulation" (p. 890) to describe the phenomenon. Finally, he also addressed the question of the stability of the outcomes resulting from horizontal competition (p. 890). No mean achievement.

the supply and "financing" of goods and services by governments. I use it in conjunction with the concepts of expenditure and revenue concentration.

7.2.   Vertical competition

In the fiscal federalism literature – the literature concerned with multitier governmental systems – the problem of centralization has two dimensions: one that relates to the division of powers among orders of government and another that pertains to the number and to the morphology of the jurisdictions that make up governmental systems and, therefore, to the structure of these systems. It is in general possible either to take the structure as given and to seek to discover an equilibrium assignment or alternatively to take the division of powers as given and to establish what the equilibrium structure looks like. One problem is the *dual* of the other.[5] For that reason it is possible to deal with only one dimension of the centralization problem without loss of generality. I focus on the one that has received most attention: the assignment or division of powers.

In the literature to which I am restricting myself, the earlier models were all based on the implicit assumption of a strict equivalence between an assignment of powers and an assignment of functions or responsibilities for the supply of particular goods and services. To put it differently, it was tacitly assumed that publicly supplied (i.e., government-supplied) goods and services could be aggregated into unambiguous classes, which were then treated as powers. The assumption led many students of federalism [for example, Oates (1972), Musgrave and Musgrave (1984), and Rubinfeld (1987)] to formulate the assignment problems as pertaining to the allocation, redistribution, and stabilization powers without, however, indicating the return passage to real-world assignments as these are embodied in, say, constitutional documents or actual practices.

However, when the assignment problem was formulated in terms of goods and services (functions), first by Breton (1965), then by Mancur Olson (1969), and finally by Oates (1972), the goods and services were invariably assumed to be *pure* Samuelsonian (1954) public goods, with the additional supposition that their "spans" varied from good to good, thus generating a more or less perfect hierarchy of goods.[6] These were then identified as local

5. This is easily seen in simple cases like that of "optimal currency areas" (Mundell, 1961). That problem can be resolved either by assigning the power over currency to a given jurisdictional level or by redesigning the frontiers of the area.
6. The span of a pure public good is the word introduced by Breton and Scott (1978) to reflect the number of persons who benefit (equally since the good is a pure public good) from the good. If the seeding of a cloud generates rain over the city of Kingston, then the span of the public good that we may call weather modification is equal to the population of Kingston (including visitors, if any). The span of a private good is accordingly equal to one person. The definition is easily adjusted to the case of nonprivate, or impure, public goods.

or municipal, metropolitan, regional, provincial, or national goods, depending on their spans. Because spans and spatial jurisdictional domains – the exogenously given structures of governmental systems – would not in general match each other (that is, map perfectly into each other), interjurisdictional spillovers were to be expected. As a consequence, the problem of the assignment of functions came to be defined as one in the efficient management of spillover flows, more or less as in the Welfare Economics conception of the State suggested by William Baumol (1969).

To illustrate, in Breton (1965) efficient management meant that the chosen assignment would minimize interjurisdictional spillovers. The remaining flows – which would obviously be larger, the more severely constrained was the minimization – would then be internalized by a system of intergovernmental Pigovian (1920) grants designed and administered by the central government. One year exactly after the publication of Breton's (1965) paper and years before the appearance of the Olson (1969) and Oates (1972) variations, Jack Weldon (1966), in a paper that went considerably beyond the assignment problem, showed that the approach itself was fundamentally flawed. His argument was simple and, for those who read it, effective. He argued that if central governments could correctly calculate the exact size of the grants needed to internalize the spillovers, all functions should be assigned to it. If, in other words, central governments could perform the difficult task of estimating all marginal spillover flows and designing the appropriate grants program, a division of functions was not only unnecessary but wasteful. The ideal governmental system was a single-tier unitary state. One should add that beyond the Weldon critique, the Breton–Olson–Oates approach suffers from another crippling defect in that it contains no body that can produce or institute the desired division of functions, except an *omniscient* central government or *omniscient* planner.

This is a convenient place to mention two other attempts to solve the assignment problem. One, of venerable vintage, can be called the *principle of responsiveness;* the other, of more recent birth, is the *principle of subsidiarity* and is very much part of current debates in Europe, where it was invented [for a good discussion, see Subtil (1990)]. Responsiveness is not modeled. Instead, it is assumed that governments that are lower in the hierarchy of governmental systems are closer to the people and ipso facto more responsive to the preferences of citizens than governments higher up in the structure (see, for example, Tullock, 1969, p. 21, and Rosen, 1985, p. 511). Because responsiveness is assumed to be a virtue, the principle simply states that a power or function (no distinction is made between the two in these discussions) should be assigned to a jurisdictional level higher in the hierarchy only if governments at lower levels cannot technically discharge the responsibilities associated with the power or function. Analysis of the technical capacity of junior governments to discharge responsibilities rapidly leads to discussion of interjurisdictional spillovers (see, for example, Rosen, 1985, pp. 511–12; and Rubinfeld, 1987, p. 631) and to issues not unlike those encountered in the Breton–Olson–Oates approach.

The problem with the principle of responsiveness is not, however, principally related to spillovers but extends to the basic intractability of the notion of responsiveness itself. Suppose, for example, that all governments are in some sense equally responsive to the preferences of citizens. Suppose also that the preferences of the citizens are more homogeneous at lower levels in the hierarchy of governmental systems. Then, if governments are equally misinformed about the preferences of their citizens, preferences will not be as well satisfied at higher jurisdictional levels as at lower ones, even though by construction governments are equally responsive, simply because there is more variability in the distribution of preferences in higher jurisdictions and, as a consequence, more information is needed by senior governments to provide goods and services in volumes that generate the same level of utility loss as that generated by junior governments. Only in a system in which everyone has the same preferences for all goods and services can the principle of responsiveness be unambiguously applied. In such a system, however, the Weldon critique applies with even more force. If all citizens have the same preferences, it makes no difference how powers or functions are assigned; furthermore, if there are costs to decentralization – even small ones – the best assignment is full centralization.

The principle of subsidiarity is essentially the same as that of responsiveness, except that responsiveness per se is not explicitly considered. The principle then reduces to the statement that a power or function should not be assigned to a jurisdictional level higher up in the hierarchy of governmental systems if the responsibilities it embodies can be discharged equally well or better by governments at lower levels. Because the notion of responsiveness is absent from the formulation, an appropriate notion of spillovers, defined by reference to the preferences of citizens, is also lacking. However, it is difficult to resist the view that when the principle is eventually fleshed out, some "technical" analog to spillovers, possibly defined by a central authority, will find its way into the analysis. Subsidiarity, like responsiveness, would then become vulnerable to the Weldon critique.

Confronted with these failures, Breton and Scott (1978) proposed a theory of the assignment of powers (not of functions) inspired by the Coasian (1960) revolution then in full swing, which suggested that the problem of externalities (spillovers) was better understood and disposed of by shifting both analytical and practical emphasis from the externalities themselves to the transaction costs of internalizing them. Breton and Scott's decision to adopt that line of analysis was to a considerable extent influenced by Gordon Tullock's (1969) seminal paper on federalism.

The basic mechanics of Ronald Coase's approach is very simple. Suppose that a negative externality inflicts a utility loss on a victim. A Coasian victim, as distinguished from a Pigovian victim, is not passive in that he or she does not expect a benevolent government to tax the source and thus internalize the externality. Instead, the victim, prompted by the loss of welfare (or money) caused by the externality and on the assumption that the source is not liable for damages, initiates negotiations with that source, negotiations that induce it, against receipt of a "bribe" or payment, to reduce the volume of the externality to the point at which the marginal damages inflicted on the victim are equal to the marginal benefits received by the source. The Coasian calculus is, however, very much a function of the size of transaction costs and, properly construed, concentrates on the effects of transaction costs (see, for example, Shavell, 1987). Breton and Scott adopted more or less the same perspective. They identified four different kinds of transaction or organization costs – mobility, signaling, administration, and coordination – which, they argued, vary as the degree of centralization or as the assignment of powers varies. They then showed that if these *ceteris paribus* cost functions satisfied certain restrictions, the minimization of the cost functions would yield an equilibrium assignment of powers. By the properties of the dual, this minimization also yields an equilibrium number of jurisdictional levels and an equilibrium number of jurisdictions per level – in other words, an equilibrium organization of government systems.

That would seem to have put an end to the matter. Breton and Scott seem to have achieved two goals: (1) the formulation of a model of the division of genuine constitutional powers as distinguished from a model of the assignment of goods and services or functions; and (2) the development of a model that did not appear to be vulnerable to the Weldon critique. Some commentators, such as Gérard Bélanger (1985), faulted the model's usefulness on the ground that the organization cost functions were difficult to measure. Although acknowledging the criticism, one must also recognize, first, that measurement problems are pervasive in the social sciences generally without being seen as insuperable barriers and, second, that the measurement problems of the Breton–Scott model are, it would appear safe to assert, no more serious than those of the Breton–Olson–Oates model or of other spillover approaches.

Immediately after the publication of *The Economic Constitution of Federal States,* John Dales, a friend and colleague at the University of Toronto, commented verbally that the Breton–Scott model had not altogether met the Weldon critique. Indeed, instead of omniscient central governments that marred the assignment models of the 1960s and early 1970s, it was omniscient constituent assemblies that, in its explicit canonical form, the model used to perform the minimization exercises that were now the stumbling block. Whatever progress may have been achieved by the Breton–Scott model, the Dales critique correctly asserted that the final equilibrium assignment was the product, as are final equilibria in conventional Welfare Economics, of a *deus ex machina*. It is true that the Breton and Scott monograph contains an institutional model of the assignment of powers, but that model has two main weaknesses. First, although recognizing that the mode of operation of constituent assemblies is different in federal and in unitary states, little by way of explicit modeling of the different bargaining and other interaction processes is provided in the book and certainly nothing that can tell us whether the equilibrium of the canonical model will be even approximately approached institutionally. Second, the analysis uses a model of bureaucracy borrowed from William Niskanen (1971), in which one of the parties involved is completely passive – an assumption Breton and Wintrobe (1982) have shown to be irrational (see also Chapter 6 of this book). It is interesting to note in this context that in their second book, which was squarely focused on constituent assemblies, Breton and Scott (1980) abandoned any attempt at explaining real-world assignments and climbed on board the normative wagon – a standard cop-out that is always a sign that the positive or descriptive apparatus is seriously defective.

How then can the Weldon and Dales critiques be met? How is it possible to obtain a division of powers that would minimize organization costs but that would dispense with omniscient decisionmakers? The idea that made it possible for me to answer this question was born of discussions of the papers presented at a Villa Colombella Seminar on federalism. Following that seminar, in what was to become my "Supplementary (or "Minority") Report" to the *Report of the Royal Commission on the Economic Union and Development Prospects for Canada* (1985), I tried to extend some of the ideas that nourished these discussions and to organize them around the notion of competitive federalism or, as I would now call it, around the idea of competitive governmental systems. (That Report and the papers presented at the Seminar were subsequently published as a Special Issue of the *European Journal of Political Economy,* Breton, 1987).

The idea that competition is ever present in governmental systems is not new. It provides the background to Alfred Marshall's (1890, Appendix G) discussion of local government finance; it is the implicit but inexorable driving force in the enormous literature on tax harmonization (see, for example, Shoup, 1967; Thirsk, 1980; Bird, 1984, 1986, Chapter 7; and McCready, 1991); it is explicit in formal models of tax competition (see, for example, Mintz and Tulkens, 1986); it underlies the Breton–Scott (1978, pp. 85–7) analysis of minimum and national standards in federal states. And in some renditions of Tiebout's (1956) theory of local public goods, competition spurred by political mobility regulates the behavior of junior governments.

In all that literature, the focus is, however, restricted (as it is in my own Report, 1985) to horizontal competition. An exception is the work on tax harmonization, but that work, being almost single-mindedly preoccupied with the nitty-gritty of harmonization, has little if anything to say about competition. None of this is an accident. It is easy to rationalize horizontal competition; the mobility of consuming households, labor, capital, and/or technology among jurisdictions is sufficient to motivate its existence. But there is no mobility among orders of government. What could drive governments located on different jurisdictional tiers to compete with one another? And what would they be competing over?

Answers to these questions were provided by Salmon (1987a) at the 1984 Villa Colombella Seminar referred to earlier and in a later (1987b) elaboration and extension. Salmon uses the economic theory of rank-order tournaments, initially proposed by Edward Lazear and Sherwin Rosen (1981) and refined by many others, to develop a mechanism to explain why governments are motivated to compete across tiers as well as within tiers. Greatly simplified, the *Salmon mechanism*, as I will call it, can be summarized as follows: Citizens use the information they acquire about the supply performance of one or more benchmark governments to appraise and evaluate the supply performance of their own governments. Opposition parties, therefore, have ready-made platforms, based on the same information as that of their citizens, from which to challenge incumbent governments. The latters' response is a manifestation of competition between them and the benchmark governments. For example, a citizen observes the performance of governments at tier i as it pertains to the supply of, say, road maintenance, education, research incentives, broadcasting, police protection, or health care, and compares that performance with the performance of governments at tier j. Because the citizen can influence government by granting or withholding consent, the governments at tiers i and j are induced to compete in supplying whatever is the object of comparison. (I look at the Salmon mechanism again in Chapter 9, Section 9.1, Subsection ii.)

In passing from the Breton–Scott organization cost model to that of competitive governmental systems based on the Salmon mechanism, I have also moved from focusing on powers to concentrating, as the early models did, on the divisions of functions (goods and services). I have not, however, returned to the initial position, because omniscient decisionmakers have been replaced by the blind force of competition. To mark this transition, I henceforth use the word *concentration* when analyzing the division of functions or supply responsibilities.

For more than 100 years, the debates on the principles that (should?) govern the assignment of powers – debates that have always been importantly influenced by jurists – have been based on the tacit assumption that the distribution of the supply flows of goods and services between orders of government is effectively determined by the constitutionally or legally specified assignment of powers. A model of vertical competition requires that this assumption be reversed. I therefore propose that we assume that the division of powers and, hence, the degree of centralization be determined by the jurisdictional distribution of supply flows and, therefore, by the degrees of expenditure and revenue concentration, and not the other way around.

To look at the matter from a different perspective, competition will force governments to specialize in the supply of the goods and services in which each is relatively most efficient and will thus help to determine the equilibrium degree of expenditure and revenue concentration. All kinds of forces have an impact on the extent of intergovernmental specialization in the supply of goods and services. These are analyzed in Chapter 8, where a model of the way they interact to generate an equilibrium governmental system is also suggested.

Replacing the assumption that constitutions and constituent assemblies, constitutional experts and judges determine the extent of specialization by an assumption that says it is competition that accomplishes that task does not mean, of course, that constitutionally entrenched assignments are irrelevant. Their role must, however, now be conceived as constraints on the competition that orders the relationship of governments engaged in the production and provision of goods and services and, therefore, on the evolution of the equilibrium degree of revenue and expenditure concentration.

An illustration of how entrenched assignments can constrain competition is useful. Suppose that a particular power – let us call it P_i – has been assigned to the provincial or state order of government sometime in the past either by a formal body that met for that purpose or by a court's interpretation of a past assignment. Governments at the provincial or state level, therefore, have the constitutional or legal authority to supply goods and services $g_{ki} = g_{1i}, \ldots,$ g_{ni} given that $g_{ki} \in P_i$. Suppose now that as a consequence of an external disturbance, relative efficiencies change and the central government finds itself in a position to out-compete provincial or state governments in supplying the entirety or a subset of g_{ki}. Over time, the constitutional or legal assignment of powers will formally be altered or the old assignment will be given a new interpretation by the courts. This new assignment will then again – in a second period, as it were – act as a constraint regulating the competition that pits governments against one another in their efforts to cater to the demands of citizens. Chapter 8, Section 8.3, looks at this process in more detail.

7.3.   Horizontal competition

That horizontal intergovernmental relations are competitive has been widely recognized. As mentioned earlier, it has been acknowledged indirectly by those who have been preoccupied with problems of tax harmonization and, one should add, by those – often political scientists – who have been concerned with what is known as "cooperative federalism" or, as I would call it, with "cooperative governmental systems" [see, for example, Elazar (1991) and Kincaid (1991) and the literature they cite]. Acknowledgment has been indirect because this literature has for the most part been particularly interested in the ways and means of squelching or controlling competition. That intergovernmental relations are competitive has also been accepted by those who assume that the mobility of citizens *qua* consuming persons or households, that of human, physical, and financial capital, and that of technology are the main driving forces generating equilibrium outcomes in the supply of goods and services, in the location of people, in housing prices, and so on, and in understanding equilibrium displacements.

As we shall discover in the next chapter (Section 8.2, Subsection ii), an equilibrium division of functions and powers among orders of governments must accord pride of place to *coordination costs* and, therefore, to tax harmonization and to other forms of "cooperation." The question at this point does not pertain to coordination costs but to the mobility of persons as a driving competitive force. In many models of intergovernmental competition based on political mobility, it is not clear, the elegance and mathematical sophistication of the models notwithstanding, how political mobility is revealed and how it stimulates competition. I do not have in mind Dieter Bös's (1983) stricture in his commentary on Roger Gordon's (1983) model of the assignment of taxation powers. Bös decries the "typical attitude of United States economists" who, in his view, "over-stress . . . the importance of migration" (p. 46) presumably even for the United States but certainly for other societies. Within the conventional paradigm, it is always possible to reply to Bös that mobility is not apparent – appears not to exist – because governments adjust the volume of goods and services they supply and/or the taxprices they charge for these goods and services so rapidly that citizens who would otherwise be moving are induced to stay put. Governmental systems of the real world, the conventional paradigm would be saying, are always in equilibrium.

The point I wish to make eventually rejoins Bös's point, but it has a different origin. It pertains to what we may call the "dilemma of mobility." I have noted earlier that all democratic governmental systems (*pace* Thatcher's Britain) are constituted of three or more – sometimes many more – jurisdictional tiers. How, then, does a citizen who lives in a three-tier system and who wishes to consume the bundle of goods and services provided by Fairfax, but does not want to consume those supplied by Virginia, choose where to reside? The problem could be simplified if there were other Fairfaxes in surrounding provinces or states, but it need not be completely resolved. Suppose that all the desired Fairfaxes outside of Virginia happen to be located in desirable Canadian provinces but that our individual is totally averse to the bundle of goods and services offered by Canada. What is this citizen then to do? Stay put in Fairfax, Virginia, U.S.A., as Bös believes generally happens?

The point, to summarize, is not that there is no political mobility of persons but that that mobility is in general so analytically intractable that it cannot be the unique reed on which to hang a theory of competition in governmental systems. It may in practice sometimes be the case that the goods and services provided by governments at all jurisdictional levels, except those at one particular tier, are nearly indistinguishable from one another or if they are distinguishable, that the intensity of preferences for these goods and services – the marginal rate of substitution between them and a numéraire – is so low compared to that for one good or service offered by the governments at the particular jurisdictional tier that an n-tier ($n \geq 3$) governmental system behaves as a two-tier system. To illustrate, suppose that education is offered by governments at a particular jurisdictional level, that in the preference ordering of parents with school-age children education dominates by a wide margin all the other goods and services (parks, sewerage, public libraries, police protection, fire protection, etc.) provided by all other governments or that the variance in the distribution of quality is seen by parents to be much greater for education than for other goods and services supplied. Then such a governmental system, even if n-tier ($n \geq 3$), would behave as a two-tier structure. In such a context, competition will exist at the level offering education, but it will be absent elsewhere in the system. I return to this *Tiebout mechanism* in Chapter 9, Section 9.1, Subsection i).

It is important to mention that because they have no preference for goods and services and because they are fungible, "the dilemma of mobility" does not affect capital and technology. As a consequence, the mobility of capital and technology – their responsiveness to differential incitations – will motivate horizontal competition among the governments of a given governmental system. If, however, competition is only weakly motivated by the obligation to respond and cater to the preferences of citizens and is strongly motivated by the imperatives of capital and technology mobility, a theory of the organization of governmental systems based on competition as its ordering principle would have only a limited explanatory power. This is why the Salmon mechanism – which is capable of motivating both vertical and horizontal competition – is of such primordial importance.

Competition can be beneficial only if it is governed by rules that we may call "rules of competition," if these rules are policed and enforced, and if infractions are penalized. I am not concerned at the moment with the rules themselves – those pertaining to barriers to mobility, to tax exporting, to conspiracies, and so on – but with the particular problems posed by the necessity that the rules be enacted and enforced. (For a discussion of some rules, see Chapter 9, Section 9.4, Subsection ii). At least since the days of *The*

Federalist (1787–8), it has been known that in any governmental system the policing and enforcement functions in respect of the rules of horizontal competition had to be the responsibility of the central government, which in respect of these activities could be called a *monitor*.[7] The need for monitors of horizontal competition and some of the instruments they make use of in stabilizing that type of competition are discussed in Chapter 9, Section 9.4, Subsections i and ii.

Assigning the responsibility for monitoring horizontal competition to central governments creates a difficulty in that these governments are also engaged in (vertical) competition with the junior governments of their respective governmental systems. The problem takes a particular configuration in federal states because in these states the divided powers are constitutionally "owned" by the jurisdictional levels to which they have been assigned. To appreciate this point, it is enlightening to recall that the Founding Fathers of the American Constitution, gathered in Philadelphia in the summer of 1787, had no great difficulty in agreeing on a division of powers.[8] After all, all the governmental systems they knew had divided powers. It was not the division of powers that posed a problem; it was their ownership. The Founding Fathers were aware that the confederal arrangement of 1778 was falling apart and, without much hesitation, decided that it could not be repaired, in flagrant violation of their "terms of reference." However, they had an horror of unitary states, which were then identified with European monarchical governments in general and in particular with the government of George III, the enemy in the recently fought War of Independence. They were therefore led to discard two obvious forms of ownership. The only alternative left was divided ownership.

The problem the Founding Fathers saw with divided ownership – to a degree the problem that nourished their aversion to unitary states – was that the central government, in devising, policing, and enforcing the rules governing horizontal competition, would have some freedom to do so in a way that could benefit itself when competing (vertically) with the junior governments. It is in resolving this problem while holding to divided ownership of powers – a task that was long and arduous and at which they nearly failed – that the

---

7. It is not easy to give a name to that role of central governments. In *The Federalist* (1787–8), Alexander Hamilton used the words "umpire," "common judge" (p. 35), and "discretionary superintendence" (p. 91) to identify what I call a monitor. Umpire is also used by Donald Smiley and Ronald Watts (1985) but in a more restrictive sense than by Hamilton. William Riker (1975) characterizes the role of central governments vis-à-vis the provincial or state governments by the verbs "control," "discipline," and "force." Like *The Federalist,* he refers to the reverse relationship as one of obedience (p. 108). I have opted for "monitor" and "monitoring" because they seem to me to be more neutral and, hence, less misleading.

8. The Fathers of the Canadian Constitution, meeting in Charlottetown in 1864, had no great problem, either, in agreeing on a division of powers.

Fathers of the American Constitution invented federalism or what *The Federalist* called a "compound republic."

Their solution was to insert into the institutional apparatus of the central
government features that would make it difficult – impossible, they hoped –
for that government to alter the de jure and/or the de facto responsibility for
the supply of goods and services by altering the rules of competition. The
main solution of 1787 was the invention of a Senate in which state representation would be equal irrespective of size, would be appointed by the States,
and would be an essential legislative component of the whole structure. Other
institutions – for example, the Electoral College – were also tending in the
same direction. How a senate achieves that end is discussed in Chapter 9,
Section 9.4, Subsection iii, where other instruments that can be applied to the
pursuit of the same end are also considered.

7.4.   Conclusion

This chapter had two objectives. First, to argue that the evolution of doctrines
on governmental systems has through some process of natural selection been
tending toward theories and models in which intergovernmental competition
is the central organizing principle; and, second, to raise in a preliminary way
some of the major problems that a theory of competitive governmental systems must address. As already indicated, the next chapter proposes a model in
which vertical competition, constrained by technological and institutional
factors, leads actual and potential governments to specialize, in part or completely (think of "special" authorities, say), in the supply of certain goods and
services and in the process to divide the overall supply of goods and services –
the functions – and ultimately the powers, among themselves. As the chapter
will make clear, the division of functions on the one hand and of powers on
the other is therefore a consequence of vertical competition constrained by
technological and institutional factors, among which the costs of coordination
play a central role. In addition, the specialization inherent in the division of
functions implies that transfers of funds between governments at different
jurisdictional tiers play a fundamental role in any concentration and centralization equilibria. These equilibria in turn have to be enforced. The chapter also
argues that the cost of enforcing intergovernmental contracts has an influence
on the division of functions. Finally, the constraining role of the constitutionally entrenched division of powers is analyzed.

In Chapter 9, after a more detailed discussion of the Tiebout and Salmon
mechanisms, I provide empirical evidence of the existence and properties of
horizontal competition among governments. On the basis of that evidence as
well as of *a priori* arguments, I suggest that intergovernmental competition –
both horizontal and vertical – may often generate unstable outcomes, from

which I conclude to the need for third-party enforcers of what I call the "rules of competition." I suggest, following *The Federalist* (1787–8), that that role is played by *central governments*. I also examine some of the instruments used for that purpose. Finally, in Chapter 10, the analysis of Chapter 9 is brought to bear on the problems of intergovernmental competition at the international level.

CHAPTER 8

The organization of governmental systems

The topics that naturally fall within the domain of this chapter – the topics of the subdiscipline of Public Finance (or Public Economics) known as Fiscal Federalism – are not only numerous, but each one is interesting and challenging in its own right. Fiscal Federalism wrestles with the question of why functions, powers, or both are divided among levels of government and examines how that division is (or should be) determined at a point in time and how it changes over time.[1] Discussions of expenditure, regulatory, redistribution, stabilization, and taxation responsibilities flow naturally into the analysis of harmonization in respect of all these powers. Problems related to vertical fiscal imbalance as reflected in intergovernmental grants also receive a great deal of attention. The attention given to fiscal imbalance and grants is not an accident. As will become apparent, all problems of Fiscal Federalism can be discussed in a model of fiscal imbalance and intergovernmental flow of funds.

The work done over the past forty years or so by a large number of economists has taught us much. However, conventional Fiscal Federalism still lacks a consistent unified treatment. Too many propositions are exclusively normative, or more exactly nominal, that is, they lack any descriptive or real-world basis. Too many are based on the premise that agents who are assumed to be rational – among them governmental decisionmakers – systematically misallocate resources and cause inefficiencies. Too many cannot be applied to governmental systems made up of three or more jurisdictional tiers – virtually all existing systems. And too many, if they are not inconsistent with one another, must live separate lives because bridges that would help us go from one to the other do not exist.

It will help give concreteness to these criticisms, as well as serve as an

---

1. As I emphasized in Chapter 7, all democratic governmental systems – except that of the United Kingdom since Prime Minister Thatcher's reform of metropolitan governments – have three or more jurisdictional levels. Many of these are not federal under any definition of the word. However, because many of the principles that govern the assignment of powers in a theory of competitive governmental systems apply to both federal and unitary states, the lack of rigor in the definition of the word *federal* is of small consequence. That is not the case, however, in standard discussions based on some presumed technical properties of public goods. The point will become clearer as we proceed.

introduction to my own analysis of the organization of governmental systems, if I begin with a discussion of the state of the art in regard to fiscal imbalance – a topic, as I have already noted, that occupies a central position in any theory of the organization of governmental systems and especially in one that rests on the hypothesis that intergovernmental relations are competitive. The literature and the models are well known. I will therefore do no more in the next section than provide a brief outline of the models that have the widest circulation, and I will offer also in that section a critical assessment of these models. In Section 8.2, I suggest an alternative approach that emphasizes how competition constrained by technology, as well as by coordination and contractual enforcement costs, determines an equilibrium division of functions. Section 8.3 examines the relation between functions and powers and looks at the influence of constitutional entrenchments on the division of functions. Section 8.4 reexamines the Wicksellian Connection and Section 8.5 concludes the chapter.

8.1.   The standard explanation

The existence of vertical fiscal imbalance – the mismatch of own revenues and expenditures of governments located at various jurisdictional tiers – and the consequent flow of funds among governments are often (sometimes implicitly or tacitly) assumed to be given or, technically speaking, to be exogenous. When this assumption is made, analysis of necessity concentrates on the *effects* of the imbalance and of the intergovernmental money flows. Exogeneity is a way of disregarding origin or motivation and of focusing on consequences on the tacit assumption that effects are unrelated in any way to origin or motivation. I note three effects on which the standard view of fiscal imbalance has concentrated. A first line of analysis has focused on the distortions in the spending priorities of recipient jurisdictions. The first, and still among the best, model is Scott (1952); see also Wilde (1971) and Gramlich (1977). A second has stressed the incentive to fiscal irresponsibility on the part of the same governments that results from the separation of expenditure and taxation decisions, which the money flows imply (see, for example, Hicks, 1978, and Walsh, 1991, 1992). And a third has underlined the promotion of fiscal illusion in citizens and the encouragement to bureaucratic manipulation, which also are caused by the separation of revenue and spending decisions (see, for example, Courant, Gramlich, and Rubinfeld, 1979; Romer and Rosenthal, 1980; and Winer 1983). Words like distortion, irresponsibility, illusion, and manipulation, if they do not automatically speak of intrinsic evil, do not signal much that should be encouraged and nurtured, either. Whenever those who focus on the effects of vertical fiscal imbalance and on the money flows among governments choose to jettison the exogeneity assumption – not systematically but as a prelude to sagacious *obiter dicta* – they almost invariably decry vertical imbalance and the consequent flows of intergovernmental funds.

The limit of the exogeneity assumption has been widely recognized, however, and this has led to the formulation of a variety of models aimed at explaining why vertical imbalance and intergovernmental flows of funds exist in all multitier governmental systems. One group of explanations derives from Welfare Economics and Keynesian macroeconomics or from Musgrave's (1959) translation of these traditions into the allocation (efficiency), redistribution (equity), and stabilization functions and branches of governments. The efficiency argument rests on the assumption or observation that there are uneven spillover flows among jurisdictions that are consequent on the supply of goods and services by "junior" governments and that in the absence of what are in effect Pigovian subsidies, these spillovers lead to nonoptimal provisions of goods and services (see Breton, 1965, and Oates, 1972).

The equity argument has two strands. According to one of them, if the level of income in a jurisdiction is so low that its government cannot match the "fiscal residuum" (Buchanan, 1950) ruling in other jurisdictions without provoking destabilizing mobility, central governments, which are necessarily less affected by this type of mobility because of the spatial dimension of their jurisdiction, should equalize fiscal residuums by using income redistributive intergovernmental transfers.[2] The second strand is based on the assumption or the fact that fiscal capacities, needs, or both differ among jurisdictions and that these differences call for some form of equalization payments from governments situated at one jurisdictional level to those at another level.

Straddling the standard efficiency and equity arguments just outlined and, in a way, intersecting both is the argument advanced by Frank Flatters, Vernon Henderson, and Peter Mieszkowski (1974) and extended by Robin Boadway and Flatters (1982a, 1982b) that if junior governments provide goods and services whose span (for a definition, see Chapter 7, footnote 6) is less than national – namely, goods and services that are private, congestible, or both – and if per capita residence-based public revenues are larger in some jurisdictions than in others because of, let us say, an uneven endowment of taxable marketable natural resources, intergovernmental transfers should be used to eliminate inefficient mobility among jurisdictions. The central government should tax the jurisdictions that are rich in natural resources and transfer the proceeds to those that are poor, thus permitting both to adopt taxation and expenditure patterns that eliminate the interjurisdictional mobility of labor that would otherwise occur. These efficiency grants would, incidentally, also contribute to an equalitarian equity objective because they lead to transfers from rich to poor jurisdictions.

2. A fiscal residuum is the difference between the utility that a citizen attaches to the goods and services provided by governments and the utility that attaches to the private goods and services that that citizen sacrifices when paying taxes.

In their monograph on the division of powers and the assignment of these powers to governments at different jurisdictional tiers, Breton and Scott (1978) argued that it was very unlikely that the minimization of organizational costs – the cost of public administration and of intergovernmental coordination on the one hand and the cost of signaling preferences and of mobility incurred by citizens to insure that their preferences are attended to on the other – would lead to an assignment of powers that would guarantee to all governments revenues and expenditures that in equilibrium would match one another. A cost-minimizing constituent assembly or a social welfare maximizing ethical observer or planner would have to create a degree of vertical imbalance and a corresponding flow of funds among governments to insure that the organization of the governmental system economizes on the use of scarce resources.

For the sake of completeness, let me note that stabilization of overall economic activity may call for cyclical budgetary imbalance at the national level, but as a matter of logic, it precludes a corresponding converse imbalance at other jurisdictional levels. It is, therefore, not related to the problem of vertical imbalance and will not, as a consequence, further retain my attention in this chapter.[3]

I begin my criticism of the foregoing explanations of vertical fiscal imbalance and of the derived intergovernmental money flows by remarking that even if these two phenomena are features of all democratic federal systems of government, they are also attributes of democratic unitary states, all of which – the word *unitary* notwithstanding – are multitier governmental systems. Vertical imbalance is, therefore, not a reflection of a constitutionally entrenched division of powers that is too costly to change, either because of rigidities in the amending formula or because of a lack of sufficient consent among decisionmakers. In unitary states the power to alter the division of powers is unambiguously nested in central governments – that is why they are called unitary – so that interjurisdictional spillovers can be easily removed by reassigning the provision of the goods and services that cause the externalities to governments higher up in the system, thus eliminating in one swoop the need for intergovernmental transfers and the concomitant vertical fiscal imbalance.[4]

Moreover, as Breton and Angela Fraschini (1992) have documented, some unitary states, such as France and Spain, have for a decade or so been doing

---

3. The argument that macroeconomic stabilization of the Keynesian variety calls for permanently larger revenues than expenditures at the national level and therefore for vertical imbalance is logically untenable. For a good discussion, see Walsh (1992).

4. From a strictly legal point of view, states are said to be unitary when *all* legislation emanates from the central government. When junior governments make decisions, as they in fact do, say, on tax rates, this is deemed not to be legislation but administration. In view of the highly nominalistic and arbitrary character of this legal conception of the state, I pay no further attention to it and consider the setting of tax rates as legislation.

exactly the opposite. Their central governments have significantly reduced the degree of expenditure concentration in their respective governmental systems. We should therefore conclude, if we adhere to the Welfare Economics credo, that they have willfully created interjurisdictional spillovers that demand intergovernmental transfers that cause vertical imbalance and, one should no doubt add, that foster distortions, irresponsibility, illusion, and manipulation. Such long-term, all-pervasive irrationality on the part of central governments cannot be presumed. It is imperative that we ask why interjurisdictional spillovers exist or, even more to the point, why they appear to be created by the multiplication of jurisdictional tiers.

The Breton–Scott (1978) model of assignment of powers can be easily adapted and used to answer such a question. The argument would be developed along the following lines. A constituent assembly in attempting to minimize organizational costs – the costs of administration and intergovernmental coordination as well as the costs of gauging the preferences of citizens, not the costs of producing and supplying goods and services – would sometimes elongate the governmental system by adding jurisdictional tiers and would increase vertical fiscal imbalance by assigning expenditure responsibilities to these new tiers, while maintaining all revenue responsibilities at the national level, because that would economize on organizational resources. That line of reasoning is not only attractive, it is also correct. The problem with it is that the postulated constituent assembly – like the planners and ethical observers who maximize social welfare functions and the decisionmakers who operate behind veils of ignorance – does not have any empirical or institutional counterpart. As already noted and will be argued, it is possible to dispense with the notion of a constituent assembly by adopting a theory of competitive governmental systems. That theory also allows us to examine a second criticism of the explanation of vertical imbalance erected on the presence of interjurisdictional spillovers. For that purpose, I immediately provide a brief preliminary sketch of that theory.

Assume, then, that there are at least two levels of government in a particular governmental system and that all the governments of the system – let me call them central and provincial or state, whether they be the governments of federal or of unitary states – provide goods and services to citizens from whom they raise revenues to pay for these supplies. Assume further that governments at various jurisdictional tiers compete with one another. Competition will force each one of these governments to specialize in the supply of the goods and services in which each is relatively efficient, that is, in the supply of the goods and services each can provide at taxprices that other governments cannot match.

It is difficult to predict with any degree of precision what the long-term equilibrium will be. For example, it could be that the goods and services whose benefit spans exceed the territory of a particular government, but are within the territory of the whole governmental system, will be supplied by the central government or by one or more coalitions of provincial or state governments. By this means, supply taxprices are brought to their competitive levels in the same way that in competitive markets economies of scale external to firms but internal to the industry are internalized and the supply of goods and services made to reflect the opportunity cost of resources. In addition to the goods and services they provide to all citizens, central governments could also supply – in total or in part – some goods and services in provinces or states or even in local jurisdictions, because they are more efficient than the junior governments in doing so. Another possibility is that a coalition made up of the central government and of some subset of provincial or state governments could together supply certain goods and services, with the remainder provided severally. In all these cases and in others like them, vertical imbalance and intergovernmental transfers may exist because the efficient (competitive) assignment of expenditures and revenue responsibilities differ, but they are not generated by interjurisdictional spillovers.

The foregoing should not be read to imply that in competitive governmental systems all externalities are always internalized. There are costs to the formation of coalitions. Coalitions may degenerate into conspiracies, barriers to entry may exist, and so on. Still, the presumption cannot be that provincial or state governments will deal with spillovers only if they are paid to do so by a perfectly informed and disinterested higher-level planner. On the contrary, the presumption must be that competition will force them to act and, as the script says, force them to act in the right way.

To summarize, the efficiency argument for vertical imbalance and intergovernmental transfers derived from Welfare Economics is based on three assumptions: first, an exogenously given or institutionally vacuous division of powers; second, the existence of interjurisdictional spillovers consequent on that division of powers; and third, the absence of intergovernmental competition. The way I have stated it, the third assumption is too vague. It is not only that competition is ruled out in the Welfare Economics paradigm but that either cooperation or a master–servant relationship between the central and provincial or state governments is required. The senior government, after having estimated the size of the externalities – more precisely, the size of the marginal damages (and/or of the marginal benefits) generated by the spillovers – must raise, in the most neutral way possible, the revenues required to deal with them, and enter into an agreement with the provinces or states that will permit an implementation of the decision to internalize the spillovers. In unitary states, because master–servant rules may obtain, the agreement may reflect instructions of senior governments. In federal states, the agreement must presumably be cooperative because the central government generally cannot impose its decisions on provincial or state governments (see, however, Section 8.2, Subsection iii). The third assumption, therefore, speaks of instructions from above or of cooperation. Welfare Economics begets autocracy or cooperation, at least as long as the division of powers begets spillovers.

These comments on competition and cooperation bring me to what may be called the "Queen's model" of vertical imbalance and transfers (both Henderson and Mieszkowski were at Queen's University when working on the problem, and Boadway and Flatters still are). This particular explanation is based on the view, explicitly acknowledged by some of its originators (Boadway and Flatters (1982b, p. 6), that from an economic perspective the ideal form of government – that is, the one that is most conducive to efficiency and equity – is the single-tier unitary state (which, as already noted, does not exist anywhere). It is a simple matter to go from that view to the argument that in real-world governmental systems, any specific advantage that improves the relative efficiency of a junior government in supplying goods and services and that thus makes it more competitive should be suppressed by taxing the advantage away and by transferring the proceeds to less-well-endowed jurisdictions. The resulting vertical imbalance and flow of funds will inhibit the mobility of labor that the advantage, left untaxed, would have provoked. The argument can be put in different words: The supply of goods and services and their taxprices should be exactly the same in multitier as in a single-tier system of government, and the role of intergovernmental transfers is to insure that this result will obtain.

In the Queen's model, vertical imbalance and intergovernmental transfers, though they extinguish intergovernmental competition, are not overtly motivated by that objective. They have a different purpose: to recapture (capture?) the efficiency and equity properties of markets and of *single-tier unitary states*. Intergovernmental competition is not needed for this goal nor is cooperation. In this case, Welfare Economics begets only itself. In addition, if intergovernmental competition leads to efficiency in governmental systems, the Queen's model of vertical imbalances and of transfers, by sacrificing that competition to achieve efficiency in labor markets, can make society worse off than it would otherwise be.

The income redistribution argument for vertical fiscal imbalance and intergovernmental transfers that derives from Welfare Economics can be sustained only if it is assumed that "donor" governments suffer from systematic chronic irrationality. Why? Because, as will be argued in the next chapter (Section 9.5, Subsection ii, c), intergovernmental transfers are not an efficient instrument for redistributing income in comparison to interpersonal transfers, namely, transfers from persons to persons mediated by governments or other agencies. However, as also argued in the next chapter, it is better not to assume that governments are irrational but to suppose instead that intergovernmental transfers are not used for the purpose of redistributing income among persons but for that of stabilizing horizontal intergovernmental competition. In this last case, Welfare Economics begets nothing.

8.2.   An alternative explanation

To be sure that it is not an exogenously given, constitutionally entrenched division of powers that creates vertical imbalance and intergovernmental transfers, I disallow this kind of entrenchment. I also exclude all divisions of powers that are imposed by constituent assemblies of any kind or by the central governments of multitier unitary states. I assume that there are no barriers, legal or otherwise, to the emergence of any division of functions called forth by the competition of governments engaged in producing and supplying goods and services to the citizens of a particular country. (I look at some of these barriers in Section 8.3.) To understand what happens under these circumstances, we must begin by taking note of the fact that intergovernmental competition will drive governments to seek to improve their productive capacity through a division of functions among levels of government. They will strive to increase their overall productivity by specializing, in most instances only partially but in some cases, as when special authorities are created, completely.

It is correct to say that to a degree the relative efficiency or comparative advantage of governments – including that of special authorities – as suppliers of particular goods and services is acquired through specialization. We shall shortly discover that a powerful incentive to specialize derives from specific characteristics of production and supply technologies that help to determine the behavior of the average cost curves of tasks and activities associated with the production of goods and services.

If the productivity of individual governmental units is a *ceteris paribus* function of the extent to which these units are specialized, the productivity of governmental systems in their entirety depends on other factors as well, among which the most important are the costs of coordinating the various production tasks and activities undertaken by governmental units whenever coordination is called for and the costs of contractual enforcement. In other words, there are limits set by coordination and contractual enforcement costs to the advantages that can be garnered through specialization.

The discussion of the remainder of this section is organized as follows: First, I examine the influence of technology (as the volume of output varies) on the division of functions – on the extent of specialization – and illustrate by looking at two functions: an expenditure and regulatory function and a revenue function. Then in Subsection ii I examine the origin, nature, and effects of coordination costs. In Subsection iii I analyze the problems posed by the fact that agreements – contracts – have to be enforced. And finally in Subsection iv I note other factors that can affect the division of functions among orders of government. Subsections ii and iv, but especially Subsection ii, repeat and extend the analysis of coordination and administration costs already accorded a central place in Breton and Scott's (1978) *The Economic Constitution of Federal States*.

i.   Technology

More than forty years ago, on the implicit assumption that the costs of market transactions as well as those of intrafirm transactions were given, Stigler (1951) proposed an elaboration of Adam Smith's (1776, p. 17) famous proposition "that the division of labor is limited by the extent of the market" or that the division of functions among firms and industries is determined by the volume of output.[5] Stigler's model begins with the fact that there is a large number of separate activities or tasks associated with the transformation of a raw material into a finished product. For example, wheat has to be grown, harvested, graded, stored, and milled; the flour, mixed with other ingredients, must be kneaded and baked; the bread must be stored, its qualities advertised; and credit possibly extended to buyers – to name only a fraction among the most obvious of all the tasks associated with what we call the making of bread. How are these activities or processes divided among firms and industries?

To answer this question, Stigler focused on a particular firm and assumed that the average cost curves of some of the activities needed to produce its output were U-shaped, that others rise, and still others fall throughout for relevant rates of flow of output. When the size of the market is small, that firm will have to assume responsibility for activities subject to continuously increasing and continuously decreasing returns (in addition, of course, to those that display increasing and then decreasing returns). It will have to do this even though the tasks that are subject to continuously increasing and decreasing costs are being operated at inefficient rates, because without the output associated with these processes, the product could not be produced. However, as the size of the product market grows, the firm will "seek to delegate decreasing and increasing cost functions [activities] to independent (auxiliary) industries" (Stigler, 1987, p. 172). As the size of the market grows, total unit costs will be reduced if the processes that display continuously increasing and continuously decreasing average costs are delegated or contracted out to other firms – if the original firm specializes. In the case of the activities characterized by decreasing costs, the adopting firms will be able to exploit the economies of scale

5. The assumption is explicit in Stigler (1966, Chapter 9, and 1987, Chapter 10).

inherent in the production technologies of these processes by meeting the demand of the firm that is delegating or contracting out and of the other firms that the expanded market has made possible. As the size of the product market continues to expand, the markets for the delegated activities will also increase and become more competitive. In the case of increasing cost processes, the original firms may produce a part of their needed input in-house and delegate or contract out for the remainder of what they need.

In effect, what is happening as a result of the expansion of the product market is an alteration in the relative efficiency or comparative advantage of firms in exploiting the economies and diseconomies of scale associated with certain activities or tasks. As the size of the market increases, the original firm will find that it will be able to compete more effectively in selling its output if it buys some inputs from another firm that can produce them at lower costs than it can itself achieve. Expansion in the size of the market, together with economies and diseconomies of scale, help explain (with other factors analyzed later) the degree of vertical integration of activities and tasks and the degree of vertical "disintegration" [Stigler's (1951, p. 135) word] of others – or, what is the same, the extent of specialization.

I suggest that the division of functions in the sort of governmental system I am, for the moment, postulating is determined in a similar fashion. To see this at its simplest, focus first on a particular expenditure and regulatory function or more precisely on the set of activities and tasks – the set of goods and services – associated with a particular function. I will concentrate on a labor policy function, though I could as easily have chosen to illustrate with functions related to, say, environmental policy, agricultural policy, housing policy, urban policy, educational policy, cultural policy, economic and development policy, defense policy, or welfare policy. In the case of labor policy, the number of tasks and activities that make up the policy is almost limitless. Among them, one finds training, labor exchanges, job security, compensation for injuries, mediation of labor strife, redress against discrimination, unemployment insurance, occupational licensing, and many others.

It is not unreasonable to suppose that the average cost curves associated with the production and delivery of some of these goods and services – with some of these tasks and activities – are U-shaped, that others rise, and that still others fall throughout for relevant rates of production. If that is the case, exactly the same forces modeled by Stigler will be at work and will lead to the vertical integration of some functions and the vertical disintegration of others, that is, to some degree of specialization and a division of functions among jurisdictional levels.

I will be more explicit by looking at a second function, namely, the revenue policy function. Conventional Public Finance discussions of tax administration and tax collection distinguish between enforcement and compliance. The first identifies a governmental activity, whereas the second pertains to the behavior of taxpayers which, one need not add, will affect enforcement. Revenue policy contains more than the tax-collection activities relating to enforcement and compliance, but for the purpose of the present exercise, it is not necessary to be concerned with the other tasks (such as selecting and defining tax bases, setting tax rates and tax brackets when appropriate, choosing exemption and credit levels, and so on).

The tasks and activities associated with the enforcement of tax laws and tax codes include the assessment of tax returns, the selection of samples of returns, the auditing of taxpayers, the prosecution of delinquents, and so on. All these activities require "large" setup expenses on personnel, computers, storage, training, and so on. The setup costs and the learning by doing associated with on-the-job training imply decreasing unit costs as volume expands [see Alchian (1959) and Arrow (1962)]. Average cost curves of that type in turn mean that gains can be realized by delegating tax collection to one or more governments at higher jurisdictional levels.

Compliance relates to tax avoidance and to tax evasion.[6] The volume of avoidance and evasion depends on factors such as the height of tax rates, economies of scale in avoidance, and evasion technologies (Scharf, 1992), "public morality" (Schwartz and Orleans, 1967; Vogel, 1974; Spicer and Lundstedt, 1976), fiscal coordination or harmonization (see Section 8.2, Subsection ii), and others.[7] In what follows, I hold these variables constant – except for coordination, which I examine in the next subsection – and focus on the effect of the number of governments at given jurisdictional levels (on the effect of revenue concentration), on avoidance and evasion.[8] First, it is easier to avoid and evade paying taxes the greater the interjurisdictional mobility of tax bases, the greater the difficulty of appraising their sizes, and the greater the ease of obtaining favorable alterations in bases and rates through political influence. Second, the strength of these factors varies from tax base

6. A literature on optimal evasion (not avoidance), based on the assumption of exogenous governments, that is, of governments that are outside the economy and above economic agents, exists (see, for example, Allingham and Sandmo, 1972; Srinivasan, 1973; and Sandmo, 1981). There is also a related empirical literature on underground economies (for a good survey, see Pommerehne and Frey, 1981). It is not clear how one should read the literature on optimal evasion once governments are endogenized and the sharp distinction between avoidance (legal) and evasion (illegal) no longer permitted (see Chapter 2, footnote 11).

7. For a survey of the literature and for new estimates of all collection costs with an emphasis on compliance costs, see Vaillancourt (1989), and also Vaillancourt and Hébert (1990). The evidence, such as it is, appears consistent with the view that unit costs fall as the size of jurisdictions increases.

8. Recall, from Chapter 7, Section 7.1, that revenue concentration can be defined, as a first approximation, to be the share of revenue collected by the central government level to total revenue collected by all governments of a governmental system.

to tax base. In what follows, I will demonstrate that these variables are related to the number of jurisdictions or governments at any jurisdictional level.

If capital is mobile, its interjurisdictional mobility will increase as the number of jurisdictions increases. As a consequence, when there are more jurisdictions it is easier for anyone to reside in a high-benefit jurisdiction and to invest in one in which tax rates on capital income are low. If jurisdictions are numerous and small enough and if labor income is taxed at source, it is easier to avoid and evade taxes by living in a high-benefit area and working in a low-tax one and easier also to purchase goods and services that are taxed at lower rates outside the jurisdiction of residence.[9] Finally, a large number of jurisdictions increases the incidence of multijurisdiction enterprises and therefore increases the capacity to shift profits among jurisdictions through the use of transfer pricing.

When the number of jurisdictions is large, the number of taxpayers who will earn income and other taxable benefits in a multiplicity of jurisdictions will be larger, thus complicating the reporting problem, that is, the problem of ascertaining the size and location of the tax bases. That too will make avoidance and evasion easier. There is finally the matter of political pressure. To the extent that the effectiveness of these pressures depends on interpersonal relations, we expect that the larger the number of jurisdictions and therefore the smaller their size, the stronger the interpersonal relations. That will also facilitate avoidance and evasion.

The burden of the foregoing discussion is that, *ceteris paribus,* an increase in the degree of revenue concentration will reduce the volume of tax avoidance and evasion and increase the amount of revenues collected. That happens because an increase in revenue concentration means that revenue collection moves to higher jurisdictional tiers where by definition the number of jurisdictions is smaller. Because the mobility of tax bases, the cost of ascertaining their size, and the responsiveness of governments to political pressure are less at higher levels of jurisdiction, more senior governments are relatively more efficient, *ceteris paribus,* than more junior ones at controlling tax avoidance and evasion and therefore at collecting revenues.

We must therefore conclude that the functions and tasks associated with the enforcement and compliance aspects of the revenue policy function possess average cost curves characterized by economies of scale. We should then in turn expect – factors so far not considered held constant – that governments, driven by competition and desirous as a consequence to reap all possible gains, will delegate tax collection to a government higher up in the hierarchy of governmental systems.

9. It is interesting that when tax bases are interjurisdictionally mobile, an increase in detection probabilities or penalty rates by one government will lead to *more,* not to less, evasion as the optimum tax evasion models, cited in footnote 6, conclude.

Before moving on to the analysis of coordination costs, there are two issues that the foregoing discussion already allows us to address. The first is suggested by the literature. Should revenue concentration be analyzed, as I have done, as a manifestation of competition operating to exploit the advantages offered by technology or, following Brennan and Buchanan (1983), as a manifestation of cartelization and monopoly? Brennan and Buchanan conceive of a situation in which lower-level governments "*cede* their powers to tax to a higher level of government in return for an appropriate share in the total revenue: the whole intergovernmental grant/revenue-sharing structure can then be treated as a means of sharing the profits from political cartelization" (1983, p. 62, emphasis added). As a consequence of the reassignment of the power to tax, the higher-level government then becomes a monopolist; lower-level governments will therefore no longer engage in beneficial tax competition.

It is sometimes difficult to decide whether a particular phenomenon is a reflection of competition or of monopoly. Take the celebrated cases of resale price maintenance and exclusive territories, which for a long time were taken to be *prima facie* evidence of monopoly in the marketplace but are now seen as consistent with, nay, called for by competition [see, for example, Klein and Murphy (1988)]. Stigler (1951, p. 133) recognized that the delegated decreasing cost process would make the receiving firm – the delegatee – at least temporarily into a monopolist. He also noted, however, that it would be a monopoly facing very elastic demands because it could not charge a price for its output higher than the average cost of that output to the firm ceding it. Lower-level governments are in the same kind of relationship with the higher-level monopoly ones.

As the language used by Brennan and Buchanan (1983) makes clear, the monopoly of central governments is not achieved by force or capture but by cession or delegation from junior governments. In such a model, as distinguished from that of Brennan and Jonathan Pincus (1990) – to which I return later – the lower-level governments are implicitly identified, in my view correctly, as the principals and the central governments as agents in principal–agent relationships. That kind of model is not consistent with cartelization and monopoly, except of the most fragile variety and of a variety that brings about a more efficient allocation of resources (however, see Section 8.2, Subsection iv).

The second issue pertains to the divisions of functions themselves. These divisions will have two characteristics. First, these divisions are not likely to be neat airtight assignments such as those called for by "classical federalism" à la Wheare (1963). Instead, we should expect governments at different jurisdictional levels to be involved in different activities and tasks – in supplying different goods and services – associated with particular functions such as police protection, road construction, international affairs, financial regulation, administration of justice, and health, in addition to those listed earlier and, of course, many others. Under the postulated circumstances, concurrency – joint occupation of functions though not, one should stress, of activities, tasks, and processes – is the rule. This is why the Salmon mechanism (for a discussion, see Chapter 7, Section 7.2 and Chapter 9, Section 9.1) is capable of motivating vertical competition.

In addition, it is important to keep in mind, first, that even if governments at different tiers supply different goods and services, that does *not* mean that all governments at a particular tier supply a given good or service. Some jurisdictions may be too small or too large to accommodate efficient technologies, and then the activities and tasks of which this is true will be assigned higher up or lower down as circumstances warrant. Second, if all processes and tasks associated with a function are characterized by economies of scale – as was the case for the activities of the revenue policy function examined earlier – all the activities and therefore the whole function will be assigned to central governments. On the other hand, if all tasks are characterized by increasing costs, all the activities and processes and therefore the whole function will be assigned to governments at a junior level of jurisdiction. The prevalence of concurrency would seem to indicate that these instances are not widespread. (On the question of overlap and duplication, see Appendix F.) The second characteristic of divisions of functions that follows from the foregoing analysis is that only by accident will revenue concentration be equal to expenditure concentration, so that vertical imbalance and the consequent intergovernmental flow of funds are features of virtually all governmental systems. I am now, however, running slightly ahead of my story. I must turn my attention immediately to the effect of coordination costs on the foregoing results.

ii.   *Coordination costs*

The division of revenue and expenditure functions (including regulatory and redistribution functions) may exceed or fall short of what competition and technology alone would call for because of the presence of other factors that also impinge on the division of functions. One of these factors, already placed in center stage by Breton and Scott (1978), is coordination costs. Three problems related to these costs need to be examined: One pertains to their origin; a second to their nature; and a third to the way they influence technical outcomes.

a. Origin: Breton and Scott (1978), still laboring under the dominion of models of the assignment of functions based on intergovernmental spillovers

– virtually all the economic models (as distinguished from the constitutional models) that had preceded their own – placed the origin of coordination and hence of coordination costs solely on spillovers, neighborhood effects, and beggar-thy-neighbor policies. Examples of these external effects are easy to come by. The development of a community center in a jurisdiction, because it would provide to young people interesting things to do, could reduce the incidence of crime in that jurisdiction *and* in a neighboring one that would then become the beneficiary of the spillover. But unless the two jurisdictions coordinate their efforts, the center will not be built if its costs exceed its benefits to the first jurisdiction in isolation. The unilateral erection of trade barriers between two provinces or states is a way of dumping local unemployment from one jurisdiction to the other. By judiciously selecting and tailoring tax bases, it is possible for a government to export a part of the burden of its taxes to the citizens of other jurisdictions. These are examples of external effects that can be addressed through coordination – that is, by expending money, time, and effort on formulating jointly acceptable solutions to the problems they pose. There can be no doubt that spillovers and neighborhood effects can create a genuine need for coordination.

In addition, coordination may be required by the existence of complementarities among activities, tasks, and processes – among the goods and services supplied – pertaining to a function or even across functions. For example, among the activities defining the labor policy function discussed earlier, training, ease of moving, information about market conditions (vacancies), and unemployment insurance may all be complementary with one another and also with activities and tasks associated with such other functions as housing, education (schooling), arts and culture, and so on. Complementarities can be upstream or downstream, that is, they can be found among activities that would on strictly technological grounds have to be assigned higher up or lower down than when coordination costs are taken into account.

In the absence of careful empirical work, it is not possible to say whether externalities or complementarities are a more important incitation to coordination, but on the basis of no more than admittedly casual evidence, I would not be surprised to learn that the second is far more important than the first.

b. Nature: There are many instances of successful coordination among the units of governmental systems – for example, the portability of pension plans, the transferability of unemployment and health insurance claims, the integration of police services in matters such as traffic violations and other offenses, the sharing of information on economic trends and crops, and so on. No doubt there are just as many, possibly more, cases of failure to coordinate. It would therefore be possible by looking at all or at a subset of these events, to acquire a solid idea concerning the nature and properties of coordination costs – the costs that allow or impede coordination.[10] That would be a major undertaking and certainly one beyond the scope of this volume. Consequently, my aim will be more modest. At a conceptual level, I will seek to assemble some of the more important elements that can explain why coordination in the area of taxation – tax harmonization – is sometimes successful and sometimes not. I leave to the reader the task of similar exercises in other areas.

Notwithstanding the existence of a considerable, though largely prescriptive, literature on the subject, tax harmonization and, more important, the cost of tax harmonization, remain poorly understood phenomena. For example, it is often tacitly assumed that the costs of adopting common definitions for variables such as income, tax brackets, deductions, exemptions, and credits are high and, therefore, that the standardization that makes it easy for junior governments, in Cliff Walsh's (1991, p. 11) words, to "piggy-back" on the tax system of the senior government difficult to achieve. Still, the marginal cost to central governments of administering special provisions in the income tax forms for each province or state is not likely to be large – depending on nothing more than a little extra complexity in computer programs and a few additional clerks and tax auditors – so that central governments could easily administer a separate rate for every deduction, credit, or special provision by simply mailing different forms to people, depending on their province or state of origin.

Tax harmonization is costly because (1) it is the product of an exercise in coming to an agreement and as such, it absorbs scarce resources; (2) it constrains junior governments by reducing or even suppressing their autonomy to exploit monopolistic or quasi-monopolistic advantages and/or to overcome idiosyncratic disadvantages; and (3) it inhibits the capacity of junior governments to compete with other governments located at the same jurisdictional level.[11]

The costs of harmonization depend on the number of jurisdictions that have to be party to an agreement to make that agreement worthwhile. These costs will increase, possibly more than proportionally, as numbers increase. Harmonization costs will also depend on precedents, on conventions derived from historical compromises, and on the distance initially separating the contracting parties. Loss of autonomy will be small – possibly nil – for a jurisdiction that possesses no natural advantage that could be exploited or no natural disadvantage that could be surmounted by adopting tax measures that departed from those incorporated in a tax harmonization agreement. But if a jurisdiction possesses a real monopolistic advantage it could exploit or a

10. For an excellent analysis of coordination between Canada's central and provincial governments in three different policy areas, see Simeon (1972).
11. The advantages are of the same kind as those that give substance to the theory of optimum tariffs (see, among many discussions, Johnson, 1953–4).

specific disadvantage it could void by special tax measures, the loss in autonomy caused by tax harmonization could be a significant cost. The ability to compete – which depends on a host of factors including, as Stanley Winer (1992, p. 359) pointedly reminds us, on the ability to fine-tune tax bases, credits, deductions, exemptions, and other provisions of the tax code – will be reduced by tax harmonization. That could impose much heavier costs on some jurisdictions than on others. The need to compete and, therefore, the cost of tax harmonization may also be less in the presence of efficient regional development policies implemented by senior governments.

The decision to harmonize and the degree of tax harmonization will, as a consequence, be the outcome of a balancing of the discounted marginal benefits of specialization (consequent on the division of the revenue function) against the marginal costs of tax harmonization. Countries and jurisdictions in which the expected benefits from the economies of scale in tax collection are large may still rationally shun tax harmonization completely if the number of jurisdictions that have to coordinate is large and the costs of lost autonomy and the hindrance to competition are significant. These countries and jurisdictions will be characterized by a relatively low degree of revenue concentration. At the other end of the spectrum, countries and jurisdictions in which the number of governments is small and none of which has significant unique advantages or disadvantages or a specific capacity to compete may still harmonize even if benefits of specialization are small. In these countries and jurisdictions the degree of revenue concentration will be relatively high.

These considerations provide a rationale, even in the presence of significant economies of scale in tax collection, for the absence of tax collection agreements between Washington and the American states such as those that exist between Ottawa and the Canadian provinces. It also allows us to understand the decision of the governments of Alberta, Ontario, and Quebec to collect their own corporation income taxes and, in part (for the rest of the explanation, see Section 8.2, Subsection iii), for the decision of the government of Quebec to withdraw from the Tax Collection Agreements in respect of the personal income tax.[12]

c. *Effects:* In their discussion of coordination costs, Breton and Scott (1978) defend the hypothesis that as these costs increase, functions – activities and tasks – will move upward in the tier hierarchy of governmental systems to economize on the resources that coordination absorbs. Conversely, as coordination costs fall, functions will travel downward, thus reducing the degree

12. In the opinion of Strick (1985, p. 93) and in that of Musgrave, Musgrave, and Bird (1987, p. 381), whom I quote, Alberta, Ontario, and Quebec "tend to consider them [the corporate tax rate differentials] a major factor [in locations decisions] and therefore engage in low-rate competition to attract capital."

of concentration (in the language of their book, the degree of centralization) of governmental systems.

That proposition, however, is true only if it is assumed that the technologies that support the activities and processes associated with functions are all characterized by constant returns to scale or long-term constant unit costs of production and supply. If we assume instead that functions, activities, and tasks are characterized by economies of large scale, low coordination costs will be associated with high concentration. In the case of revenue collection, for example, it appears that the tax collection technologies display significant economies of scale. Assuming this to be the case, high coordination costs would prevent the exploitation of these economies and lead to a lower degree of revenue concentration than technological considerations alone would have dictated. Consider another case. Suppose that the production technologies of the activities and tasks associated with the housing policy function are all characterized by significant diseconomies of scale calling for a low degree of concentration of the function. High coordination costs in respect of the function's various activities and tasks would call, on grounds of efficiency, for a higher degree of concentration than technology alone would.

The general conclusion must therefore be as follows:

1. In the presence of constant average costs of producing activities and tasks, low coordination costs call for low concentration, and high coordination costs for high concentration – the traditional result.
2. In the presence of increasing unit costs of production, low coordination costs require low, possibly lower, concentration, and high coordination costs demand higher concentration, than technology alone would call for.
3. In the presence of decreasing average costs of production, low (high) coordination costs call for more (less) concentration than technology alone does.

iii.   Contractual enforcement costs

To proceed, I assume that the equilibrium outcome of the workings of competition constrained by technology and coordination costs is a governmental system in which there is more concentration in revenue collection than in the provision of goods and services, which conventional treatment identifies, not always felicitously, with the expenditure, regulatory, and redistribution functions. For the sake of completeness, I should mention that a high level of revenue concentration can be achieved in one of two ways but that one dominates the other. First, lower-level – local and provincial or state – governments can delegate all or part of the revenue collection function to a more senior government and, through this choice, give rise to a governmental system characterized by vertical imbalance and intergovernmental flows of funds from the top to the bottom. Or, second, they may decide to create their own tax collection agency. If economies of scale in tax collection are at all significant, the first alternative will always be chosen because the second, though it leads to the exploitation of some economies of scale, leads to an exploitation that is necessarily less than that which is possible when the collection of the senior government's revenue is also part of the package.

Lower-level governments will delegate the revenue collection function to a more senior government to be able to deliver goods and services to their citizens at lower unit costs and, through the consequent reduction in (marginal) taxprices, to minimize the utility losses inflicted on these same citizens. That will be possible only if senior (sometimes federal and sometimes provincial or state) and junior (sometimes provincial or state and sometimes local) governments can enter into contractual agreements that make it possible for the first to guarantee that taxes will be efficiently collected and efficiently transferred to the second. If an enforceable contract cannot be drawn up, the competition that is calling for a greater degree of revenue concentration than of expenditure concentration will not be allowed to yield its beneficial effects.

To understand the nature of contractual relations between senior and junior governments and in particular the nature of the contractual enforcement problem in the presence of vertical fiscal imbalance, it is important to be aware that this imbalance can be accommodated in one or both of two ways. First, the senior government can act as a revenue collection agency for the junior governments, much in the way the central government in Canada, through the Tax Collection Agreements, does for the provinces (except Quebec) in respect of the personal income tax. I will henceforth call the sums thus collected by senior governments and returned to junior governments, *remittances*. Second, the senior government can raise revenues that it delivers to the junior governments as conditional transfers. I will call these second sums *revenue payments*.[13]

Intergovernmental contracts relating to vertical fiscal imbalance and to the resulting flow of funds between governments are both necessarily incomplete and implicit contracts. A complete contract would specify all relevant contingencies over the life of the contract, foresee a course of action for each of these contingencies, deny the signatories the possibility of renegotiation so as not to deprive the original agreement of its credibility, and provide for each contingency, before the contract is signed, a mechanism for dispute settlement that is satisfactory to all parties. Most contracts are, given these requirements,

13. This chapter is not concerned with the intergovernmental transfers, which are sometimes used to stabilize horizontal intergovernmental competition and which I call "stabilizing grants." These are discussed in Chapter 9, Section 9.4, Subsection ii, c.

incomplete. If incomplete contracts are supplemented with unarticulated and generally shared expectations and understandings, they are said to be *implicit*.

In regard to intergovernmental flows of funds, the idea that relations between governments have characteristics that place them (the relations) in the category of incomplete and implicit contracts is not new. It can be traced back at least to the work of Martin McGuire (1975, 1979) and to that of Ernst Zampelli (1986). Recently, Brennan and Pincus (1990) have argued that contracts regulating grants from central to provincial or state governments contain tacit "provisos, riders, or contingencies" (p. 129) and that, as a consequence, all grants are conditional. The tacit provisos, riders, or contingencies imply that in the conventional framework of analysis, all grants have substitution as well as income effects. Brennan and Pincus in effect tell us that donors are not disinterested or neutral in regard to the sums they grant. They do not tell us, however, why these donors are concerned and interested in the behavior of recipients. Brennan and Pincus, like McGuire and Zampelli, though they allude to or make use of the concept of implicit contracts, do not use the rich economic theory that has developed in respect of these contracts.

In the present context, namely, the one in which senior governments are, as it were, hired by junior governments to collect their revenues, incomplete and implicit contracts have two particularly important facets. First, even if junior governments (the principals) through monitoring can observe, say, a degree of shirking in tax collection by the senior government (their agent), they cannot demonstrate to a third party (a court, say) that the senior government has indeed breached the contract and caused them damages – the contract is said to be nonverifiable. Incompleteness and implicitness also mean, and that is the second crucial facet of these contracts, that reverse cheating is possible: Principals can breach contracts just as well as agents can. Specifically, junior governments can renege on contractual undertakings as much as senior governments can.

If, as is dictated by the fact of nonverifiability, enforcement by third parties is not possible and if trust is ruled out on the ground that intergovernmental relations are too fickle for trust to form the basis of long-term enforcement, contractual relations will be possible only if contracts are self-enforcing. Self-enforcement requires that both principals (in the case under analysis, junior governments, namely, provincial or state or municipal governments) and agents (central or provincial or state governments) can credibly commit to perform the tasks specified in the implicit incomplete contractual agreement. Put differently, each must be seen by the other as having something to lose from the termination of the contract consequent on nonperformance.

From theory (for example, Klein, Crawford, and Alchian, 1978; Klein and Leffler, 1981; and Williamson, 1975, 1985) we know that if junior governments choose to rely on a self-enforcing contract, they must be able to create a valuable stream of (political) quasi-rents and deliver that stream to the senior government. The capital loss that the principals can then impose on the agent by extinguishing that stream will be sufficient to induce the agent to perform as long as the present value of the delivered stream exceeds the present value of the advantages of nonperformance. Can junior governments create such streams of quasi-rents? The answer to this question is "yes." A demonstration of the affirmation requires, however, that we distinguish between remittances and revenue payments.

In the case of remittances – the sums returned by the senior to the junior governments on the basis of some revenue collection agreement – the quasi-rents are created, as already argued, by the exploitation of economies of scale consequent on the greater ability of senior governments to control tax avoidance and evasion than that of junior governments. Note that the flow of quasi-rents accruing to senior governments will be greater, the larger the fraction of their own tax revenues that junior governments delegate for collection to the senior government. Indeed, given the economies of scale, the unit cost of tax funds *to the senior government* will diminish as that fraction increases.

In delegating tax collection to senior governments, junior governments create a stream of quasi-rents that *can* benefit those senior governments. It *will* do so, however, only if a particular condition is satisfied. To appreciate what that condition is, consider what would happen, in an admittedly extreme case, if the factors discussed in the last two subsections called for a division of functions that demanded that the tax revenues of the entire governmental system had to be raised by senior governments and that all of them had to be spent by the junior governments. The only expense of senior governments under these circumstances would be remittances to the junior governments. As a consequence, the value of low-cost tax funds to senior governments would be zero and so would the value of the stream of quasi-rents. Only if senior governments provide some goods and services to citizens can they themselves benefit from the low unit cost of tax funds. These benefits will rise as the volume of goods and services supplied increases, or to put it differently, the value of the stream of political quasi-rents increases as expenditures concentration also increases.

More generally, if the factors governing the division of functions call for a low degree of expenditure concentration and if there are economies of scale in tax collection that can technically be exploited, the required volume of remittances may be so large and the value of the stream of political quasi-rents accruing to the senior government consequently so low that that stream will be unable to insure performance on the part of that government. To guarantee performance – to control shirking, negligence, and other forms of inefficient behavior in tax collection – the volume of remittances will have to be reduced below what would be possible in a world in which the cost of insuring performance was zero. The inherent conflict between the benefits of a high degree of revenue concentration and the benefits of a low degree of expenditure concentration implies that there are limits in the extent to which remittances can be used to create a stream of valuable political quasi-rents that can be delivered to senior governments to insure performance.

The volume of remittances will therefore be determined by two factors: (1) the cost of tax harmonization; and (2) the value of reductions in the unit cost of tax revenues to senior governments. If, for example, the expenditures of senior governments on own-goods and own-services decline significantly so that low-cost tax funds generate only a limited stream of quasi-rents and if the costs of harmonization increase, senior and junior governments may not be able to enter into contractual arrangements in respect of remittances that would permit much exploitation of the economies of scale in tax collection.

Does that limit on the volume of remittances imply that relevant economies of scale in tax collection cannot be exploited, or that the degree of expenditure concentration has to be greater, or both, than that called for by the division of functions reflecting the relative efficiencies or comparative advantage of competing governments as reflected in production technologies? The answer is "no." All economies of scale in tax collection can be exploited, and the optimal division of functions can be achieved by making use of what I have earlier called revenue payments. These transfers permit the exploitation or, if remittances already exist, the further exploitation of economies of scale in tax collection, and they allow junior governments to spend the sums transferred on the goods and services that they produce and deliver relatively efficiently.

The revenue payments must be conditional, and the conditions have to be specified in terms of particular goods and services supplied. Why? Remember that the problem remains one of insuring that senior governments find it in their own interest to abide by the terms of an incomplete contract and act as efficient tax collectors for the junior governments. That can happen only if the revenue payments create a sufficiently large stream of political quasi-rents for senior governments that they will not want to risk losing it through nonperformance. These conditions will in the first instance, therefore, attach the revenue payments to goods and services that are in high demand and for which demand is relatively easy to estimate, thus reducing the utility losses resulting from supply. Typically, these goods and services will be educational services, health and hospital care, vocational and other forms of training, transportation services, care of the blind and of other disabled persons, and so on. As times and circumstances change, the demand for goods and services may change, the volume demanded may become more difficult to appraise, or both – thus increasing the chances of providing quantities and qualities that differ more markedly from those desired – and the conditions that attach to the revenue payments will also change.

Two complementary points should be made. First, the conditions that attach to the transfers are willed by the junior governments; these are the governments that wish to create the stream of political quasi-rents for the benefit of the senior government. Second, senior governments will as a rule have a say in the formulation of the conditions and will monitor how well the conditions are adhered to, simply because the conditions are the factors that cause the stream of quasi-rents accruing to them to be created. The available evidence indicates that the conditions are, indeed, negotiated as suggested earlier [see, for example, Bella (1979), Chernick (1979), and Strick (1971)].

Two other problems must be addressed to complete the analysis. The foregoing discussion tells us that junior governments are capable of creating a stream of political quasi-rents to induce senior governments to exploit the relevant economies of scale in tax collection and to pay the sums collected to junior governments either as remittances or as revenue payments. That discussion did not, however, tell us why senior governments could expect the junior governments to adhere to their side of the contract. It did not tell us why senior governments should expect the junior governments to continue to deliver the stream of quasi-rents they are capable of creating if circumstances change in such a way that it becomes advantageous for them not to deliver. It does not tell us, either, why junior governments would be efficient suppliers of the goods and services to which the conditions of the revenue payments attach. Both problems are easily dealt with. I consider them in turn.

Junior governments must not only be able to create a stream of political quasi-rents for the benefit of the senior governments; they must also be able to make a credible commitment that they will continue to deliver that stream as long as senior governments perform, that is, do not shirk on tax collection. Such a commitment is possible for both remittances and revenue payments if the costs to the junior governments of raising their own revenues – of forgoing the economies of scale in tax collection – exceed the sums that have to be paid to senior governments for the collection service *plus* the costs, expressed in comparable monetary units, of creating the political quasi-rents.

We must recognize that the costs of contracting or, more precisely, the costs of contractual enforcement may be so high that the division of functions called for by competition constrained by technology and coordination costs may not be possible. In other words, if the supply price of tax collection or the costs of creating a stream of (political) quasi-rents are "high," it may not be possible to achieve the division of functions called for by the unit costs of producing and supplying activities and tasks on the one hand and the cost of coordinating these activities and tasks on the other. For example, in some federations at certain times, because of widespread negative feelings vis-à-vis the senior government in one or more junior units, the costs of creating a flow of

political quasi-rents to the benefit of that senior government are so high that
these units will choose to forgo the benefits of an optimal division of functions. That, I suggest, is what led the government of the province of Quebec
as early as 1947 to seek and to gain control of the personal and corporate tax
fields and to continue to stay out of the collection agreements. In general,
such decisions inflict losses on the whole governmental system – the supply
price of goods and services is higher for all – but the losses are larger for the
unit or units that choose to collect their own taxes.

Turning to the second problem, that of the efficient performance of junior
governments in supplying the goods and services to which the conditions of
revenue payments apply, it is sufficient to recognize that if the stream of
political quasi-rents is appropriately divided between the senior and junior
governments or, put differently, if the conditions that attach to the revenue
payments generate large enough political quasi-rents for both levels of government, junior governments will have an incentive to perform efficiently.
To see why, consider what would happen if the whole stream of quasi-rents
accrued to the senior government. Under such circumstances, the junior governments would have no incentive to perform, that is, to be efficient providers
of the goods and services financed by the revenue payments. An appropriate
division of the political surpluses is needed to deal with the reverse cheating
problem.

The conventional model of intergovernmental grants based on the assumption that the origin of grants is exogenous to the analysis makes a prediction
that has been tested empirically by a number of scholars [the classic paper is
Gramlich (1977); see also, for a good survey of the empirical literature, Fisher
(1982)]. The prediction is the following: If \$X is received by a junior govern-
ment in the form of an unconditional transfer, a fraction of \$X will be spent on
the goods and services supplied by that junior government. The rest will serve
to reduce taxes and thus lead to an increase in private- or market-supplied
goods and services bought by citizens, as long as privately and publicly
provided goods are normal goods. When tested, the evidence indicated that if
not all of \$X, at least a larger fraction than expected is spent by junior
governments and, as a consequence, little, relative to what should have been
expected, takes the form of tax reductions. Edward Gramlich (1977) called
the anomaly the "flypaper effect," a colorful expression designed to describe
the fact that money appears to stick where it hits.

This chapter does not deal with unconditional grants proper, that is, with
stabilizing transfers, which I will later associate with equalization payments
and revenue-sharing. But because of the position taken by Bird and Jack
Mintz (1992, pp. 22–3) and others [see Musgrave, Musgrave, and Bird
(1987, p. 512)] that, in Canada at least, "so-called conditional grants pro-

grams (such as grants for education) actually have few conditions attached to them," I must consider the various views taken with respect to the flypaper effect and state what the model proposed here implies about this effect.[14]

Early explanations of the flypaper effect appealed to fiscal illusion and to bureaucratic empire building. More recently – in recognition, no doubt, of the inherent weakness of explanations based on assumptions of irrationality and inefficient behavior – analysts have been arguing that whatever the legal and formal terms in which grant programs are embodied, there are always, often only very implicit, provisos that effectively transform all grants into matching conditional grants. In the more recent framework of analysis, all grants – whether formally unconditional or whether effectively untied as is the case, except for corner solutions, with specific-purpose grants – have substitution effects, so that it is not necessary to appeal to a flypaper effect to explain why money sticks where it hits.

More recently still, Brennan and Pincus (1991), building on an earlier analysis of Fisher (1982), have argued that because the citizens of governmental systems are citizens of both junior and senior jurisdictions and, *a fortiori*, are taxpayers and consumers of the goods and services at the two levels, intergovernmental grants have no net income effects whatsoever, only substitution effects. The positive income effect enjoyed by individuals in their role as citizens of a grant-receiving junior jurisdiction is canceled by the negative income effect suffered by those same individuals as citizens of the grant-paying senior jurisdiction. Redistributional effects may exist, but overall the positive and negative income effects will cancel each other out to yield a zero net income effect. Brennan and Pincus (1991, p. 2) claim that the conventional model of intergovernmental grants is really a model of international aid, not one of federal aid.

The difficulty with the first "new" explanation of intergovernmental money flows – that based on implicit adjustments by recipients à la McGuire or on implicit provisos by donors à la Brennan and Pincus – is that it provides no rationale for these flows (grants are exogenously determined), and it assumes that decisionmakers are always and exclusively senior governments. In the McGuire (1975, 1979) and Zampelli (1986) explanation, the junior governments, unhappy to be victims of particular grant programs they do not like, seek redress by disguised manipulations of the terms of the contract, and hapless senior governments do nothing about it. In the Brennan and Pincus

14. The view of Brennan and Pincus (1990) that (in Australia at least) unconditional grants always have implicit conditions attached to them seems in contradiction with the position of Bird and Mintz (1992) that (in Canada at least) conditional grants are really unconditional. I suspect that the contradiction is superficial and will dissolve once an appropriate model of intergovernmental money flows is accepted.

(1990) earlier explanation, senior governments, unwilling to give funds without attaching strings to them, covertly tie conditions to the grant. Why senior governments would act that way is unclear; the easiest explanation is that they behave like empire-building leviathans. If so, the presumption must be that the outcome is socially inefficient.

In Brennan and Pincus's (1991) most recent attempt, the existence of intergovernmental grants derives from the preferences of median voters and from the assumption that the excess burden of federal tax funds is smaller than the excess burden of provincial or state tax funds. The explanation for the existence of unconditional grants rests on the assumption that there is a unique median voter – the same at the federal and provincial or state levels of government – who, through grants, economizes on the cost of tax revenues. These grants are therefore efficient. For matching grants, two different median voters are needed – one at each jurisdictional tier. It is assumed that the median voter at the senior level makes the grant. The resulting expenditure level and tax mix are inefficient. This most recent attempt appears to be headed in the direction of producing results not much different from those of conventional models, except that the income effect has been removed.

The model suggested in this chapter is based on an accepted theory of incomplete and implicit contracts, which rests on the assumption that all agents are rational and that resources are used efficiently by them. It does away with the assumption that intergovernmental relations, at least as regards intergovernmental flows of funds, are necessarily master–servant relations. It does not assume that intergovernmental flows of funds are Pigovian subsidies aimed at interjurisdictional spillovers – a plus in a world in which that policy instrument is rarely if ever used; but it does not assume that Pigovian subsidies could not be used to deal with interjurisdictional spillovers. It is able to explain why the degree of expenditure and revenue concentration varies between governmental systems and from period to period. It is able to explain why revenue and expenditure concentration usually differ and, therefore, why vertical fiscal imbalance and the accompanying flows of funds exist. It can explain why transfers from senior to junior governments are often conditional and efficient.[15] It is consistent with the observed fact that governmental systems are sometimes lengthened and sometimes contracted (Breton and Fraschini, 1992). It can explain why the degree of tax harmonization varies from time to time and from context to context. Finally, it establishes naturally that the flypaper effect is not an anomaly of the real world, only an anomaly of a particular theoretical *weltanschauung*.

---

15. I have not analyzed the case when tax funds flow from junior to senior governments, but the model can be adapted to that case relatively easily.

iv.   Caveats

Many other factors no doubt help to determine the division of functions between orders of government. Most, I believe, are insignificant, but two deserve to be mentioned: (1) information costs and (2) conspiracies or collusive arrangements.

a. Information costs: Governments, whatever the location they occupy in governmental systems, can inflict utility losses on their citizens by providing goods and services in quantities (and qualities) that differ from those that at given taxprices and incomes are desired. Scholars have examined a number of factors that are taken to be structural components of governmental systems and that are presumed to induce utility losses. Among them is the "bundling" of goods and services, that is, the provision in a single package of a number of goods and services. Yoram Barzel (1969) has shown that bundling can impose utility losses on citizens.

It has been suggested (Borcherding and Deacon, 1972) that the goods and services supplied by junior governments are more in the nature of (technical) private goods, whereas those provided by senior governments are more like Samuelsonian (1954) public goods. It has also been suggested that populations sort themselves by preferences – or by traits such as language, upbringing, customs, and religions that mold preferences – in such a way that preferences tend to be more homogeneous at lower than at higher tiers of governmental systems. Finally, Tullock (1969) has argued that bundling increases as both the number of goods and services *and* the number of persons to whom they are supplied increases. It then follows, as a matter of definition, that there will be more bundling at higher than at lower jurisdictional levels.

These arguments would seem to imply that in addition to coordination and contractual enforcement costs, the division of functions would also be constrained by the greater ability of governments at lower jurisdictional tiers to unbundle supply, that is, to provide citizens with goods and services in quantities and qualities that better match what they desire. A function, which on the basis of economies of scale alone – and disregarding coordination and contractual enforcement costs – would have to be assigned to a more senior jurisdictional tier would, as a consequence, be located with more junior governments.

Notwithstanding the importance of this line of reasoning in the literature, I believe that it is seriously flawed. In Chapter 2, I have argued that governments impose utility losses on citizens because they lack information about demand functions. As the reader will recall, the reasoning is simple. With perfect information about demand functions, governments can always alter taxprices or find goods and services that are either substitutes for or complements to those that have the character of (technical) public goods and to those that are bundled and, by fine-tuning supply, reduce everyone's utility losses to zero.

To defend the traditional line of reasoning, it is therefore essential to be able to argue that more junior governments can acquire information about demand functions at lower costs than can governments located higher up in the system. That may be the case. Casual observation, however, points to economies of scale in polling, canvassing, and consulting and to economies of size in interest groups or demand lobbies that convey information on the preferences of their members (see Chapter 2, Section 2.3). Furthermore, cliques, family compacts, and other cabals that filter information to governments may be easier to create at more junior levels. Given these possibilities, it is prudent to assume that information costs do not vary systematically with jurisdictional level and have as a consequence no systematic effect on the degree of expenditure and revenue concentration, that is, on the division of functions.

b. Collusion: I have discussed collusion and conspiracies in Chapter 3, Section 3.3 and again in Chapter 5, Section 5.3. I have nothing new to add on the phenomenon here, except to say that collusion may, indeed, exist and when it does, it will affect the resulting division of functions. Although acknowledging the possibility of collusion, I hold to the view that it is better to analyze the division of functions in a model in which competition is sometimes marred by conspiracies than in one in which collusion is the rule, except for brief flashes of competition.

8.3.   The constitutional factor

Although it is not possible to assume, for reasons that have already been suggested, that the formal division of powers determines the distribution of functions, we must recognize that together with other constitutional provisions it does sometimes constrain – John Whyte's (1985) words are "condition . . . , restrict . . . or frustrate . . . " (p. 29) – changes that may be required in the assignment of functions. I do no more in what follows than indicate in broad terms how constitutions and formal divisions of powers constrain what is mandated by competition and technology adjusted for coordination and contractual enforcement costs.

I start with the assumption that in the beginning, before the appearance of any constitution and of any division of powers, competition between governments produces a distribution of functions between jurisdictional levels, resulting in an equilibrium degree of revenue and expenditure concentration. During this initial period, we can presume that rules exist to insure that competitive outcomes are enforced, but there is no formal division of powers to restrict or frustrate the workings of competition. I now assume that in a second period the country we are looking at is given to constitutional experts who, after having deciphered the distribution of functions reflected in the equilibrium degree of revenue and expenditure concentration and in the flows of remittances and revenue payments determined during the initial period, codify all of this in a constitution. As a consequence, they are thereafter known as the Fathers (and/or Mothers) of the Governmental System or simply as the Founding Fathers (and/or Mothers).

Why do the Fathers (and/or Mothers) translate a degree of expenditure and revenue concentration – a division of functions – into a degree of centralization – a constitutional division of powers? They do so to define and fix a pattern of ownership of functions by, as it were, converting functions into powers. As we shall have occasion to ascertain once more in the next chapter (Section 9.4), there are three fundamental patterns of ownership of functions, and each is associated with a particular form of governmental systems, to wit confederalism, unitarianism, and federalism. In the first, all powers are owned by the junior governments, even if some functions have been assigned to senior governments. In the second, all powers are owned by senior governments, even if functions are assigned to junior ones. And, in the third, the ownership of powers is divided among orders of government, though at any one moment some of the functions embodied in a particular central government power may have been assigned to junior governments, or vice versa.

The patterns of ownership and assignments – the division of powers and functions – are especially important when exogenous disturbances require changes in one or in both. Change always reflects the influence of history, political culture, prejudice, interests, and last but not least, political power. These various factors are, however, necessarily channeled or work themselves through one or the other pattern of ownership. Specifically, decisions pertaining to changes in assignment are unilateral in confederal and unitary states, but they are bilateral and more often multilateral in federal states. One should, therefore, expect that the biases imparted by history, political culture, and prejudice and the distorting influence of interests and power to be less in federal than in confederal and unitary states. It is not the division of functions among orders of government or intergovernmental competition that accounts for the superiority of federalism over confederalism and unitarianism, since functions are divided and competition exists in all governmental systems. It is in the pattern of ownership of powers and in the procedures (based on the equality of all participants) used to alter that pattern of ownership that one finds the fundamental superiority of the federal form of government. These procedures serve as a protection against abuse of power, trespass, legerdemain, and unilateral abrogation of agreements, which, even if they are not illegal may not be efficient.

Assume that in a third period there is an exogenous disturbance that leads to a change in the equilibrium degree of concentration established in the initial period. Should we expect this change to produce a corresponding change in the degree of constitutional centralization? The answer depends on the nature of the disturbance. Suppose, to illustrate, that the constitution drafted during the second period entrenches the power over education in provinces or states. An exogenous shock that called for an increase in expenditures on that function might or might not call for a change in the division of powers. If the increase in expenditures was large, the need for more revenues could lead to a further concentration of revenue collection and to a larger flow of revenue payments to the provinces or states, requiring adjustments that could be accommodated within the framework of the constitution of the second period. However, if the greater concentration of revenue collection cannot be achieved because the formal constitutional division of powers raises the costs of coordination, of contractual enforcement, or of both, then the formal assignment of powers will be altered.

Changes can be effected in many ways – through formal amendments of the constitution, through judicial reinterpretation based on jurisprudence, or through negotiations between the various units of governmental systems. In federal governmental systems, formal constitutional amendments are difficult to achieve and are, as a consequence, little used. They are, however, a preferred instrument for change in unitary states because constitutional amendments are often no more than changes in the legislation of central governments. In federal states, the assignment of powers – their division as well as the functions they embody – is continuously tested in the courts, so that judicial review and reinterpretation are important instruments to alter constitutions. These instruments are not as widely used and for obvious reasons in unitary states. Negotiations over powers (and other related matters) have been identified by some students of federalism [for example Friedrich (1968)] as being central to an understanding of how federal governmental systems work. These writers distinguish between the structure of governmental systems – the degree of concentration and of centralization – and what they call "the process of federalism," and they claim that we should focus on the latter in analyzing federal states. One reason for the claim is that structure, it is argued, can explain little of what we observe in intergovernmental relations. Another is that those federal structures – the former Soviet Union, for example – in which process has been suppressed are not federal states in any meaningful sense [for a good discussion of the matter, see Elazar (1987)]. One need not accept fully the conception of governmental systems advocated by that school of thought to recognize that process plays an important role in federal systems in moving ownership patterns from one configuration to another and that it is less salient in confederal and unitary states.

8.4.   The Wicksellian Connection remembered

The forces described in Part I that foster and tighten Wicksellian Connections operate in the same way in governmental systems as they do in single governmental units. The only reason for recalling the Wicksellian Connection in this chapter is the long and solidly held conviction of many Public Finance economists that vertical fiscal imbalance and the intergovernmental flows of funds that it necessarily implies breaks the connection between revenues and expenditures and leads to fiscal illusion, bureaucratic manipulation, and waste (see Section 8.1 for some references to the relevant literature). In view of the assumption strongly held by mainstream Public Finance that there is no relationship between revenues and expenditures except an accounting one, in the budget making of single isolated governments, that position is somewhat mysterious.

The purpose of Part I was to establish that a Wicksellian Connection between taxprices and quantities demanded is forged by intragovernmental competition. Must that conclusion be rejected when the analysis moves from single governments to governmental systems? The foregoing discussion has made it clear that vertical fiscal imbalance under competitive conditions does not lead to an undoing or unfastening of the Wicksellian Connection built earlier. Indeed, how could a division of functions and of powers that minimizes the real resource cost of supplying goods and services through specialization, the coordination costs of harmonizing spillover flows and complementarities, and the contractual enforcement costs of insuring efficient performance destroy Wicksell–Lindahl efficiency? On the contrary, we should expect intergovernmental competition to reinforce the results of intragovernmental competition and to generate an overall allocation of resources in which utility losses are even smaller than they would be in single-tier unitary states.

It is true that collusion and conspiracies among governments can lead to insufficient or to excessive specialization. It is also true that what I have called the "constitutional factor" can lead to the same outcomes. However, given that multilateral negotiations between equals, litigation involving equals, and constitutional amendments accepted by equals will generate changes in the formal constitutional division of powers that more faithfully track alterations in expenditure and revenue concentration – in the division of supply responsibilities – in federal than in confederal and unitary governmental systems, we should expect the constitutional factor to be less an obstacle to efficient adjustments in the first than in the second types of governmental systems. We should expect patterns of ownership of powers in federal, more than in confederal and unitary states, to accommodate smoothly the modifications in the division of functions that are needed and thus insure the minimization of all costs – production, delivery, coordination, and contractual enforcement – called for by competition. Under these circumstances, we expect the Wicksellian Connection to be such that utility losses are small in all governmental systems but especially in federal systems. We expect intergovernmental competition in all types of governmental systems but especially in federal states to lead to the revelation of the citizenry's true demand functions for government-supplied goods and services.

The reader will recall that in Chapter 4 we established a presumption that utility losses would be smaller in parliamentary than in congressional systems of government. This presumption combined with the foregoing discussion implies that it is in federal parliamentary systems of government that utility losses are the smallest and the Wicksellian Connection the tightest – a conclusion that I myself would have rejected only a few years ago (Breton, 1985).

8.5.   Conclusion

After a review of earlier work, this chapter has proposed a model of the causes and consequences of vertical fiscal imbalance in governmental systems in which vertical competition exists. In that model, governments specialize in the production and supply of certain goods and services. Specialization in turn calls for coordination; it also leads to vertical imbalance and to the necessity of intergovernmental flows of funds. These can be effected only if self-enforcing contracts can be "signed," because the necessarily implicit and incomplete nature of contracts among governments precludes third-party enforcement. The self-enforcing contracts provide an explanation for conditional grants and for other characteristics of intergovernmental relations. The model suggested also implies that it is specialization in response to the obligation to minimize production, coordination, and contractual enforcement costs forced on governments by competition that determines the formal constitutional division of powers and not the other way around. Finally, it is argued that contrary to a prevalent belief, the Wicksellian Connection is not weaker but stronger in governmental systems than in isolated governments and that that proposition is especially true for federal systems of government.

CHAPTER 9

Competition, stability, and central governments

In many models of governmental systems, the focus is exclusively on the division of powers between two or more jurisdictional levels of government.[1] When that orientation is forced on the analyst by a political theory of sovereignty in which states are assumed to be independent and separate entities, the analyst is compelled, as was Wheare (1963), to a view of federal governmental systems in which the assignment of powers is so airtight that there can be no interaction between central governments and the constituent units – which I will continue to call provinces or states. Furthermore, if the assignment of powers is optimal in the sense that all relevant spillovers are internalized when powers are divided (Breton, 1965; Olson, 1969; Oates, 1972), there is no interaction between the provinces or states, either.

When, however, the analysis of the division of powers is governed by observation of real-world governmental systems, intergovernmental interactions – originating in spillovers of various sorts (including the transfer of tax burdens), in overlapping or concurrent powers, in interjurisdictional mobility, and in other factors – play a role in the modeling of these systems, but strangely enough that role has historically often been a largely prescriptive one. It is these interactions that have provided the grounds for discussion of "cooperative federalism" (see, among many, Elazar, 1966; Grodzins, 1966; and Riker, 1975) and of "executive federalism" (Smiley, 1980).

As we have seen (Chapter 8), the division of powers is an important, indeed fundamental, feature of all governmental systems, but if one's motivation and preoccupation are an understanding of how these systems behave in the real world, it is not a feature that should be finessed into eliminating horizontal and even vertical intergovernmental competition. There is a relationship between the division of powers and its formal entrenchment on the one hand and the vigor and character of competition on the other, but neither the division of powers nor its entrenchment are the causes or sources of competition, whether horizontal or vertical, though they can be used to reduce or even to extinguish competition.

1. An exception is Riker (1975), who argues that the division of powers in federations is of no consequence and, in any case, has given rise to no solid body of theory. Another exception is the political science literature concerned with intrastate federalism (see Section 9.5, Subsection iii.b).

One way of understanding this point is by reference to standard economic theory. The organization of industry – the number of firms, their distribution by size, the extent of vertical and horizontal integration – helps to determine the degree and character of interfirm competition, but the origin of the competition is the efforts of firms to maximize profits or some other index. In a similar fashion, the organization of governmental systems helps to determine the degree and character of intergovernmental competition, but organization is not its origin. To illustrate, assume that when a large fraction of all constitutional powers, appropriately weighted, is assigned to the center, the federation is centralized and in the opposite case that it is decentralized. Then, in a highly centralized federation, even if horizontal competition is vigorous, it will be over few and insignificant powers and, as a consequence, not of great significance in terms of the overall allocation of resources. Vertical competition, moreover, will be weak because the junior governments are deprived of the wherewithal to compete with the more senior governments. For example, the former Soviet Union was a highly centralized federation in which competition among the republics was always evanescent and that between Moscow and the governments of these republics insignificant. The American and Canadian federations, on the other hand, are incomparably more decentralized, and as a consequence, both horizontal and vertical competition are brisk and pervasive. In some unitary states, a large proportion of all powers is vested in the central government and, as a consequence, intergovernmental competition in these states resembles that among governments in the former Soviet Union.

The next section returns in more detail than hitherto (Chapter 7, Section 7.1, Subsection i) to the Tiebout and Salmon mechanisms that motivate competition between governments. Section 9.2 presents some secondary empirical evidence that documents that horizontal competition exists as well as some of the forms it can take. (For a discussion of other forms, see Kenyon, 1991). Section 9.3 addresses the problem of stability under horizontal competition and Section 9.4, under vertical competition. Section 9.5 focuses on central governments as monitors of the rules of competition and on the instruments these governments can use to insure stability of competitive outcomes. Section 9.6 briefly reconsiders the Wicksellian Connection, and Section 9.7 concludes the chapter.

9.1.   The inducements to compete

As already noted in Chapter 7, the Tiebout mechanism, as it applies to persons, is analytically intractable in a world, like the real world, in which governmental systems are made up of three or more jurisdictional tiers. In the absence of the more general and more powerful Salmon mechanism, the motivation for competition in governmental systems would be weak, though, as argued in Chapter 8, it could still exist in particular circumstances. In addition, a Tiebout mechanism, however feeble for persons, exists because of the mobility of capital and technology. In discussing the mechanism, I follow the literature and assume a two-tier governmental system in which the senior tier is completely passive; competition regulates the relations of governments at the junior tier. The Salmon mechanism is of more recent vintage; I turn to it after looking at the more ancient Tiebout mechanism.

i.   *Tiebout's potential entry and exit mechanism*

The idea of horizontal intergovernmental competition entered the literature of Public Finance and Public Choice with Tiebout's (1956) seminal paper on local public goods. Assumption 7 of the Tiebout model states "that communities below the optimum size *seek to attract* new residents to lower average costs [and] [t]hose above optimum size *do just the opposite*" (p. 419, my italics), that is they seek "to get rid of residents" (p. 420). That surely is competitive behavior. The discussion that follows the statement of the assumption is, however, disconcerting. The decisionmakers are identified as "chambers of commerce" (p. 419) and "aldermen" (p. 420), and there is a reference to "zoning laws," which evokes governments because these laws are usually designed and implemented by such authorities, but there are no references to governments per se in Tiebout's elaboration of the assumption.

The difficulty is to a large extent artificial. Tiebout was not developing a model of local government but instead was suggesting a preference revelation device for local public goods. Given his preoccupation, Assumption 7 would have been better formulated as: Communities below optimum size will receive new residents, whereas those above optimum size will lose residents. Because the model imposes no restrictions on the number of communities (Assumption 3), the population distributes itself in such a way that in each community all residents have identical preferences. The equilibrium partition of the population, therefore, shows that a preference revelation device, "choosing by moving" or "voting with one's feet," is efficient. There are many problems with the Tiebout revelation device to which a generation of scholars have pointed, but they need not retain our attention here.[2]

But even if we grant the existence of governments, there are difficulties in the Tiebout framework with the derivative notion of intergovernmental competition. If communities are in unlimited supply and if the flow in and out of

2. To illustrate, let me mention a few of these difficulties. For example, the number of persons with the same preferences might not be large enough to exhaust the economies of scale associated with the provision of a bundle of goods and services by the marginal community. Or a full equilibrium may be possible only if a fraction of a person is available – the equilibrium requires, say, $4,510^{3/8}$ persons – but persons come in units of one. And so on.

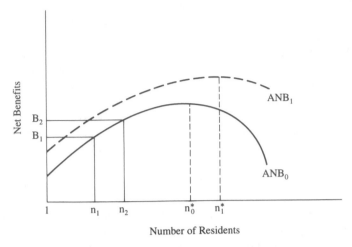

Figure 9.1. Adjustments to potential entry and exit.

communities is of people who all have the same preferences as those already there, the idea that governments compete with one another is artificial and has no force. Assume, then, that jurisdictions are in limited supply – sometimes, as is the case for Australia (six states and two territories), Canada (ten provinces and two territories), and Germany (sixteen läender), or even Switzerland (twenty-six cantons and half-cantons), and the United States (fifty states and the District of Columbia), in quite limited supply – and also that the people in each jurisdiction do not have identical preferences and, therefore, that migrants to and migrants from these jurisdictions are not homogeneous, either.

Assume also that an average net benefit curve defined over the number of residents can be constructed and that it looks like ANB_0 in Figure 9.1. Except at n^*_0 where there are constant returns to size, the curve displays a region of economies of size up to n^*_0 and diseconomies of size beyond that point. The ANB_0 curve is constructed as follows: All of a jurisdiction's current and potential population is ranked in order of decreasing contributions to the net welfare of the resident population.[3] For example, assume that when the population is equal to n_1, the average net benefits of residents are B_1. Adding one more person, thus increasing the size of the jurisdiction to $n_2 (= n_1 + 1)$ will increase the welfare of the n_1 initial resident by $W_1 = (B_2 - B_1)$. To the right of n^*_0, increases in population reduce the welfare of residents.

Following Buchanan's (1965) "Theory of Clubs," average net benefits can

---

3. That notion is clear, except for the first entrant for whom there is no resident population. One could adopt the convention of defining the origin as 1 instead of 0, as I do in Figure 9.1.

be defined as the per capita difference between the reduction in the average tax burden of financing publicly supplied goods and services and the congestion added by the new entrant.[4] That definition is, as a formal definition, broad enough to encompass all situations. Assume now that the population of a country – which, without loss of generality, we can take as fixed – is completely distributed over its J jurisdictions. Assume also that in this arbitrary distribution some jurisdictions find themselves to the left of their optimum point, whereas others are to the right. It is reasonable to suppose that the first seek to attract people and the second to turn them away. That by itself need not be competitive behavior. Indeed, if the people the first group of jurisdictions wants to attract are exactly those that the second want to lose and exactly in the same number, there is no competition. That, however, is a very special situation that we can disregard.

A more likely situation results when two or more jurisdictions seek to attract or to turn away the same people, which stimulates competitive behavior. Consider the following hypothetical case. Suppose that a jurisdiction (j_1) is at an optimum such as $n*_0$ in Figure 9.1. If the government of another jurisdiction (j_2) introduces policies of interest to residents of j_1, some of them may consider leaving. It is this potential exit of some of its citizens in response to actions in j_2 that will drive the government of j_1 to undertake actions that are by nature competitive.

If the actions of the government of j_2 have the effect of driving out some of its residents, it is the potential entry into j_1 and the consequent lowering of welfare there that will induce the government of j_1 to undertake competitive responses. One implication of this, of which Tiebout and Buchanan were already aware, is that we cannot assume that governments seek to attract more residents all the time. They may also wish to turn them away.

Governments have a number of ways of responding to undesired potential entry and exit. Local governments can deal with entry via zoning and other kinds of land use regulations. National governments have access to the whole panoply of measures identified as "immigration policy." Provincial governments, at least in Canada, have fewer or less powerful instruments than do local and national governments. This may explain why provincial governments respond to excessive immigration by seeking to attract capital. The ANB_0 curve in Figure 9.1 is drawn for a given stock of capital. If the government of a jurisdiction is successful in attracting more capital, the ANB curve will shift to (say) ANB_1. Capacity will have been increased so that the new optimum size may be given by $n*_1$ ($> n*_0$). Governments can deal with undesired potential entry and exit by a variety of measures. Restrictions on the use of some measures will simply intensify the use of others.

4. In Buchanan's model all preferences are homogeneous, but that has no effect on the notion of net benefits.

ii.   *Salmon's external benchmark mechanism*

In two-tier governmental systems or in those that can in particular circumstances be reduced to such dimensions, the Tiebout potential entry and exit mechanism may act as a stimulus to intergovernmental competition. But if the mechanism for one reason or another is inoperative, competition would be present because of the existence of an altogether different mechanism, which I introduced in Chapter 7 (Section 7.1, Subsection i) and called the Salmon mechanism. Salmon (1987a, 1987b) has persuasively argued that if the citizens of a jurisdiction use information about the goods and services supplied in other jurisdictions as a benchmark to evaluate the performance of their own government and if they decide to grant consent (see Chapter 2) to their own governing politicians or to withhold it from them on the basis of that assessment, governments in different jurisdictions will compete with one another as long as there is competition among centers of power within the jurisdiction. As also noted in Chapter 7, the Salmon mechanism is an application of the theory of rank-order tournaments in labor markets developed by Lazear and Rosen (1981) and extended by, among others, Barry Nalebuff and Joseph Stiglitz (1983).

The basic idea underlying the theory of labor market tournaments is fairly simple. Suppose, first, that the cost of measuring the effort exerted by workers is high and, second, that the cost of measuring the productivity of workers *relative* to that of other workers is low compared to the cost of measuring the *absolute* productivity of workers. Then, if productivity is a random variable, risk-averse workers, to avoid the burden of excessive risk, will want a remuneration for their effort that is independent of their output. Such a reward system is, however, an incentive for workers to exert less than optimal effort.

To see this, assume that the productivity (P_j) of worker j depends on j's effort (e_j), on a random variable *common* to all workers (r), and on another random variable *unique* to j, namely u_j, so that $P_j = f(e_j, r, u_j)$. Assume now that the employer can observe P_j but not e_j, r, or u_j. Then as soon as the contract is signed, j will observe r and choose some level of e_j. Therefore, though the employer observes P_j, the employer does not know if its level depends on e_j or on r. If the reward to the worker depends on P_j alone, a risk-averse worker will insist that his or her pay be independent of P_j, lest he or she lose because P_j has fallen following a severe exogenous adverse movement of r. But such a remuneration system means that as soon as the worker observes r, he or she can choose to exert a small e_j.

By setting up a tournament, an employer makes it attractive for each worker to increase the probability of winning the larger prize by exerting more effort. This is true whether the random variables are correlated across workers or are mostly independent. Tournaments, however, are more effective when disturbances are greater in respect of the common (the r's) than in respect of the unique or idiosyncratic (the u_j's) random variables.

To be able to apply this theory of labor market tournaments to intergovernmental relations, Salmon had to confront the fact that, in the absence of interjurisdictional mobility of persons, capital, and technology, governments located in different jurisdictions do not interact directly with one another. Governing and opposition politicians and the inhabitants of other centers of power, as well as citizens, interact with one another within a given jurisdiction. However, by postulating that citizens in a jurisdiction assess their government's performance by comparing it to that of governments in other jurisdictions, Salmon was able to apply the theory of tournaments to intergovernmental relations and to establish that competition between governments for rank order on some ordinal scale or scales exists. Because of performance comparisons, "[e]ach government has an incentive to do better than governments in other jurisdictions in terms of levels and qualities of services, of levels of taxes or of more general economic and social indicators. The strength of this incentive depends on the possibility and willingness of citizens to make assessments of comparative performance . . . and [on] the impact these assessments have on the well-being of politicians. . . . " (Salmon, 1987b, p. 32). As was the case with labor market tournaments, in intergovernmental tournaments, the relationship between the effort of public sector actors and their reward, although always stochastic, will be stronger if random disturbances are common, that is, affect all participants in the contest.

In addition, the competition grounded in the assessment of a government's performance on the basis of comparisons with the performance of one other government presupposes that there are citizens possessing the same preferences in the two jurisdictions. Other things being equal, we would expect the competition to be stronger, the larger the subgroups with identical preferences in the two localities and, conversely, the competition to be weaker, the smaller these subgroups. As a consequence, in a strict Tiebout partition of the population according to preferences in which the residents of each community have identical preferences and these preferences are different from those of citizens in neighboring communities, intergovernmental competition based on the Salmon mechanism vanishes altogether.

In the real world, for a variety of reasons, of which the economic impossibility of creating enough jurisdictions to insure that all "alikes" reside together is not the least (see Subsection i), there are many subgroups whose preferences with respect to certain goods and services are the same as those of subgroups in other jurisdictions. One can, therefore, be confident that the incitation to compete based on external benchmarks exists. The strength of the mechanism will obviously depend on the ability of citizens to make intergovernmental performance comparisons. The existence of "iron" and "bamboo" curtains – measures designed to insure that policies implemented else-where are not used as external norms to evaluate internal performance – is evidence that the Salmon mechanism is not only operative but powerful. But as we shall see immediately, other more precise evidence is also available.

9.2.   Some empirical evidence on intergovernmental competition

I cannot be exhaustive in presenting evidence to support the view that horizon-tal intergovernmental relations are competitive. I simply suggest that they are by pointing to three bodies of data that are easily interpreted as evidence that behavior is competitive and that are, with only much difficulty, given a differ-ent meaning. There are surely other bodies of data that further research will bring to light. Here I limit myself to the following: (1) studies of the rate of diffusion among jurisdictions of legislative policies and programs; (2) esti-mates of the elasticity of population migration to fiscal and other policy changes; and (3) observations of "price" adjustments by governments to se-cure particular objectives.

i.   Indices of policy and program diffusion

The literature on the diffusion of legislative policies and programs is enor-mous and goes back at least to Ada Davis's (1930) analysis of the diffusion of mothers' pensions, or more exactly of widows' allowances, designed to make it possible for dependent children "to remain in their own home" (p. 575). The number of legislative enactments studied is also large, running into the hun-dreds.[5] From the moment of first adoption, the cumulative distributions over time of the number of jurisdictions enacting particular measures all graph as ogives (S-curves), indicating that the proportion of jurisdictions adopting a particular measure – for example, fluoridation – increases with the passage of time, first at a slow rate, then at an accelerated pace, and finally again at a slow rate, thus describing a stylized S such as S_1 in Figure 9.2. There appears to be no exception to that proposition except that sometimes the lower hori-zontal portion of the S is very short or nonexistent, as is the case for curve S_2 in Figure 9.2. One should mention, however, that some classes of legislative enactments have not been studied. In particular, measures that have not dif-fused among jurisdictions, or whose diffusion is very limited (as represented by S_2), do not appear to have retained much scholarly attention. That is regrettable because analyses of these cases would help us to better understand

5. Walker (1969) examined 88 programs. In addition to this important piece of research and to Davis's study, which I have just mentioned, there are McVoy (1940), Sutherland (1950), Crain (1966), Hofferbert (1966), Savage (1985), Scott (1968), Sharkansky (1968), and Gray (1973).

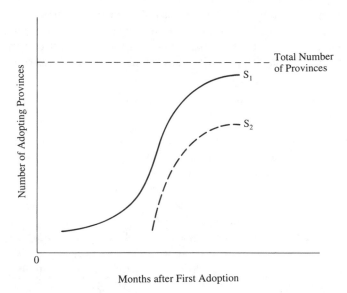

Figure 9.2. The diffusion of innovations.

the reasons for diffusion and the characteristic S-shape. Finally, the density of the cumulative distributions – the rate of diffusion or the "process of diffusion," to use James Coleman, Herbert Menzel, and Elihu Katz's (1959) expression – and the extent of diffusion vary considerably among legislative measures.

Explanations for the S-shape of the distributions abound. There are, for example, hypotheses centered on the way information propagates (Coleman et al., 1959), on the presence of internal adjustment costs (Reinganum, 1981), on regulatory barriers (Oster and Quigley, 1977), on the mode of operation of pressure groups and "propaganda," or advertising, by these groups (Davis, 1930), on the size of units (Mansfield, 1963), and on the "bounded rationality" of decisionmakers (Walker, 1969). Why policies and programs diffuse in the first place has received less attention. True, some of the factors just listed provide part of an explanation, but these are not articulated as a consistent hypothesis. Walker (1969) was the first to suggest that intergovernmental competition was the driving force behind the diffusion indices he was trying to explain. The idea, in a game theoretic framework, was also important in Jennifer Reinganum's (1983) work. Roberta Romano (1985) used measures of diffusion as indicators of competition in an explicit way.

To understand how competition can lead to the diffusion of policies and programs, consider the case of a measure that has been implemented in some jurisdictions but not in others. What could move public sector actors (officials) to introduce a new policy or program that has been successfully implemented elsewhere? Given the assumption that officials maximize expected consent (see Chapter 2), the answer to this question must be that they will be so moved if implementing the new policy or program will cause an improvement in expected consent.

It is easy to identify forces that can cause such an outcome. For example, the threat of exit by persons, capital, or both as described in Subsection i, could alter the consent expected by politicians and other public officials. It is potential, not actual, exit that spurs competition; actual exit is a measure only of the unwillingness or inability of a jurisdiction to compete effectively. Potential exit is the exact counterpart of potential entry in the theory of monopoly and oligopoly. If the threat of entry is effective, potential entrants will not enter, but the incumbents will set the price of their output nearer the competitive price. Actual entry, in this case also, is a measure of the unwillingness or of the incapacity to provide a competitive response. An analogous argument can be made *mutatis mutandis* for the potential (political) entry of (undesired) persons into a jurisdiction if the new policy or program is not implemented.

Potential exit and entry are sufficient, but they are not necessary to cause changes in the consent expected by governing politicians and officials. If, for the reasons suggested earlier (Subsection i), potential exit and entry are weak forces, expected consent would still adjust as a consequence of the operation of benchmark or rank-order competition à la Salmon. That mechanism, incidentally, would seem to imply that diffusion curves are not only S-shaped but look like logistic curves according to which the rate of diffusion is proportional to the number of jurisdictions that have already implemented the policy *and* to the number that will eventually implement it. It is as if each jurisdiction that has adopted a policy or program could, as it were, transmit it to a constant proportion of all the other jurisdictions per unit of time, recognizing that a certain proportion of these other jurisdictions will already have adopted the measure.[6] Inspection of diffusion curves indicates that their shape is in most cases that of the familiar logistic curve, and therefore there is a presumption that the Salmon mechanism governs the diffusion of policies and programs through governmental systems.

6. Let j be the number of jurisdictions that have adopted a particular policy measure at any point of time, t be time, k be a diffusion constant of proportionality, and J be the total number of jurisdictions. Then

$$dj/dt = kj \, (J - j)$$

or letting j = 1 at t = 0

$$j = Je^{kt}/J - 1 + e^{kt}$$

is the logistic growth curve. See Coleman (1964, pp. 42–3).

ii.   *Estimates of political mobility*

In a path-breaking article based on the tacit assumption that the part of the American governmental system he was analyzing could be treated as if it were a two-tier system, Wallace Oates (1969) inverted the Tiebout mechanism by assuming that differences in property taxes and in the provision of local public goods would be reflected in property values. Accordingly, if taxes were lower in community A than in community B, but the supply of local goods and services was the same in both, migration from B into A would cause the price (rental value) of real property (assumed to be in fixed supply) to rise in A and fall in B. Tax and expenditure levels would be capitalized in property values. The degree of capitalization would be both a measure of the extent to which citizens take tax and expenditure levels into account in deciding where to locate and also a measure of the differential attractiveness of communities.

Critics of the Oates model, among them Matthew Edel and Elliot Sclar (1974) and Bruce Hamilton (1976), have correctly argued that capitalization is an indication of the absence, not of the presence, of a Tiebout equilibrium, because in such an equilibrium property taxes are benefit taxes: They are the real efficiency prices of the goods and services provided. As a consequence, neither taxes nor expenditure levels are capitalized in property values. If a steady-state Tiebout equilibrium can be presumed to exist, estimates of capitalization point to a disequilibrium – in Hamilton's words (p. 648) to a situation "in which there is a temporary shortage of fiscal havens."[7] Because they assume, explicitly or implicitly, the existence of a Tiebout *equilibrium,* some scholars (for example, Epple and Zelenitz, 1981, and Gramlich and Rubinfeld, 1982) have been able to interpret statistically significant estimates of capitalization as evidence of the presence of a Tiebout mechanism. However, as Mark Pauly (1976) as well as Dennis Epple, Allan Zelenitz, and Michael Vischer (1978) have noted, nothing can be surmised about the existence and properties of an equilibrium from an empirical analysis of disequilibrium states.

Suppose, however, that a Tiebout equilibrium is assumed as well as the presence of natural and economic scarcities – the latter being the product of entrepreneurship. In the equilibrium, some communities will be "more desirable places to live" (Meadows, 1976, p. 870), because the environment and the scale as well as the mix of goods and services provided will make them so. These scarcities (or specific qualities) will command higher prices and will, thus, generate rents that will be capitalized in property values. If one reads the empirical studies of Oates (1969), George Meadows (1976), Andrew Reschovsky (1979), Kenneth Rosen (1982), and other students of local public

---

7. The word "temporary" is surely an indication that an equilibrium is postulated.

finance [for an able review, see Bloom, Ladd, and Yinger (1983)] in that spirit, they indicate that political mobility spurs competitive intergovernmental relations.

There is another body of literature, not unrelated to the Tiebout mechanism, but addressed to a different problem – namely, that of the effect of intergovernmental grants and other fiscal variables, such as tax rate and expenditure differences, on mobility – which is relevant in the present context. Among noteworthy contributions to that empirical literature are those of Thomas Courchene (1970), Stanley Winer and Denis Gauthier (1982), Kenneth Norrie and Michael Percy (1984), and Kathleen Day (1992). The conclusion of this research is that mobility is to a degree responsive to fiscal variables. It seems reasonable to assume that if such is the case, governments would take that mobility into account in making fiscal decisions. When they do so, they are, of course, competing among themselves.

iii.   Analysis of price rivalry

The widespread use of direct (cash and in-kind) subsidies, tax holidays, purchase agreements, and land grants and of credits and abatements of various sorts, to name but a few of the "price" instruments that governments use to attract labor, capital, and technology, is an unequivocal testimony to the fact that intergovernmental relations are competitive. At the risk of overstating the notion of "price," one should add to the instruments just listed such policies as the subsidization or outright provision of concert halls, museums, public libraries, conference centers, sports arenas, and the host of other projects intended to make a jurisdiction or a community more attractive.

A large fraction of the literature concerned with this type of price competition derives from Public Finance's normative analysis of the optimality of neutral taxation and spending and is, as a consequence, condemnatory. But there also exists a positive literature related to the matter. Daphne Kenyon's (1991) competent summary of that very large literature for the United States documents the widespread existence of price competition, at least if one is willing, as she and I are, to interpret, as evidence of competitive responses and adjustments on the part of local and state governments, successful statistical explanations of phenomena such as plant location, capital investment per worker, growth of employment, and others as they are related to tax levels, tax rates, and expenditure levels.[8]

In the international arena, it is particularly easy to document (see Nurkse,

---

8. One should also mention the large number of case studies of service delivery at the local level (see, among the best, Young, 1972 and Bish, 1987, which all confirm the fact that intergovernmental relations are competitive).

1944, and Kindleberger, 1986, among many) the competitiveness of governments. Instruments that cannot be used in the home economy, such as tariffs, exchange rate devaluations, and quotas – voluntary or not – as well as innumerable nontariff barriers, have been and continue to be widely used. They are all *prima facie* evidence that governments compete with one another.

9.3.   Horizontal competition and stability

If a mechanism or a configuration of forces moves an institutional structure from *any* position of disequilibrium to one of equilibrium, that equilibrium is said to be globally stable. The equilibrium is locally stable (stable in the small) when the mechanism or the configuration of forces can move the institutional structure to equilibrium only from states or positions already close to it. (See Samuelson, 1953, Chapter IX.) Intergovernmental competition, conceived as a configuration of forces can generate outcomes that are globally or locally unstable. One must avoid identifying instability with collapse; sometimes instability means just that, but at other times it means "restoring forces" (Lancaster, 1974, p. 287) are set in motion that prevent collapse. Following upon Kelvin Lancaster, we could say that when this happens instability is "bounded." To illustrate, he writes that "[p]erhaps the unemployment levels in the thirties represented the boundary of disequilibrium" (p. 287) for that phenomenon.

Stability and efficiency are closely related phenomena, but they are distinct and must be analyzed separately. This is especially true when we are considering global, as distinguished from local, stability. For example, intergovernmental price competition may be shown to be efficient or inefficient, but that matter is clearly different from the question of whether intergovernmental price competition degenerates into unstable price wars. The point can be illustrated by reference to standard discussions of externalities. As is well known, externalities cause inefficiencies in the allocation of resources. In general, however, the analysis of externalities and of the remedies to deal with them is conducted within a framework of assumptions that guarantee that the institutional structure is stable.[9]

The remainder of this section is concerned with institutional instability; efficiency questions are set aside, if only because stability must be assumed when addressing questions of efficiency. Matters pertaining to efficiency can be studied within a given institutional framework, whereas problems of stability require changes in that framework, so that the latter has priority over the former. As a matter of convenience, I will follow the order of Section 9.2. I

9. If negative externalities are strong enough, they may, as Baumol (1964) and Baumol and Bradford (1972) have shown, lead to a reversal in the sign of the second-order, or stability, condition and thus cause instability.

will first discuss issues related to stability as they pertain to the diffusion of policies and programs and then move on to political mobility and to price competition.

i.   Policy and program diffusion

Although Walker (1969, p. 890) had already recognized that a problem of institutional stability could exist, the first systematic discussion of the problem of stability as it pertains to the diffusion of policies and programs is that of William Carey (1974). He argues that competition for the revenues produced by the supply of corporate charters has led state governments in the United States to make corporate statutes increasingly more appealing to managers – namely, to those who "buy" the incorporation or reincorporation charters – by increasing their freedom vis-à-vis stockholders. As a consequence, both the stockholders and the general public receive inadequate legal protection. Carey writes of a "movement toward the least common denominator" (p. 663), of a "race for the bottom" (p. 666), and of an "application of Gresham's law" (p. 698). Phrases like these could imply either global or local instability. His argument would, however, appear to be more consistent with a notion of local instability.

Carey's methodology of proof is one common in legal writings and standard in legal and jurisprudential proceedings. By marshaling and analyzing cases that are deemed to be relevant, Carey (1974) seeks to establish that in matters pertaining to "fiduciary responsibility and fairness" and to "shareholder's rights," corporate law in the state of Delaware has been "shrinking" and been "water[ed] down" (p. 696). The "race for the bottom" language and the regular use of the word "competition" leads one to believe that what is happening in Delaware is a response to competitive pressures from the outside, although Carey does not offer any analysis of what other states are doing in the area. Furthermore, because the evidence brought forward to document what could be called complicity between the courts and the Delaware legislature to explain the "watering down" of legislation can be interpreted as a response to competitive pressures from the outside, I assume that the "complicitous" arrangements and other behaviors noted by Carey were the result of competitive pressures.

Carey's paper was not long without a response. In particular, his policy prescription that to deal with competitive instability, the responsibility for corporation–shareholder relationships should be transferred extensively to the national government, provoked a number of rejoinders, among which are Ralph Winter (1977) and Daniel Fischel (1982). Carey's ideal solution would have been "federal incorporation"; however, because that solution was in his view "politically unrealistic," he proposed the adoption of federal minimum standards of regulation. There can be little doubt that in Carey's mind instability is removed by eliminating horizontal intergovernmental competition. He writes (1974): "[t]he third [principle on which we should proceed] is to emphasize the need for uniformity, so that states shall not compete with each other by lowering standards for competitive reasons or for the purpose of generating revenue" (p. 697). To a Canadian, and to many others no doubt, that solution has a familiar ring to it: It was the solution proposed to perceived problems of competitive instability by the famed, though seldom read, *Report* (1940) of the Rowell–Sirois Royal Commission on Dominion–Provincial Relations in Canada.

The corporate charter debate is not an easy one to enter. It seems to be constantly menaced by strong philosophical and even ideological positions. I will therefore tread lightly and remain close to my own special concern. In my opinion, Carey's major point has not been addressed by his critics. The notion that any stockholder who does not like the activities of the corporation in which he or she owns stock has only to sell and buy elsewhere would appear to conflict with the fact, central to Carey's analysis, that shareholders sometimes litigate. Carey's main point is that because of competitive adjustments in corporate law, the chances of successful litigation by shareholders in Delaware have eroded over time. That is where the instability lies.

That Carey limited his analysis to Delaware weakened his argument. Is it only in Delaware that "shareholders' rights" are being "water[ed] down," or is one witnessing a genuine "race for the bottom"? If competition is producing what Carey alleges, then one also has to look at what is happening elsewhere because Delaware is either responding to, or acting in anticipation of, actions in other jurisdictions. If what is happening in Delaware is not governed by competitive pressures, then the argument of Carey's critics – that shareholders in Delaware corporations should rearrange their portfolios by substituting non-Delaware for Delaware shares – could be adapted to imply that would-be litigators should buy into non-Delaware, instead of Delaware, corporations, although the management of an asset portfolio governed by expected returns is surely very different from that governed by expected litigations.

Peter Dodd and Richard Leftwich (1980) and, more unequivocally, Romano (1985) have shown that the earnings of corporations changing their charter domicile to Delaware do not fall. In other words, if Delaware is pro-management, it is so in a way that allows management to maintain and even increase the present value of the firm. These results, both based on econometric event analysis, appear to be incontrovertible. However, it is not clear that the kind of instability Carey has in mind could not happen in the presence of the price stability revealed by these apparently robust results. After all, price stability can exist in markets characterized by quality deterioration or by what we could call quality instability.

Romano (1985) noted that respondents in her survey "consistently alluded . . . [to] Delaware's well-developed case law, which provides a pool of
handy precedents, and the basis of obtaining almost instantaneously a legal
opinion on any issue of Delaware law" (p. 274) as an important reason for
Delaware's dominance in the reincorporation market. Delaware, in other
words, has specialized in corporate law; hence what one observes is not
instability but a division of labor and its consequences. The argument is
appealing, but it is difficult to reconcile with the fact that 66 of all 140
reincorporations of New York Stock Exchange firms that took place between
1928 and 1977 occurred between 1966 and 1970, after a "major revision" of
the Delaware corporate code (Dodd and Leftwich, 1980, pp. 267–8).

The question, I suggest, is still open. It would be unwise on the basis of this
one case to conclude that the competitive forces underlying interjurisdictional
diffusion processes cannot be unstable. However, if they are unstable, it does
not follow, as suggested by Carey and others, that intergovernmental competition should be suppressed by reassigning the power to a higher level of
government. That solution would be optimal only if other means of stabilizing
competition did not exist or were shown to be less efficient.

ii.   Political mobility

A pure Tiebout equilibrium is stable because the adjustment mechanism that
describes behavior when the system is in disequilibrium is based on U-shaped
average (per capita) cost curves for local goods and services. This is an
acceptable assumption when the number of communities is postulated to be
large enough to allow a partition of the entire population according to preferences (total utility) into strictly homogeneous groups. If the number of communities is smaller than needed to achieve this degree of homogeneity because there is, say, "a scarcity of community sites" (Westoff, 1979, p. 537),
then equilibrium can be unstable, as has been demonstrated by Frank Westhoff
(1979) and Susan Rose-Ackerman (1979). Other causes of instability
have been analyzed (see, for example, Stiglitz, 1977). There is no need to
review that literature here, although the logic of instability that it describes is
always fairly simple: A movement from A to B worsens the situation in A and
improves it in B, so that it induces further movement in the same direction.

There is another literature that, if it does not explicitly deal with instability
or even make use of the concept, is, in the guise of solutions to federalist
problems, implicitly concerned with it.[10] I am referring to the normative
discussions of the assignment of the constitutional power to redistribute income among individuals. A long list of eminent scholars, including Buchanan
(1950), Stigler (1957b), Musgrave (1959), and Oates (1972), have argued that

10. An exception is Frederick Mueller (1957) who uses the word in the same sense as I do.

that power should be assigned to the national or central government – that it should be centralized – essentially because competition between jurisdictions in this policy area is unstable. Oates (1972, p. 7) makes the point succinctly: ". . . in view of the relatively high degree of individual mobility that characterizes a national economy, [an income redistribution program] would create strong incentives for the wealthy to move out to neighboring municipalities and for the poor to migrate into the community."[11] This process leads to less than the optimal amount of redistribution – at the limit, to none at all – or to a redistribution that does not satisfy the principle of horizontal equity, which is the "equal treatment of equals."

Notwithstanding what appears to be complete unanimity among scholars, the notion that centralization is the solution to the problem of competitive instability in the provision of income redistribution among individuals is mistaken. The fact that redistribution policies are implemented by governments at the subnational level in virtually all governmental systems is testimony to that fact. Because the theoretical analysis that points to instability is most certainly correct, the existence of redistribution at other than the national level indicates the presence of institutions or mechanisms that effectively stabilize intergovernmental relations in this policy area.

Another body of empirical evidence bearing on the stability of political mobility relates to the urban crisis in the United States. The urban crisis can be described as the presence in the central city of "undernourished and poorly educated children, dilapidated housing and abandoned neighborhoods, or rising unemployment and high rates of crime" (Bateman and Hochman, 1976, p. 283). The causes of this crisis, this analysis asserts, can be attributed to a "fiscal imbalance," which in turn is the consequence of migration to the suburbs. To the extent that the urban crisis is real it can be interpreted as a manifestation of unstable intergovernmental competition.

The literature on the subject is enormous and so specialized that I cannot do it justice. It comprises at least three strands: one that is preoccupied with the forces that have caused the crisis, a second that is concerned with the morphology of the phenomenon, and a third that is prescriptive, in search of remedies to deal with the problem. I am concerned here exclusively with the first strand, and I follow such writers as Worth Bateman and Harold Hochman (1976), Edwin Mills (1980), and Harvey Rosen (1985), who, addressing the question in the framework of the Tiebout model, viewed the crisis as being caused by migratory adjustments. None of these authors, nor any other, to my knowledge, has interpreted the crisis as a sign of competitive instability, but that is surely what it is.

11. Though the argument refers to "municipalities," Oates concludes that "a policy of income redistribution has a much greater promise of success if carried out on the national level" (p. 8).

In *Urban Public Finance in Canada,* Richard Bird and Enid Slack (1983) are enlightening on the matter. They make the point that (at the time they were writing) there was no "urban crisis" in Canada and said that one is not "likely to emerge . . . with anything like the same force" as in the United States. They give three reasons: (1) the relative youth of Canadian cities and the consequent continued significant growth in property tax bases; (2) a more centralized division of powers between provincial and local governments in Canada than between state and local governments in the United States; and (3) a much tighter control of local finance by provincial governments in Canada than by state governments in the United States (p. 13). The second and especially the third of these three reasons imply that there is less intergovernmental competition among local governments in Canada than in the United States. That by itself would mute competitive instability in Canada. But as Bird and Slack also note, "provincial support of municipal finance . . . is much greater in Canada" (p. 13). This means that interjurisdictional mobility will not erode tax bases as much as occurs in the United States; consequently, a process of migration that would otherwise have been unstable can operate in a stable manner. In the next section, I return to the role of interjurisdictional grants in promoting stability.

iii.   Price rivalry

The theoretical literature on optimal tariffs and on retaliation [for example, Scitovsky (1941) and Johnson (1958)] indicates that tariff wars can be unstable, although they need not be. The enormous economic and political science literature on hegemonic stability, which holds that in the absence of a hegemon international relations will unravel, also points to the view that price competition is unstable (see Chapter 10).

Even if tariff wars and competitive exchange devaluations need not always be unstable, there can be little doubt that when they were allowed to develop unchecked during the interwar years (1919–39), they were unstable [see Nurkse (1944) and Kindleberger (1986)]. I mention these events, even though they are removed from the context under consideration in this chapter, because a dominant explanation for their occurrence is particularly revealing in a search for competitive stability in governmental systems.

9.4.   Vertical competition and stability

An instructive way of looking at the stability problem as it pertains to vertical competition is to contrast three different types of governmental systems, namely, confederalism, unitarianism, and federalism. This not only allows us some insight into the problem of stability, but it also helps us at the same time to discover the specificity of federalism among the variety of multitier governmental systems. The first type of system – to wit, confederalism – is best conceived as a system in which the powers that are assigned to a more senior level of government remain in the possession or ownership of the junior governments. With the second – unitarianism – exactly the opposite is true: Powers assigned to lower jurisdictional levels are always owned by the senior government. In a federal governmental system, powers are constitutionally owned by the jurisdictional level to which they are assigned: national powers by central governments, provincial or state powers by provincial or state governments, and so on.

There are many unitary states in existence, but the confederal states that have existed in the past have now all disappeared. This is not an accident. Unitary states – even those with many competing jurisdictional tiers – are more capable than confederal states of adjusting to exogenous shocks and of insuring that the rules of competition are implemented; they are, in a word, more stable. Why? If junior governments, following some exogenous shock, become relatively more efficient in supplying goods and services hitherto supplied by senior government and if the latter refuses to decentralize the assignment of powers, which by definition of unitarianism it can unilaterally do, citizens can fairly easily establish that the senior government is responsible for the utility losses they have to suffer and can simply withhold consent from that government. It is the normal functioning of democracy that in this case leads to deconcentration and to decentralization. In the case of confederal states, if, following an external disturbance, the senior government becomes relatively more efficient in supplying one or a number of goods and services, the citizens can again withhold consent from their respective junior governments for refusing to reassign powers upward, but that withholding will necessarily be less effective because it is usually difficult to identify which one among the junior governments that make up the confederation is responsible for the obstruction. As a consequence, inefficiencies in the supply of goods and services will eventually become excessively burdensome and lead to the eventual collapse of the system. Furthermore, if some or all junior governments not only refuse to reassign powers upward but also respond to the external disturbance, as they have historically often done, by "repossessing" through one means or the other most or all powers, the confederation will simply disintegrate.

It is interesting to note that the authors of *The Federalist* (1787–8), who had lived through ten years of confederation and who had studied older confederations with care, also believed that confederalism was unstable. Though they did not formally distinguish between vertical and horizontal competition, they recognized the existence of the two. Indeed, in making their case against confederalism, they seem to be arguing that both led to instability.

In *Federalist,* 18, Alexander Hamilton and James Madison wrote:

> The powers [of the Amphictyonic council of the Grecian republics], like those of the present [U.S.] Congress, were administered by deputies appointed wholly by the cities in their political capacities; and exercised over them in the same capacities. Hence the weakness, the disorders, and finally the destruction of the confederacy. The more powerful members, instead of being kept in awe and subordination, tyrannized successively over all the rest. (p. 107)

Earlier (*Federalist,* 9), Hamilton had written about the "infinity of little jealous, clashing, tumultuous commonwealths [as being] the wretched nurseries of unceasing discord" (pp. 49–50) in describing the relationships of neighboring states. Again, in *Federalist,* 15, Hamilton writes that:

> [t]he measures of the Union have not been executed; the delinquencies of the States have, step by step, matured themselves to an extreme, which has, at length, arrested all the wheels of the national government, and brought them to an awful stand. (p. 94)

These several quotations point to a belief on the part of Hamilton and Madison that both horizontal and vertical competition are the source of instability in confederal states.

Let us accept for a moment the views of the authors of *The Federalist* and ask whether the instability of confederalism derives primarily from horizontal or from vertical competition. I suggest, as proposed earlier, that it derives mostly from the latter. To see this, let us begin by recalling that some confederations – such as the 500-year-old Swiss Confederacy (from 1291 to the Napoleonic wars) – survive for long periods. However, in these cases, one power only is typically assigned to the central authority: defense against foreign aggression. Given the technologies of deterrence and aggression, it is reasonable that, with only one centralized power, there is not much competition between the two orders of government. It is only when a significant number of powers is assigned to the center, as in the American Confederation of 1781, that competition between jurisdictional tiers can cause instability. It was a recognition of that fact that led Tocqueville (1835–40, p. 157) to observe that "the real weakness of federal [i.e., central] governments [in confederation] has almost always increased in direct proportion to their nominal powers."

Unitary states, though more stable than confederal states, are less stable than federal states in arrangements that pertain to the delivery of goods and services, essentially because the federal states have mechanisms that allow the constitutionally entrenched assignment of powers to track – albeit sometimes with longish lags – the changing configuration of relative supply efficiencies of the various orders of government as reflected in the changes taking place in the degree of expenditure and revenue concentration. The mechanisms are more effective because they rest on divided ownership and, therefore, in the rights of all parties to challenge any division of powers by sometimes requiring constitutional amendments, more often by eliciting judicial review and reinterpretation, and more often still by provoking intergovernmental recontracting through negotiation and coordination.

9.5.   Securing stability

> There are a set of functions which are intrinsically national because they are indivisible. [Among them] [o]ne may cite . . . the control of relationships among lower governmental levels.
>
> G. J. Stigler (1957b, p. 218)

Just as there is a problem of stability and one of efficiency, there is a need *at the institutional level* for two different sorts of instrumentalities or agencies to deal with these problems: one to insure that the rules that secure the stability of competitive outcomes are monitored and implemented; and another to insure that agreements, bargains, transactions, and contractual undertakings are enforced. I am concerned in this section with the first of these only; the matter of contractual enforcement has been addressed in the last chapter.

I assume that the stability of competitive outcomes is, in all governmental systems, the responsibility of central governments. The assumption, to repeat, is not new. It has been part of the theory of federal governmental systems at least since the days of *The Federalist* (1787–8). Central governments, therefore, have two logically distinct functions to perform. They must supply the goods and services that they are most efficient at providing, and they must guarantee the stability of competitive outcomes. The supply function of central governments is usually the only one considered in the literature on governmental systems, either because it is implicitly assumed that intergovernmental competition is inherently stable or because it is presumed that intergovernmental relations are not competitive. As mentioned earlier, in the remainder of this chapter, I am concerned exclusively with what we may call the stabilizing function – with what I associate with the monitoring function of central governments (see Chapter 7, Section 7.1, Subsection ii, and footnote 7).

Central governments must monitor both vertical and horizontal competition, that is, the competition among themselves and the other governments of the system and that among junior governments. In monitoring vertical competition, central governments are both judges and juries. That poses a difficult problem that different governmental systems resolve differently. In what follows, I first ask why the stability problem has historically been addressed by making use of monitors and not in some other way. I then examine how horizontal and vertical competition are, in practice, monitored.

i.   *Why use monitors?*

Every one of the units that make up governmental systems want the problem of competitive instability resolved – they want rules or precepts to be put in place to prevent the predatory pricing of goods and services, the exportation of tax bases, the dumping of negative externalities, the erection of trade and of other barriers, the formation of conspiracies, the encouragement of excessive duplication, and so on. Why is it that in real-world governmental systems the responsibility for preventing these destabilizing practices is assigned to central governments? Why do not provincial or state governments enter into covenants that would prevent such practices? Put simply, the answer to these questions is that such covenants are not possible.

First, let us establish that competitive stability cannot be achieved through cooperation. Before addressing this point, let me insist that if this be true, the proposition is not an indictment or at least not a complete indictment of what is known as "cooperative federalism." Recall the distinction between horizontal and vertical intergovernmental relations. Discussions of cooperative federalism are mostly concerned with vertical relationships: They are largely tacit on the question of horizontal competition. The point is that horizontal cooperation is not a solution to horizontal competitive instability.

Cooperation would achieve stability by suppressing competition, but it is not the only way of suppressing competition. It is easy to generate a division of powers among jurisdictional levels that will also extinguish competition by simply overcentralizing the governmental system. The argument, then, is not that cooperation is impossible because it suppresses competition but because it cannot deliver stability. Let me illustrate by referring to market calisthenics. If each oligopolists in a particular market behaves as a Bertrand player in that each conjectures that the other players will keep the current price of their output unchanged when any one of them changes his or her own price and if each of them has sufficient capacity to supply the entire market demand, the stage is set, as is well known, for the instability sometimes called "cutthroat competition." The formation of a collusive (cooperative) cartel is not a solution to the problem of instability, because cartels are also generally unstable (Stigler, 1964).

Why are the cooperative covenants of governmental systems unstable? Even a casual look at the behaviors these covenants would seek to prevent (refer to the short list in the first paragraph of this subsection) reveals that for each it is profitable for any one governmental unit to engage in them if the other units do not. Put differently, it is advantageous for one government to cheat on the others if the others refrain from cheating. Could a cooperative covenant that would prevent such cheating be self-enforcing, that is, not require a monitor? The answer is "no" because the problems posed by self-enforcement are most acute when the time horizon of the covenant is finite and nearly certain. In other words, if A knows that two years hence, B cannot be assumed to be a party to the covenant, A must assume that B will violate the covenant before the two years are over. That expectation on A's part is sufficient by itself to prevent the emergence of a covenant. Is that not the kind of expectation that electoral politics necessarily fosters? Which provincial premier or state governor can assume that other premiers or governors will be reelected in the next electoral contest?

When self-enforcement is not possible, another way of ensuring cooperation is to have all the parties to a covenant post a bond (Becker and Stigler, 1974). Violation causes loss of the bond. Let me first note, as Lester Telser (1980) has already done, that it is not obvious that bond posting does not require a third party or monitor. Who decides whether there has been a violation? In any case, governments do not post bonds!

Trust, as defined by Breton and Wintrobe (1982, Chapter 4) and by Coleman (1983), can also lead to cooperation and therefore to relationships that do not require the presence of a monitor. But trust requires repeated interaction, which periodic electoral contests make difficult, if not impossible. Bureaucratic relationships may, however, be more permanent and trust as a result more likely to accumulate. That, in turn, would reduce the need for a monitor. In general, the necessity of a monitor would be reduced or, more precisely, fulfilling the function of monitor would be less onerous if circumstances were such as to permit the self-enforcement even of only parts of convenants, the posting of bonds or of substitutes, and the accumulation of some amount of trust among the relevant parties. We should then observe less reliance on monitors to stabilize competition and more reliance on covenants or similar devices.

ii.   *Monitoring horizontal competition*

The number and variety of instruments that central governments can use to monitor horizontal competition – to insure that member governments follow the rules adopted to stabilize competition – are numerous, and the precise subset that will be used in any particular context will vary over time as circumstances change. In this subsection, I illustrate by considering three instruments that are frequently employed, often in conjunction with one another: (1) the use of prohibitions and standards; (2) the use of regional policies; and (3) the implementation of intergovernmental grants programs.

a. Prohibitions and standards: It is impossible to list all the different prohibitions that central governments may use to stabilize competition. The following short list illustrates the grounds the prohibitions may cover:

Central governments may disallow the use by any provincial or state government of measures aimed at exploiting other provincial or state governments or out-of-province or out-of-state residents. For example, central governments may prohibit the exportation of tax burdens and of negative externalities from one province or state to another.

Central governments may regulate barriers to the movement of goods, services, and factors of production.

Central governments may prevent conspiracies of two, three, or more provincial or state governments directed at outbidding another provincial or state government that is seeking to attract, say, human or physical capital to its jurisdiction.

In other words, central governments will be concerned with the whole panoply of beggar-thy-neighbor policies that provincial and state governments may be tempted to use, and central governments may choose to inhibit their use.

In addition to prohibitions such as the foregoing, central governments may choose to enforce minimum or even maximum standards of performance and provision. The use of minimum standards to stabilize competitive markets affected by moral hazard resulting from asymmetric information has already been recognized (Leland, 1979).[12] One must acknowledge that it is often difficult to use standards as a monitoring device, because if the minimum is set too high or the maximum too low, competition will not be stabilized but suppressed. Still, they can do the job if appropriately designed. For a further discussion of this topic, see Breton and Scott (1978, pp. 85–7).

b. *Regional policies:* I am principally concerned with the regional policies of the central governments of governmental systems and should probably call these policies provincial or state development policies. However, I defer to custom and remain close to tradition. I do so because what I have to say applies to all governments that are higher up in the hierarchy of multitier governmental systems. What I have to say can be used to understand and evaluate not only the regional policies of central governments in provinces or states but also the regional policies of provincial or state governments in municipalities within provincial or state boundaries and the regional policies of municipal governments in jurisdictions (such as land-use authorities, school boards, water boards, police commissions, and other special district governments) under them.

Regional development policies include all the policies of central govern-

12. Carey (1974, p. 701) proposed seven minimum standards, to be embodied in a "Federal Corporate Uniformity Act," to stop what he saw as the instability of the competitive diffusion of innovations.

ments that affect regional development. They often include basic infrastructure policies related to the construction of railways, canals, airports, communication networks, street, road and highway systems, water supply and water storage reservoirs, port facilities, and many others. Most infrastructure projects are mechanical engineering undertakings that the provinces or states could very easily coordinate and implement by themselves. The reason they are virtually always joint ventures is that if central governments were not active partners in the undertakings, intergovernmental competition would not lead necessarily to more stable outcomes – it could lead to more unstable ones.

Basic infrastructure undertakings are just one of many regional development policies implemented to insure competitive stability. Central governments are also active in research and development. Examples of R and D activity are experimental agricultural and forestry farms, as well as the operation of more conventional laboratories. In this connection, one should mention the role of military and defense R and D, which is additional to the production of military hardware. Over the past thirty or forty years, the central government in the United States has progressively reduced its direct concern for regional issues, to the point that at present regional matters seem totally absent from the national agenda. This absence, I suggest, is an illusion because regional policies are now embodied in defense expenditures.[13]

That "fact" makes it difficult to evaluate the efficiency of these regional policies or to identify the component of defense expenditure that is truly regional in character, but the task of stabilizing interstate competition is still accomplished. Defense expenditures have historically not been as large a component of regional policy in Canada as they have been in the United States. It is, however, easy to imagine a change in that situation. Suppose that under the North American Free Trade Agreement among Canada, Mexico, and the United States, the International Panel – which has the responsibility of determining what is a subsidy and what is not – strikes down a significant part of Canada's regional policy arsenal as inconsistent with free trade. One should then expect an increase in defense expenditures in Canada as a conduit for regional policies. The evidence in respect of both regional policies and defense expenditures in Canada in recent years is consistent with the foregoing conjecture. Interprovincial or interstate competition must be stabilized.

In addition to infrastructure undertakings and to research and development activities, central governments give subsidies, whether direct or indirect, in money or in kind, to labor, capital, and technology with the object of inducing them to locate in particular areas. There is no limit, it would seem, to the variety of forms the subsidies can take. They include loan guarantees, lower

13. That view is also taken by Robert Reich (1983).

interest rates, lower tax rates, and lower rents on central government land, in addition to capital grants and labor subsidies of various sorts.

On what basis should one appraise the efficiency of the regional policies? The first point to note in addressing this question is that the answer depends on whether other policies exist that contribute to competitive stability. I will argue later that in some contexts a fraction of the total flow of intergovernmental grants must be conceived as a policy instrument aimed at competitive stability. I will refer to that fraction of total grants as "stabilizing" grants. Consequently, if a stabilizing grants system is in place and if it has been optimally designed to produce stability, regional policies would be wasteful. If, however, the stabilizing grants system is not optimal, regional policies would have to be seen as complementary to the stabilizing grants program.

The simplest case to look at is the one that obtains when there is no system of stabilizing intergovernmental grants. That case provides us with the elements we need to analyze the efficiency dimension of regional policies. In some governmental systems, only a subset of all the constituent units compete with one another in certain policy areas. The literature on the diffusion of legislative measures clearly indicates that this is sometimes the case (see Section 9.2, Subsection i). However, if one considers development policies, broadly defined, it would seem reasonable to assume that all the constituent units partake in the competition. However that may be, I will assume, without any loss of generality, that all the units in a given governmental system compete with one another. Furthermore, I will assume that the number of competing units is fixed – there is no exit and entry of units, no bankruptcy, and no new province or state. The last assumption reflects not a fact – though a fact it may be – but a constraint needed for the following analysis.

To proceed, I assume two jurisdictions (provinces or states) J_1 and J_2 which, given their sizes, have unit production and delivery (supply) costs for a particular (Hicksian) bundle of goods and services equal to C_1 and C_2 respectively. That is shown in Figure 9.3, which is drawn on the assumption that the two jurisdictions face the same average cost curve (AC); it should be obvious that I have made this assumption only because it simplifies the diagram. It would be easy to draw two different cost curves and get the same result. I have also drawn the cost curve sloping downward through its whole length. That too is a simplifying assumption, at least as long as the smaller jurisdiction operates at a unit cost that is higher than the minimum. Under the conditions depicted in the diagram, J_1 will always lose out to J_2 in the competitive struggle for talent, capital, and technology, and as a consequence its relative position will worsen continuously. Eventually, competition would drive J_1 to bankruptcy. By disallowing this possibility, I am forced to consider a stabilizing policy such as regional development (or grants).

Regional development policies would stabilize the outcomes of competition

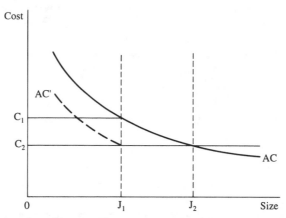

Figure 9.3. The stabilization of intergovernmental competition through regional policies.

if the unit costs of the goods and services supplied by the provincial or state governments were equalized, as would happen if the average cost curve of J_1 in Figure 9.3 was shifted by policy from AC to AC′. Three points should be made abut this property of development policy. First, efficient regional development policies are discriminatory: Not all provincial or state governments will be treated in the same way. Some jurisdictions will be the target of significant attention by central governments, whereas others will receive little or no attention. Second, virtually all governments in the system will be affected by regional development policy, some adversely. Third, regional policies will reduce interjurisdictional mobility, but not all mobility will be eliminated. But because jurisdictions will be competing on a more or less equal footing, the interjurisdictional mobility that will take place will be stable and productive.

In Section 9.3, Subsection ii, I pointed to the urban crisis in the United States as a manifestation of competitive instability. Following Bird and Slack (1983), I imputed the crisis, in part at least, to excessive intermunicipal mobility causing the competition between governments at that level to generate outcomes that are somewhat unstable. If the foregoing analysis is correct, a municipal development policy, implemented by the central or by state governments, could alleviate the problem.

c. Intergovernmental grants: The economic literature on intergovernmental grants programs derives from many traditions – an interjurisdictional spillover tradition [for example, Breton (1965) and Oates (1972)], an income redistribution tradition [for example, Buchanan (1950)], a fiscal imbalance tradition [for example, Musgrave (1961)], and an inefficient mobility of labor tradition [for example, Flatters, Henderson, and Mieszkowski (1974), and Boadway and Flatters (1982b)] – which are still not integrated and unified in any meaningful sense.[14] The *theoretical* work in these various traditions has, however, one assumption in common: It treats provincial or state governments – the recipients of money from central governments – as conduits for transfers directed to individuals or firms for the purpose of achieving certain objectives (the sources of the various traditions just noted): internalization of spillovers, redistribution of net fiscal benefits, and so on.

Sometimes the assumption of the provincial or state government as conduit is camouflaged by a prior supposition that all citizens have identical preferences.[15] But even in these cases, the assumption delivers its payload: To see this, it suffices to recognize that all the objectives that are assigned to grants programs can be more efficiently achieved by an interpersonal than by an intergovernmental transfer system, at least if we acknowledge, as we must, that preferences differ. One can probably make the case that, as a matter of historical fact, to the extent that governments have been preoccupied with the objectives that grant theorists impute to them and to the extent that they have used grants to achieve these objectives, they have resorted to interpersonal grants, namely, to grants made to persons (families) and firms but mediated by or effected through governments. In this connection, it is well to recall that in most societies income redistribution policy is embodied in a variety of "welfare" programs based on the age, the employment situation, the family status, the health conditions, and other characteristics of the individuals, families, and groups that are recipients. Proposals to streamline these programs have often been made by academics and others on the basis of little-known research that shows, one presupposes, that they are inefficient. George Akerlof (1978) has shown, however, that a strong case can be made that the patchwork of programs that form the income redistribution policy of societies is more efficient than some proposed streamlined systems would be, because for any given volume of redistribution the excess burden of the revenues needed to pay for it is smaller in the patchwork than in the streamlined system. What Akerlof calls "tagging," namely, the use of certain characteristics to identify the individuals and groups in need, is simply a device that insures that resources are not transferred to those who are not in need.

On the basis of the foregoing, one would have to conclude that from an income redistribution point of view, intergovernmental transfers are inefficient because the governments of some jurisdictions in which rich and poor

14. One could possibly add a Keynesian-stabilization tradition (see Raynauld, 1971, and Rabeau, 1986) to the list in the text, but it has never been a very active tradition.
15. This assumption in turn may be disguised by the adoption of a technique introduced into the theory of government grants by Scott (1952), which treats recipient governments as if they were individual consumers.

citizens reside receive funds, whereas the governments of other jurisdictions in which rich and poor citizens also reside do not receive any funds as a result of the fact that average per capita income, say, is lower in the first than in the second. Intergovernmental transfers, in other words, are inconsistent with "tagging" and, therefore, with efficient behavior.

If interpersonal grants are more efficient than intergovernmental grants, why do central governments sometimes use the second type of grants? Is it that central governments are not pursuing, through these grants, the objectives analysts think they ought to be pursuing? Is it possible, in other words, that the objectives that central governments are pursuing require intergovernmental grants programs in addition to the interpersonal grants programs they are implementing?

To see that the objectives pursued by governments are different from those that analysts believe they should be pursuing, refer to Courchene's (1984) *magnum opus* on equalization payments and recall his assertion "that the nature of Canada's equalization programs, past and present, owes much more to 'political' rationales then [sic] it does to any notion of economic efficiency" (quotation marks on political in the original). And to tell us what he means by "political," a few lines later, Courchene adds: "[i]s there any doubt that this consensus [on the principles of equalization that led to the Constitution Act, 1982] was rooted in the nationhood, federalist, and tax decentralization rationales, rather than in, say, a concern over efficiency?" He concludes by adding: "[d]espite all of this, the remainder of the chapter is devoted to a detailed discussion and evaluation of the economic underpinnings of equalization" (p. 92).

This makes clear that the policy objectives sought by decisionmakers and those the analyst would have them pursue are not the same. I am tempted to add that the view that the analyst is preoccupied with efficiency and "economic underpinnings," whereas the decisionmakers are not, is a gratuitous slur on the latter. Suppose that in the absence of equalization payments, the competition between provincial or state governments would produce outcomes unstable enough that the governmental system would, if not collapse, be subjected to severe disturbances, but that with a program of stabilizing intergovernmental grants it would not. Would one not have to conclude that the grants are efficient from a strict economic point of view? Notions of economic efficiency have meaning only in respect of the objectives of decisionmakers, but they have meaning in respect of any and all these objectives.

Robin Boadway and Frank Flatters (1982b) in their monograph on equalization, in effect come to the same conclusion as Courchene, although the road they travel is different. After discussing the equity arguments for equalization, arguments that they insist point to the superiority of interpersonal grants programs, they conclude in favor of intergovernmental systems on the ground that only with the latter will the central government not be able to override "all redistribution decisions of provincial governments." The central government should not have this latitude because "[i]n the Canadian federal system, federal and provincial governments jointly determine the extent of redistribution . . ." – a state of affairs that "is inherent in the distribution of tax and expenditure responsibilities between levels of government" (p. 52). They conclude by a policy recommendation according to which "the federal government [should] equalize in such a way as to *make it financially possible* to achieve full horizontal and vertical equity for all individuals. "But," they immediately add, "the provinces must be permitted to redistribute their own tax revenues as they see fit" (p. 53, italics in original).

I suggest that nationhood, federalism, equity, and efficiency – as understood in the various traditions to which I have referred – are not the rationales for intergovernmental grants. The necessity to stabilize interprovincial competition is the *raison d'être* of some of them. This does not mean that these transfers do not have effects on income distribution, mobility, the expenditure patterns of recipient governments, and other variables, but it means that grants programs should be analyzed and evaluated in terms of their contribution to the stability of horizontal intergovernmental competitive outcomes, not on some other basis.

How do intergovernmental grants contribute to competitive stability? Simply by allowing all provincial or state governments to compete with one another on a more equal footing than they could without them. If the grants were interpersonal instead of being intergovernmental, the relative positions of provincial or state governments would be unchanged by grants, even if the positions of their constituents were changed, unless of course the provincial or state tax rates were such as to fully recapture, province by province or state by state, the sums granted by central governments. If it is recalled that the jurisdictions in which governments are recipients of grants are made up (like those from which the funds are derived) of both rich and poor persons, a tax recapture scheme would of necessity be quite complicated and not obviously constitutional in democracies.

To visualize how an intergovernmental grants program helps to stabilize competition, consider how it would affect the operation of one of the modes of competition examined earlier. Assume, therefore, that a province or state innovates by introducing a new policy that receives support not only in the province or state in which it is implemented but elsewhere by serving as a Salmon benchmark (see Section 9.1, Subsection ii). The expected response within the competitive paradigm is for other provinces or states to follow. But what if one or more other provinces or states cannot follow because they lack the necessary resources to do so? Presumably, labor, capital, and technology will leave these jurisdictions, worsening the jurisdictions' positions relative to the preinnovation positions and improving those of the host provinces or states. That describes instability (see Section 9.3, Subsections i and ii); an intergovernmental grants program can prevent this from happening.

Viewing intergovernmental grants programs as instruments to stabilize horizontal competition not only provides us with a rationale for their existence as intergovernmental grants; it also helps to explain their perdurance in many governmental systems decades after decades. In addition, it allows us to do away with the idea that those who designed these programs and supported them over long periods were either ignorant of the dictates of Welfare Economics, moved by imperatives that were less than honorable, or simply irrational. Decisionmakers who opt for grants to promote competitive stability should and will choose intergovernmental grants. Finally, the recognition that intergovernmental transfers are only one in a series of possible instruments that can be used to stabilize competitive outcomes leads us to expect that grant systems will vary considerably from one governmental system to another both in terms of importance and in terms of design. It is even possible for some governmental systems not to have any grant systems because other instruments serve to achieve sufficient competitive stability.

Before concluding, I should repeat the point made in Breton (1985) that these grants will be unconditional. To see this it suffices to note that if they were conditional and if the conditions were set by central governments, as they would have to be, the grants programs would simply suppress competition. Central governments may want to do this in certain circumstances or in respect of specific policy areas – to, for example, realize minimum standards (see Section 9.4, Subsection ii) – but if they did this on a broad front, it would simply extinguish the governmental system itself. Conditional grants can be equivalent to a centralization of constitutional powers.

I have called these intergovernmental transfers stabilizing grants. In Chapter 8 I introduced and analyzed two other types of intergovernmental transfers, which I called remittances and revenue payments. In equilibrium, these are the only types of transfers. In the United States, Revenue Sharing was a stabilizing grant scheme, whereas the other grants programs are part of the revenue payment systems. In Canada, the Tax Collection Agreements give rise to remittances, the Equalization Payments – entrenched as Section 36 of the Canadian Constitution (1982) – are stabilizing grants, and the Established Programs Financing and Canada Assistance Plan are revenue payments.

iii.   Monitoring vertical competition

As already noted, in monitoring vertical competition, central governments confront an irreducible difficulty, namely, that they are themselves competing with provincial or state governments in the provision of goods and services.

As agents whose responsibility is to stabilize vertical competition between themselves and the provinces or states of governmental systems, central governments are, as it were, both judges and juries and will, unless constrained, have a tendency to police and enforce the rules of competition to their own advantage. The problem that a theory of competitive governmental systems must of necessity address relates to the constraints that will persuade or impel central governments to monitor vertical competition in as neutral a way as possible. As was the case with the monitoring of horizontal competition, there is no unique or singular set of constraints that will guarantee that vertical competition is appropriately monitored. Different governmental systems will address the matter differently. Still, there will be a tendency for the constraints on monitoring to have a family resemblance. Accordingly, in the remainder of this subsection, I look at three institutions and practices that have served or continue to serve as constraints: (1) a bicameral parliament or congress; (2) a provincial or state presence in the central government (intrastate federalism); and (3) a degree of entrenchment in the constitution.

a. Bicameralism: The legislative branch of central governments in many governmental systems – in virtually all federal governmental systems – is often bicameral with the added feature that one of the two chambers is structured to represent the preferences – interests, concerns, and demands – of provincial or state citizens *qua* provincial or state citizens. Sometimes representatives in second chambers are elected by the citizens and have, as a consequence, greater effectiveness because of the increment in legitimacy, which in our age elections confer. Sometimes the delegates are appointed either by the central government itself or by the provincial or state governments. When appointments are made by the junior governments, the delegates will still be able to contribute to the monitoring of vertical competition, albeit less effectively than if they were elected or appointed by central governments, unless they are the servants (in a master–servant relationship) of those junior governments as was, no doubt, the intention for United States Senators in the 1787 American Constitution (see Riker, 1955). As servants of junior governments, delegates would, on difficult matters, be forced by their appointors to obstruct the operations of central governments.[16]

How is vertical competition monitored? Simply by insuring that central governments do not seize or arrogate or, conversely, discard or relinquish, the responsibility for the provision of certain goods and services because of hubris, annoyance with junior governments, vexations, adventurousness, or a desire to be provocative. Vertical competition is monitored when central

16. For a discussion of how Canada's second chamber – the Senate – could be reformed to become a more effective monitor of vertical competition, see Breton (1985).

governments do not make use of their position to bend the rules of competition to their advantage by establishing control over the supply of goods and services or by discarding an obligation to supply goods and services that would be provided in the first instance more efficiently and in the second instance less efficiently. An example of a temporarily effective monitoring of vertical competition is the British House of Lords' opposition to Prime Minister Thatcher's elimination of seven Metropolitan county governments. Another example of effective monitoring of vertical competition is the Canadian Senate's defeat of a bill that would have amalgamated two granting bodies – the Canada Council and the Social Sciences and Humanities Research Council – making the merged body less efficient and leading to an eventual inefficient devolution to the provinces of the responsibility for supplying certain services. Finally, an example of a failure to monitor vertical competition is the American Senate's failure to block President Reagan's imposition of a minimum drinking age at the cost of federal funds to the states.

b. Intrastate federalism: My concern is with all governmental systems of which federalism is only one; I use the expression "intrastate federalism" because it is an established idiomatic term for the matter I now discuss. The reader should not, however, restrict its application to federal governmental systems. The words "interstate" and "intrastate" federalism were introduced into the literature by Karl Loewenstein (1965). However, the relevant substance now attached to these words was put there first by Donald Smiley (1971) and then by a number of Canadian political scientists among whom we find Alan Cairns (1979), Peter McCormick, Ernest Manning, and Gordon Gibson (1981), Roger Gibbins (1982), and Smiley and Ronald Watts (1985). Interstate federalism is mostly concerned with problems centered on the division of powers. The literature to which it has given rise is not very satisfactory, having adopted too many elements from the now essentially defunct "spillovers model" of governmental systems. Intrastate federalism is preoccupied with the design of some and possibly all the agencies that make up central governments: executive, legislative and judicial branches, regulatory boards, public corporations, and so on. The principle that the literature asserts should be embodied in the design of these agencies is that the values, preoccupations, and interests of provincial or state citizens be institutionally present in an effective way in decision making and policy implementation at the level of central governments.

The literature on intrastate federalism is not cast in the framework of a theory of competitive governmental systems. On the contrary the outlook of some, if not all, contributors is that competition is a destructive force that must be reined in or, better still, altogether suppressed. In addition, it is not an easy literature to read because, though essentially normative, the model of intrastate federalism is used, more or less at the same time that prescriptions are being formulated, to diagnose and analyze real-world problems.

That notwithstanding, the idea that vertical competition can be stabilized if provincial or state "values and interests" (Smiley and Watts, 1985, p. 155) are present in many (all?) agencies of central governments is surely correct. At the risk of oversimplifying, let me summarize in the language of this chapter the way intrastate federalism can stabilize vertical competition in governmental systems. First, the representation of provincial or state "values and interests" in the agencies of central governments increases the legitimacy (trustworthiness) of these agencies, which will then be reluctant to espouse practices that would impair the stock of accumulated legitimacy (trust). Second, that same representation will make it more difficult for central governments to use their power against the provinces or states in distortive ways, because of the provincial or state presence in the decisions of central governments. Third and last, that representation increases the knowledge that provincial and state governments have of the plans of central governments and allows the first to act before being confronted with *faits accomplis* by the second. Smiley and Watts (1985) have documented that elements of intrastate federalism such as these can be found in all real-world federations. They may, indeed, be important in all real-world governmental systems. Pierre Salmon has suggested to me that there is probably an element of intrastate federalism in the French governmental system's *cumul des mandats,* that is, in the practice whereby many members of parliament and most cabinet ministers are also mayors of cities, presidents of *conseils généraux* (such as *assemblées départementales*), of regional councils, and the like.

c. Constitutional entrenchment: Entrenchment is always relative. Constitutional provisions, even when well established and well founded and even when their wording remains unaltered, change. When the basic text is untouched, changes are made through bilateral or multilateral agreements or covenants or through judicial reinterpretation; when the basic text is modified, changes take the form of amendments and redrafting. Still, however great the variation in entrenched constitutional provisions, entrenchment makes a difference, as we have seen in the Section 9.4 discussion of confederal, unitary, and federal constitutions.

The difference, it will be recalled, has its roots in the fact that the constitutional ownership of powers is different among these various types of governmental systems. In both confederal and unitary states, constitutional provisions are embodied in *legislative* documents of the junior or of the senior governments and can be modified unilaterally by one or the other. In federal states, powers are incorporated in *constitutional* documents which can be formally (excepting the case of judicial interpretation) altered only with the explicit, though not necessarily unanimous, consent of central and provincial or state governments.

Entrenchment – whether legislative or constitutional – can therefore serve as a more or less solid barrier that constrains central governments to be more effective monitors of vertical competition. Entrenchment can prevent capricious occupation or desertion by central governments of one or the other particular supply responsibility when these governments perceive the possibility of exploiting a particular advantage that would destabilize socially beneficial competition.

9.6.   The Wicksellian Connection reconsidered

At this stage, only one more word is needed on the Wicksellian Connection. That word is simply that Wicksellian Connections will be more robust – the link between taxprices and quantities demanded tighter – the more effective central governments are in monitoring intergovernmental competition both horizontal and vertical and in insuring that the rules governing the efficiency of that competition are respected. In turn, effective monitoring and enforcement of rules will depend on the extent to which central governments can access instruments that allow them to monitor horizontal competition and on the extent to which central governments are designed to monitor vertical competition without bias. Failure to access instruments, failure to use them, and failure to do necessary reforms called by "intrastate" considerations will make Wicksellian Connections weaker than they would be otherwise. *The Federalist* (1787–8) and a short list of genuine political leaders have understood the very central role of central governments in promoting Wicksell–Lindahl efficiency in governmental systems. It must be acknowledged that by proposing models of governmental systems in which central governments are altogether absent, many scholars have often forgotten about that crucial role.

9.7.   Conclusion

This chapter has been concerned with intergovernmental competition. After a discussion of the *modus operandi* of the Tiebout and Salmon intergovernmental competition mechanisms, it has provided empirical evidence that is consistent with the view that governments compete with one another in the provision of goods and services. It has also sought to document the fact that the various identified types of competition will generate outcomes that are often unstable. The evidence presented in support of this second point is not as transparent as one would desire because there are institutions in place that generally prevent the instability from manifesting itself.

The institutions that secure stability, the chapter has argued, are reflections or products of the actions, instruments, and policies of central governments when they act as monitors of horizontal and vertical competition. A range of practices and features of governmental systems are interpreted as being consistent with the proposition that central governments do, in fact, effectively monitor horizontal and vertical competition. To the extent that they do so, they make an added contribution to the creation of robust Wicksellian Connections, and to the extent that they fail to monitor as well as they could, they forge Wicksellian Connections that are weaker than need be.

CHAPTER 10

The world order

In the ongoing search for a robust theory of the international political economy or world order and of the place of international organizations in that order, economists, political scientists, and others have borrowed an impressive number of ideas and propositions from neoclassical economics. There now exists an assortment of models that make one use or another of concepts taken from the theory of externalities – including of course Coase's (1960) theorem – from the theory of public goods, and from the derived theory of collective action. Other models rely more heavily on the theory of games, especially on variants of the prisoners' dilemma game.[1] Finally, in recent years, ideas borrowed from the theory of property rights, from that of self-enforcing agreements, and from the emerging theories of reputation and trust have also found their way into these models.[2]

As is well known, these economic theories in their original, or natural, settings are associated with the notion of market failure and with the analysis of the "spontaneous" forces or of policy alternatives that can either mitigate these failures or eliminate them altogether. In the international organizations literature, the same theories are similarly associated with what could be called "world order failure" and with the attendant question of the desirability or undesirability of international cooperation, and on the assumption of desirability, of ways and means of generating cooperative outcomes to deal with the failure problem.

Traditionally, the expression "market failure" has been used as a shortcut for "failure of competitive market forces." The stylistic power brought about by the excision has been acquired, it would appear, at a price. It is not, of course, the mere existence of public goods, externalities, and other like phenomena, such as technological economies of scale, that produce failure but their existence in the presence of competitive forces (see Samuelson, 1954, p. 389); the same phenomena in certain noncompetitive contexts would not be associated with failure. But the absence of competition from the analytical stage has had an important consequence: Approaches that would focus on institutions and policies designed to make competition efficient and produc-

1. See Keohane (1984) and Frey (1984a) for references to the literature.
2. See, for example, Conybeare (1980), Yarbrough and Yarbrough (1986), and Keohane (1984).

tive are given short shrift or not even contemplated. This is very much in the tradition of conventional Welfare Economics, which assigns the solution of market failures to governments – bodies that are assumed to be monolithic.

In the international political economy literature, there is considerable disagreement on the extent of world order failure (see Corden, 1981, Vaubel, 1983, and Keohane, 1984, for a sampling of the different views), but when it is acknowledged to exist, the solutions center on the desirability of cooperation,[3] which is then seen as the outcome of actions taken by hegemonic powers such as Rome, Britain, and the United States, which have given the world or parts thereof Pax Romana, Pax Britannica, and Pax Americana – metaphors intended to convey the idea that cooperation induced by hegemonic powers leads to beneficial resolutions of problems of world order failure. Those hegemonic powers are assumed to be monolithic and to operate through what political scientists call "international regimes" (I define and discuss these in Section 10.3).

This chapter is not offered as a solution to the problems of world order failure. The reader should approach it as if it was a digression, which it is. It is presented as no more than an exploration of what the theory of competitive governmental systems developed in the two preceding chapters has to say about intergovernmental competition at the international level. For that purpose, it places the idea of competition at center stage and accepts the notion of international regimes but enwrapped in a frame of reference different from the one in which it is usually embodied. I start from the premise that the problems of the international community of nations are not primarily problems related to the control of externalities originating either in the supply of international public goods, or in international interjurisdictional spillovers, or in both, nor are they primarily problems of cooperation and noncooperation, but problems of ensuring that the competitive forces that array and govern international relations are stable and efficient. This is more than a simple change of emphasis. Focusing on competition and on the institutions which guarantee that it is stable and efficient will reveal important difficulties with the notion of a hegemon who produces cooperation. Instead, I will be forced by the logic of competition to concentrate on the conditions that must be satisfied if a hegemon is to be able to fulfill the role assigned to it in the theory of hegemonic stability (Morgenthau, 1948/66; Gilpin, 1981; and Keohane, 1984).

To repeat, my purpose will be to apply to the world order and to international organizations some of the building blocks of the theory of competitive governmental systems. There are important and significant differences between a governmental system – whether federal or not – and a world order,

3. Not everyone, among those who diagnose failure, recommends cooperation (see Rogoff, 1985).

but it is better to let them emerge from the theory than to impose them as a matter of definition. There are also similarities between the two orders. For example, the competition that exists between the provinces or states of a governmental system and that between the states of the world appear to be of the same kind and very much governed by the same Salmon and Tiebout mechanisms that rule inside governmental systems (see Chapter 9, Section 9.1 for a discussion of these mechanisms), so that the instruments that ensure efficient and stable competition in one framework should be the same in the other.

The proof of the pudding is in the eating. If the theory of competitive governmental systems can serve as a blueprint for a theory of a competitive world order, significant and worthwhile theoretical simplifications will have been achieved. More important, however, theories of the world order, such as imperialism, which not so long ago still had wide currency, or the "dependency" hypothesis, still popular in Latin America, could be examined in a new light, since on one interpretation at least, both of these hypotheses pertain to pathological manifestations of competition. In that case, these theories would find a natural habitat in a more general theory of the world order.

In his review of Robert Keohane's (1984) book, Salmon (1986) has suggested that a number of propositions in that book would have been different if Keohane had paid more attention to smaller subsystems instead of focusing on the world of which the United States is taken to be the hegemon. Coming to the theory of the world order via a model of competitive governmental systems is a natural protection against criticisms of that kind. But it is more than that. It makes it possible to shed new light on these subsystems themselves. In that spirit, I will try to demonstrate that proposition by suggesting a perspective, derived from the theory of competitive governmental systems, for some aspects of the structure of the European Union.[4] In the same review, Salmon also noted that Keohane had underestimated the role of the (former) USSR in his analysis of postwar developments. Reviewing all the evidence goes beyond my own project; I will, however, examine the influence of competing hegemons on the world order. To be precise, in the next two sections I examine the nature of international competition and the place and characteristics of international regimes in a stable and efficient competitive world order. Section 10.3 looks at Europe and Section 10.4 concludes the chapter.

My ambition is to provide in this chapter a new way of looking at a competitive world order and to suggest an analysis of the conditions under which international organizations are not only required but truly efficient. In the process, I hope that the theory of governmental systems itself will be enriched.

4. What was first called the European Economic Communities, then the European Communities is now, after the Maastricht Treaty, called the European Union. I use that expression in the text.

10.1.   International competition

The purpose of this section is *not* to argue that the world order is competitive. That it is has, to my knowledge, never been denied. The enormous literature concerned with the need for international cooperation or with the uselessness or wastefulness of such cooperation is a vibrant testimony, albeit mostly backhanded, of the competitive nature of international relations. What is not sufficiently recognized and, consequently, must be emphasized is that this competitiveness is grounded in the obligation, not legal but behavioral, of all governments – democratic and nondemocratic, though more so for the first than for the second – to be sensitive to the interests and preferences of their citizens and to respond to them. This does not deny that governments would like to be more autonomous of their citizens so as to compete on only their own terms. But the evidence is overwhelming that their behavior in the international arena is dictated by citizens as much as it is on the domestic front.

One can point to tariff formation [for an able summary of the literature on the subject see Frey (1984b)], to foreign aid and the role of interest groups in donor countries in trying to ensure that the aid is "tied," to the direct involvement of citizens in bringing the Vietnam War to an end against the will of the Establishment, or to any number of similar events to bring home the point that citizens are a strong driving force behind international competition. But there is evidence that goes much further back. In his study of foreign policy in the seventeenth and eighteenth centuries, Jacob Viner observes that "major political considerations, including the very safety of the country [Holland] or its success in wars in which it was actually participating, had repeatedly to give way to the cupidity of the merchants . . ." [Viner (1948), as quoted by Keohane (1984), p. 23]. Viner's "major political considerations" are, of course, the government's own considerations or private objectives; these had to be modified as a result of the action of citizens, and consequently Holland's competitive posture was different than it would have otherwise been.

Citizens are very often absent from the formal international political economy literature.[5] Explicitly or implicitly, governments (or states) are then the basic units of analysis to which utility functions, defined over wealth and power as sole arguments, are imputed.[6] Keohane (1984, p. 23), who surveys a

---

5. In Keohane's (1984) *magnum opus* on international organizations, citizens make appearances when real world events are discussed and analyzed (see, for example, the narratives on pp. 103 and 147), but they are absent from the theory.
6. Ruggie (1972) under the label of "modified Westphalia system" provides a rationale for the assumption and, as a by-product, for the hold that the assumption has on the minds of political scientists. Citizens have never had much of a role to play in economists' approach to government.

wide literature, refers, in the spirit of Viner's remarks that I quoted above, to "the long-term power/wealth interests of the state and the partial interests of individual merchants, workers, or manufacturers." The assumption comes, no doubt, from a world in which governments are all nondemocratic and, as a consequence, entertain only minimal relationships with their citizens (called in that context "subjects"). From such a perspective, it is difficult to understand what forms the basis of "the long-term power/wealth interests" of democratic governments, and it certainly makes the analysis of many real-world problems awkward. If one follows a competitive governmental systems approach to world order and international organizations, utility functions have to be imputed to the citizens of democratic states, with significant consequences, as will transpire later. The arguments of these utility functions are the goods and services citizens want, including internationally provided goods and services.

In Chapters 7 and 9, I have identified and examined two different mechanisms that can motivate centers of power in one jurisdiction to compete with centers of power in another. I called them the Salmon and Tiebout mechanisms. It is clear that these mechanisms operate in the international order as well and that they help us to understand why governments compete the way they do. They help us to interpret the kind of evidence I have just sketched. I also note that if democratic governments (states) do pursue wealth and power, it is only because these pursuits are derived from the preferences of their citizens.

The recognition that democratic governments compete with one another because they have to respond to their citizens' interests and preferences has some important theoretical consequences for the analysis of international competition. I mean, in particular, that the use of Prisoners' Dilemma games to model that competition and to derive propositions about the need for cooperation is misleading. The reason for this is simply that in a context in which citizens have a say, cooperation may not be sustainable or if it is imposed, it is equivalent to collusion, because it serves only to curb and even suppress the interests and preferences of citizens.

To illustrate, consider the tit-for-tat strategy that has been shown to dominate all other strategies in computer tournaments of iterated Prisoners' Dilemma games (Axelrod, 1984). Tit for tat is a strategy that consists in being cooperative on the first move and of doing, on all successive moves, what the other player did on the previous one. The strategy is dominant in that it has the largest payoff. Since the strategy leads to cooperation, one concludes that in Prisoners' Dilemma contexts, the most appropriate way to compete must be tit for tat. That view is reinforced by the fact that, under reasonable conditions, tit for tat is "collectively stable," that is, it is a strategy that, when it has been adopted by a population, cannot be "invaded" by any other more successful strategies (Axelrod, 1984, pp. 55–61).

Given all these virtues why do we not generally observe the practice of international competition evolving toward tit for tat? At its most basic, a government that represents the interests and preferences of citizens may not have the capacity or freedom to tit (or to tat) when it is time to do so. In the international competition in which citizens count, there are costs (including the loss of political consent) as well as benefits (the payoffs of the mathematical models) to titting and tatting, and it is reasonable to assume that sometimes the cost of these actions will exceed their benefits. In such circumstances a rational decisionmaker will jettison tit for tat and adopt other modes of competing that are designed to sustain the consent of citizens: The decisionmaker will behave like a Schumpeterian entrepreneur. In addition, political actors may not have the resources required for engaging in a tit-for-tat game. Such games tend to favor the wealthiest players and to be detrimental to the poorest, who are often not in a position to respond optimally because they lack the wherewithal to do so.

In discussing the virtues of a tit-for-tat strategy, Robert Axelrod (1984, p. 18) asserts that to use the Prisoners' Dilemma model it is not necessary to assume "a unified actor pursuing a single goal. On the contrary, they [the actions of players] might well be the result of an incredibly complex bureaucratic politics involving information processing and shifting political coalitions." That will be true, if and only if, when it is time to tit (or to tat), the "shifting political coalitions" are not an obstacle to that action. It must be remembered that, even if to tit (or to tat) in computer tournaments is a very simple action, it will always correspond in the world of international relationships to complex, intricate, and even convoluted behavior. In general, I would expect Axelrod's assertion not to hold in the world of democratic competitive politics.

If the reality of international competition is accepted and the elaborate and complicated nature of that competition acknowledged, we can move on to a more difficult and inherently more contentious question, namely, the matter of the "public goods" character – in the sense given that term by Samuelson (1954) – of the goods and services internationally provided. The question is contentious because to some extent it turns on a problem of definition. There is a long and respectable tradition in economics – born of the protracted debates on how best to define the concept of public goods – that consists in identifying as public good *anything* that is the same for two or more persons. In that view, a price, such as the price of labor, is a public good, because once determined (through bargaining, let us say,) it is equally available to all labor services to which it pertains (see Olson, 1965). As noted, that approach is legitimate and has produced many interesting results. But it can be confusing if it is not used with care.

To illustrate, let me consider the (intentionally) nonexhaustive list of international public goods in Charles Kindleberger's (1986) Presidential Address to the American Economic Association. The list begins with peace and then goes on to include "an open trading system, including freedom of the seas, well-defined property rights, standards of weights and measures that may include international money, or fixed exchange rates, and the like" (pp. 7–8). There is no doubt that these are all (technical) public goods and as such are, for standard reasons, associated with market failure. That is Kindleberger's point. But looked at in a different way, they are also components or dimensions of what comes to mind when one thinks of competition. That is surely the case for the freedom to buy and to sell and for the property rights that ensure the enforcement of contracts as well as for the property rights implied in standardized, easily policeable weights and measures; it is even the case for peace, since wars, like divorces and strikes, are a sign that relationships, whether competitive or not, have broken down.

There is nothing wrong in treating these various goods and services as public goods, but there is one advantage at least in thinking of them as components of a competitive framework that is not to be had when one thinks of them as public goods: It does away with the idea that the goods and services can be produced by a higher-level government – an international government – alone, and it forces us to focus on the conditions under which competition can be made efficient and stable through efficient monitoring.

The advantage is real. There are some (true) international public goods that are *not* components of the international competitive system: control of malaria, abatement of acid rain, weather modification, and others. These have to be produced by world bodies or through international arrangements. Recall the discussion in Chapter 9 (Section 9.5) and the distinction between the supply and the monitoring responsibilities of central governments. If there was an international division of functions and of powers, those embodying the responsibility to supply goods and services that were truly international public goods would presumably be assigned to some body such as a world government. But that *of itself* does not mean that that government would also have been given the capacity to monitor international competition. Assigning only the authority to provide goods and services to a world body would produce something that would be in the nature of a world confederation. Such a structure, for the reasons advanced in Chapter 9, Section 9.4, would be unstable. To mimic a world federation and achieve stability and efficiency would require that the world body be also given the power to monitor international competition. I look at this matter in more depth immediately.

10.2.   International regimes

It is fair to say that the question of the international division of powers is not *explicitly* on the research agenda of scholarship concerned with issues that relate to world order and to international organizations.[7] The word "explicitly" is appropriately emphasized. Important parts of the literature dealing with the international supply of goods and services [for example, Ruggie (1972), Keohane (1984), and Kindleberger (1986)] would be directly relevant to any investigation of how that division is (or should be) effected. It is the assumption of *national sovereignty* that has removed the matter from the agenda; what has taken its place are debates over the incidence and significance of market failure and the desirability of dealing with it through international cooperation. Because cooperation is almost antithetical to the notion of assigning responsibility, the existing state of affairs is not surprising.

If one approaches the problems of world order and international organizations from the perspective of the theory of competitive governmental systems, an international division of functions and of powers must be presumed. In the language of Chapter 9, one would then have to say that the existing international division of functions is very deconcentrated and that it is not constitutionally entrenched and protected. As we know from that chapter, this state of affairs has implications for vertical competition. Before discussing this problem I must, however, inquire into the nature and characteristics of the institutions that compete vertically in the international order.

"Realists," both in political science and in economics [Bryant (1980) and Kindleberger (1986)], who diagnose market failure and argue for cooperation as a solution, use the notion of international regimes to describe the loci or sites of such cooperation.[8] First introduced in the literature by John Ruggie (1975), the idea of regimes has received considerable attention. Keohane (1984, p. 57), quoting Stephen Krasner (1983), defines them as "sets of implicit or explicit principles, norms, rules and decision-making procedures around which actors' expectations converge in a given area of international relations." Reference to "principles, norms, rules and . . . procedures," in my opinion, complicates matters more than is necessary. Adopting the language of the theory of property rights, one can simplify by saying that international regimes are the implicitly or explicitly accepted behaviors that can be permitted and those that have to be proscribed if the competitive pursuit of

7. To my knowledge, the only explicit discussion is by Vaubel (1986) who, using the expression "division of labor" (p. 47), discusses the problem without, however, any references to the federalist literature on the assignment of functions and powers.
8. For a thorough discussion of the schools of thought among political scientists and what they stand for, see Keohane (1984), Chapter 1.

self-interest by governments is to be stable and efficient. It is worth noting that the very existence of regimes is an implicit recognition that unrestrained international competition is unstable. Such a proposition is obvious to anyone who has reflected on the place and role of property rights in guaranteeing orderly behavior in all institutions, including markets.

For a variety of reasons, among which the dynamic and changing nature of international circumstances which demand a virtually continuous updating and interpretation of the accepted conventions of regimes, these regimes are incorporated in international organizations. It is recognized that these bodies do not have the formal power to monitor competition and to enforce the rules of competition (see Chapter 9). There is, as a consequence, an ongoing debate on whether international competition or the search for cooperation, in the framework of international regimes, is self-policing. Notwithstanding Keo-hane's (1984) valiant efforts to demonstrate that it is, I believe that the weight of the evidence is that it is not. The fact that regimes are valuable does not mean that they will not be sabotaged when the cost of not doing so is a significant loss of consent from one's own citizens. To be stable and efficient, international competition, like all intergovernmental competition, has to be monitored and the rules of competition enforced. This is one instance when the assumption that citizens do not count is misleading.

Ruggie (1983), Keohane (1984), and others attribute to the principle of sovereignty the fact that international organizations do not monitor interna-tional competition and enforce the necessary rules. That is also misleading: Sovereignty gives governments the power to accept being monitored by a third party and being forced to adhere to agreed upon rules in the same way that it gives them the power to accept the convention of international regimes. The fundamental reason international organizations, which embody the exist-ing regimes, cannot monitor international competition and enforce the rules is that they do not have the resources to do so.

As we have seen in earlier chapters, monitoring and enforcement are car-ried out through the implementation of negative and positive measures. This requires resources. Indeed, if competition is rife, effective monitoring and enforcement will require abundant resources. If the resources are not forth-coming, the international order will unravel or, to avoid the unraveling, com-petition will be suppressed through the use of various devices (see Section 10.5).

The reason we observe stable and efficient international competition, some-times for fairly long periods, is that competitive behavior during these periods is monitored and the rules of competition enforced by an hegemonic power. It is generally accepted that international organizations and the regimes they embody are promoted by hegemons. The existing international regimes, for example, are largely the product of the efforts of the United States government in the years following World War II. Monitoring and the enforcement of rules is not done, however, by regimes but by hegemonic powers. These powers create the regimes to facilitate monitoring and the enforcement of rules. It is easy to understand why this is so: International regimes reduce the costs of monitoring and enforcement, and, the more effective the regimes, the lower those costs. If governments abide by the conventions laid down in regimes, monitoring will be easier. Still it will not be inexpensive. In the twenty-five years following World War II, while a system of international regimes was being erected under the aegis of the United States, that country expended a very large volume of resources to stabilize international competition. However, if the regimes had not been built, it would have had to allocate considerably more resources to achieve the same result. The argument is a familiar one: The enforcement of property rights is less costly in a law-abiding society.

Without any fundamental changes in the structure of regimes, beginning in the mid-1970s and until the demise of the Soviet Union, it would appear that the United States monitored international competition less effectively than it had heretofore and, as a consequence, one could observe an incipient unraveling of the world order. That fact, on the assumption that it is a fact, poses a fundamental theoretical question: When will a hegemonic power choose to monitor international competition and enforce the necessary rules, and when will it abdicate that role? If I interpret the literature on hegemons and regimes within my own framework of analysis, I would have to conclude that a hegemonic power monitors and enforces in direct proportion to its degree of hegemony. In that perspective, the decline in monitoring and enforcement that began in the mid-1970s and persisted until the fall of the Soviet Union would be attributed to the fact that during that period the United States had more or less ceased to be a hegemon.

I would like to suggest a different view of things. As I have noted, there are costs to monitoring and to enforcing rules, but there are also benefits. Benefits derive in the last analysis from the fact that a hegemonic power's interests are everywhere within the domain of its hegemony. The question, then, is whether monitoring and enforcement costs rose or the benefits decreased during the period under consideration. It would be hard to argue convincingly that either changed. So we must look elsewhere to understand what happened. Did the United States's command over resources decline at that time? Keohane (1984, Chapter 3) and others have argued that it did. But their argument is cast in terms of command over resources *relative* to that of others, which is hardly relevant; that tells us only that the United States was less of a hegemon, not that it had ceased to be one. Did the U.S. government decide to allocate less of the country's command over resources to the international order during that period? A casual look at the data, if it tells us anything, tells us the opposite.

What, then, did happen during that period? To understand that, it is necessary to recognize that even if it was a hegemonic power, the United States was *not* a world hegemonic power. It was a hegemon in a particular space; in another space, the Soviet Union was the hegemon; and in a third space, China was emerging as the hegemon. (Because China's hegemony is only incipient, I neglect it in what follows.)

Hegemonic powers compete with one another. In the present instance, the competition was between two radically different *social systems* to which all the vital interests of each were attached. In the mid- and late-1970s, after the defeat of the United States in Vietnam, the invasion of Afghanistan by the USSR, and the extension of Soviet influence in the Horn of Africa, there developed a widespread perception in the United States that the hegemonic competition with the Soviets was being lost. In the years that followed, the American government successfully reallocated a considerable amount of resources to that competition, forcing a reduction in the volume of resources that in the previous decades had been allocated to monitoring competition and enforcing the rules of competition in the geographic space of its own hegemony.

The reallocation of resources – of money, of preoccupation and attention, and of priorities – was successful vis-à-vis the USSR, but why did it adversely affect monitoring of horizontal competition and the enforcement of rules within the United States's own sphere of influence? Earlier, I noted that international regimes can reduce the cost of monitoring to the extent that the parties that are members of these regimes adhere to their conventions. However, during the period we are discussing, the regimes' conventions were broken by virtually all members, not least by the United States government itself.

One of the reasons the conventions were breached is that a hegemonic power is an inefficient monitor of horizontal competition and an inefficient enforcer of the rules of competition; the source of the inefficiency is to be found in the fact that the interests, concerns, and preoccupations of the countries in the hegemon's domain or sphere of influence are not represented in the hegemon's deliberations and decision making. The precepts of intrastate federalism are violated. It is well to be clear on the meaning of that violation. The interests and concerns of the governments in the hegemon's sphere of influence are represented in the international regimes but not in the hegemon itself. Because it is the latter and not the former that monitors and enforces rules, hegemonic monitoring and enforcement are always inefficient, though at times the inefficiency can be minimal.

Could hegemonic powers be made into efficient monitors of horizontal competition and enforcers of rules? My own view is that this is not likely. Why? Because that would require that vertical competition between the hegemon and the governments in its sphere of influence be stabilized by a "constitution" in which a division of powers would be entrenched and protected. "World federalists" are possibly idealistic when they advocate such a constitution, but applying the logic of competitive governmental systems to the world order indicates that they are correct, even if world federalism is not in the cards. The stability of competitive outcomes in the international domain or in parts of that domain is not always achieved through regimes and hegemons. When these do not exist, stability is still possible through different means. It is interesting, from that perspective, to look at the European Community and to inquire into how competition is stabilized in that part of the world order.

10.3. The European Union

There is no doubt that the creation and growth of the European Union are remarkable achievements. Through the Treaty of Rome, proud nations, which in the past had often resolved conflictual situations by aggression and war, agreed to form a community. For some community members, the project was a midway house on the road to a "United States of Europe" or to a federal structure; for others, the community was the end – a permanent *"Europe des patries."* However that may be, Europe is still not a federation. True, there is an elected European Parliament, which meets in Strasbourg, but a large fraction of important Union decisions are made by the Council of Ministers – that is, by the national ministers of the various member countries in general meetings – whose decisions are made on the basis of weighted majority voting. Furthermore, the division of functions between the member nations and the center is a very deconcentrated one, and there is no constitutionally entrenched division of powers. Finally, the center – the Parliament and the Council – has only limited power to monitor horizontal competition among the member countries and to enforce rules of competition.

The theory of competitive governmental systems tells us that under these circumstances the outcomes of horizontal competition will be unstable. Should one then conclude that the European Union is an unstable structure likely to unravel under the impact of a severe exogenous shock? I do not believe that to be the case. I believe that the European Union is quite stable but that the stability has been acquired by the virtual suppression of intercountry competition through excessive policy harmonization.

Let me underline this point. Within the confines of Europe, there is no hegemonic power ready to monitor horizontal competition and to enforce the rules of competition; in addition, the central bodies of the community are poorly equipped for these tasks. Unmonitored and the rules not enforced, competition is unstable. To prevent the occurrence of instability, competition is minimized through the excessive harmonization of a substantial fraction of social, economic, and other policies. Harmonization is not complete, but if one compares the degree of harmonization in Europe with that in Canada, the United States, and other federations, one is impressed by the extent to which it is greater in Europe than in the federations.

Policy harmonization reduces competition by neutralizing and, at the limit, by extinguishing the Salmon and Tiebout mechanisms. Minimizing competition in this way ensures stability but at the cost of forgoing the benefits that come with competition. This provides us with a somewhat ironic paradox. The national governments of the member countries of the European Union do not assign more entrenched and constitutionally protected powers to the European Parliament and do not give it the power to monitor horizontal competition among themselves and the power to enforce the rules of competition because doing so, it is thought, would infringe on their sovereignty and their indivisible, autonomous, and independent status. But to be able to enjoy a stable Union structure, they impose on themselves a series of harmonizing measures that transforms them into the simile of a unitary state – thereby metamorphosing their individual sovereignty and independence from reality into symbol!

There is only one way for Europe to enjoy the benefits of intergovernmental competition: through a constitution that assigns significant powers to a supranational Parliament and thus allows that government to monitor competition and to enforce the necessary rules. The straitjacket of excessive harmonization could then be jettisoned and the provision of differentiated goods and services tailored to the preferences of citizens in each jurisdiction adopted.

10.4.   Conclusion

This chapter, which is no more than a digression, has tried to apply some of the propositions developed in the analysis of domestic governmental systems to the problem of intergovernmental competition at the international level. In an indirect way, it has confirmed once more that what was invented in Philadelphia in the summer of 1787 – the logically unappealing idea of "divided sovereignty" – was of great significance. The idea behind the chapter's development is simply that if the institutions that guarantee the stability of federal systems of government could be applied to a world government at the international level, citizens of member states could benefit from goods and services produced at lower cost – because of a more efficient specialization between orders of government and because of more stable competitive relationships between these governments.

PART III

Socio-political structures

CHAPTER 11

The size of the nonmarket sector

In their capacity as suppliers of goods and services, governmental centers of power do not only compete with one another, with other centers of powers within their own governmental systems, and with those centers of power outside these systems, but they also compete with a broad range of institutions that are actually or potentially engaged in the provision of similar goods and services. Among these institutions, one must include families – extended, nuclear, and monoparental – churches, religious, humanitarian and other eleemosynary organizations, clubs, unions, cooperatives, business enterprises, and others. The size of the nonmarket sector is therefore quite large, encompassing as it does all these nongovernment–nonmarket bodies in addition to the governments themselves. I stress that the nongovernment–nonmarket part of that sector is considerably larger even today – and was certainly much larger only a few decades ago – than the nonprofit or not-for-profit sector that has retained the attention of scholars like Burton Weisbrod (1977, 1988) and Henry Hansmann (1980). The reason for this is that the nonprofit sector has not been defined to include institutions like families, churches,[1] and corporate businesses,[2] which have historically been and remain even today important suppliers of goods and services that compete with those provided by governments.

To a degree, the neglect of nongovernment–nonmarket institutions – and the consequent tacit assumption that the only rivals of governments in the provision of goods and services are privately owned business enterprises operating in markets – has its roots in a simple semantic problem. Goods and services like care of the elderly, of the sick and the convalescent, of the unemployed, and of the physically and mentally challenged are not given bureaucratic labels when supplied by families, charities, and other nongovernment–nonmarket organizations but are classified as old age pension programs, health insurance programs, unemployment insurance programs, and rehabilitation programs when provided by governments, though the goods and services offered by the

---

1. In some societies, churches are themselves, or have created, nonprofit organizations, but that is not true everywhere and has not historically been a very important phenomenon even where churches were deeply involved in the care of infants, the sick, the elderly, and the indigent.
2. Not in their role as market suppliers of goods and services, but as providers of goods and services to their employees and to their families.

279

latter differ not at all or only in degree from those supplied by the former. As a consequence of the labeling, they are in addition often taken to be genuine goods and services in the first instance but treated as transfers in the second.

As I will suggest anew in Chapter 12, the growth of governments over the past two centuries or so has been, on the basis of the available evidence, the result of a reallocation of the responsibility for the provision of many goods and services from families, churches, humanitarian and other organizations to governmental centers of power. Such a redirection implies that whatever transformation the goods and services may have been subjected to in the process of reallocation, they are of the same class after the move as they were before.

If the idea that centers of power in a given government and governments in governmental systems compete with one another is difficult to accept, the notion that governments on the one hand and nongovernment–nonmarket institutions such as those listed earlier on the other are competing among themselves is, for some, simply preposterous. It will be one of the tasks of this and the next chapter to seek to convince that the assumption that the nonmarket sector is competitive permits a logically consistent and empirically satisfactory explanation of the available evidence. Before undertaking that assignment, I must, however, briefly consider the literature on nonprofit organizations and explain how that body of literature relates to what I have to say on the nongovernment–nonmarket sector. That will retain my attention in the next two sections. Then, in Section 11.3, I will state and illustrate an assumption that is essential to the supposition that the nonmarket sector is competitive. Section 11.4 will conclude the chapter.

11.1.   Nonprofit organizations

I have already hinted at the fact that there are two major models of that part of the nongovernment–nonmarket sector known as the nonprofit sector: One was suggested by Weisbrod and the other was introduced into the literature by Richard Nelson and Michael Krashinsky (1973) and was fully developed by Hansmann. Both have elements common to those underlying the model of "the growth of competitive governments" proposed in my Presidential Address to the Canadian Economics Association (1989) and reproduced, with some important changes, in the next chapter.

In his second book on the subject, Weisbrod (1988) has assembled and synthesized many of the ideas put forward to explain the existence of nonprofit organizations. He does, however, give pride of place – and rightly so – to the model that he himself has developed. That model, reduced to its minimum expression and therefore stripped of much of its richness, states that nonprofit organizations exist to provide collective-type goods in quantities and qualities different from what is provided by governments, which in democracies, Weisbrod assumes, must respond to the interests of the majority. In other words, the nonprofit sector exists to respond to a greater diversity of demand than the governmental sector can satisfy because of the majoritarian constraint to which it is bound. Weisbrod recognizes that to fulfill that function, nonprofit organizations will have to address and resolve a free-rider problem and that in fact they do (Weisbrod, 1988, pp. 25–31).[3]

From the point of view of this study, the main problem with Weisbrod's bare-bone paradigm – the one in which he attempts to integrate all the contributions he finds pertinent – is not that many nonprofits supply other than collective-type goods or that what nonprofit organizations do could just as well be done by for-profit enterprises (see Hansmann, 1987), but the tacit assumption that governments are monolithic structures. That assumption is implicit in the use made of the so-called majoritarian principle.[4] Weisbrod uses the fact that the "nonprofit sector does seem to be particularly noteworthy in the United States, a country of unusual diversity" as evidence that nonprofits are a response to the desire to diversify the bundle of goods and services provided to a multiplicity of distinct groups of citizens. He goes on to argue that "[t]his is what the demand-diversity model would predict – if government responds to the demands of the majority and the nonprofit sector responds to the demands of the undersatisfied, then the greater the diversity of demand the larger the size of the nonprofit sector will be, other things being equal" (Weisbrod, 1988, p. 27). Someone writing on federalism or on governmental systems generally would make exactly the same argument doing no more than substituting in this quotation the words "provincial or state governments" or "local governments" for those of "nonprofit sector." A recognition that a single government, by adding centers of power to its apparatus, could do the same thing as nonprofit organizations would make even clearer how much Weisbrod's formulation is a victim of a particular conception of politics that restricts that activity to periodic electoral contests in which electoral platforms that (implicitly) contain the whole program of the elected party (or candidate) is implemented without any changes whatsoever.

Later in this chapter, however, I will argue that if we jettison the majoritarian principle and the implied notion that governments are monopolists during election periods – the time span between elections – Weisbrod's fundamental intuition is correct: that, to put it simply, in the conventional language of microeconomic theory, nonprofit organizations are a source of product

3. Weisbrod's discussion of how nonprofits, in fact, resolve the free-rider problem is not only fascinating, it is also a major contribution to an understanding of this most elusive phenomenon.
4. This is a good example of how the assumption that governments are monoliths or monopolies creeps into analyses that are otherwise fully articulated on the real world.

differentiation whose role is to satisfy diversified demands. Why, we must then ask, is product differentiation generated by nonprofit organizations and not by for-profit enterprises or by governmental centers of power? Simply because in some circumstances nonprofits are more efficient in providing certain goods and services – in these circumstances, they have a comparative advantage. Where does the comparative advantage come from? The next chapter is devoted to answering that question. For the time being, let me simply state that it comes from a greater capacity to resolve the free-rider problem and to ascertain the relevant parameters of the demand functions for goods and services that citizens wish to consume.

Reference to information provides the occasion to consider, also very briefly, Hansmann's model of nonprofit organizations. The model has two basic building blocks: The first is that in a number of instances "consumers feel unable to evaluate accurately the quantity or quality of the service a firm produces for them." This incapacity of consumers may be due to "the circumstances under which the service is purchased or consumed or to the nature of the service itself" (Hansmann, 1987, p. 29). Under these circumstances, Hansmann argues, for-profit firms can gain by "exploiting" consumers, whereas nonprofit organizations, bound by "nondistribution constraints" – the sort of constraints that "prohibits the distribution of residual earnings to individuals who exercise control over the firm, such as officers, directors or members" (Hansmann, 1987, p. 28) – cannot gain in that way. The nondistribution constraints that prevent shirking and cheating is the second basic building block of the model.

Hansmann has applied his model to a variety of situations and has been able to explain some otherwise intriguing phenomena. That notwithstanding, it seems to me that the model contains a basic inconsistency. How can one assume that nonprofit organizations are able to meet the demands of consumers who do not themselves know what it is that they are demanding? Hansmann's fundamental intuition is that nonprofit organizations, because of the existence of nondistribution constraints, will have a lesser incentive to exploit consumers than for-profit firms do. It is to give meaning and force to nondistribution constraints that consumers are assumed to be vulnerable to actions of for-profit enterprises. It is hard, however, to imagine that in the presence of ignorant and defenseless consumers, nonprofit organizations would behave differently than do for-profit firms. Profits do not have to be distributed to yield amenities to people who choose to shirk and cheat. Another rationale for nondistribution constraints is needed.

11.2.   An alternative perspective

As I have indicated earlier, I accept Weisbrod's idea that nongovernment–nonmarket institutions exist to permit a wider diversification of supply or a wider differentiation of product than would exist in their absence. I differ from him by *not* requiring that the supply thus diversified be that of collective-type goods and services. The nongovernment–nonmarket sector supplies goods and services of all sorts with differentiation characterizing a large variety of these, which are completely private in the technical sense given to that expression by Samuelson (1954).

As is well known, differentiation may, however, require that equilibrium be on the downward sloping portion of the average cost curve both in the short and the long run simply because differentiation prevents the full exploitation of economies of scale. In the conventional analysis of this problem of "monopolistic competition," equilibrium quantities of output on that section of the average cost curve are associated with the notions of excess capacity and of waste. However, it must be recognized that if consumers are willing to pay for more differentiation of production there will be no waste but, on the contrary, an increase in well-being. In the conventional analysis, differentiation is wasteful because it is assumed to be contrived; hence the label of "monopolistic competition."

Could the greater diversification of demand that consumers (or citizens) want be generated by governments? Does increased differentiation have to come from institutions such as nonprofit organizations? My answer to these questions, as the reader now well knows, is that differentiation could easily be provided by governments, as it is in some societies at certain periods of their history. The reason why it is sometimes nonprofit organizations that provide the differentiation is that these bodies will sometimes be more efficient than other organizations at doing so. Efficiency, or more precisely relative efficiency, as I have stressed throughout this study and as I will emphasize anew in the next chapter, depends on a number of factors, of which two, already noted, are particularly important in the present context: (1) the capacity to control free-riding that does not take the form of preference falsification but of avoiding and evading payment of one's share of the cost of the good or service consumed; and (2) the ability to obtain information about the parameters of the relevant demand functions.

The institutions that supply goods and services to people are those that are relatively more efficient – those that have a comparative advantage in production, supply, and financing. Sometimes the institution is a governmental center of power or a subset of centers, sometimes it is a nonprofit organization, and sometimes it is a kind of nongovernment–nonmarket body different from a nonprofit one. If it is relative efficiency that determines supply and, therefore, who is the victor in the competitive struggle that pits these various organizations against one another, why is it that virtually all nonprofit organizations are subsidized by governments, whether directly or indirectly? Why do governments subsidize their competitors? The answer to these questions is provided in Chapter 2, Section 2.3, but can be stated briefly here: It is simply that subsidies are a contribution to the resolution of the free-rider problem confronting all suppliers. The subsidies are on the same footing as the "legally enforced property rights" governments provide to resolve the free-rider problem in the marketplace where free-riding takes the form of fraud and breach of contract. In that framework, Hansmann's nondistribution constraints are devices imposed by governments to control the volume of subsidies and the uses to which they are put.

11.3.   Goods are goods

A basic, though usually implicit, assumption of neoclassical demand theory is that consuming households are indifferent about the provenance or source of the goods and services they buy and consume. Given the information at their disposal, their preferences, and their incomes, households are assumed to choose quantity and quality by reference to prices (including the various costs of transacting). This does not mean that some characteristics of suppliers are not, at least in the short run, of importance for an understanding of consumption behavior. We now recognize that reputation (Shapiro, 1983) is a characteristic of firms that has an impact on demand. Others, such as the color and ethnicity of suppliers, may also be of significance. If we neglect these factors, the assumption simply says that there is competition among all suppliers, or that phenomena such as firm and brand loyalty do not repeal the law of demand. For the sake of brevity, I shall call this assumption the "goods are goods" assumption instead of using the more precise, but more clumsy, "goods and services are goods and services."

I suggest that a necessary first step in analyzing the growth of competitive governments consists in extending the "goods are goods" assumption to *all* goods and services, including, in addition to private goods and services, pure and impure Samuelsonian (1954) public goods and income redistribution as defined in Chapter 1, Section 1.1.

The assumption that households are indifferent about sources of supply or that "goods are goods" has implications for the last of the items in the foregoing list, namely income redistribution. Consider old-age pensions. As I have already noted, when these are provided by governments, they are identified as redistribution and classified as transfers, but when they are supplied by families or by charitable organizations, say, they are treated as services, though they will not generally be incorporated in national accounts. The same is true of unemployment relief, aid to unwed mothers, day care, nursing, compensation to victims of criminal acts, disintoxication assistance, convalescent help, and a host of other services. The point does not pertain to whether the provision of these services has income redistribution effects, which they no doubt have (see Strotz, 1958; Aranson and Ordeshook, 1981), but to the common practice of treating these activities as services when they are provided by families, churches, humanitarian bodies, cooperatives, and corporations and as transfers or welfare payments when they are supplied by governments. I shall treat them as services in the remainder of this study in conformity with the demands of the "goods are goods" assumption and the definition of goods and services used throughout the book.

In that framework, let me illustrate the "goods are goods" assumption by supposing that people have a demand for security of life, well-being, and property. That service is available in a wide range of qualities and quantities from governments, from the market, and from households themselves (Becker, 1965) – to limit myself to only three possible sources of supply. The quantity and quality demanded by a typical person will depend on his or her information, income, and preferences, and on prices. All of the service may be acquired from the government or from the market, or all may be produced by the household itself. Alternatively, a fraction of the total that is demanded may be obtained from the government, a fraction from the marketplace, and the remainder produced by the household. The individual, assumed to be indifferent about provenance, will therefore choose the volume and quality of security needed from the source or sources supplying it at the lowest price.

That illustration and any number of others that could be provided should make clear that the "goods are goods" assumption means that from the individual's or household's point of view there are no such things as goods that are intrinsically or technically government goods or market goods. Because of this, the assumption means that the goods and services that enter as multiplicands in government expenditures at one time may have been at some other time supplied in whole or in different proportion by markets, households, or other agencies.

11.4.   Conclusion

In the preceding pages, I have argued that the size of the nonmarket sector is larger than most of us have been accustomed to assume. That is not only because that sector is made up of nonprofit organizations in addition to governments, but also and very important because the sector includes institutions such as families, churches, and corporate enterprises in their nonmarket role (see footnote 2). These institutions have been and in some cases remain important suppliers of the goods and services that in other societies are provided by governments. I have also argued that the basic intuitions underlying existing theories of nonprofit organizations – those pertaining to the need to meet a diversified demand and to the importance of nondistribution constraints – can, with some modification, be retained within the framework of analysis I am proposing.

CHAPTER 12

The growth of governments

Few topics have received more attention than that of the growth of governments. Alan Peacock (1978) has reminded us that as early as 1835 Alexis de Tocqueville (1835/1840) was already speculating on the subject; Adolph Wagner's (1883/1890) well-known "Law of Increasing State Activity" has been and remains an object of scholarly attention; and, following Peacock and Jack Wiseman's (1961) path-breaking monograph, we have witnessed not only a multiplication of hypotheses, the construction and exploitation of new data bases, and the estimation of countless regression equations but also the publication of many excellent critical reviews of the literature and at least one review of reviews.

As a result, we can endorse Borcherding's (1985) judgment that considerable progress has been made in identifying and modeling the forces that have propelled a growth process that appears to have been in operation, at least in the more "advanced" countries, for nearly two centuries (see Mueller, 1987, p. 116). The unabated research activity is also, however, an indication that our knowledge of that growth process remains profoundly unsatisfactory. There are two main reasons for this state of affairs: unresolved difficulties with the available data and the almost complete lack of a theory of supply.

I do not consider data problems in this chapter. I simply note that the continuing inability to fit the regulatory activities of governments as well as practices such as loan guarantees, tax concessions to individuals, businesses and charitable organizations, and other off-budget items into conventional measures means that much inductive work in the field has been focused on problems that probably have no real-world existence and that many statistical tests of significance used empirically to appraise deductive models have no real force. The enormous portfolio of empirical work on the growth of governments must, sad to say, be interpreted and evaluated against this background.[1]

1. For example, if the growth in the regulation of economic activity (including so-called tax expenditures), which appears to have taken place, at least in Canada and the United States, in the 1960s and especially in the 1970s is a reflection of a resistance to further increases in taxation, does that not have profound implications for Peacock and Wiseman's (1961) Displacement Effect hypothesis?

Neither is it my object to survey the theoretical literature. As I have just noted, excellent reviews (among which I note Bird, 1970, 1979; Larkey, Stolp, and Winer, 1981; Borcherding, 1985; Louvet, 1986; Usher, 1986; and Mueller, 1987) have appeared in recent years, and a new one would only be a waste of everyone's time. However, as backdrop or introduction to what I wish to say, I would like to adopt and amplify two criticisms of the theoretical work that have been made in the reviews just noted and add a third of my own.

First, normative welfare economics theories of market failure, such as the theory of public goods and the theory of externalities, are often assumed, generally without much defense, to be capable of explaining the growth of government. Such an assumption is invalid. Indeed, even if a genuine demand for public goods and for the abatement of negative externalities exists, nothing can be presumed about the behavior of public provision and public expenditures without analyzing supply. Public goods and services, like market goods and services, are produced and supplied, and it is just as unacceptable to disregard the forces that govern that production and supply as it would be to jettison those forces when one is analyzing the growth of economies. Even if we postulate a world of fully informed rational agents and efficient resource allocation, we cannot conclude that the growth of governments is a consequence of the removal by governments of Pareto inefficiencies resulting from market failures. That should become abundantly clear as the discussion proceeds.

Second, the problem of the *size* of governments is sometimes not well enough distinguished from that of the *growth* of governments. If it is the latter that we wish to explain, then theories of public goods, externalities, median voters, interest (or pressure) groups, and bureaucracy – assuming the validity of one or more of these for *positive* analysis – have to be supplemented by hypotheses that explain why the demand for public goods and for the abatement of negative externalities and their supply have changed over time, or why median voters, interest groups, and bureaucracies are willing and capable of generating a larger public sector today than they were 50, 100, and 200 years ago.

One implication of the foregoing is that in discussing the size of governments, some of the variables that are treated as exogenous or are simply neglected must, when growth is analyzed, be endogenized, whereas other variables must be introduced as new exogenous forces. Douglass North (1985), in one of the more important recent contributions to the analysis of the growth of governments, has stressed the point, though it had already been made by Bird (1970).

Second, there are two ways of empirically approaching the problem of the growth of governments: (1) by focusing on long-term trends as revealed in the time series data of particular countries and (2) by concentrating on comparisons among countries through cross-sectional analysis of data. Patrick Larkey, Chandler Stolp, and Mark Winer (1981) and Borcherding (1985) have noted that it is difficult not to violate significant *ceteris paribus* assumptions in cross-country studies. A careful identification of what is endogenous and what is exogenous should help to obviate this problem.

Third and last, though most writers distinguish between supply and demand, there appears to be no agreement as to the variables that determine demand and those that condition supply. As regards the latter, we mostly have catalogues of the various cost components of the goods and services provided by governments, such as resource costs, decision-making costs, deadweight costs, and others. How the behavior of these costs affects supply has not, to my knowledge, been modeled. Furthermore, if we take standard microeconomic theory as our benchmark, neither William Baumol's (1967) model of unbalanced growth – which I examine shortly – nor Niskanen's (1971) model of bureaucracy provides us with a solid theory of supply. Because of this, but also because the analysis of the demand for goods and services proposed in Chapter 2 – with the added assumption suggested in Chapter 11 that "goods are goods" (and "services are services") – is the one relevant for the analysis of the growth of governments, I shall focus in the remainder of this chapter on the analysis of supply.

12.1.   The determinants of supply

Let me begin the analysis of supply by remarking that with very few exceptions the goods and services that are nowadays usually provided by governments can be and as a matter of historical record are or have been supplied by nongovernmental agencies. This statement applies to goods and services that are public in a technical sense (see Samuelson, 1954; Buchanan, 1968), such as national defense (Frey and Buhofer, 1988), lighthouses (Coase, 1974; Peacock, 1979), mail delivery (Coase, 1961), police and fire protection, roadways, parks, and even diplomacy. It is also the case that technically private goods and services that we currently associate with nongovernmental provision have at times been supplied by governments. Among them are bread, circuses, baths, baking ovens, milk, and orange juice. Furthermore, many goods and services are offered by both governmental and nongovernmental bodies at the same time. That is the case at present in Canada with, for example, health services, education, care of the physically challenged, broadcasting, telecommunications, rail and road transportation, mail delivery, police protection, refuse collection, snow removal, income redistribution, and censorship.

i.   Some preliminaries

As argued in Chapter 11, many types of organizations supply goods and services. I retain five for the present discussion: families, whether they be extended, nuclear, or monoparental families; religious, humanitarian, and other eleemosynary bodies; cooperatives; private business enterprises operating in markets; and governments. I am not claiming that all goods and services are at all times supplied by all these different supply sources. I am simply saying that some goods and services are in some circumstances supplied by one or another source and in other circumstances by a multiplicity of sources. I am arguing, in other words, that as is the case in international commerce, there will sometimes be specialization in, and at other times diversification of, supply sources.

The economics of governmental supply is, therefore, an economics of relative efficiency or of comparative advantage.[2] Before I analyze the forces that determine the choice of supply sources, let me pause briefly to illustrate the reality of multisource supply with the case of income redistribution defined to include such goods and services as old-age pensions, unemployment insurance, day care facilities, aid to the sick and the needy, and any other transfer of one person or group to another person or group. I have chosen income redistribution, first, because it illustrates well the point I am trying to make, though the number of candidates that would serve that purpose as well is large, but also because income redistribution currently happens to be the focus of competing views of how one should approach the analysis of governments and of their growth. I hope, by focusing on this example, also to shed light on this second issue.

Income redistribution has at different times and places been enacted by all five agencies enumerated in the foregoing paragraph. Let me look briefly at each one to document this point, if only in an impressionistic way. A typical extended family system or kinship network provides shelter, food, protection, security, and insurance to its members. This provision does not require that family members or kin live under one roof, but it does necessitate some degree of physical and geographic proximity. The family or kinship system will be a more effective provider of child care, nursing and convalescence services, unemployment relief, assistance to the elderly and to single mothers, loan guarantees, and protection against homelessness and destitution in soci-

---

2. Though North's (1985) analysis of government growth is different from mine, the two approaches have a number of things in common, in particular the view that the economics of supply is one of comparative advantage. Similarly, though focused on a different problem – that of the instrumentalities of supply – Borcherding's (1983) analysis of governmental modes of supply also rests on a notion of relative efficiency.

eties characterized by a low degree of geographic mobility and a strong attachment to ancestral homes and places of residence. For reasons that are obvious, the nuclear family is much less capable of supplying many of the income redistributional services just listed, and the monoparental family is still less effective.

Bélanger (1987, 1988) has already stressed the extent to which before the Quiet Revolution in Quebec the provision of hospital services, the care of orphans and elderly persons, and other similar social services as well as education, were in that province provided by church-sponsored religious bodies. Bird (1970, 1979) has argued that the reassignment of responsibility for health services from the private to the public sector has accounted for a considerable fraction of the growth of government expenditures in Canada. That private sector, there is no need to insist, was very largely made up of charitable and religious bodies. For that matter, the wide network of hospitals, leprosariums, orphanages, homes, and dispensaries created and operated by churches and religious orders is testimony that for centuries many of the functions of the modern welfare state were in effect vested in these institutions. To a degree this is still the case today, though more so in Third World countries than in the advanced ones in which church-sponsored institutions have to a significant extent been replaced in the nongovernmental sphere by voluntary humanitarian organizations.

I mention cooperatives not because they historically have been important suppliers of income redistributional goods and services but because their evolution enables us better to circumscribe the forces that help to determine the relative efficiency of alternative supply sources. There are still a number of cooperative ventures in operation today – such as mutual aid groups and mutual insurance and building societies – but the kind of cooperation that Robert Owen envisaged for the settlements at New Harmony (Indiana), Orbiston (Scotland), Ralahine (Ireland), and Queenwood (England) or that Charles Fourier contemplated for his *phalanstères*[3] have not only disappeared altogether but have had relatively short lives.[4] That, it would appear, seems to be the fate of Israel's kibbutzim also. One cannot deny, however, that cooperative settlements, such as the ones just mentioned and many others, organized on the basis of sharing, can be and have historically been, for short periods at least, suppliers of income redistribution.

3. Fourier (1772–1837), a contemporary of Owen (1771–1858), conceived of a building (or a complex of buildings) that would be occupied by a "phalanx" or socialist community of some 1,800 persons living together as one family and holding property in common. The building that housed the phalanx was called a *phalanstère,* or phalanstery. (A word constructed from phalanx – group – and from monastery).
4. In some cases, cooperative enterprises are closely tied to religious institutions. In these cases, they tend to have longer life spans.

Business enterprises sell a variety of instruments, such as insurance policies and trusts, which facilitate the redistribution of income. Market transactions, whether consummated at equilibrium or disequilibrium prices, generally alter the pretransaction distribution of incomes. I have neither of these phenomena in mind when suggesting that private enterprises supply income redistribution. I shall discuss later how the provision of goods and services through markets, which may or may not be competitive, influences the relative efficiency of different supply sources. For the present, I am focusing on the redistribution effected by enterprises within their own organizational confines. Some firms do provide health and hospital insurance programs as well as pension plans to their employees; some guarantee lifetime employment. Others offer scholarships, day care, free membership in associations and clubs to their employees and to members of employees' families and dispense free credit cards or extend signing privileges to some employees. A number of these practices and others like them must be understood as efficiency-enhancing rewards or payments (see Chapter 6). But all entail life-cycle or intrapersonal redistribution, and those that possess significant public goods characteristics and hence cannot serve as rewards for better performance also contain elements of interpersonal redistribution.

Governments, especially since the end of World War II, but even before (see Hughes, 1977; Anderson and Hill, 1980), have also been important suppliers of income redistribution. That is such a well-known fact that it does not need to be documented here. Instead, let me consider the tendency in the rent-seeking and interest-group literature to assume that most (all?) public policies are responses to the activities of individuals trying to change the distribution of income in their favor. It is impossible to deny that some policies are the result of such a process. Before Tullock (1967) had suggested a model of what Anne Krueger (1974) later labeled "rent-seeking," I had proposed (Breton, 1964) a theory of nationalism that is in effect a theory of rent-seeking. Economic nationalism remains in my view an instance of that kind of activity.

However, as Assar Lindbeck (1985, p. 314) has noted, many policies, such as "agricultural protectionism, rent control, and tax concessions to home-owners all indicate that a group which benefits from redistribution policy does not necessarily have to be well organized, or indeed organized at all, in a democratic state." Lindbeck argues that competitive electoral politics in effect motivates these policies. This is not a minor point. Rent-seeking and electoral competition are models that have so far not been effectively reconciled with each other. Becker's (1983, p. 392) defense of rent-seeking on the ground "that voter preferences are frequently not a crucial *independent* force in political behavior," because "[t]hese 'preferences' can be manipulated and created through the information and misinformation provided by interested pressure groups, who raise their political influence partly by changing the revealed 'preferences' of enough voters and politicians" (italics and quotation marks on 'preferences' in original) is difficult to accept if only because the people whose preferences are assumed capable of being "manipulated and created" are the very same people whose preferences were generally assumed to be stable – and for good reason – in the conventional analysis of demand.[5]

In addition, if the income redistribution enacted by governments is a substitute for that which at other times or in different circumstances was or is provided by families, by religious and humanitarian organizations, and by other agencies, logic would seem to require that we also motivate the actions of these suppliers by reference to rent-seeking. That would seem to necessitate that we assume that lepers, orphans, and other indigent and destitute individuals, for example, have – in the past and to a degree even today – organized themselves as pressure groups to create the religious orders through which they thenceforth were able to engage in rent-seeking. I am doubtful that the facts would support this view of the mechanism of income redistribution. I prefer the view, not inconsistent with the evidence, that income redistribution is either a by-product of the utility- or wealth-augmenting effects of the supply of goods and services or, except for some policies, a response to demand (see Chapter 1, Section 1.1).

If the proposition is accepted that for virtually all goods and services there exists a multiplicity of *potential* supply sources, we must ask which one or ones will be selected to be the effective or *actual* source or sources. We must ascertain the factors that determine the relative efficiency of alternative supply sources.

Let me begin this discussion by underlining an important point. The concept of relative efficiency or comparative advantage carries within itself the notion of competition. The idea that supply sources are selected on the basis of relative efficiency implies that the sources are competing with one another. Families, voluntary organizations, cooperatives, business enterprises, and governments are engaged in a competitive struggle to supply the goods and services the members of society are demanding.

I should stress, however, that even though economists rightly assume that business firms compete with one another and would, I am quite certain, easily concede that religious and humanitarian organizations as well as cooperatives compete among themselves, these economists, without much apparent reluctance, assume that governments are monopolies and that they have sole control over coercion (see Chapter 1, Section 1.2). Taken at its face value, this means that no other institution in society possesses that kind of power. That is

---

5. "The combined assumptions of maximizing behavior, market equilibrium, and *stable preference*, used relentlessly and unflinchingly, form the heart of the economic approach [to human behavior] as I see it" (Becker, 1976a, p. 5, italics added); see also Stigler and Becker (1977).

manifestly not the case. On any meaningful definition of the word, it is easy to show – as I have argued in Chapter 1 and will endeavor to do again later – that decisionmakers in families, in religious and other voluntary organizations, in business enterprises, in addition to those in governments, coerce.

That is, however, not the only point. What must also be underlined is that institutions with the capacity to coerce can do so only within the domain of their authority or jurisdiction. As a consequence, to say that governments have a monopoly over coercion tells us nothing about the volume of coercion they inflict on society unless we also know the set of activities over which they exercise authority. It is a fact that the jurisdiction of today's governments in advanced countries is extensive, but if we are concerned with the growth of governments, that is precisely the phenomenon that has to be explained, because such vast governmental authority was not always the case. We must explain why there is now more coercion or the potential for more coercion by governments and presumably less by other sources than in years gone by. The assumption that governments are monopolies is of no help in that quest.

Moreover, even if governments are assumed to be monopolies, we must acknowledge, by virtue of what we as social scientists have to consider a fundamental character of society, that all institutions, whether directly or indirectly, interface and interact with one another. If, in addition, we accept the "goods are goods" (and "services are services") assumption, we must then also agree with the proposition that the relationships underlying the interfacing and the interaction are essentially competitive in character. If there are no fixed technical lines of demarcation between sources of supply, it must be that *ceteris paribus* rational demanders will "purchase" the goods and services they want from the lowest price source. That by itself will encourage competition between supply sources.

Governments, however, are not monopolies. As we have seen in Part I, each is a conglomerate of centers of power that compete with one another. It is true, as Part I also noted, that centers of power or some subset of them may try to collude and may at times and for some periods succeed in doing so. In the end, this is an empirical matter. However, I assume, as economists are wont to do, that collusion among centers of power, like the collusion that may from time to time exist in a subset of market suppliers, is not in the long run an enduring phenomenon.

ii.   *Differential productivity growth of conventional inputs*

It is time to consider the determinants of relative efficiency. It would certainly be presumptuous to claim at this early stage in the formulation of a theory of the supply of nonmarket goods and services that all the determinants can be identified. The modern theory of international trade, which is 200 years old and has attracted over its lifetime the attention of many of the best minds in economics, continues to add factors to an already longish list in its search for explanations of the observed patterns of international commerce. But if I cannot claim completeness, I am confident that the factors I have identified are among the significant ones. In any case, they appear to explain, as I endeavor to show later, some important facts related to the growth of governments. As research progresses and new empirical puzzles become manifest, new determinants will no doubt be added to the list.

Let me begin by focusing, in the spirit of David Ricardo's theory of comparative advantage, on the rate of growth of productivity of conventional inputs – land, labor, capital, and organization – employed by different supply sources. A natural point of departure for this discussion in the context of public sector growth is Baumol's (1967) model of unbalanced growth. The model is easily sketched. There are two output sectors and one competitive labor market. In one sector labor productivity grows exponentially; in the other it remains constant. Assuming that there is only one wage rate and that sectoral output shares remain constant, expenditures on the output of the stagnant sector will rise, and those on the output of the progressive sector will decline.

The growth of labor productivity in the progressive sector need not be exponential, nor that in the stagnant sector zero – it suffices that the rate of growth be different in the two sectors. Nor is it important that there be only one wage rate – it is sufficient that the rewards of labor converge. As is generally acknowledged (see Baumol, Batey Blackman, and Wolff, 1985), the assumption that sectoral output shares have to be constant is, however, fundamental. This assumption is in turn based on the notion that the boundaries between sectors are fixed and exogenously given or alternatively that the demand for the output of each of the sectors is completely price inelastic.

There is much that is worthwhile in Baumol's hypothesis, but in making use of it it is essential to keep in mind its assumption that sectoral shares of governmental and nongovernmental output are and have been constant over time.[6] That is especially important because these shares have not in fact been constant. At the beginning of this chapter I remarked on the data problems that derive from our inability to incorporate regulations, tax expenditures, and other off-budget items in estimates of government output. In measuring the growth of governments relative to the total output of the economy, a no less serious problem arises from the fact that our measure of this aggregate places

---

6. Peacock's (1969) criticism of the differential productivity element in Baumol's hypothesis is not principally concerned with the constant sectoral output shares on which I focus here. He makes the point, which I fully accept, that even with fixed shares, the productivity of actors, say, can increase because of the use of records, videos, broadcasting, and other instruments that enlarge audiences and thus increase derived demand.

too low a value – in some instances a value of zero – on the output of important supply sources. For example, the household labor of women is not included in national accounts. As a consequence, the in-house supply of day care, nursing services, convalescent help, and other similar services is given a value of zero in these accounts. However, if some women convert a fraction of their household labor into market labor and if governments undertake to supply the services previously supplied by women – which will in the process stop being called services and become identified as transfers – both government and market shares of output will increase, their ratio may even remain more or less constant, but the output share of families will have fallen. Unavoidable reliance on the available data may hide this fact; if it does, it will simply have biased our perception and understanding of the real world.

In addition to differential growth in the productivity of basic inputs, other conventional determinants of relative efficiency such as differential technological change and differential economies of scale in production processes will help to shape supply. I have nothing new to say about these factors. I therefore immediately move on to a discussion of two other important determinants of relative efficiency on which I have something to say, namely, the capacity to control free-riding and the ability to amass information about demand.

iii.   Differential growth in the capacity to control free-riding

A person free-rides whenever he or she participates in the benefits of a good or service but does not share proportionately in the costs. The capacity to control free-riding is, therefore, the capacity to insure that those who benefit from goods and services carry a commensurate burden of the costs. Free-riding is a widespread behavior readily observable in all supply sources identified earlier. It can be caused by public goods, whether these possess a small or a large degree of Samuelsonian publicness; by all or virtually all remedies designed to deal with externalities; by income redistribution even when that redistribution is a utility-augmenting argument in people's utility functions; and by purely private goods whenever their allocation is rationed by nonprice mechanisms such as promotion committees,[7] referees, queues, credit-

7. Let me illustrate with tenure, an institution central to the life of academia in that it absorbs much valuable time of promotion committee members, often nourishes epic intramural wars, and is deemed to insure quality. Given the median academic's propensity to ideology and dogmatism, there is no doubt that tenure is essential to academic freedom. At the same time, it must be recognized that the institution makes it possible for those who have obtained tenure to free-ride, that is, to appropriate over their lifetime a stream of benefits in excess of the stream of costs they have to bear simply by "working to rule," as it were. It would be a simple matter, space allowing, to show that all the devices listed in the text are, in one way or another, sources of free-riding.

rationing agencies, signing privileges (the "there is no such thing as a free lunch" problem), insider trading, and by poor law enforcement that allows fraud. As a consequence, free-riding is a much more pervasive phenomenon than is usually acknowledged in standard treatment of the subject.

What instruments can be used to control this basic behavior? To review all those that have been examined in the literature would take me too far afield. Indeed, under names such as opportunism, moral hazard, and shirking, the literature on contracts, on principal–agent relations, and on efficiency wages – to name only a few of the more important strands – has analyzed a roster of instruments capable of controlling free-riding. In the discussion that follows, I focus on four: tie-ins, social pressures, moral codes, and tax enforcement. My purpose is not to be exhaustive but simply to examine some instruments that decisionmakers in the various sources of supply introduced earlier can and do use to control free-riding.

In his model of collective action, Olson (1965) has suggested that in the presence of public goods decisionmakers deal with free-riding by supplying these goods tied in with one or more private goods. The desire to obtain the private goods then acts as a control on the urge to free-ride on the public goods. Olson's careful analysis of a number of institutions that supply public goods and at the same time provide private goods that are tied to the public goods is evidence of the power of his hypothesis.

It seems reasonable, moreover, to assume that the Olson tie-in instrument is capable of long-term technological improvement. Given that in one application or another it has been or could be used by all the supply sources identified earlier, including governments (see Breton, 1974) and market enterprises,[8] differential growth of its productivity could therefore explain changes in the relative efficiency of these different sources. Whether that is in fact what historically has happened can be established, however, only by turning to the facts. But there is a dimension of the tie-in instrument – first noted by Stigler (1974) – that must be taken into account in ascertaining its effective power as a determinant of relative efficiency.

Stigler made the point that the private goods used as a control instrument can often be untied from the public goods and made available to the same clientele at lower prices, thereby reducing the capacity of the instrument to control free-riding. In other words, the market provision of the same goods and services that suppliers of public goods would like to use to control free-riding will place limits on the effectiveness of the Olson instrument and may even prevent its use. The more competitive the markets, the greater the threat they pose to the effectiveness of the instrument. The point is not that markets

---

8. I am not thinking here so much of standard or conventional tied goods – razors and blades – as of such tie-ins as news and advertising in the mass media.

substitute for other nongovernmental supply sources. However, by undermining the ability of these supply sources to control free-riding, they weaken and possibly even destroy their capacity to supply any goods subject to free-riding. We shall see later on (Section 12.2) that this effect of market forces on nongovernmental suppliers is a closed-economy phenomenon; in an open economy, market competition will weaken the government's ability to control free-riding.

Free-riding can also be controlled by social pressures and moral codes (or norms) – two different but related instruments. Among recent economic discussions of these instruments are Thomas Ireland and David Johnson (1970), Burton Weisbrod (1977), Akerlof (1980), Wintrobe (1983), and Coleman (1988). Social pressures may be subtle or blunt, as when they lead to ostracism, expulsion, or excommunication. In all cases, they operate to induce people to conform to some norm or other. It is therefore easy to imagine that they would be used to induce people to contribute their just share of the cost of any endeavor and therefore to forgo free-riding.

It may be difficult for *fin de siècle* Europeans and North Americans to accept that significant groupings have existed in which a majority of members would not free-ride simply because they lived according to certain moral rules of conduct. Still, there is considerable anthropological and historical evidence that this was sometimes the case among significant groups of humankind. It remains true today in some limited environments.

What are the factors that allow social pressures and moral codes to appear and grow or to vanish? Wintrobe (1983, pp. 262–3) has shown that a moral code may not only survive but may even, in his words, be contagious "if those who adhere to it enforce the code in binary encounters, i.e., they rationally refuse to trade with anyone who does not adhere to it." This implies that codes would be more efficient in certain contexts than in others. To be specific, it implies that moral codes and social pressures will more effectively control free-riding – will be better at eliciting contributions that reflect the share of the costs of the goods and services subject to free-riding – in families and in religious and other voluntary organizations than in market (and government) surroundings in which repeat binary interactions are less likely.

This is very much in the spirit of Stigler's critique of Olson's tie-in instrument. The more closely a society adjusts itself to the requirements of efficient market organization, the more mobile will its labor force become. This mobility will tend to dislocate social relationships and foster anomie. As a consequence, social pressures will lose some of their ability to control free-riding, and for reasons that follow from Wintrobe's line of reasoning, moral codes will erode. The two instruments will become less efficient as control devices.

In addition to tie-ins, social pressures, and moral precepts as instruments of free-rider control, there also exist what we may call legally based tax enforcement technologies. Taxation in the form of tributes or exactions from subjugated peoples, of more of less compulsory gifts from wealthy citizens as practiced in ancient Greece and Rome, of dues imposed by feudal lords on their serfs, and of custom duties levied on trade has existed for as long as states have. Modern systems of taxation have become possible, however, only with the diffusion of accounting and bookkeeping practices, the spread of formally recorded commercial transactions, and the transformation of the labor force from a largely self-employed into a salaried and wage-earning population with the resulting possibility of tax withholding at source. It is these changes that have made the implementation of modern tax enforcement technologies possible.

Buchanan (1967, especially pp. 117–21) has demonstrated that when tax institutions – bases and rates – are given and, one must add, when tax laws are perfectly enforced, free-riding vanishes. Tax institutions are not, however, fully exogenous, and enforcement is never costless. As a consequence, taxation is always subject to free-riding. The effect of costly enforcement is underscored by the documented existence of "underground economies" (see Fortin and Fréchette, 1988 and the literature they cite). There are many reasons to go underground aside from the desire to evade taxes, among which one can mention illegal residency status and violations of minimum wage legislation. As a consequence, even if measures of the aggregate size of underground economies were exact, they would not tell us as much as we would like about the effectiveness of tax enforcement technologies as an instrument to control free-riding.

Tax avoidance and evasion and the responsiveness of tax institutions to political forces are not the only factors undermining the capacity of enforcement procedures to control free-riding. In the spirit of Stigler's critique of Olson, I note that markets reinforce that tendency, as is illustrated by the case of police protection. Assume that the amount demanded by citizens is fully provided by the government and paid for by taxation. In terms of what I have said so far, the reason for this is that the government is relatively more efficient in producing the service and in controlling free-riding. Now assume that for whatever reason, markets become capable of supplying, at lower prices than hitherto, police personnel, guns, dogs, door locks, and the other factors used in producing protection. As a result, the demand for publicly supplied protection will fall and so will the acceptability of taxation to pay for it. Competitive market supply of substitutes will have reduced the public provision of protection because the relative efficiency of the government as producer (provider) of protection is now obviously less than it was, but also because its relative efficiency in controlling free-riding has been reduced – the productivity of its enforcement technology has been eroded.

This is not, however, the only, or necessarily the more important, channel through which markets can frustrate the capacity of enforcement mechanisms to control free-riding. There is a growing awareness, due significantly to the work of my colleagues Bird (for example, 1988) and Donald Brean (1984), that global economic integration is making it more difficult for governments to tax international income flows. As both Bird and Brean have stressed, in the final analysis the reason, in the words of the OECD, "tax avoidance and evasion [are becoming] increasingly complex and more difficult to detect" (quoted by Bird, p. 293) is that tax legislation and enforcement procedures are essentially national – even though governments compete with one another by reducing tax rates and sometimes by exempting from taxation certain types of incomes – whereas capital movements and income flows are increasingly international in character. Bird and Brean have stressed that unless a new supranational tax enforcement technology is devised, the ability of governments to tax incomes will be seriously impaired or, to put it in the language of this chapter, their capacity to control free-riding will be severely undermined. The point is that in open economies and without supranational coordinating machinery, market forces work to undermine the ability of governments to operate efficient tax enforcement procedures.

Now that we know the circumstances under which free-riding arises and have identified some of the instruments that can be used to control it, we must ask whether the familial, commercial, voluntary, religious, and governmental organizations introduced earlier make use of these instruments, namely, whether all of them must address a free-rider problem.

Let me begin with governments. Pressures to alter the tax system, tax avoidance, and tax evasion all are indices that governments face an enormous free-rider problem. But the auditing of selected taxpayers, the prosecution of suspected derelictions, the more or less regular reimplementation of tax reform and a continuous policing of accounts is also an indication that a legally based enforcement technology exists and that governments are actively preoccupied with the free-rider problem.

When we turn from governments to the other sources of supply, the evidence that they have to deal with a free-rider problem is more indirect but no less compelling. With respect to churches and religious organizations, Weisbrod (1977) was able to establish that one measure of social pressure – solicited pledges of monetary contributions – was related in a statistically significant way to the size of donations. Laurence Iannaccone (1988, 1992) has proposed an empirically compelling model of the behavior of church and sect members in which two of the driving forces are the application of sanctions and the withdrawal of rewards by the groups. It is noteworthy that in the model, tie-ins – what Iannaccone calls "essentially secular rewards" (1988, p. S259) – have to be provided to sect members to sustain their production of "religious goods."

Weisbrod (1977, p. 65) and his students were able to establish "that voluntary organizations do employ coercive and compulsive powers, just as do governments, although the penalties are social rather than governmentally sanctioned fines or imprisonment. While pressures to 'donate' to the United Fund, Red Cross, Cancer Society or private colleges, are (sometimes) somewhat more subtle than the pressure to pay one's taxes, the difference is one of degree, not of kind." Ireland and Johnson (1970) had earlier made the same point.

The news stories on insider trading, embezzlements, and abuses of corporate privileges are indices that shirking or free-riding exists in commercial organizations also. The recent literature on efficiency wages (for example, Shapiro and Stiglitz, 1984) as a "worker discipline device" – a kind of Olsonian tie-in – points to one way that decisionmakers in business firms try to deal with the phenomenon.

What about intrafamily relationships? Are they sometimes characterized by free-riding? Two economic approaches to family relations can be found in the literature. One (Becker, 1976b) assumes that in dealing with their children parents are altruists; the other (Bernheim, Shleifer, and Summers, 1985; Cox, 1987) postulates exchange relationships between parents and children. For the problem at hand, one fortunately does not have to decide which is the correct approach, because free-riding is possible under both.

In an important paper, Becker and Murphy (1988, pp. 7–8) have implicitly acknowledged the possibility of free-riding in the altruistic family and have rationalized government intervention in three areas of family relations – education, social security, and divorce – as a way of dealing with the phenomenon.[9] They have shown that government intervention can serve to recapture the optimality properties of altruism that derive from the Rotten Kid Theorem (Becker, 1974) but are not attainable because of free-riding or because parents for whatever reasons will not make gifts or bequests to their children. Twice in their paper (pp. 6 and 8), Becker and Murphy recognize that "social norms" can act as pressures that would substitute for government intervention, but they add that in modern societies social norms are probably too weak to deal with the free-riding. On this point, Becker and Murphy's and my own analysis have much in common.

If one chooses to model family relationships as exchange relationships, free-riding will result if the objects traded have some of the characteristics of public goods. So far, the traded objects that have been studied have been restricted to visits, telephone calls, and monetary transfers, all of which are technically pure private goods. Extension of the set of traded goods and services to day care, nursing, unemployment relief, and the many other ser-

---

9. The possibility that the Rotten Kid will free-ride had previously been noted by Hirshleifer (1977) and by Wintrobe (1983).

vices that sometime enter family transactions and that have some degree of publicness will bring the free-rider problem to the fore and with it the possibility that it can be resolved by tie-ins, social pressures, norms, and ethical codes. The current literature is understandably focused on the modern American family. A broader perspective would reveal, I suspect, that the extended family is more capable of moral and social pressures than the nuclear family and the latter more so than the monoparental family. The ability to deal with free-riding is, therefore, greater in the first, less in the second, and least in the third.

On a priori grounds, it is not possible to determine which of legal enforcement procedures, ethical codes, social pressures, or tied-in private goods and services is the most efficient instrument of free-rider control. That will depend on contexts and circumstances. However, it seems clear that the various sources of supply identified earlier will not as a rule access the same instruments. Families and voluntary organizations, for example, will not make much use of law and law enforcement to obtain the resources needed to conduct their business but will employ one variation or another of Olson's tie-ins, will resort to social pressures, and will try to cultivate ethical norms in their members. Governments, on the other hand, will, as a broad characterization, rely more on regulations and law enforcement.

If, therefore, conditions are such that *ceteris paribus* free-riding is effectively controlled by social pressures, moral codes, and Olsonian tie-ins, families and voluntary organizations could easily have a comparative advantage over, say, governments in supplying goods and services. A transformation of society that reduced the effectiveness of these instruments and increased that of legal enforcement would alter the comparative advantage in favor of governments.

On a widely accepted reading of the last 200 years' historical record, that is precisely what has happened.[10] According to that reading, the industrial revolution of the eighteenth century, what North (1985) has called the "second economic revolution" of the nineteenth, and their extension into our own century have brought about a dislocation of the extended family and its replacement, first, by the nuclear family and, now with increasing incidence, by the monoparental family. The forces associated with these events have led to an increased secularization of life and of social arrangements and have in-

10. The record, as we should expect, is a complicated one to track. North (1985) makes technological change the primary motor of change, though he also gives an important role to "ideological conviction." Bélanger (1987), while seeming to agree with North, gives importance to the fact that certain explanatory factors, which at one time are consequences of certain events, later in the process of growth become causes. Although suspicious of unidirectional causation and therefore sympathetic to Bélanger's "general equilibrium" outlook, I do not want to engage the issue in this chapter.

duced a diminished presence and, in a number of instances, a complete displacement of religious and charitable organizations from such areas as hospitals, orphanages, hospices, homes for the elderly, and educational establishments.

These same forces did not simply dislocate extended families and foster secularization; they also promoted commercialization and market relationships, which in turn encouraged the recording of transactions, the use of accounting, and the change of status from self-employed to employee for members of the labor force. These developments not only permitted the introduction of relatively efficient tax enforcement technologies to control free-riding but at the same time undermined the other instruments by making available at competitive prices substitute goods and services and by promoting labor mobility. The transformation of societies over the past 200 years has reduced the effectiveness of those very instruments of free-rider control that made it possible for families, firms, and voluntary and religious organizations to compete against governments as supply sources of goods and services subject to free-riding, while at the same time increasing the effectiveness of those instruments used by governments.

iv.   Differential growth in the ability to acquire information

In addition to the differential productivity growth of labor, capital, and other inputs used to produce goods and services and to the differential growth in the efficiency of the instruments used to control free-riding, there is another factor that plays a central role in determining the relative efficiency of various supply sources. From the discussion in Chapter 2, the reader will recall that whenever goods and services are supplied in quantities and qualities that, at given taxprices, are different from those desired by citizens, the citizens suffer a loss in utility that must be associated, not with the taxprices themselves, but with the whole of the supply response. The discussion in that chapter also made it clear that to be able to reduce utility losses – and, therefore to maintain and enhance their capacity to compete – suppliers must find the means to acquire information about the relevant dimensions (own-price elasticities, cross-elasticities, etc.) of the population's demand functions for goods and services.

We know so little about the internal workings of families, religious and other voluntary bodies, cooperatives, business enterprises, and even governments that it is difficult, indeed impossible, to rank these various sources of supply in terms of their ability to acquire information about the preferences and demands of their clienteles. Better information about demand parameters, it will be remembered, permits a firmer link – a tighter Wicksellian Connection – to be built between costs and benefits and, therefore, between revenues and expenditures in different decision-making contexts. In the absence of reliable measures of the differential changes in the ability of different supply sources to access information, the only research strategy, at least for the near future, would appear to consist in including in regression equations relating to the growth of governments variables that would act as proxies for the degree of tightness in different Wicksellian Connections.

Let me illustrate with two examples. In the analysis of budgetary processes in congressional and parliamentary governments proposed in Chapter 4, I reached the conclusion that Wicksellian Connections are tighter in the second type of system than in the first and that, as a consequence, utility losses will tend, *ceteris paribus*, to be smaller in that second type of government. Looking at that factor alone and normalizing for the effects of demand variables, we would expect governments to be larger in parliamentary than in congressional systems, because their relative efficiency is greater in respect of reductions in utility losses. One would therefore expect a proxy for the type of government to be significant in cross-sectional regressions on the size of government, with, if parliamentary systems are indexed one and congressional systems zero, coefficients having positive signs.

My second example pertains to utility losses associated with direct democracies and with representative democracies defined to encompass both *representative* and *responsible* governments. The argument is sometimes made that the Wicksellian Connection is tighter in the first than in the second. The opposite must be the case, however. First, referenda – the hallmark of direct democracies – relate to goods and services one by one, not recognizing that some have substitutes and others complements, whereas budgetary debates and negotiations in representative democracies generate information about these interrelationships. Second, referenda do not recognize variations in the intensity of preferences, whereas representative democracies make use of that information in the bargaining and logrolling that characterize their mode of operation. Third, referenda seldom place costs and benefits on the same ballot, whereas budgetary bargaining, in parliamentary systems at least, consider them together. Fourth, as Galeotti and Breton (1986) have demonstrated and documented, citizens participate less in referenda than in elections. All these elements suggest that utility losses are less in representative than in direct democracies and may help to explain why Switzerland, a country in which referenda are widely used, has a public sector smaller than that of comparable societies.[11] (See also the discussion in Appendix E on the role of representation in disclosing Wicksellian Connections.)

11. It is a fact that the central and the cantonal governments in Switzerland often propose increases in expenditures which are then vetoed by the citizens in referenda. That is not contrary to expectations. Bargaining and logrolling are ways of reducing the utility losses of public policies. No equivalent mechanism is present in referenda, so that *ceteris paribus* the

Let me conclude this discussion of supply by simply noting that there is no reason to believe that the operation of the determinants of relative efficiency will lead to specialization – that is, to the complete localization of supply in one source alone. That may happen, but diversification with two or more suppliers is not an unlikely outcome given the number of factors that help determine comparative advantage.

12.2.   Equilibrium and growth

To understand the growth of governments we must combine supply and demand and examine how they interact. This means, among other things, that we cannot use (reduced-form) regression equations to study the influence of supply variables without normalizing for demand, nor can we analyze the effect of different demand variables without taking supply into account.

Before looking at some empirical implications of this proposition, let me use it to comment on a practice, akin to that of identifying nursing and day care, say, as transfers when supplied by governments and as services when provided by other supply sources. In effect, such identification consists in discussing the public supply of transfers (services) in the language of welfare, justice, and entitlements. The practice plays an important role in the work of Scott Gordon (1977) and of Thomas Courchene (1980) – two of the most articulate users of this method of analysis. Gordon and Courchene acknowledge the presence of historical forces that brought about a displacement in the provision of a multitude of services from families and social networks to governments. But they argue that in the process charity not only became institutionalized but that "it was transferred 'from the realm of benevolence into that of justice'" (Courchene, p. 561; the inside quotation is from Gordon).

Such an assumption – it is nothing else – can help to shed light on the question of growth, but it skips over a lot of problems. First, even if we accept the underlying notion that families and social networks were engaged in noninstitutionalized charity, we must recognize that they were providing services that were subject to free-riding and, therefore, that that free-riding had to be controlled through the use of coercion. The only way out of this problem is to assume that people engaged in charitable activities never free-ride. This is not an easy assumption to defend.

Second, the assumption does not by itself tell us much about the behavior of

marginal excess burden of $1.00 of expenditure on a project will be higher when decisions are controlled by referenda than when they are made in bargaining or logrolling contexts. Frey (1994) has recently stated that there is an underlying logrolling mechanism at work in referenda. His paper does not, however, elaborate on the nature and properties of the mechanism.

supply and demand. To be able to tell us about that behavior, it would have to tell us how the concepts of entitlement, welfare, and justice affect price and income elasticities of demand and how they alter the relative efficiency of alternative supply sources as determined, *ceteris paribus,* by the ability of these sources to control free-riding and their capacity to reduce the marginal utility losses associated with supplies that, at the levies that have to be exacted to pay for the services provided, fall short or exceed the quantities and the qualities desired by the population.

I have remarked earlier on the unreliability of the data used to describe and to explain the growth of governments. There are facts, however, that appear to be so robust that it is difficult to conceive of improvements in the underlying information that would contradict their message. I have selected a few of these and will make brief comments on them.

One of these facts, noted by a number of scholars (among them, Bird, 1970, 1979; Peltzman, 1980; Wildavsky, 1985) and central to the Gordon and Courchene discussions, is that in advanced countries transfers as a ratio of aggregate measured income have been growing at a rapid pace for some years. The fact is dramatic enough to have induced Sam Peltzman (1980) and Allan Meltzer and Scott Richard (1981) to develop models of the growth of governments that are based on the assumption that governments, in effect, do nothing else but redistribute income. These models have been examined and criticized by Dan Usher (1986) and Dennis Mueller (1987), both of whom have concluded that the models cannot explain the available evidence.

The model suggested in this chapter offers a better explanation of the growth of *government* transfers. However, a growth in public transfers is not necessarily a growth in total transfers. We can measure the volume and the expansion of public transfers, but we have no worthwhile data on the total volume of transfers made by all supply sources combined – families, churches, voluntary bodies, cooperatives, businesses, and governments – over the past 50, 100, and 200 years. It is not impossible that, relative to income or to some other pertinent benchmark, this all-inclusive magnitude not only has not increased but has declined or remained more or less constant.

A second fact that seems quite robust pertains to the fraction of total measured income spent by governments in rich and in poor countries – with economic status measured by per capita income. Borcherding (1985, p. 360, Table I), using information from Yair Aharoni (1977), documents that, in the mid-1960s, for the eleven rich countries on which he focuses, taxes plus social security payments averaged 36.9 per cent of GNP, whereas for the poor countries, the average was 12.6 per cent.[12] Some of this difference is no doubt

---

12. Borcherding's own figure is 11.8 per cent, but that is an arithmetical error if the country numbers he cites are the correct ones.

due to differences in incomes, and therefore in demand. However, there appears to be more variation in relative public sector sizes within each income group than intragroup income variation can account for. For example, the average for the United Kingdom, Austria, France, and West Germany was 42.4 per cent, whereas for the richer Canada, Belgium, and United States, it was only 36.3 per cent. Italy at 34.1 per cent had a public sector that in relative size was the same at that of the richer United States at 34.5 per cent. The same kind of variation characterized the poor countries.

The very sparse secondary evidence that is available appears to be consistent with the view that a significant fraction of this variation between rich and poor countries can be explained by the kind of supply variables I have been discussing: the importance and role of families, the extent of secularization, the degree of labor mobility, the reach and competitiveness of markets, and other variables that have an impact on the capacity of organizations to control free-riding and to fashion tight Wicksellian Connections by gathering information about demand and through that medium reduce the utility losses inflicted on people.

In this connection there is a third fact that also appears to have considerable robustness: the statistical correlation between the growth of governments and changes in agricultural employment. Harold Demsetz (1982) and North (1985) have taken this measure of urbanization to be a proxy for the division of labor and the specialization of the labor force. North's explanation for the positive correlation is that the increased division of labor and specialization "led to *increased demands* on government . . . to assume functions previously performed by private organizations" (p. 388, my italics).

I would suggest that if the effect of a greater division of labor and of specialization was to increase demand, it was not to increase demand for goods and services that governments alone could supply.[13] Instead, I would argue that the greater division of labor and specialization led to a decline in the ability of private organizations to compete with governments, in such a way that the increased demand had to be met by governments. Urbanization, as a consequence, should be treated as a proxy for changes in the capacity of private organizations to control free-riding and in their ability to forge tight Wicksellian Connections.

There is another, less robust fact on which I would like to comment as much for the illumination it gives to the model as for the light the model sheds on it. In 1978 David Cameron argued that the "openness of the economy is the best single predictor of the growth of public revenues relative to the economic product of a nation" (p. 1254) because openness implies vulnerability to

13. Borcherding, who has given such careful thought to matters of supply (see Borcherding, 1983), also seems, in his masterful recent survey of the literature (Borcherding, 1985, p. 372), to confuse the operation of supply and demand.

outside forces and, therefore, the need for public income supports and other social security schemes. In Cameron's reasoning, openness operates on the demand side. There is no reason to believe that in a properly specified structural model, openness would not enter on the demand side with the sign suggested by Cameron. However, his is a reduced-form model, and on the basis of a similar model Peter Saunders (1988) showed that when the degree of openness is distinguished from the size of the economy, the influence of openness is greatly weakened if not eliminated. The size of the economy is a proxy for economies of scale and should, as we have seen, be negatively correlated with governmental growth at least over some range of sizes.

But the story is more complicated than this. We have seen earlier that market competition in a closed economy strengthens the capacity of governments to deal with free-riding, essentially by undermining the ability of other supply sources to control the phenomenon. In an open economy, however, market competition, as we have also seen, weakens that ability in governments by eroding the effectiveness of national tax enforcement technologies. Relative efficiency, as it is determined by the ability to control free-riding, will then depend on the relative impact of market forces on alternative supply sources.

It seems reasonable to assume that until a few years ago the degree of openness of advanced economies was still limited enough that the ability of governments to deal with free-riding was not seriously impaired by market forces. However, the growing economic integration that has been taking place over recent years and the consequent strengthening of market forces have begun to affect adversely the ability of governments to control free-riding. It would be interesting to speculate on the implication of this fact for the supply of all those goods and services that are liable to free-riding and are currently provided by governments, because there is no indication that the demand for these goods and services is declining. That issue, however, would take me too far afield.

Let me conclude by remarking on Borcherding's (1985, pp. 364–5) estimate that 31 per cent of the growth of government expenditures in the United States between 1902 and the mid-1980s can be attributed to an increase in the price of government over nongovernment output of 1.5 per cent per annum, given a compensated price elasticity of demand of − 0.40.[14] The 1.5 per cent per annum figure is based on Baumol's (1967) "unbalanced growth" hypothesis and therefore reflects the assumption that there was no switching of de-

14. Let $\dot{g}_p$ be the annual growth rate of public spending relative to aggregate income due to price changes, e be the compensated price elasticity of demand, and $\dot{p}$ be the annual growth rate in the price of public output over that of private output. We then have $\dot{g}_p = (1 + e)\dot{p}$. Given the estimates reported in the text, $\dot{g}_p$ equals 0.009. Because the growth rate of public expenditures for the period is 2.9 per cent per year, $\dot{g}_p$ is equal to 31 per cent of that rate.

mand – no alteration in relative efficiency – among supply sources during those years.

That assumption is not acceptable. Indeed, during the first eight decades of the twentieth century, American society witnessed a prolongation of the trends that had begun in the previous century: The dislocation of extended kinship networks and even of nuclear families; the secularization and the consequent reduction in the number of recruits into church-related bodies; the increased mobility of the labor force; the expansion of the reach and scope of markets; and, since the 16th Amendment to the Constitution in 1913, the greatly expanded capacity of the central government in Washington to levy taxes.[15] All these developments have increased the relative efficiency of the government as supplier of goods and services subject to free-riding and have weakened the efficiency of alternative supply sources and continue to do so. They have done so by reducing the capacity of these alternative sources to control free-riding and, where that capacity has not been fully extinguished, by loosening the Wicksellian Connection and thus increasing utility losses. For this reason, I suggest that Borcherding's estimate that 31 per cent of the growth of government can be imputed to a Baumol effect is much too high.

12.3.   Conclusion

I have argued in this chapter that to understand the growth of governments one needs a theory erected on a recognition that there are many possible sources of supply for the goods and services wanted by demanders and that these sources compete with one another. In that theory, the allocation of output among the various supply sources is determined by their relative efficiency, which in turn depends on, among other things, the differential capacity to control free-riding and the differential ability to acquire information about demand, and therefore on the differential aptitude to forge tight Wicksellian Connections. The reason for this is that every supply source – in this chapter, limited to families, churches, voluntary organizations, business firms, and governments – has to resolve the same fundamental problems of free-riding and of information gathering.

In his presidential address to the David Hume Institute, Stigler noted that "the propensity to use the state is like the propensity to use coal: we use coal when it is the most efficient resource with which to heat our houses and power our factories. Similarly, we use the state to build our roads or tax our consum-

15. For an interesting, if somewhat specialized, discussion of some aspects of the trends related to the problem that I am now considering, see Lee and Swenson (1986) and the voluminous literature they cite.

ers when the state is the most efficient way to reach these goals" (1986, pp. 3–4). This chapter has suggested a model of the conditions under which governments are most efficient in supplying certain goods and services and those under which families, religious and humanitarian organizations, business firms, and cooperatives are most efficient at the same task.

Conclusion

In the preparation and writing of this book I have pursued two distinct but closely related objectives. First, I have tried to model a number of different manifestations of competition and of competitive behavior in domains in which governments operate or are involved in one way or the other. With that objective in mind, I have in Part I looked at different forms or configurations of competition inside single governmental units. Then, in Part II, I examined intergovernmental competition in federal, confederal, and unitary governmental systems where, the label affixed to the last-mentioned system notwithstanding, competition and competitive behaviors are easy to observe. Finally, in Part III, I considered the competition that organizes and regulates the relations of governments with social institutions like families, churches, labor unions, businesses, clubs, and others that are also involved in supplying goods and services to people. There are other manifestations and forms of intra-, inter-, and extragovernmental competition besides those considered in the preceding pages that could be analyzed with great benefit. (In Chapter 4, I noted the regulatory process as one obvious candidate, but the eligible population is large, especially when we recall how great is the diversity of democratic systems that exist.)

My second objective was to argue that intra-, inter-, and extragovernmental competition operates in such a way as to build or forge a link between the taxprices that citizens pay and the (marginal) value they put on the goods and services provided them by governments and by other sources of supply – that competition operates in such a way as to induce a revelation of demand for government-supplied goods and services. That link or revelation mechanism I have called the Wicksellian Connection, because Wicksell (1896) was, to my knowledge, the first person to see that if certain conditions were satisfied a Pareto-optimal link or connection between costs and benefits would emerge. In his classic elaboration, Wicksell explored the modifications that would be required in parliaments and parliamentary procedures for the connection to appear. He did not, however, explore whether competition could achieve the same result. That is not difficult to understand, especially when we remember that some 100 years ago, when governments were still relatively small and often dominated either by a monarch or by an aristocracy and when families and churches were still the main suppliers of many of the goods and services now provided by governments, competition was probably not vigorous enough to generate visible Wicksellian Connections.

My concern, as anyone who has read the preceding pages as been able to ascertain, has been to focus on the workings of competition. At a number of junctures I have noted the possibility of collusion and have even discussed the conditions conducive to that phenomenon. I am often astonished by the schemes that politicians and bureaucrats put forward which, if they were adopted, would simply lead to collusion. As I have stressed, coordination is an important governmental activity, just as it is an important marketplace activity. However, many coordination schemes are nothing but screens to hide effective collusive arrangements. Currently in Canada, with governments of virtually all political persuasion in office at the national and provincial levels, the most popular schemes, supported by all governments, are schemes aimed at eliminating excess duplication between jurisdictional tiers, even though the best studies indicate that there is no excess duplication. A successful implementation of the schemes would simply reduce intergovernmental competition and weaken – possibly destroy – existing Wicksellian Connections and make some citizens worse off without making anyone better off except the colluding politicians and bureaucrats.

In the face of all this and well aware of the existence and possibility of collusion, I have nevertheless not emphasized it in the preceding pages because collusion and monopoly have been and to a considerable degree still remain the dominant assumptions in the economic analysis of politics and in the literature of Public Choice. Economists do not deny the existence and the possibility of some collusion in the marketplace, but being aware of the ubiquitousness and pervasiveness of the drive to compete, they have, at least since the time of Adam Smith – with the possible exception of the 1930s – made competition the most basic of the assumptions that define the dominant paradigm of the profession. That has proved to be a very rewarding research strategy. It is because I have come to believe that the analysis of politics should be given the same foundations that I have emphasized competition throughout this book.

Appendices

Long-term budget deficits

Sometimes the budgetary deficits of governments in certain jurisdictions are so large and persistent that a more or less general consensus forms that the deficits cannot be sustained. However, even in the face of such a consensus, the large fiscal imbalance may endure for long periods. How can such events be explained? Is one obliged to appeal to ideology, to irrationality, to capture, or to some other phenomenon that points to inefficiency to understand the persistence of deficits in the presence of a consensus that something must be done about them?

In a recent insightful and factually dense paper, Alberto Alesina and Allan Drazen (1991) have suggested that the long delays that precede the resolution of certain fiscal imbalances as well as the process that leads to them can be modeled as a war-of-attrition game, more or less as is done in biology to formalize what goes on when two animals fight over a prize. Two assumptions are particularly important for the precise formalization of the war-of-attrition model proposed by Alesina and Drazen. The first is that the population of the jurisdiction suffering from a long-term budget deficit be heterogeneous, that is, that it be made up of "different socioeconomic groups with conflicting distributional objectives" and that, as a consequence, "delays in stabilization [be] due to a political stalemate over distribution" (p. 1171). Specifically (and to simplify), Alesina and Drazen postulate that society is constituted of two groups and that "the 'loser' [in the war of attrition] assumes a fraction $\alpha > 1/2$ of the tax burden at [date of stabilization] T, [and that] the 'winner' [pays] a fraction [equal to] $1 - \alpha$". That fraction is not the prize over which war breaks out but "is a given parameter meant to capture the degree of polarization in society" (p. 1176). The second assumption is that the tax burden is more distortionary before an agreement is reached to deal with the deficit problem – before time T – than after such an agreement has been concluded. To simplify, Alesina and Drazen assume that the utility loss associated with distortions is positive before and zero after the moment of resolution.

With these two assumptions and a few supplementary ones used only to facilitate presentation, Alesina and Drazen show that the behavior of the two groups in society can be described by "concession functions" defined over utility losses and that the war-of-attrition game played by the two groups using these functions has a Nash equilibrium. The authors also make clear that what happens at T – at the time of agreement or resolution – is not the elimination of the deficit but "the beginning of a successful program" (p. 1183) of fiscal stabilization. The period over which that program is implemented is not determined in their model.

Interest groups sometimes compete over spoils. However, that need not always be the case. It is possible to assume that long-term deficits are not the product of a conflict over how the burden of a resolution will be distributed among heterogeneous groups, but, in the spirit of the model proposed by Gary Becker and Kevin Murphy (1988), the product of the difficulty of renegotiating an outstanding implicit and incomplete intergenerational contract.

Recall that Becker and Murphy argue, among other things, that parents who are too poor to make gifts and bequests to their children do not have the option to withhold all or a part of these gifts and bequests to insure the repayment of investments in the human capital of these children and as a consequence may not optimally invest in them. They go on to argue that this contractual failure can be remedied by an implicit intergenerational "social compact" put in place and enforced by governments. In Becker and Murphy's approach, governments are the agents of both children and parents and in that capacity levy taxes on the parents to create human capital (education, health, etc.) in the children, on the understanding that when the children have grown up and become productive they will in turn be taxed to repay the parents, with the repayments taking the form of pensions, medical care and so on. Governments can play that role only if the promises made to both children and parents over succeeding generations are credible. A solution to a budget deficit caused by an exogenous shock which, let us say, reduced available tax revenues or increased the expenditures necessary to service the outstanding predeficit debt, and which curtailed or destroyed the credibility of governments, would not only void existing implicit intergenerational contracts but would impair, possibly for generations, the ability to negotiate such contracts and would, therefore, reduce investments in human capital, thus lowering growth and average future incomes. In addition, because these contracts cover the poorer sections of society, destroying the capacity of governments to put them in place would increase income and wealth inequalities in society with the social consequences that often attach to increments in these inequalities.

In that view of the world, persistent long-term budget deficits can be efficient. That is likely to be true even in the strictly neoclassical conception of a country's public finances that imputes utility losses not to the failure of supply to match the quantities desired at given taxprices, but to taxes alone. It would generally take truly massive deadweight costs of taxation to match the costs of the unrest and disruption that would likely accompany the suppression of social programs like old age pensions, medicare, schooling, and so on.

The problem facing governments confronted with adverse exogenous disturbances that produce large budget deficits is to renegotiate intergenerational contracts that are acceptable to all parties and that as a consequence do not undermine the ability of these governments to act as agents for parents and children in the present as well as in the future. There are, no doubt, circumstances that make that task more difficult (like changes in the size of age cohorts consequent on alterations in fertility rates, mortality rates, or both) and others that make it easier (like changes in migration flows), but if the disturbances are at all severe, coming to a resolution of the problem – as understood by Alesina and Drazen (1991, p. 1183–4) – is likely to be a protracted process. However, if renegotiations are successful and the credibility of governments is not impaired, there will be no losers, only winners, both in the present and the future, more or less as when contracts are renegotiated in the marketplace.

The power of "small" groups

The Buchanan–Eaton–White preferences-based rationale for redistribution appears capable of providing an explanation for a phenomenon that has been and remains puzzling. There is evidence that groups that are small relative to the total population of a jurisdiction often gain from redistribution, whereas groups that are relatively larger lose. The classic example, often noted in the literature, is agriculture. Farming is often subsidized when it is a relatively small sector of economies and taxed when it is a relatively large one.

An early explanation of the phenomenon was based on the assumption that the cost of organizing small groups – the cost of controlling free-riding in small groups – is significantly lower than the cost of organizing large groups. Once organized, small groups can exert pressure on governments to obtain subsidies, whereas large groups, being incapable of controlling free-riding and therefore of collective action, become the victims of exactions. It is a fact that in many societies the number of farmers is relatively small. Still, in a country of 50 million people in which 2 per cent – certainly a small percentage – are engaged in agriculture, the number of farmers is equal to 1 million; in a population of 250 million with the same percentage of farmers, their number would be 5 million. Numbers like 1 and 5 million are in the circumstances relatively small, but they are absolutely so large as to leave the free-rider problem whole. Organizational costs, it would appear, cannot provide an explanation for the phenomenon (see Salmon 1987a).

An alternative explanation of more recent origin is due to Becker (1983).[1] Although integrating organizational costs, that explanation is more squarely based on the proposition that when the number of taxpayers is larger, the marginal deadweight cost of taxation for each taxpayer is smaller, inducing taxpayers to allocate fewer resources to the production of political pressure, which by itself increases the relative effectiveness of pressure by those seeking subsidies. These subsidies, on a per capita basis, will be larger, the smaller the number of beneficiaries. If we disregard for a moment the explicit balancing at the margin of the excess burden of taxes and subsidies that is admittedly at the core of Becker's model, the essence of his argument in respect of the phenomenon under discussion can be put in the following

1. Becker's contribution to the subject had, however, been anticipated by Pareto, Downs, and Stigler.

words: When benefits are concentrated on a few and costs diffused among many, the first will be more effective than the second in making an advantageous use of the political process.

A main difficulty with both the early and the more recent explanations of the greater political effectiveness or power of small groups is that they appear unable to explain why, among small groups, some seem to be able to do better for themselves than others. For example, in a city like Toronto, sanitary engineers (garbage collectors and street cleaning employees), public transportation workers, and primary school teachers do better for themselves than publicly employed social workers; medical doctors throughout the country do better than dentists, and engineers better than architects. (All these occupations are regulated or self-regulating under a publicly approved protocol.)

The Buchanan–Eaton–White preferences-based rationale for redistribution suggests that if the problem of free-riding by group members is resolved (see Chapter 2, Section 3, Subsection ii for a discussion of how this is done) the groups that are able to gain most through income redistribution are those that are capable of causing significant social disturbances because redistribution, by giving them, in Eaton and White's words, "more to lose," reduces the incentive they have to disrupt. Sanitary engineers, transportation workers, and teachers (schools, remember, perform a basic baby-sitting and day-care service in addition to offering education) are capable of more widespread disruption than are social workers; doctors can cause more harm than dentists by withholding services, and engineers more than architects. In all cases, larger sums are transferred to the first than to the second to forestall the disruptive actions they could undertake.

Which groups are more capable of causing social disruption or, to put it differently, which groups have the most power to interfere with the orderly, peaceful, and stable operation of society or of significant parts thereof? Milton Friedman's (1951) analysis of the power of labor unions tells us that there is no better source, in seeking an answer to this question, than Alfred Marshall's (1890, Book 5, Chapter 6) theory of derived demand. Adapted to the present context, the theory rests on four principles which establish that the derived demand for the services of a group will be more inelastic and, therefore, the capacity or power of that group to disrupt correspondingly greater:

1. The more essential the services supplied by that group because an interruption in the supply of the service causes more disruption and turmoil;
2. The more inelastic the demand for the service of that group because the capacity to endure disruptions and disturbances is low and the willingness of the relevant population to yield higher;
3. The lower the cost of the services provided by that group relative to

the total cost of services provided by all groups because the cost of averting the disruption and the turmoil is relatively low – a situation that is more likely, the smaller the size of the group;[2]

4. The more inelastic the supply of the services provided by complementary groups because interruptions in deliveries will concern all groups and disruption, therefore, will be more widespread.

The four principles that regulate the derived demand for the services of groups are interrelated, but in particular circumstances one or the other may dominate.[3] For example, principles (1) and (2) are likely the most relevant in explaining the power differential between sanitary engineers and social workers. The extent to which the services of a group are essential will be smaller in the long run when substitutes are likely to be more readily available. The increasing production of day-care centers by private firms and governments is therefore likely to reduce the power of primary school teachers to disrupt, and consequently they are likely to benefit less from redistribution as the cost of protecting property rights from their actions diminishes. However, day-care centers are imperfect substitutes for the services of teachers; their increasing availability will therefore only marginally affect the power of teachers. Even if the services of midwives, chiropractors, therapists, and other healers are imperfect substitutes for the services of medical doctors, citizens will redistribute income toward them to protect themselves against the disruption the medical doctors are capable of generating.

The extent to which the services of groups are essential will be less and the elasticity of demand for these services greater in open economies than in jurisdictions that are closed or self-sufficient. Redistribution to secure the enforcement of property rights – to avert disruptions and turmoil – will be less in the first than in the second. Even in open jurisdictions, however, citizens may transfer income to certain groups – depressed enterprises, say – on the basis of principle (4) to avert the disturbances a sudden shutdown would entail. But because elasticities of supply are likely to be larger in the long than in the short term, these transfers more likely occur in the short run.

2. Marshall's third principle of derived demand has, therefore, a family resemblance to the explanations of the power of groups, mentioned earlier, based on the size of groups and on the concentration of benefits and the diffusion of costs, but it is obviously not the same.
3. Friedman's analysis of the power of labor unions is mainly based on principles (1) and (2).

The independence of judiciaries

In a provocative paper written some twenty years ago, William Landes and Richard Posner (1975) suggested a model of politics in which a number of autonomous centers of power are active but in which checks and balances do not exist. The model is principally concerned with the American system of government, though the authors' reference to the British system (p. 887) and the canonical form of the economic model they develop seem to indicate that the analysis is intended to be general.

In the model, an "independent," or autonomous, judiciary – independent because it is "above" the politics of interest-group pressures – has the role of enforcing "the 'deals' made by effective interest groups in earlier legislatures" (p. 894). The conclusion is that even though the judiciary is independent, it in fact always behaves as if it were colluding with the legislature, not temporarily but as a matter of design. There is, in other words, no effective checking by centers of power.

Landes and Posner would not deny that some governmental centers of power need consent, but their model is not concerned with that problem.[1] Instead, it rests on an analysis of "the benefits received by legislators" (p. 880) – measured by triangles formed by intersecting demand and supply curves for legislation (see their Figure I) – and of those received by judges. The benefits received by judges are not portrayed in a diagram, though they are carefully discussed. In reviewing and criticizing their model, I will therefore also focus on the interest of legislators and judges. I will not, in other words, discuss Landes and Posner's view of checks and balances using the logic of consent, but their own views. I begin by summarizing briefly the main lines of their model.

Assume first that all relevant legislation is special-interest legislation and second that it is sold spot to the highest bidder.[2] Landes and Posner then argue that *ceteris paribus* the discounted present worth of any piece of legislation varies directly with its expected longevity, which in turn depends on two

---

1. They write: "If courts are not valued highly . . ." (p. 885), a proposition that must refer to the consent they have secured. The authors are not explicit about who should value the courts highly, but one must assume that it is the public.
2. It is difficult to be clear about whether *all* legislation is special-interest legislation in the interest-group theory of politics, hence the word *relevant*.

factors: (1) the legislature's procedural rules that, combined with a limited time budget and "the press of other legislative business" (p. 878), increase the transaction costs of repealing already enacted legislation; and (2) a judiciary that interprets "the 'contracts' of earlier legislatures according to the original understanding of the 'contract'" (p. 885), an element which, it is said, derives from the judiciary's independence.

And as Landes and Posner argue, if judges were not independent but were instead "merely agents of the current legislature, they [would] utilize their *considerable interpretive leeway to rewrite legislation* in conformity with the views of the current rather than the enacting legislature and they [would] thereby impair the 'contract' between the enacting legislature and the group that procured the legislation" (p. 879, italics added). Referring to the authors' own example on the same page, the foregoing statement means that legislation which had imposed "a heavy tax on margarine" for the benefit of the dairy industry would be rewritten by a compliant judiciary in such a way as to repeal the tax whenever a new legislature wished to benefit margarine interests but could not change the old probutter law. A truly compliant judiciary would presumably rewrite the law so as to impose a heavy tax on butter!

Legislators, it would seem to follow, will not want subservient and compliant agents in the judicial branch but independent individuals who will enforce contracts and thus raise the present value of legislation, which can then be sold at a high spot price in the interest-group marketplace.[3] That, of course, is what enacting (first-generation) legislators would want, but what about current (second-generation) legislators who may want "judicial interpretations that [would] gut some existing laws" (p. 885)? Would they not want compliant judges in the judicial branch? The answer must be that they may or may not depending on whether the value to them of having existing legislation gutted exceeds or falls short of the value of enacting new legislation. It must therefore be the case that legislators will sometimes want an independent judiciary, whereas in other circumstances these very same individuals will want compliant judges. The Landes–Posner model in fact assumes that a first legislature designs the judiciary and makes it independent to serve its own purposes. A second legislature, it is implicitly contended, must then accept the first's legislation and presumably serve a different clientele because of the high transaction costs of repealing legislation. However, that assumption about

3. Crain and Tollison (1979) argue that the Landes–Posner model can be applied with benefit to the use of the veto by American presidents – few if any executives outside the United States have a formal veto power – because "the veto power of the chief executive raises the cost of repealing a law, once it is enacted" (p. 560) and therefore also serves to enforce deals made between interest groups and earlier legislatures. It is not clear whether that means that legislators do not want an acquiescent executive but one who sustains the high present value of enacted legislation by striking down their own.

transaction costs cannot do what Landes and Posner want it to do. What they need is an assumption that transaction costs are higher for repealing old legislation than for enacting new law. If the transaction costs of rescinding old legislation are equal or lower than those of enacting new laws, the calculus of legislators in the second and in all subsequent assemblies will relate to the value to them of gutting old legislation versus enacting new law. Which of the two transaction costs – of repeal or of new enactments – is the larger can be determined only by reference to the facts. However, unless the costs of repeal are always higher than those of new enactments, legislators, except those of the very first assembly, will not automatically want an independent judiciary.

Landes and Posner, I believe, would not disagree. For that reason, in the subsection of their paper entitled "A Closer Look at the Concept of Judicial 'Independence'," they in effect deal with the matter by arguing that the self-interest of judges is best served by that independence. They regret the lack of a theory of judicial behavior that would allow them to rationalize this assumption but claim that such a theory is unnecessary for the argument of their paper (p. 887).

That this is not the case can be seen in the fact that Landes and Posner do make use of an implicit theory of judicial behavior. Such a theory surely underlies the view that judges who possess, as Landes and Posner claim, "considerable leeway to rewrite legislation in conformity with the views of the current rather than the enacting legislature" (p. 879) (and, one must suppose, in conformity with the views of any constituency), forgo that privilege, which must be assumed to be enormously profitable, for the sake of independence. One's instinct, governed by observation and experience, is to assume that any individual – even a judge – who had the effective, *de facto* power to "rewrite legislation" and therefore to write it, would close his or her eyes to the thin gruel of independence and simply bankrupt the hapless legislators by taking over the total supply of special-interest legislation. The notion that judges would choose independence in such circumstances cannot be postulated but must be argued, and, on the basis of self-interest, it is doubtful whether judges having the power given them by Landes and Posner would choose to be independent.

But even if judges did not have "considerable leeway to rewrite legislation" – which given legal procedures, time constraints, and the pressure of other business must, at most times, be a very restricted and circumscribed leeway – it is hard to see why they would accept enforcing legislation for the benefit of others. They must be assumed to know that without them special-interest laws would be very diluted deals. Consequently, if they act without recompense as enforcers of special-interest legislation, it is not because they have themselves decided to play that role. It is simply not the one that self-interest dictates they would choose.

The burden of the foregoing discussion is that neither the legislators' nor the judges' self-interest is in general well served by an independent judiciary that enforces legislation enacted for the benefit of interest groups. An independent judiciary is not what these actors would generally design for themselves if we assume that they act rationally and that they have the power to design the institutional structure. But independence could be imposed on the judicial branch by, let us say, a constituent assembly or a constitutional convention at the constitution-writing stage (Buchanan and Tullock, 1962). That is not an unreasonable assumption to make. The question then arises of whether it makes sense to assume that a rational constituent assembly, governed by a desire for efficiency, would make the judiciary independent for the purpose of enforcing deals between legislatures and interest groups. The answer, I believe, must be negative. First, if the purpose of independence is to make the judiciary an efficient enforcer of contracts, the constituent assembly would never give it the power of judicial review; it would probably even deny that power or, at the very least, circumscribe its use to very specific and limited areas far removed from the domain of special-interest legislation – if that domain is not all inclusive! Second, in federal states at least, it is easy for constituent assemblies to make judges much more independent than they now are in the United States, by, for example, assigning the responsibilities for the determination and the payment of judges' salaries and for the general administration of justice to governments and legislatures at a jurisdictional level different from the one at which the judiciary is located. The Canadian Constitution goes part of the way in that direction in that judges of the main *provincial* courts (Superior, District, and County Courts) are appointed by the *federal* Cabinet and paid by the Canadian Parliament.[4] Constituent assemblies could go even further. Judges do not have to be appointed by one or both other branches of government. Selection could be the product of an anonymous competition – exams and other procedures – adjudicated by an independent tribunal, more or less as is currently done in, for example, Italy.

Because, prior to 1982, judicial review was a limited practice in Canada and because of the way the judicature is divided between the federal and provincial jurisdictional levels (see the previous paragraph), one would expect the incidence of special-interest legislation to be greater in Canada than in the United States, since the absence of judicial review and the more limited capacity for "budgetary harassment" (Landes and Posner, 1975, p. 885) of judges, at least in respect of provincial laws, means that *ceteris paribus* the present value of special legislation is greater in Canada than in the United States. I do not know the relevant facts. These same factors make it difficult, however, to understand why Canadian legislatures have so often chosen

---

4. See Gilles Pépin (1985).

Crown Corporations instead of regulation in enacting what Landes and Posner would call special-interest legislation, because Crowns were and are surely less independent than a judiciary not capable of judicial review and free of "budgetary harassment."[5]

I conclude that whoever designs judiciaries as independent bodies does not do so to allow them to enforce special deals between legislators and interest groups. They design them as independent, autonomous and balanced centers of power that can and do check other centers of power, including legislatures.

5. Landes and Posner (1975) write: "Administrative agencies [Crown Corporations?] will be established most frequently when the probability of *de facto* judicial nullification of legislation is high" (p. 888). For a hundred years that probability hovered only marginally above zero in Canada, at the same time as hundreds of Crown Corporations were created by governments at the federal and provincial levels.

Information and pressure

Recent work on lobbying [see Pross (1986), Potters and van Winden (1990, 1992), and Potters (1992)], as well as slightly older work on advertising [for example, Leffler (1981)], rest on the assumption, sometimes more implicit than explicit, that those who seek to pressure or to persuade have to offer something in what must be conceived as a surrogate exchange. The point of the assumption is that the persons who are subjected to pressure or to persuasion would not, if they are rational, accept being handled in that way unless they are offered something as *quid pro quo*. The argument can be put in a still different way: Even though it may be rational for lobbyists (typically interest or pressure groups) and for entrepreneurs to expend resources to create and apply pressure or to persuade, it is not rational for anyone to give in to pressure or persuasion, unless he or she is compensated for yielding to one or the other.

The *quid pro quo* that has retained the attention of scholars who have sought in effect to formulate rational theories of lobbying and of advertising is information. The intuition behind this assumption is eminently reasonable. Information allows the party that is subjected to pressure or to persuasion to test the consequences of yielding to that pressure or persuasion.

Consider an advertising example. A new product is offered for sale to the public. The producer decides to allocate some resources to promote the sale of the product. To persuade households that the product is worth a try, the advertisement will contain information about the product that will not only induce households to buy but will also allow them to verify that the producer is credible, that in other words, the information supplied is correct, and therefore that other characteristics of the product that are not as easily ascertained are genuine components of the product. The information provided by the producer is, as a consequence, an essential element in the willingness of households to eventually yield to the persuasion of the producer. Keith Leffler (1981, p. 55) put it well for the case he studied of prescription drugs, which, for obvious reasons, are advertised to medical doctors. He wrote: "If patients frequently experience less favorable effects than the physician has been led to expect from the products of a particular firm, that firm's detail man will likely lose access to the physician."

The same kind of mechanism underlies rational lobbying. A lobbyist who wishes to be provided with a particular good or service or with a good or service that possesses certain characteristics will, in exerting pressure to obtain these goods, services, or characteristics, offer information about the demand functions of lobby members that will allow the center of power being pressured to test whether it is to its advantage to yield; to test, in other words, whether yielding to pressure will generate net gains in expected consent. What the center of power is able to test is the general credibility of the lobbyist. The mechanism belongs to the same family as the one described by Leffler in the earlier quotation. That is why information is the *quid pro quo* to pressure or persuasion.

The preceding brief discussion does not mean that we now possess a full-blown theory of rational lobbying, but it does mean that we do not have to adhere to the fundamental irrationality of the conventional view. The next few years should therefore witness the emergence of a complete substantive theory of rational lobbying. The recent work is a splendid beginning.

An empirical Wicksellian Connection?

In a recent paper, not unrelated to much of what constitutes the prime focus of this study but published after the relevant chapter had been finished, Lawrence Summers, Jonathan Gruber, and Rodrigo Vergara (1993) have proposed a fascinating hypothesis to explain the considerable variation that can be observed to exist in the rates of taxation of a group of seventeen developed economies. Their point of departure, which is not materially different from that of Wicksell (1896) on which I have based my own theory of the Wicksellian Connection and of demand revelation, is that "[i]n a Robinson Crusoe economy with an all-comprehending Robinson, taxes would not be distortionary," because Robinson would "recognize the linkage between the taxes [he] pay[s] and the benefits that [he] receive[s]" (p. 385). The authors go on to demonstrate that "[i]f individuals fully perceive the benefits of taxation, then there is no deadweight loss from taxation; the "net" (of benefits) tax rate has fallen to zero" (p. 398). The context of their demonstration makes it clear that the perception they are referring to is the perception that the benefits would accrue to the taxpayers themselves.

In real-world non–Robinson Crusoe economies, the linkage between taxes and the benefits that these taxes permit is recognized, they suggest, by union leaders when bargaining between management and workers is conducted in centralized contexts. They argue that "[w]hen there is one encompassing union that negotiates with employers, g ["the degree of encompassment"] approaches one, and there is full perception by the union leaders that the taxes paid by their workers will come back to these same workers as the benefits of government spending" (pp. 396–7). Later in the paper, they expand on this point by noting that for individual workers "the typical 'free-rider' problem remains; they [the workers] do not see that more labor input from them raises the tax base upon which the public goods that they use is financed. However, [the authors reassert] the linkage is seen by the union bosses, who establish the level of employment and hours of work in the negotiation of the union contract" (p. 401).

Summers et al. make use of indexes of "corporatism" developed by a number of economists and political scientists – indexes that have been extensively used to study macroeconomic performance – as measures of the degree of encompassment. That assumption seems consistent with the definition of corporatism proposed by Michael Bruno and Jeffrey Sachs (1985) and adopted by Summers et al., according to which corporatism is "a mode of social organization in which functional groups rather than discrete individuals wield power to transact affairs" (quoted by Summers et al., p. 385–6). They then provide evidence that the relationship between total tax revenue as a percentage of GNP (as well as other measures of the burden of taxation) and the index of corporatism that they select is "robust." Tax levels are indeed on the average higher, the greater the degree of corporatism. So much seems clear.

The assumption about the "perception" of labor unions is incorporated in a representative union's utility function [equation (1)] from which all the theoretical propositions and the specification of the empirical tests follow in straightforward fashion. One question not addressed by Summers et al. is why union bosses, when g is high, would be motivated to "maximize . . . social surplus". Why, in other words, would union leaders in more encompassing unions care about the level and, one must assume, the composition of the bundle of the goods and services supplied by governments to their members? This question suggests that corporatism (and encompassment) may be no more than a proxy for the kind of variables suggested in this study and especially for variables like information about the parameters of the demand functions of the unions' membership for the goods and services supplied by governments and by other agencies, including private markets, and variables like governmental competition. That possibility becomes more insistent when one remembers that "high" corporatism often involves governments in one capacity or another in the bargaining process. The point is not that governments are formal participants in bargaining but that, when the degree of corporatism is high, informal discussions on all sorts of matters among governments and labor and management groups are easy to provoke and organize.

These informal discussions would, however, have limited impact unless union leaders knew what their members demand by way of government-provided goods and services. Consequently, the conditions that make it easier for union bosses to know what unionists want from governments should be explicitly introduced in the analysis. Among these conditions one would surely want to include the degree of preference homogeneity of union members as well as the extent to which the tastes of unionists differ from those of nonunion members. Union bosses are only one source of information. Information can also be obtained by governmental centers of power when they are forced to do so by the competition of other governmental centers of power. The degree of intra- and intergovernmental competition should, therefore, be incorporated into the analysis. The basic Figure I (p. 388) of Summers et al. appears consistent with the view, based admittedly on nothing more than impressions, that many countries would be much closer to the regressions line

– assuming that that line would remain where it is even after the incorporation of other variables – if a measure of governmental competition was embodied in the analysis.

Be that as it may, I read the Summers, Gruber, and Vergara contribution as consistent with the idea that there are forces in operation in the real world directed at the construction of Wicksellian Connections and at the revelation of demand for government-supplied goods and services.

Overlap and duplication

In large institutions like governments and governmental systems, as in markets, there are two organizational or structural consequences of competition which, if they are suppressed, extinguish the beneficial effects of that otherwise powerful regulatory force. The two consequences are distinct and separately observable, but they are closely interrelated. They are specialization and duplication. Few people understand the meaning of these two concepts and of the reality they identify and describe. It is very important always to keep in mind that specialization is seldom, if ever, complete and that duplication is never perfect. One of the great discoveries of economists and of trade practitioners and a source of wonderment for them both was the fact that as trade barriers were reduced in Europe as the Treaty of Rome was implemented, a particular country did not completely specialize in the production of, say, cars and another completely specialize in the production of, say, wines, but that both countries specialized in certain types of cars and certain types of wines. Competition, following the removal of trade barriers, led to specialization and maintained duplication. If that is not acknowledged, the actual manifestations of specialization – which is known to be a major source of increased efficiency – will not be recognized.

In what sense, then, can it be said that competition leads to duplication? I do not have in mind the fact that duplication is essential to the existence of competition. Instead, I am referring to the fact that because specialization is in virtually all cases partial and imperfect, there is always potential duplication and, hence, potential competition. Consider the case of cars. Two countries, let us say, have erected trade barriers vis-à-vis each other such that each is autarchic in cars. Now as trade barriers are reduced, instead of all production originating in one country, both specialize in the production of different kinds of cars. That means that if producers in one country become sloppy and inefficient, it is a relatively simple matter for producers in the other country to tool up and invade the first country's market. In that sense there is duplication or, shall we say, potential duplication. Duplication reduces the transaction cost of exploiting opportunities and as such increases competition and therefore efficiency. Outside observers, noting that both countries are producing cars, may conclude that there is no specialization and only wasteful duplication. They would be wrong. In the absence of trade and other barriers, competition will lead to partial, but optimal, specialization and to optimal duplication, which will in turn act as a spur to further competition.

All of this applies almost word for word to the problem of assembling inputs for the production of goods and services in governments and governmental systems and in other large organizations. I will make the point by looking at the case of economic policy. It is easy to extend the analysis to all the other goods and services produced and supplied by governments.

The production – formulation and implementation – of economic policies (of macroeconomic management policies, of industrial, commercial and environmental policies, of taxation policies and so forth) involves a large number of departments, committees, councils, and other governmental agencies or centers of power. Each one of these is to a degree specialized in a particular domain of analysis and activity, but all of them are capable of extending their jurisdiction to other domains and activities. What is sometimes called, with barely muted condemnatory overtones, bureaucratic "empire building" is a manifestation of the capacity of centers of power to extend their jurisdiction and is incidentally a manifestation of competitive behavior. Instead of being ridiculed and damned, it should be applauded and encouraged. The alternative to competition is planning, which is as wasteful inside organizations as in economies generally.

For example, as regards macroeconomic management policy in Canada, the prime players in the government are the Department of Finance and the Bank of Canada, but the Prime Minister's Office, the Department of Labor, Central Mortgage and Housing, the Economic Council of Canada (now abolished), and other centers of power can and do contribute to the process of policy formulation – either as advocates or as critics of certain orientations – even if they are not directly involved in policy implementation. The provincial governments do not have constitutional jurisdiction over macroeconomic management policy, but there are regular meetings of First Ministers (the Canadian Prime Minister and the provincial Premiers), of Ministers of Finance, and of Deputy Ministers of Finance to discuss macroeconomic management. The provincial governments, in turn, have departments responsible for various aspects of economic policies, all of which have views and make contributions to macroeconomic management policy. For other areas – such as social policy, education, arts and culture, housing, income redistribution, communication, police protection, international affairs, transportation – the same is true in varying degree, as is easy to document.

In view of this and in view of the widespread belief that there is too much overlap – a view that parallels the now defunct idea that competitive market organization is tantamount to anarchy and should be replaced by planning – one must ask whether wasteful or excess duplication can exist. The answer to this query is "yes;" excess duplication is possible. In the market economy, the phenomenon is known as excess capacity, an inappropriate expression that describes a situation in which the number of individual supplying firms is too large and each one too small. The phenomenon derives from increasing returns or (if we neglect pecuniary changes in factor prices resulting from industry-wide adjustments, which have nothing to do with the phenomenon) from decreasing unit costs generated by the production of a variety of differentiated products. It is not known how serious a problem – how wasteful – excess capacity is in the market economy. However, noisy econometric estimates of cost functions indicate that unit cost curves are saucer shaped, that is, they begin with a region of falling costs, followed by a significant region of constant costs succeeded by a region of increasing costs. Put differently, the average variable cost curves are U-shaped but have a flat stretch over a range of output at the bottom of the U. To the extent that this is the case and to the extent that output flows are "large enough," waste is not a very serious problem.

We have few estimates of the unit cost of producing goods and services in governments – certainly none about the unit cost of producing economic policies – and consequently cannot adopt the same conclusion for governmental centers of power as is done for market enterprises. It is well to recall, however, that to a considerable degree, the saucer shape of average cost curves is not a product of physics, chemistry, and other natural and technological forces alone, but also of the ability of management, through a variety of means, to introduce flexibility into the operation of the enterprise [see, for example, Stigler (1939)]. Consequently, if excess duplication exists, closing down centers of power is an appropriate policy – one that will improve efficiency – only if it is not possible to create a flat stretch in the unit cost curve and to operate somewhere on that stretch; only if, in other words, managers of centers of power in governments and governmental systems are not efficient or, more precisely, are less efficient than managers in the market sector. In view of the considerable two-way traffic of managers between the two sectors that can be observed in many countries – France and the United States being notable examples – this would appear to be a difficult position to defend. On that reasoning, the noisy econometric estimates of cost functions for market goods and services can be used with care to argue that the cost functions of government-supplied goods and services are also probably U-shaped, implying little if any excess duplication in governments and governmental systems.

The structure and stability of federal states

William Riker and Jonathan Lemco (1980),[1] on the basis of a detailed and provocative statistical analysis of forty federations[2] that exist today or have existed over the period from 1798 to the present, have argued that the stability of federal structures is positively associated with the degree of centralization of the federation. Stability is taken to be a measure of the capacity to survive. Unstable federations are defined as those that have failed, partially stable ones as those which, in 1980 (see footnote 1), were "threatened by separatism, secession or civil war," and stable federations as those that were not so threatened. This is a definition of stability which is consistent with the one used in Chapter 9.

Centralization, a notoriously difficult concept to measure in view of its inherent multidimensionality, is defined in two ways. First, by a dichotomous variable based on the authors' knowledge and judgment of which federations are centralized and which are not; second, by the number of constituent units and by the presence or absence of "oversized" units in the federation. The relationship of numbers to centralization is as follows: federations, in Riker and Lemco's view, are essentially arrangements for defense against, or for the pursuit of, aggression. Therefore, if numbers are small, the gain in military strength from federalizing does not much outweigh the loss in freedom of action, but when numbers are larger it does outweigh the loss so that the members accept transferring real power to the center. Variance in size relates to centralization in that differences in it lead members to entertain different expectations about the value of the federation: Large units want more influ-

1. The paper on which I will comment was written in 1980 and presented at "a conference on Canadian reforms". It was first published in Riker (1987) after excision of "topical references to Canada" (Riker, 1987, p. 113). Professor Riker has graciously made available to me a copy of the original conference paper to allow me to examine what he and Lemco had said about Canada. All page references in what follows are to Riker (1987); when I quote from the original, I simply refer to the "original."

2. Riker and Lemco's work – as well as earlier work of Riker on federalism – treats federations, confederations, leagues, and some other associations of states as belonging to one class. The distinguishing mark of these various systems is the degree of centralization: Federations are more centralized than confederations and the latter more than leagues. I do not look at the matter in this way, but because of the relevance and interest of Riker and Lemco's findings for my own approach, I have chosen to read their paper within the terms of their own framework.

ence, small units want equality of influence. That prevents a strong center. Other variables besides centralization – language differences, wealth, democracy – were considered as explanations of stability but were found to be statistically insignificant.

On the basis of their analysis, Riker and Lemco conclude that "[c]entralization and stability are closely related" (p. 127). In the language of the theory of competitive federal governmental systems suggested in Chapter 9, Riker and Lemco could be said to be arguing that when the number of units in a federal structure is small and when there are "oversized" units in the structure, horizontal competition is unstable.

If Riker and Lemco are right, where does their analysis leave the discussion of monitoring by central governments and of competitive stability suggested in Chapter 9? I argue that Riker and Lemco's analysis, contrary to possible first impressions, reinforces my argument about monitoring in two different ways. The first derives from the fact that central governments' task of monitoring the rules of competition will be easier if the number of constituent units is large and the variance in their size-distribution small. This is analogous to the argument that competition policy in a market context is easier to implement in similar circumstances – many nearly equal size firms (see, for example, Edwards, 1949).

The second way in which the Riker and Lemco analysis reinforces my own – a way that is much more important than the first for an understanding of stability – is by pointing to the existence of substitutes for numbers and variance in size-distribution as sources of stability. Riker and Lemco would not, I believe, disagree. The original version of their paper (see footnote 1) contains a discussion of the problems of the Canadian federation, circa 1980, which concludes: "Insofar as our measurement is reliable, this association [of stability with centralization] means that [Prime Minister] Trudeau has done what he must to prolong the political stability of Canada by encouraging the centralization process." It is not possible to know what this sentence really means, but since former Prime Minister Trudeau did not change the number of provinces in Canada, or change their size-distribution, he must have put in place measures that were substitutes for these things!

The relevance of the Riker and Lemco analysis, from my perspective, is that structure helps, but that if the structure is not optimal, the problems that that poses can be circumvented by measures that promote stability. Structure is important, but effective monitoring is the more significant phenomenon.

References

Acheson, Keith, "Bureaucratic Theory: Retrospect and Prospect," in Albert Breton, Gianluigi Galeotti, Pierre Salmon, and Ronald Wintrobe, eds., *Villa Colombella Papers on Bureaucracy, European Journal of Political Economy* (Vol. 4, Extra Issue, 1988), 17–46.

Aharoni, Yair, *Markets, Planning, and Development: The Private and Public Sectors in Economic Development* (Cambridge, MA: Ballinger, 1977).

Akerlof, George A., "The Market for 'Lemons': Quality Uncertainty and the Market Mechanism," *Quarterly Journal of Economics* (Vol. 84, No. 3, August 1970), 488–500.

"The Economics of 'Tagging' as Applied to the Optimal Income Tax, Welfare Programs, and Manpower Planning," *American Economic Review* (Vol. 68, No. 1, March 1978), 8–19.

"A Theory of Social Custom, of Which Unemployment May Be One Consequence," *Quarterly Journal of Economics* (Vol. 94, No. 4, June 1980), 749–75.

"Labor Contracts as Partial Gift Exchange," *Quarterly Journal of Economics* (Vol. 97, No. 4, November 1982), 543–69.

Alchian, Armen, "Costs and Outputs," in Paul A. Baran, Tibor Scitovsky, and Edward S. Shaw, eds., *The Allocation of Economic Resources* (Stanford: Stanford University Press, 1959), 23–40.

"Corporate Management and Property Rights," in Henry G. Manne, ed., *Economic Policy and the Regulation of Corporate Securities* (Washington: American Enterprise Institute, 1969), 337–60.

Alesina, Alberto, "Macroeconomics and Politics" in Stanley Fischer, ed., *NBER Macroeconomics Annual* (Cambridge, MA: MIT Press, 1988), 13–52.

"Politics and Business Cycles in Industrial Democracies," *Economic Policy,* (Vol. 4, No. 1, April 1989), 55–98.

Alesina, Alberto, and Allan Drazen, "Why Are Stabilizations Delayed?," *American Economic Review* (Vol. 81, No. 5, December 1991), 1170–88.

Alesina, Alberto, and Nouriel Roubini, "Political Cycles in OECD Economies," (Mimeo, 1990).

Allen, Douglas W., "Homesteading and Property Rights; or, 'How the West Was Really Won'," *Journal of Law and Economics* (Vol. 34, No. 1, April 1991), 1–23.

Allingham, Michael G., and Agnar Sandmo, "Income Tax Evasion: A Theoretical Analysis," *Journal of Public Economics* (Vol. 1, No. 3/4, November 1972), 323–38.

Anderson, Terry L., and Peter J. Hill, *The Birth of a Transfer Society* (Stanford: Hoover Institution Press, 1980).

Aoki, Masahiko, ed., *The Economic Analysis of the Japanese Firm* (Amsterdam: North-Holland, 1984).

"Horizontal vs. Vertical Information Structure of the Firm," *American Economic Review* (Vol. 76, No. 5, December 1986), 971–83.

"Toward an Economic Model of the Japanese Firm," *Journal of Economic Literature* (Vol. 28, No. 1, March 1990), 1–27.

Aranson, Peter H., and Peter C. Ordeshook, "Regulation, Redistribution, and Public Choice", *Public Choice* (Vol. 37, No. 1, 1981), 69–100.

337

Arendt, Hannah, *The Origins of Totalitarianism,* Second Edition (New York: Harcourt Brace Jovanovich, 1973).

Arrow, Kenneth J., *Social Choice and Individual Value* (New York: Wiley, 1951; Revised Edition, 1963).

"Toward a Theory of Price Adjustment," in Paul A. Baran, Tibor Scitovsky, and Edward S. Shaw, eds., *The Allocation of Economic Resources* (Stanford: Stanford University Press, 1959), 41–51.

"The Economic Implications of Learning by Doing," *Review of Economic Studies* (Vol. 29, No. 3, June 1962), 155–73.

"Informational Structure of the Firm," *American Economic Review* (Vol. 75, No. 2, May 1985a), 303–7.

"The Economics of Agency," in John W. Pratt and Richard J. Zeckhauser, eds., *Principals and Agents: The Structure of Business* (Boston: Harvard Business School Press, 1985b), 37–51.

Auerbach, Alan, J., and Laurence J. Kotlikoff, *Dynamic Fiscal Policy* (New York: Cambridge University Press, 1987).

Auster, Richard D., and Morris Silver, *The States as a Firm: Economic Forces in Political Development* (Hingham: Martinus Nijhoff, 1979).

Axelrod, Robert, *The Evolution of Cooperation* (New York: Basic Books, 1984).

Bacharach, Samuel B., and Edward J. Lawler, *Power and Politics in Organizations* (San Francisco: Jossey-Bass, 1981).

Bagehot, Walter, *The English Constitution,* with an Introduction by R. H. S. Crossman, (Glasgow: Fontana/Collins, 1867/1963).

Barro, Robert J., "Are Government Bonds Net Wealth?" *Journal of Political Economy* (Vol. 82, No. 6, November/December 1974), 1095–1117.

Barzel, Yoram, "Two Propositions on the Optimum Level of Producing Collective Goods," *Public Choice* (Vol. 6, Spring 1969), 31–7.

Bateman, Worth, and Harold M. Hochman, "Social Problems and the Urban Crisis: Can Public Policy Make a Difference?" in Harold M. Hochman, ed., *The Urban Economy* (New York: Norton, 1976), 283–93.

Baumol, William J., *Welfare Economics and the Theory of the State,* Second Edition (Cambridge, MA: Harvard University Press, 1969; First Edition, 1952).

Business Behavior, Value and Growth, Revised Edition (New York: Harcourt Brace Jovanovich, 1967; First Edition, 1959).

"External Economies and Second-Order Optimality Conditions," *American Economic Review* (Vol. 54, No. 4, Part 1, June 1964), 358–72.

"Macroeconomics of Unbalanced Growth: The Anatomy of Urban Crisis," *American Economic Review* (Vol. 57, No. 3, June 1967), 415–26.

Baumol, William J., and David F. Bradford, "Detrimental Externalities and Non-Convexity of the Production Set," *Economica* (Vol. 39, No. 154, May 1972), 160–76.

Baumol, William J., Sue Anne Batey Blackman, and Edward N. Wolff, "Unbalanced Growth Revisited: Asymptotic Stagnancy and New Evidence," *American Economic Review* (Vol. 75, No. 4, September 1985), 806–17.

Baumol, William J., John C. Panzar, and Robert D. Willig, *Contestable Markets and the Theory of Industry Structure* (San Diego: Harcourt Brace Jovanovich, 1982).

Beard, Charles A., *An Economic Interpretation of the Constitution of the United States* (New York: Macmillan, 1913/1960).

Becker, Gary S., "A Theory of the Allocation of Time," *Economic Journal.* (Vol. 75, No. 299, September 1965), 493–517.

Human Capital and the Personal Distribution of Income: An Analytical Approach (Woytinski

Lecture, University of Michigan, 1967). Reprinted in Becker, *Human Capital,* Second Edition (New York: National Bureau of Economic Research and Columbia University Press, 1975), 94–144.

"A Theory of Social Interactions," *Journal of Political Economy* (Vol. 82, No. 6, November/ December 1974), 1063–93.

The Economic Approach to Human Behavior (Chicago: University of Chicago Press, 1976a).

A Treatise on the Family (Cambridge, MA: Harvard University Press, 1976b).

"A Theory of Competition Among Pressure Groups for Political Influence," *Quarterly Journal of Economics* (Vol. 98, No. 3, August 1983), 371–400.

"Public Policies, Pressure Groups, and Dead Weight Costs," *Journal of Public Economics* (Vol. 28, No. 3, December 1985), 329–47.

Becker, Gary S., and Kevin M. Murphy, "The Family and the State," *Journal of Law and Economics* (Vol. 31, No. 1, April 1988), 1–18.

Becker, Gary S., and George J. Stigler, "Law Enforcement, Malfeasance, and Compensation of Enforcers," *Journal of Legal Studies* (Vol. 3, No. 1, January 1974), 1–18.

Bélanger, Gérard, "The Division of Powers in a Federal System: A Review of the Economic Literature, with Applications to Canada," in Richard Simeon, ed., *Division of Powers and Public Policy* (Toronto: University of Toronto Press, 1985), 1–27.

"Un changement institutionnel majeur: la croissance du secteur public", dans *Mémoires de la Société Royale du Canada,* Cinquième Série, Tome II (Ottawa: Société Royale du Canada, 1987), 57–73.

Croissance du secteur public et fédéralisme: perspective économique, (Montréal: Agence d'Arc, 1988).

Bella, Leslie, "The Provincial Role in the Canadian Welfare State: The Influence of Provincial Social Policy Initiatives on the Design of the Canada Assistance Plan," *Canadian Public Administration* (Vol. 22, No. 3, Fall 1979), 439–52.

Bénard, Jean, *Economie Publique* (Paris: Economica, 1985).

Bendor, Jonathan, Serge Taylor, and Roland Van Gaalen, "Bureaucratic Expertise Versus Legislative Authority: A Model of Deception and Monitoring in Budgeting," *American Political Science Review* (Vol. 79, No. 4, December 1985), 1041–60.

Bennett, James T., and Thomas J. DiLorenzo, *Destroying Democracy. How Government Funds Partisan Politics* (Washington: Cato Institute, 1985).

Bennis, Warren G., "Leadership Theory and Administrative Behavior: The Problem of Authority," *Administrative Science Quarterly* (Vol. 4, No. 3, December 1959), 259–301.

Bergstrom, Theodore C., and Robert P. Goodman, "Private Demands for Public Goods," *American Economic Review* (Vol. 63, No. 3, June, 1973), 280–96.

Berle, Adolf A., and Gardiner C. Means, *The Modern Corporation and Private Property* (New York: Macmillan, 1932).

Bernheim, B. Douglas, Andrei Shleifer, and Lawrence H. Summers, "The Strategic Bequest Motive," *Journal of Political Economy* (Vol. 93, No. 6, December 1985), 1045–76.

Beveridge, William H., *Social Insurance and Allied Services,* American Edition (New York: MacMillan, 1942).

Full Employment in a Free Society (New York: Norton, 1945).

Bird, Richard M., *The Growth of Government Spending in Canada* (Toronto: Canadian Tax Foundation, 1970).

Financing Canadian Government: A Quantitative Overview (Toronto: Canadian Tax Foundation, 1979).

"Tax Harmonization and Federal Finance: A Perspective on Recent Canadian Discussion," *Canadian Public Policy* (Vol. 10, No. 3, September 1984), 253–66.

Federal Finance in Comparative Perspective (Toronto: Canadian Tax Foundation, 1986).

"Shaping a New International Tax Order," *Bulletin of the International Bureau of Fiscal Documentation* (July, 1988), 292–303.

Bird, Richard M., and Jack M. Mintz, "Introduction," in Bird and Mintz, eds., *Taxation To 2000 and Beyond* (Toronto: Canadian Tax Foundation, 1992), 1–28.

Bird, Richard M., and Enid Slack, *Urban Public Finance in Canada* (Toronto: Butterworth, 1983).

Birdsall, William C., "A Study of the Demand for Public Goods," in Richard A. Musgrave, ed., *Essays in Fiscal Federalism* (Washington: Brookings Institution, 1965), 235–94.

Bish, Robert L., *Local Government in British Columbia* (Victoria: Union of British Columbia Municipalities and University of Victoria School of Public Administration, 1987).

Black, Duncan, *The Theory of Committees and Elections* (Cambridge, UK: Cambridge University Press, 1958).

Bloom, Howard S., Helen F. Ladd, and John Yinger, "Are Property Taxes Capitalized Into House Values?" in George R. Zodrow, ed., *Local Provision of Public Services: The Tiebout Model After Twenty-Five Years* (New York: Academic Press, 1983), 145–63.

Boadway, Robin, and Frank Flatters, "Efficiency and Equalization Payments in a Federal System of Government: A Synthesis and Extension of Recent Results," *Canadian Journal of Economics* (Vol. 15, No. 4, November 1982a), 613–33.

Equalization in a Federal State: An Economic Analysis (Ottawa: Supply and Services Canada, 1982b).

Borcherding, Thomas E., "Toward a Positive Theory of Public Sector Supply Arrangements," in J. Robert S. Prichard, ed., *Crown Corporations in Canada. The Calculus of Instrument Choice* (Toronto: Butterworth, 1983), 99–184.

"The Causes of Government Expenditure Growth: A Survey of the U.S. Evidence," *Journal of Public Economics* (Vol. 28, No. 3, December 1985), 359–82.

Borcherding, Thomas E., and Robert T. Deacon, "The Demand for the Services of Non-Federal Governments," *American Economic Review* (Vol. 62, No. 5, December, 1972), 891–901.

Bös, Dieter, "Commentary on Roger Gordon's 'An Optimal Taxation Approach to Fiscal Federalism'," in Charles E. McLure, Jr., ed., *Tax Assignment in Federal Countries* (Canberra: Centre for Research on Federal Financial Relations, Australian National University, 1983), 43–7.

Bothwell, Robert, Ian Drummond, and John English, *Canada Since 1945: Power, Politics, and Provincialism* (Toronto: University of Toronto Press, 1981).

Boulding, Kenneth E., "Notes on a Theory of Philanthropy," in Frank G. Dickinson, ed., *Philanthropy and Public Policy* (New York: National Bureau of Economic Research, 1962), 57–71.

Bracher, Karl D., *The German Dictatorship,* Translated by Jean Steinberg (New York: Praeger, 1969/1970).

Brean, Donald J. S., *International Issues in Taxation: The Canadian Perspective* (Toronto: Canadian Tax Foundation, 1984).

Brennan, Geoffrey, and James M. Buchanan, *The Power to Tax. Analytical Foundations of a Fiscal Constitution* (New York: Cambridge University Press, 1980).

"Normative Tax Theory for a Federal Polity: Some Public Choice Preliminaries," in Charles E. McLure Jr., ed., *Tax Assignment in Federal Countries* (Canberra: Centre for Research on Federal Financial Relations, Australian National University, 1983), 52–65.

Brennan, Geoffrey, and Jonathan Pincus, "An Implicit Contract Theory of Intergovernmental Grants," *Publius: The Journal of Federalism* (Vol. 20, No. 4, Fall 1990), 129–44.

"A Minimalist Model of Federal Grants," (Typescript 1991).

Breton, Albert, "The Economics of Nationalism," *Journal of Political Economy* (Vol. 72, No. 4, August 1964), 376–86.

"A Theory of Government Grants," *Canadian Journal of Economics and Political Science* (Vol. 31, No. 2, May 1965), 175–87.

The Economic Theory of Representative Government (Chicago: Aldine, 1974).

"Supplementary Report," in *Report* of the (Macdonald) *Royal Commission on the Economic Union and Development Prospects for Canada* (Ottawa: Supply and Services, 1985). Reprinted as "Towards a Theory of Competitive Federalism," *European Journal of Political Economy* (Vol. 3, Nos. 1–2, 1987), 263–329.

"The Growth of Competitive Governments," *Canadian Journal of Economics* (Vol. 22, No. 4, November 1989), 717–50.

Centralization, Decentralization and Intergovernmental Competition. The 1989 Kenneth R. MacGregor Lecture (Kingston: Queen's University, Institute of Intergovernmental Relations, 1990).

Breton, Albert, and Angela Fraschini, "Free-riding and Intergovernmental Grants," *Kyklos* (Vol. 45, No. 3, 1992), 347–62.

Breton, Albert, and Gianluigi Galeotti, "Is Proportional Representation Always the Best Rule?" *Public Finance* (Vol. 40, No. 1, 1985), 1–16.

Breton, Albert, and Anthony Scott, *The Economic Constitution of Federal States* (Toronto: University of Toronto Press, 1978).

The Design of Federations (Montreal: Institute for Research on Public Policy, 1980).

Breton, Albert, and Ronald Wintrobe, "The Equilibrium Size of a Budget-Maximizing Bureau: A Note on Niskanen's Theory of Bureaucracy," *Journal of Political Economy* (Vol. 83, No. 1, February 1975), 195–207.

"Bureaucracy and State Intervention: Parkinson's Law?" *Canadian Public Administration* (Vol. 22, No. 2, Summer 1979), 208–26.

The Logic of Bureaucratic Conduct. An Analysis of Competition, Exchange, and Efficiency in Private and Public Organizations (New York: Cambridge University Press, 1982).

"The Bureaucracy of Murder Revisited," *Journal of Political Economy* (Vol. 94, No. 5, October 1986), 905–26.

Breton, Margot, "Reflections on Social Action Practice in France," *Social Work with Groups* (Vol. 14, No. 3/4, 1991), 91–107.

Brown, Robert E., *Charles Beard and the Constitution: A Critical Analysis of 'An Economic Interpretation of the Constitution'* (Princeton: Princeton University Press, 1956).

Brown, Wilfred B. D., *Exploration in Management* (London: Heinemann, 1960).

Browning, Edgar K., "The Marginal Cost of Public Funds," *Journal of Political Economy* (Vol. 84, No. 2, April, 1976), 283–98.

Bruno, Michael, and Jeffrey Sachs, *The Economics of Worldwide Stagflation* (Cambridge, MA: Harvard University Press, 1985).

Bryant, Ralph C., *Money and Monetary Policy in Independent Nations* (Washington: The Brookings Institution, 1980).

Bryce, James, *The American Commonwealth* (New York: Macmillan, 1888/1911).

Buchanan, James M., "Federalism and Fiscal Equity," *American Economic Review* (Vol. 40, No. 4, September 1950), 583–99. Reprinted in Richard A. Musgrave and Carl S. Shoup, eds., *Readings in the Economics of Taxation* (Homewood: Irwin, 1959), 93–103.

"The Economics of Earmarked Taxes," *Journal of Political Economy* (Vol. 71, No. 5, October 1963), 457–69.

"An Economic Theory of Clubs," *Economica* (Vol. 32, February, 1965), 1–14.

Public Finance in Democratic Process. Fiscal Institutions and Individual Choice (Chapel Hill: University of North Carolina Press, 1967).

The Demand and Supply of Public Goods (Chicago: Rand McNally, 1968).

The Limits of Liberty. Between Anarchy and Leviathan (Chicago: University of Chicago Press, 1975).

"The Constitution of Economic Policy," *American Economic Review* (Vol. 77, No. 3, June 1987), 243–50.

Buchanan, James M., and Marilyn R. Flowers, *The Public Finances* (Homewood: Irwin, 1987).

Buchanan, James M., and Gordon Tullock, *The Calculus of Consent. Logical Foundations of Constitutional Democracy* (Ann Arbor: University of Michigan Press, 1962).

Burke, Edmund, *Burke's Politics: Selected Writings and Speeches on Reform, Revolution and War.* Ed. Ross J. S. Hoffman and Paul Levack (New York: Knopf, 1949).

Burns, Tom, and G. M. Stalker, *The Management of Innovation* (London: Tavistock, 1961).

Cairns, Alan C., *From Interstate to Intrastate Federalism* (Kingston: Queen's University, Institute of Intergovernmental Relations, 1979).

Cameron, David R., "The Expansion of the Public Economy: A Comparative Analysis," *American Political Science Review* (Vol. 72, No. 4, December 1978), 1243–61.

Campbell, Colin, and George J. Szablowski, *The Super-Bureaucrats: Structure and Behavior in Central Agencies* (Toronto: Macmillan, 1979).

Canada, Royal Commission on Dominion-Provincial Relations, *Report* (Ottawa: King's Printer, 1940). [Rowell–Sirois Report].

Carey, William L., "Federalism and Corporate Law: Reflections Upon Delaware," *Yale Law Journal* (Vol. 83, No. 4, March 1974), 663–705.

Chandler, Alfred D., Jr., *Strategy and Structure* (Cambridge, MA: MIT Press, 1962).

Chapple, Elliot R., and Leonard Sayles, *The Measure of Management* (New York: Macmillan, 1961).

Charreaux, Gérard, "La théorie des transactions informelles: une synthèse," *Economies et Sociétés* (Série Sciences de Gestion no. 15, mai 1990), 137–61.

Chernick, Howard A., "An Economic Model of the Distribution of Project Grants," in Peter M. Mieszkowski and William H. Oakland, eds., *Fiscal Federalism and Grants-in-Aid* (Washington: The Urban Institute, 1979), 81–103.

Cheung, Steven N. S., "The Fable of the Bees: An Economic Investigation," *Journal of Law and Economics* (Vol. 16, No. 1, April, 1973), 11–52.

Clarke, Edward H., "Multipart Pricing of Public Goods," *Public Choice* (Vol. 11, Fall 1971), 17–33.

Coase, Ronald H., "The Problem of Social Cost," *Journal of Law and Economics* (Vol. 3, October 1960), 1–44.

"The British Post Office and the Messenger Companies," *Journal of Law and Economics* (Vol. 4, October 1961), 12–65.

"The Lighthouse in Economics," *Journal of Law and Economics* (Vol. 17, No. 2, October 1974), 357–76.

Coleman, James S., *Introduction to Mathematical Sociology* (Glencoe: Free Press, 1964).

"The Possibility of a Social Welfare Function," *American Economic Review* (Vol. 56, No. 5, December, 1966), 1105–22.

"Recontracting, Trustworthiness, and the Stability of Vote Exchanges," *Public Choice* (Vol. 40, No. 1, 1983), 89–94.

"Social Capital in the Creation of Human Capital," *American Journal of Sociology* (Vol. 94, Supplement, 1988), S95–S120.

Coleman, James, Herbert Menzel, and Elihu Katz, "Social Processes in Physicians' Adoption of a New Drug," *Journal of Chronic Diseases* (Vol. 9, No. 1, January 1959), 1–19.

Collier, Kenneth E., Richard D. McKelvey, Peter C. Ordeshook, and Kenneth C. Williams, "Retrospective Voting: An Experimental Study," *Public Choice* (Vol. 53, No. 2, 1987), 101–30.

Conybeare, John C., "International Organization and the Theory of Property Rights," *International Organization* (Vol. 34, No. 3, Summer 1980), 307–34.

Cooter, Robert, and Stephen Marks, with Robert Mnookin, "Bargaining in the Shadow of the Law: A Testable Model of Strategic Behavior," *Journal of Legal Studies* (Vol. 11, No. 2, June 1982), 225–51.

Corden, W. Max, *The Logic of the International Monetary Non-System* (Canberra: Centre for Economic Policy Research, Australian National University, Discussion Paper No. 24, 1981).

Courant, Paul N., Edward M. Gramlich, and Daniel L. Rubinfeld, "The Stimulative Effects of Intergovernmental Grants: Or Why Money Sticks Where It Hits," in Peter M. Mieszkowski and William H. Oakland, eds., *Fiscal Federalism and Grants-In-Aid*, (Washington: The Urban Institute, 1979), 5–21.

Courchene, Thomas J., "Interprovincial Migration and Economic Adjustment," *Canadian Journal of Economics* (Vol. 3, No. 4, November 1970), 550–76.

"Towards a Protected Society: The Politicization of Economic Life," *Canadian Journal of Economics* (Vol. 13, No. 4, November 1980), 556–77.

Equalization Payments: Past, Present and Future (Toronto: Ontario Economic Council, 1984).

Cox, Donald, "Motives for Private Income Transfers," *Journal of Political Economy* (Vol. 95, No. 3, June 1987), 508–46.

Crain, Robert L., "Fluoridation: The Diffusion of an Innovation Among Cities," *Social Forces* (Vol. 44, No. 4, June 1966), 467–76.

Crain, W. Mark, and Robert D. Tollison, "The Executive Branch in the Interest-Group Theory of Government," *Journal of Legal Studies* (Vol. 8, No. 3, June 1979), 555–67.

Cross, Rod B., and G. Keith Shaw, "The Evasion–Avoidance Choice: A Suggested Approach," *National Tax Journal* (Vol. 34, No. 4, December, 1981), 489–91.

Crossman, Richard, *The Diaries of a Cabinet Minister,* Vol. I (London: Hamish Hamilton and Jonathan Cape, 1975).

Crozier, Michel, *Le phénomène bureaucratique* (Paris: Seuil, 1963). Translated by Crozier as *The Bureaucratic Phenomenon* (Chicago: University of Chicago Press, 1964).

Dahl, Robert A., *A Preface to Democratic Theory* (Chicago: University of Chicago Press, 1956).

Dalton, Melville, *Men Who Manage: Fusion of Feeling and Theory in Administration* (New York: John Wiley, 1959).

Darnton, Robert, *The Great Cat Massacre and Other Episodes in French Cultural History* (New York: Random House, Vintage Books, 1985).

Davies, David G., "The Concentration Process and the Growing Importance of Noncentral Governments in Federal States," *Public Policy* (Vol. 18, Fall 1970), 649–57.

Davis, Ada J., "The Evolution of the Institution of Mothers' Pensions in the United States," *American Journal of Sociology* (Vol. 35, No. 4, January 1930), 573–87.

Davis, Otto A., and Andrew B. Whinston, "Welfare Economics and the Theory of Second Best," *Review of Economic Studies* (Vol. 32, No. 1, January 1965), 1–14.

Day, Kathleen M., "Interprovincial Migration and Local Public Goods," *Canadian Journal of Economics* (Vol. 25, No. 1, February 1992), 123–44.

Deacon, Robert T., "Private Choice and Collective Outcomes: Evidence from Public Sector Demand Analysis," *National Tax Journal* (Vol. 30, No. 4, December 1977), 371–86.

"A Demand Model for the Local Public Sector," *Review of Economics and Statistics* (Vol. 60, No. 2, May 1978), 184–92.

Deacon, Robert T., and Perry Shapiro, "Private Preference for Collective Goods Revealed Through Voting on Referenda," *American Economic Review* (Vol. 65, No. 5, December, 1975), 943–55.

Demsetz, Harold, "Why Regulate Utilities?" *Journal of Law and Economics* (Vol. 1, No. 1, April 1968), 55–65.

Economic, Legal, and Political Dimensions of Competition (Amsterdam: North-Holland, 1982).

Denzau, Arthur T., and Robert J. Mackay, "Tax Systems and Tax Shares," *Public Choice* (Vol. 45, No. 1, 1985), 35–47.

Dicey, Albert, *Introduction to the Study of the Law of the Constitution,* Tenth Edition (New York: St. Martin's Press, 1962).

Dodd, Peter, and Richard Leftwich, "The Market for Corporate Charters: 'Unhealthy Competition' Versus Federal Regulation," *Journal of Business* (Vol. 53, No. 3, July 1980), 259–83.

Downs, Anthony, *An Economic Theory of Democracy* (New York: Harper & Row, 1957).

Inside Bureaucracy (Boston: Little, Brown, 1967).

Eaton, B. Curtis, and William D. White, "The Distribution of Wealth and the Efficiency of Institutions," *Economic Inquiry* (Vol. 29, No. 2, April 1991), 336–50.

Eavey, Cheryl L., and Gary J. Miller, "Bureaucratic Agenda Control: Imposition or Bargaining?" *American Political Science Review* (Vol. 78, No. 3, September 1984), 719–33.

Edel, Matthew, and Elliot Sclar, "Taxes, Spending, and Property Values: Supply Adjustment in a Tiebout–Oates Model," *Journal of Political Economy* (Vol. 82, No. 5, September/October 1974), 941–54.

Edwards, Corwin D., *Maintaining Competition. Requisites of a Governmental Policy* (New York: McGraw-Hill, 1949).

Elazar, Daniel J., *American Federalism: A View from the States* (New York: Crowell, 1966).

Exploring Federalism (Tuscaloosa: University of Alabama Press, 1987).

"Cooperative Federalism," in Daphne A. Kenyon, and John Kincaid, eds., *Competition Among States and Local Governments* (Washington: Urban Institute, 1991), 65–86.

Epple, Dennis, and Allan Zelenitz, "The Implications of Competition Among Jurisdictions: Does Tiebout Need Politics?" *Journal of Political Economy* (Vol. 89, No. 6, December 1981), 1197–1217.

Epple, Dennis, Allan Zelenitz, and Michael Visscher, "A Search for Testable Implications of the Tiebout Hypothesis," *Journal of Political Economy* (Vol. 86, No. 3, June 1978), 405–25.

Ellis, Richard E., *The Jeffersonian Crisis. Courts and Politics in the Young Republic* (New York: Norton, 1971).

Fama, Eugene F., "Agency Problems and the Theory of the Firm," *Journal of Political Economy* (Vol. 88, No. 2, April 1980), 288–307.

Fayol, Henri, *Administration industrielle et générale: prévoyance, organisation, commandement, co-ordination, contrôle* (Paris: Dunod et Pinat, 1917). Translated by Constance Starrs as *General and Industrial Management* (London: Pitman, 1949).

Ferejohn, John, and Charles Shipan, "Congressional Influence on Bureaucracy," *Journal of Law, Economics, and Organization* (Vol. 6, Special Issue, 1990), 1–20.

Finkle, Peter, Kernaghan Webb, William T. Stanbury, and Paul Pross, *Federal Government Relations with Interest Groups: A Reconsideration* (Ottawa: Mimeo, 1991).

Fiorina, Morris P., *Retrospective Voting in American National Elections* (New Haven: Yale University Press, 1981).

"Legislative Choice of Regulatory Forms: Legal Process or Administrative Process?" *Public Choice* (Vol. 39, No. 1, 1982), 33–66.

Fischel, Daniel R., "The 'Race to the Bottom' Revisited: Reflections on Recent Developments in Delaware's Corporation Law," *Northwestern University Law Review* (Vol. 76, No. 6, 1982), 913–45.

Fisher, Ronald C, "Income and Grant Effects on Local Expenditure: The Flypaper Effect and Other Difficulties," *Journal of Urban Economics* (Vol. 12, No. 3, November 1982), 324–45.

Flatters, Frank R., J. Vernon Henderson, and Peter M. Mieszkowski, "Public Goods, Efficiency, and Regional Fiscal Equalization," *Journal of Public Economics* (Vol. 3, No. 2, May 1974), 99–112.

Fortin, Bernard, and Pierre Fréchette, "Estimating the Size and Determinants of the Underground Economy with Survey Data: The Case of Quebec," (Mimeo, 1988).

Frank, A. Gunder, "Administrative Role Definition and Social Change," *Human Organization,* (Vol. 22, No. 4, Winter 1963–64), 238–42.

Frey, Bruno S., "Why Do High Income People Participate More in Politics?," *Public Choice,* (Vol. 11, Fall 1971), 101–105.

"Politico-Economic Models and Cycles," *Journal of Public Economics* (Vol. 9, No. 2, April 1978), 203–20.

International Political Economics (Oxford: Oxford University Press, 1984a).

"The Public Choice View of International Political Economy," *International Organization* (Vol. 38, No. 1, Winter 1984b), 199–223.

"Direct Democracy: Politico-Economic Lessons from Swiss Experience," *American Economic Review* (Vol. 84, No. 2, May 1994), 338–42.

Frey, Bruno S., and Heinz Buhofer, "Prisoners and Property Rights," *Journal of Law and Economics* (Vol. 31, No. 1, April 1988), 19–46.

Frey, Bruno S., and Friedrich Schneider, "An Empirical Study of Politico-Economic Interaction in the United States," *Review of Economics and Statistics* (Vol. 60, No. 2, May, 1978), 174–83.

Friedman, Milton, "The Significance of Labor Unions for Economic Policy," in David McCord Wright, ed., *The Impact of the Unions* (New York: Harcourt Brace, 1951), 207–15. Reprinted in Friedman, *Price Theory* (New York: Aldine Publishing, 1976), 160–65.

Friedrich, Carl J., *Trends of Federalism in Theory and Practice* (New York: Praeger, 1968).

Galbraith, Jay, *Designing Complex Organizations* (Reading: Addison-Wesley, 1973).

Galeotti, Gianluigi, "Rules and Behaviors in Markets and Bureaucracies," in Albert Breton, Gianluigi Galeotti, Pierre Salmon, and Ronald Wintrobe, eds., *Villa Colombella Papers on Bureaucracy, European Journal of Political Economy* (Vol. 4, Extra Issue, 1988), 213–28.

"The Number of Parties and Political Competition," in Albert Breton, Gianluigi Galeotti, Pierre Salmon, and Ronald Wintrobe, eds., *The Competitive State. Villa Colombella Papers on Competitive Politics* (Dordrecht: Kluwer Academic Publishers, 1991), 113–27.

Galeotti, Gianluigi, and Albert Breton, "An Economic Theory of Political Parties," *Kyklos* (Vol. 39, Fasc. 1, 1986), 47–65.

Galeotti, Gianluigi, and Antonio Forcina, "Political Loyalties and the Economy: The U.S. Case," *Review of Economics and Statistics* (Vol. 71, No. 3, August, 1989), 511–17.

Gibbins, Roger, *Regionalism: Territorial Politics in Canada and the United States* (Toronto: Butterworths, 1982).

Gilbert, Felix, "Venetian Secrets," *New York Review of Books* (Vol. 34, No. 12, July 16, 1987), 37–9.

Gilpin, Robert, *War and Change in World Politics* (Cambridge, UK: Cambridge University Press, 1981).

Gordon, Roger H., "An Optimal Taxation Approach to Fiscal Federalism," in Charles E. McLure, Jr., ed., *Tax Assignment in Federal Countries* (Canberra: Centre for Research on Federal Financial Relations, Australian National University, 1983), 26–42.

Gordon, H. Scott, *The Demand and Supply of Government: What We Want and What We Get* (Ottawa: Economic Council of Canada, Discussion Paper No. 79, 1977).

Guarding the Guardians. An Essay on the History and Theory of Constitutionalism (Mimeo., 1986).

Gouldner, Alvin W., *Patterns of Industrial Bureaucracy* (Glencoe: Free Press, 1954).

"The Norm of Reciprocity: A Preliminary Statement," *American Sociological Review* (Vol. 25, No. 2, April 1960), 161–78.

"The Importance of Something for Nothing," in *For Sociology: Renewal and Critique in Sociology Today* (New York: Basic Books, 1973), 260–99.

Gramlich, Edward M., "Intergovernmental Grants: A Review of the Empirical Literature," in Wallace E. Oates, ed., *The Political Economy of Fiscal Federalism* (Lexington: D.C. Heath, 1977), 219–39.

Gramlich, Edward M., and Daniel L. Rubinfeld, "Micro Estimates of Public Spending Demand Functions and Tests of the Tiebout and Median-Voter Hypothesis," *Journal of Political Economy* (Vol. 90, No. 3, June 1982), 536–60.

Gray, Virginia, "Innovation in the States: A Diffusion Study," *American Political Science Review* (Vol. 67, No. 4, December 1973), 1174–85.

Grodzins, Morton, *The American System: A New View of Government in the United States* (Chicago: Rand McNally, 1966).

Groves, Theodore, "Incentives in Teams," *Econometrica* (Vol. 41, No. 3, July 1973), 617–31.

Hage, Jerald, and Michael Aiken, "Routine Technology, Social Structure, and Organization Goals," *Administrative Science Quarterly* (Vol. 14, No. 3, September 1969), 366–76.

Hamilton, Alexander, John Jay, and James Madison, *The Federalist* (New York: Random House, The Modern Library, 1787–88/1937).

Hamilton, Bruce W., "The Effects of Property Taxes and Local Public Spending on Property Values: A Theoretical Comment," *Journal of Political Economy* (Vol. 84, No. 3, June 1976), 647–50.

Hansmann, Henry, "The Role of Nonprofit Enterprises," *Yale Law Journal* (Vol. 89, No. 5, April 1980), 835–901.

"Economic Theories of Nonprofit Organization," in Walter W. Powell, ed., *The Nonprofit Sector, A Research Handbook* (New Haven: Yale University Press, 1987), 27–42.

Harris, Milton, and Artur Raviv, "Some Results on Incentive Contracts with Applications to Education and Employment, Health Insurance, and Law Enforcement," *American Economic Review* (Vol. 68, No. 1, March 1978), 20–30.

Hart, Oliver D., and Bengt Holmström, "The Theory of Contracts," in Truman F. Bewley, ed., *Advances in Economic Theory, Fifth World Congress* (New York: Cambridge University Press, 1987), 71–155.

Hartle, Douglas G., *The Revenue Budget Process of the Government of Canada: Description, Appraisal, and Proposals* (Toronto: Canadian Tax Foundation, 1982).

The Expenditure Budget Process of the Government of Canada: A Public Choice – Rent-Seeking Perspective (Toronto: Canadian Tax Foundation, 1988).

Hashimoto, Masanori, and John Raisian, "Employment Tenure and Earnings Profiles in Japan and the United States," *American Economic Review* (Vol. 75, No. 4, September 1985), 721–35.

Heclo, Hugh, *A Government of Strangers: Executive Politics in Washington* (Washington: Brookings Institution, 1977).

Heiner, Ronald A., "Imperfect Decisions in Organizations. Toward a Theory of Internal Structure," *Journal of Economic Behavior and Organization* (Vol. 9, No. 1, January 1988), 25–44.

Hettich, Walter, and Stanley L. Winer, "Economic and Political Foundations of Tax Structure," *American Economic Review* (Vol. 78, No. 4, September, 1988), 701–12.

Hibbs, Douglas, A., Jr., "Political Parties and Macroeconomic Policy," *American Political Science Review* (Vol. 71, No. 4, December, 1977), 1467–87.

The American Political Economy (Cambridge, MA: Harvard University Press, 1987).

"Partisan Theory After Fifteen Years," *European Journal of Political Economy* (Vol. 8, No. 3, 1992), 361–73.

Hicks, John R., "The Theory of Monopoly," *Econometrica* (Vol. 3, No. 1, January 1935), 1–20. Reprinted in George J. Stigler and Kenneth Boulding, eds., *Readings in Price Theory* (Homewood: Irwin, 1952), 361–83.

Hicks, Ursula, K., *Federalism: Failure and Success* (London: Macmillan, 1978).

Hickson, David J., "A Convergence in Organization Theory," *Administrative Science Quarterly* (Vol. 11, No. 2, June 1966), 224–37.

Hickson, David J., Derek S. Pugh, and Diana C. Pheysey, "Operations Technology and Organization Structure: An Empirical Reappraisal," *Administrative Science Quarterly* (Vol. 14, No. 3, September 1969), 378–97.

Hirshleifer, Jack, "Shakespeare vs. Becker on Altruism: The Importance of Having the Last Word," *Journal of Economic Literature* (Vol. 15, No. 2, June 1977), 500–2.

Hochman, Harold M., "Public Choice Interpretations of Distributional Preference," (Mimeo., 1992).

Hochman, Harold M., and James D. Rodgers, "Pareto Optimal Redistribution," *American Economic Review* (Vol. 59, No. 4, Pt. 1, September 1969), 542–57.

Hofferbert, Richard I., "Ecological Development and Policy Change in the American States," *Midwest Journal of Political Science* (Vol. 10, No. 4, November 1966), 464–83.

Holmström, Bengt, R., "Moral Hazard and Observability," *Bell Journal of Economics* (Vol. 10, No. 1, Spring 1979), 74–91.

Holmström, Bengt R., and Jean Tirole, "The Theory of the Firm," in Richard Schmalensee and Robert D. Willig, eds., *Handbook of Industrial Organization,* Volume I (Amsterdam: North-Holland, 1989), 61–133.

Hotelling, Harold, "Stability in Competition," *Economic Journal* (Vol. 39, March 1929), 41–57. Reprinted in George J. Stigler and Kenneth E. Boulding, eds., *Readings in Price Theory* (Homewood: Irwin, 1952), 467–84.

Huchon, Jean-Paul, *Jours tranquilles à Matignon* (Paris: Grasset et Fasquelle, 1993).

Hughes, Jonathan R. T., *The Governmental Habit: Economic Controls from Colonial Times to the Present* (New York: Basic Books, 1977).

Iannaccone, Laurence R., "A Formal Model of Church and Sect," *American Journal of Sociology* (Vol. 94, Supplement, 1988), S241–S268.
   "Sacrifice and Stigma: Reducing Free-Riding in Cults, Communes, and Other Collectives," *Journal of Political Economy* (Vol. 100, No. 2, April 1992), 271–91.

Inman, Robert P., "Markets, Governments, and the 'New' Political Economy," in Alan J. Auerbach and Martin Feldstein, eds., *Handbook of Public Economics,* Vol. II (Amsterdam: North-Holland, 1987), 647–777.

Ireland, Thomas R., and David B. Johnson, *The Economics of Charity* (Blacksburg: Center for Study of Public Choice, 1970).

Jackson, Peter M., *The Political Economy of Bureaucracy* (Oxford: Philip Allan, 1982).

Jensen, Michael C., and William H. Meckling, "Theory of the Firm: Managerial Behavior, Agency Costs and Ownership Structure," *Journal of Financial Economics* (Vol. 3, No. 4, October, 1976), 305–60.

Johansen, Leif, *Public Economics* (Amsterdam: North-Holland, 1965).

Johnsen, D. Bruce, "The Formation and Protection of Property Rights among the Southern Kwakiutl Indians," *Journal of Legal Studies* (Vol. 15, No. 1, January 1986), 41–67.

Johnson, Harry G., "Optimum Tariffs and Retaliation," *Review of Economic Studies,* (Vol. 21, No. 2, 1953–4), 142–53. Reprinted in Johnson, ed., *International Trade and Economic Growth* (Cambridge, MA: Harvard University Press, 1958), 31–55.

Johnson, Ronald N., and Gary D. Libecap, "Bureaucratic Rules, Supervisor Behavior, and the Effect on Salaries in the Federal Government," *Journal of Law, Economics and Organization* (Vol. 5, No. 1, Spring, 1989), 53–82.

Johnston, Richard, *Public Opinion and Public Policy in Canada: Questions of Confidence* (Toronto: University of Toronto Press, 1986).

Kalt, Joseph P., and Mark A. Zupan, "Capture and Ideology in the Economic Theory of Politics," *American Economic Review* (Vol. 74, No. 3, June 1984), 279–300.

Kaplan, Robert S., "The Evolution of Management Accounting," *The Accounting Review* (Vol. 59, No. 3, July 1984), 390–418.

Kau, James B., and Paul H. Rubin, "Self-Interest, Ideology, and Logrolling in Congressional Voting," *Journal of Law and Economics* (Vol. 22, No. 2, October 1979), 365–84.

Kenyon, Daphne A., *Interjurisdictional Tax and Policy Competition: Good or Bad for the Federal System?* (Washington: Advisory Commission on Intergovernmental Relations, 1991).

Keohane, Robert O., *After Hegemony. Cooperation and Discord in the World Political Economy* (Princeton: Princeton University Press, 1984).

Key, Valdimer O., *The Responsible Electorate. Rationality in Presidential Voting, 1936–1960*, (Cambridge, MA: Harvard University Press, 1966).

Kincaid, John, "The Competitive Challenge to Cooperative Federalism: A Theory of Federal Democracy," in Daphne A. Kenyon and John Kincaid, eds., *Competition Among States and Local Governments* (Washington: The Urban Institute Press, 1991), 87–114.

Kindleberger, Charles P., *The World in Depression, 1929–1939*, Second Edition (Berkeley: University of California Press, 1986; First Edition, 1973).

"International Public Goods Without International Government," *American Economic Review* (Vol. 76, No. 1, March 1986), 1–13.

Kirkpatrick, Jeane, "Dictatorships and Double Standards," *Commentary* (Vol. 68, No. 5, November 1979), 34–45.

Kirzner, Israel, *Competition and Entrepreneurship* (Chicago: University of Chicago Press, 1973).

Klein, Benjamin, Robert G. Crawford, and Armen A. Alchian, "Vertical Integration, Appropriable Rents, and the Competitive Contracting Process," *Journal of Law and Economics* (Vol. 21, No. 2, October 1978), 297–326.

Klein, Benjamin, and Keith B. Leffler, "The Role of Market Forces in Assuring Contractual Performance," *Journal of Political Economy* (Vol. 89, No. 4, August, 1981), 615–41.

Klein, Benjamin, and Kevin M. Murphy, "Vertical Restraints as Contract Enforcement Mechanisms," *Journal of Law and Economics* (Vol. 31, No. 2, October 1988), 265–97.

Knight, Frank H., *The Ethics of Competition* (London: George Allen and Unwin, 1935).

Kolm, Serge-Christophe, "La production optimale de justice sociale" dans *Economie Publique*, sous la direction de Henry Tulkens (Paris: Editions du Centre National de la Recherche Scientifique, 1968), 109–77.

Kraan, Dirk-Jan, *Budgetary Decisions* (Ph.D. Dissertation, Erasmus University, Rotterdam, 1990).

Krasner, Stephen D., ed., *International Regimes* (Ithaca: Cornell University Press, 1983).

Krueger, Anne O., "The Political Economy of a Rent-Seeking Society," *American Economic Review* (Vol. 64, No. 3, June 1974), 291–303.

Lafay, Jean-Dominique, "L'opposition dans le système politico-économique: analyse théorique et étude empirique du cas français," *Journal des Economistes et des Etudes Humaines* (Vol. 1, No. 1, Hiver 1989–1990), 43–59.

"La théorie probabiliste du vote," *Revue d'économie politique* (Vol. 102, No. 4, Juillet-Août, 1992), 487–518.

"Les prévisions des modèles politico-économiques," *Le Figaro* (Vendredi, 19 mars, 1993), 11.

Laffont, Jean-Jacques, "Hidden Gaming in Hierarchies: Facts and Models," *Economic Record* (Vol. 64, No. 187, December 1988), 295–306.

"Analysis of Hidden Gaming in a Three-Level Hierarchy," *Journal of Law, Economics, and Organization* (Vol. 6, No. 2, Fall 1990), 301–24.

Lammers, Nancy, ed., *Powers of Congress,* Second Edition (Washington: Congressional Quarterly Press, 1982).

Lancaster, Kelvin J., "A New Approach to Consumer Theory," *Journal of Political Economy* (Vol. 74, No. 2, April 1966), 132–57.

Introduction to Modern Microeconomics, Second Edition (Chicago: Rand McNally, 1974).

Landes, William M., and Richard A. Posner, "The Independent Judiciary in an Interest-Group Perspective," *Journal of Law and Economics* (Vol. 18, No. 3, December 1975), 875–901.

Landsberger, Henry A., "The Horizontal Dimension in Bureaucracy," *Administrative Science Quarterly* (Vol. 6, No. 3, December 1961), 299–332.

Larkey, Patrick D., Chandler Stolp, and Mark Winer, "Theorizing About the Growth of Government: A Research Assessment," *Journal of Public Policy,* (Vol. 1, No. 2, Part 2, May 1981), 157–220.

Laski, Harold J., "The Obsolescence of Federalism," *The New Republic* (Vol. 98, May 1939), 367–69. Reprinted in Ashner N. Christensen and Evron M. Kirkpatrick, eds., *The People, Politics, and the Politician: Readings in American Government* (New York: Holt, 1941), 111–17.

Lazear, Edward P., "Why Is There Mandatory Retirement?" *Journal of Political Economy* (Vol. 87, No. 6, December 1979), 1261–84.

"Agency, Earnings Profiles, Productivity, and Hours Restrictions," *American Economic Review* (Vol. 71, No. 4, September 1981), 606–20.

Lazear, Edward P., and Sherwin Rosen, "Rank-Order Tournaments as Optimum Labor Contracts," *Journal of Political Economy* (Vol. 89, No. 5, October 1981), 841–64.

Lee, Judith A. B., and Carol Swensen, "The Concept of Mutual Aid," in Alex Gitterman and Laurence Shulman, eds., *Mutual Aid Groups and the Life Cycle* (Itasca: F. E. Peacock, 1986), 361–80.

Leffler, Keith B., "Persuasion or Information? The Economics of Prescription Drug Advertising," *Journal of Law and Economics* (Vol. 24, No. 1, April 1981), 45–74.

Leland, Hayne E., "Quacks, Lemons, and Licensing: A Theory of Minimum Quality Standards," *Journal of Political Economy* (Vol. 87, No. 6, December 1979), 1328–46.

Leibowitz, Arleen, and Robert Tollison, "A Theory of Legislative Organization: Making the Most of Your Majority," *Quarterly Journal of Economics* (Vol. 94, No. 2, March 1980), 261–77.

Levinthal, Daniel, "A Survey of Agency Models of Organizations," *Journal of Economic Behavior and Organization* (Vol. 9, No. 2, March 1988), 153–85.

Lévy-Garboua, Louis, "General Interest and Redistribution with Self-Interested Voters: Social Contract Revisited," *Public Choice* (Vol. 69, No. 2, February (II) 1991), 175–96.

Lewis, Bernard, "Muslims, Christians and Jews: The Dream of Coexistence," *New York Review of Books* (Vol. 39, No. 6, March 1992), 48–52.

Lewis-Beck, Michael S., and Tom W. Rice, *Forecasting Elections* (Washington: Congressional Quarterly Press, 1992).

Libby, Orin G., *The Geographical Distribution of the Vote of the Thirteen States on the Federal Constitution, 1787–8,* in the *Bulletin of the University of Wisconsin, Madison. Economics, Political Science, and History Series* (Vol. 1, No. 1, June 1894), 1–116.

Lindahl, Erik, "Just Taxation – A Positive Solution," in Richard A. Musgrave and Alan T. Peacock, eds., *Classics in the Theory of Public Finance* (London: Macmillan, 1919/1964), 168–76. Translated by Elizabeth Henderson from "Positive Lösung," *Die Gerechtigkeit der Besteuerung* (Lund, 1919), 85–98.

Lindbeck, Assar, "Redistribution Policy and the Expansion of the Public Sector," *Journal of Public Economics* (Vol. 28, No. 3, December 1985), 309–28.

Lipsey, Richard G., and Kelvin Lancaster, "The General Theory of Second Best," *Review of Economic Studies* (Vol. 24, No. 1, October, 1956), 11–32.

Loewenstein, Karl, *Political Power and the Governmental Process* (Chicago: University of Chicago Press, 1965).

Louvet, Philippe, *Essais sur les choix publics et la demande de consommation collective* (Paris: Université de Paris I, Panthéon-Sorbonne, Thèse pour le doctorat, 1986).

Main, Jackson T., "Charles A. Beard and the Constitution: A Critical Review of Forrest McDonald's *We The People*," *William and Mary Quarterly,* Third Series (Vol. 17, No. 1, January, 1960), 86–102.

The Anti-Federalists (New York: Norton, 1961/1974).

Mansfield, Edwin, "The Speed of Response of Firms to New Techniques," *Quarterly Journal of Economics* (Vol. 77, No. 2, May 1963), 290–311.

Marshall, Alfred, *Principles of Economics,* Eighth Edition (New York: Macmillan, 1890/1952).

Maslove, Allan M., Michael J. Prince, and G. Bruce Doern, *Federal and Provincial Budgeting* (Toronto: University of Toronto Press, 1986).

Mayo, Elton, *The Social Problems of an Industrial Civilization* (Cambridge, MA: Harvard University Press, 1945).

McCormick, Peter, Ernest C. Manning, and Gordon Gibson, *Regional Representation: The Canadian Partnership* (Calgary: Canada West Foundation, 1981).

McCready, Douglas J., *Tax Harmonization in Canada, 1991* (Mimeo., 1991).

McDonald, Forrest, *We The People: The Economic Origins of the Constitution* (Chicago: University of Chicago Press, 1958).

Alexander Hamilton. A Biography, (New York: Norton, 1979/1982).

McGuire, Martin C., "An Econometric Model of Federal Grants and Local Fiscal Response," in Wallace E. Oates, ed., *Financing the New Federalism* (Baltimore: John Hopkins University Press, 1975), 115–38.

"The Analysis of Federal Grants into Price and Income Components," in Peter M. Mieszkowski and William H. Oakland, eds., *Fiscal Federalism and Grants-in-Aid* (Washington: The Urban Institute, 1979), 31–50.

McKee, Michael, "In Networks We Trust: All Others Pay Cash – Competition in Public Sector Bureaus," in Albert Breton, Gianluigi Galeotti, Pierre Salmon, and Ronald Wintrobe, eds., *Villa Colombella Papers on Bureaucracy, European Journal of Political Economy* (Vol. 4, Extra Issue, 1988), 185–211.

McKee, Michael, and Ronald Wintrobe, "The Decline of Organizations and the Rise of Administrators: Parkinson's Law in Theory and Practice," *Journal of Public Economics* (Vol. 51, No. 3, July 1993), 309–27.

McManus, Maurice, "Private and Social Costs in the Theory of Second Best," *Review of Economic Studies* (Vol. 34, No. 3, July 1967), 317–21.

McVoy, Edgar C., "Patterns of Diffusion in the United States," *American Sociological Review* (Vol. 5, No. 2, April 1940), 219–27.

Meadows, George R., "Taxes, Spending, and Property Values: A Comment and Further Results," *Journal of Political Economy* (Vol. 84, No. 4, Part I, August 1976), 869–80.

Meltzer, Allan H., and Scott F. Richard, "A Rational Theory of the Size of Government," *Journal of Political Economy* (Vol. 89, No. 5, October, 1981), 914–27.

Merton, Robert K., "The Unanticipated Consequences of Purposive Social Action," *American Sociological Review* (Vol. 1, No. 6, December 1936), 894–904.

"Bureaucratic Structure and Personality," *Social Forces,* (Vol. 18, 1940). Reprinted in Merton, *Social Theory and Social Structure* (Glencoe: Free Press, 1957), 195–206.

Migué, Jean–Luc, "The Economic Theory of Representative Government: A Review," *Public Choice* (Vol. 20, Winter 1974), 117–28.

Migué, Jean–Luc, and Gérard Bélanger, "Toward a General Theory of Managerial Discretion," *Public Choice* (Vol. 17, Spring 1974), 27–43.

Mill, John Stuart, *Considerations on Representative Government* (London: J. M. Dent, 1863/1910).

Miller, Gary J., *Managerial Dilemmas: The Political Economy of Hierarchy* (New York: Cambridge University Press, 1992).

Miller, Gary J., and Terry M. Moe, "Bureaucrats, Legislators, and the Size of Government," *American Political Science Review* (Vol. 77, No. 2, June 1983), 297–322.

Miller, William, *A New History of the United States* (New York: Dell Publishing, 1969).

Mills, Edwin, S., *Urban Economics*, Second Edition (Glenview: Scott, Foresman, 1980).

Mintz, Jack, and Henry Tulkens, "Commodity Tax Competition Between Member States of a Federation: Equilibrium and Efficiency," *Journal of Public Economics* (Vol. 29, No. 2, March 1986), 133–72.

Mintzberg, Henry, *The Structuring of Organizations. A Synthesis of the Research* (Englewood Cliffs: Prentice-Hall, 1979).

Power In and Around Organizations (Englewood Cliffs: Prentice-Hall, 1983).

Mirrlees, James A., "The Optimal Structure of Incentives and Authority Within an Organization," *Bell Journal of Economics* (Vol. 7, No. 1, Spring 1976), 105–31.

Mnookin, Robert, and Lewis Kornhauser, "Bargaining in the Shadow of the Law: The Case of Divorce," *Yale Law Journal* (Vol. 88, No. 5, April 1979), 950–97.

Moene, Karl O., "Types of Bureaucratic Interaction," *Journal of Public Economics* (Vol. 29, No. 3, April 1986), 333–45.

Moore, Thomas J., "The Purpose of Licensing," *Journal of Law and Economics* (Vol. 4, October 1961), 93–117.

Morgenthau, Hans J., *Politics Among Nations* (New York: Knopf, 1948/1966).

Mougeot, Michel, *Economie du secteur public* (Paris: Economica, 1989).

Mount, Ferdinand, *The British Constitution Now* (London: Heinemann, 1992).

Mueller, Dennis C., "The Possibility of a Social Welfare Function: Comments," *American Economic Review* (Vol. 57, No. 5, December, 1967), 1304–11.

"The Growth of Government. A Public Choice Approach," *IMF Staff Papers* (Vol. 34, No. 1, March 1987), 115–49.

Public Choice II (New York: Cambridge University Press, 1989).

Mueller, Frederick H., "Area Development Expenditures and Economic Stability in Local Areas," in Joint Economic Committee, Subcommittee on Fiscal Policy, *Federal Expenditure Policy for Economic Growth and Stability* (Washington: U. S. Gov't. Printing Office, 1957), 803–4.

Mundell, Robert A., "A Theory of Optimum Currency Areas," *American Economic Review* (Vol. 51, No. 4, September 1961), 657–65.

Musgrave, Richard A., "The Voluntary Exchange Theory of Public Economy," *Quarterly Journal of Economics* (Vol. 53, No. 2, February 1938), 213–37.

The Theory of Public Finance (New York: McGraw-Hill, 1959).

"Approaches to a Fiscal Theory of Political Federalism," in NBER, *Public Finances: Needs, Sources, and Utilization* (Princeton: Princeton University Press, 1961), 97–122.

Fiscal Systems (New Haven: Yale University Press, 1969).

"Pareto Optimal Redistribution: Comment," *American Economic Review* (Vol. 60, No. 5, December 1970), 991–993.

Musgrave, Richard A., and Peggy B. Musgrave, *Public Finance in Theory and Practice*, Fourth Edition (New York: McGraw Hill, 1984).

Musgrave, Richard A., Peggy B. Musgrave, and Richard M. Bird, *Public Finance in Theory and Practice*, First Canadian Edition (Toronto: McGraw-Hill Ryerson, 1987).

Nalebuff, Barry J., and Joseph E. Stiglitz, "Prizes and Incentives: Towards a General Theory of

Compensation and Competition," *Bell Journal of Economics* (Vol. 14, No. 1, Spring 1983), 21–43.

Newman, Peter C., *Renegade in Power* (Toronto: McClelland and Stewart, 1973).

Nelson, Richard R., and Michael Krashinsky, "Two Major Issues of Public Policy: Public Policy and Organization of Supply," in Richard R. Nelson and Dennis Young, eds., *Public Subsidy for Day Care of Young Children* (Lexington: D.C. Heath, 1973).

Niskanen, William A., Jr., *Bureaucracy and Representative Government* (Chicago: Aldine-Atherton, 1971).

"Bureaucrats and Politicians," *Journal of Law and Economics* (Vol. 18, No. 3, December 1975), 617–43.

"Reflections on *Bureaucracy and Representative Government,*" in André Blais and Stéphane Dion, eds., *The Budget-Maximizing Bureaucrat. Appraisal and Evidence* (Pittsburgh: University of Pittsburgh Press, 1991), 13–32.

Nordhaus, William D., "The Political Business Cycle," *Review of Economic Studies* (Vol. 42, No. 2, April 1975), 169–90.

Norrie, Kenneth H., and Michael B. Percy, "Province-Building and Industrial Structure in a Small, Open Economy," in Douglas D. Purvis, ed., *Economic Adjustment and Public Policy in Canada* (Kingston: John Deutsch Memorial Institute for the Study of Economic Policy, 1984).

North, Douglass C., "The Growth of Government in the United States: An Economic Historian's Perspective," *Journal of Public Economics* (Vol. 28, No. 3, December 1985), 383–99.

Nurkse, Ragnar (with William A. Brown, Jr.), *International Currency Experience* (League of Nations, 1944).

Oakland, William H., "Theory of Public Goods," in Alan J. Auerbach and Martin Feldstein, eds., *Handbook of Public Economics,* Vol. II (Amsterdam: North-Holland, 1987), 485–535.

Oates, Wallace E., "The Effects of Property Taxes and Local Public Spending on Property Values: An Empirical Study of Tax Capitalization and the Tiebout Hypothesis," *Journal of Political Economy* (Vol. 77, No. 6, November/December 1969), 957–71.

Fiscal Federalism (New York: Harcourt Brace Jovanovich, 1972).

"Book Review of *The Economic Theory of Representative Government,*" *Canadian Journal of Economics* (Vol. 8, No. 1, February 1975), 146–8.

"The Changing Structure of Intergovernmental Fiscal Relations," in Horst C. Recktenwald, ed., *Secular Trends of the Public Sector* (Paris: Cujas, 1978), 151–60.

Olson, Mancur, Jr., *The Logic of Collective Action* (Cambridge, MA: Harvard University Press, 1965).

"The Principle of Fiscal Equivalence," *American Economic Review* (Vol. 59, No. 2, May 1969), 479–87.

The Rise and Decline of Nations (New Haven: Yale University Press, 1982).

Orzechowski, William, "Economic Models of Bureaucracy: Survey, Extensions, and Evidence," in Thomas E. Borcherding, ed., *Budgets and Bureaucrats: The Sources of Government Growth* (Durham: Duke University Press, 1977), 229–59.

Oster, Sharon M., and John M. Quigley, "Regulatory Barriers to the Diffusion of Innovation: Some Evidence from Building Codes," *Bell Journal of Economics* (Vol. 8, No. 2, Autumn 1977), 361–77.

Ostrom, Vincent, *The Political Theory of a Compound Republic,* Second Edition, Revised and Enlarged (Lincoln: University of Nebraska Press, 1987; First Edition, 1971).

Paldam, Martin, "A Preliminary Survey of the Theory and Findings on Vote and Popularity Functions," *European Journal of Political Research* (Vol. 9, No. 2, June 1981), 181–99.

"Does Politics Matter After All? A Comparative Test of Partisan Cycles on Data for 17 Countries" (Paper presented at the *European Public Choice Society Meetings,* Linz, Austria, 1989).

Palmer, Matthew S. R., "The Economics of Organization: Towards a Framework of Constitutional Design" (Mimeo., 1992).

Panagopoulos, Epaminondas P., *Essays on the History and Meaning of Checks and Balances* (Lanham: University Press of America, 1985).

Parkinson, C. Northcote, *Parkinson's Law and Other Studies in Administration* (New York: Ballantine, 1957).

Pauly, Mark V., "A Model of Local Government Expenditure and Tax Capitalization," *Journal of Public Economics* (Vol. 6, No. 3, October 1976), 231–42.

Peacock, Alan T., "Welfare Economics and Public Subsidies to the Arts," *Manchester School of Economic and Social Studies* (Vol. 37, No. 4, December 1969), 323–35.

"The Problem of Public Expenditure Growth in Post-Industrial Society," in Alan T. Peacock, ed., *The Economic Analysis of Government and Related Themes* (Oxford: Martin Robertson, 1979; paper first published in 1978), 105–17.

"The Limitations of Public Goods Theory: The Lighthouse Revisited," in Alan T. Peacock, ed., *The Economic Analysis of Government and Related Themes* (Oxford: Martin Robertson, 1979), 127–36.

Peacock, Alan T., and Jack Wiseman (assisted by Jindrich Veverka), *The Growth of Public Expenditure in the United Kingdom* (Princeton: NBER and Princeton University Press, 1961; reissued with a new Introduction by Allen and Unwin, 1967).

Peltzman, Sam, "Toward a More General Theory of Regulation," *Journal of Law and Economics* (Vol. 19, No. 2, August 1976), 211–44.

"The Growth of Government," *Journal of Law and Economics* (Vol. 23, No. 2, October 1980), 209–87.

"Constituent Interest and Congressional Voting," *Journal of Law and Economics* (Vol. 27, No. 1, April 1984), 181–210.

Pépin, Gilles, "The Problem of Section 96 of the Constitution Act, 1867," in Claire Beckton and A. Wayne MacKay, eds., *The Courts and the Charter* (Toronto: University of Toronto Press, 1985), 223–77.

Perrow, Charles, "A Framework for the Comparative Analysis of Organizations," *American Sociological Review* (Vol. 32, No. 2, April, 1967), 194–208.

Pfeffer, Jeffrey, *Power in Organizations* (Boston: Pitman Publishing, 1981).

Phillips, Susan D., "Meaning and Structure in Social Movements: Mapping the Network of National Canadian Women's Organizations," *Canadian Journal of Political Science* (Vol. 24, No. 4, December 1991), 755–82.

Pigou, Arthur C., *The Economics of Welfare* (London: Macmillan, 1920/1951).

Plott, Charles R., "A Notion of Equilibrium and its Possibility Under Majority Rule," *American Economic Review* (Vol. 57, No. 4, September, 1967), 787–806.

Polinsky, A. Mitchell, "Imperfect Capital Markets, Intertemporal Redistribution, and Progressive Taxation," in Harold M. Hochman and George E. Peterson, eds., *Redistribution Through Public Choice* (New York: Columbia University Press, 1974), 229–58.

Polsby, Nelson W., *Congress and the Presidency,* Fourth Edition, (Englewood Cliffs: Prentice-Hall, 1986).

Pommerehne, Werner W., "Quantitative Aspects of Federalism: A Study of Six Countries," in Wallace E. Oates, ed., *The Political Economy of Fiscal Federalism* (Lexington: Heath, 1977), 275–346.

"Institutional Approaches to Public Expenditure: Empirical Evidence from Swiss Municipalities," *Journal of Public Economics* (Vol. 9, No. 2, April, 1978), 255–80.

Pommerehne, Werner W., and Bruno S. Frey, "Two Approaches to Estimating Public Expenditures," *Public Finance Quarterly* (Vol. 4, No. 4, October, 1976), 395–407.

"Les modes d'évaluation de l'économie occulte," *Futuribles* (Vol. 50, décembre 1981), 3–32.

Popitz, Johannes, "Der Finanzausgleich," in *Handbuch der Finanzwissenchaft* (Tübingen, 1927).

Potters, Jan, *Lobbying and Pressure. Theory and Experiments* (Amsterdam: University Thesis, 1992).

Potters, Jan, and Frans van Winden, "Modelling Political Pressure as Transmission of Information," *European Journal of Political Economy* (Vol. 6, No. 1, 1990), 61–88.

"Lobbying and Asymmetric Information," *Public Choice*, (Vol. 74, No. 3, October 1992), 269–92.

"Models of Interest Groups. Four Different Approaches," in Norman Schofield, ed., *Social Choice and Political Economy* (Boston: Kluwer, 1993).

Presthus, Robert V., "Toward a Theory of Organizational Behavior," *Administrative Science Quarterly* (Vol. 3, No. 1, June 1958), 48–72.

Pross, A. Paul, *Group Politics and Public Policy* (Toronto: Oxford University Press, 1986).

Pryor, Frederic L., *Public Expenditures in Communist and Capitalist Nations* (London: Allen and Unwin, 1968).

Rabeau, Yves, "Regional Stabilization in Canada," in John Sargent, ed., *Fiscal and Monetary Policy* (Toronto: University of Toronto Press, 1986), 151–97.

Radner, Roy, "Monitoring Cooperative Arguments in a Repeated Principal–Agent Relationship," *Econometrica* (Vol. 49, No. 3, September 1981), 1127–48.

Rawls, John, *A Theory of Justice* (Cambridge, MA: Harvard University Press, 1971).

Raynauld, André, "Pour une politique de stabilisation régionale," *Administration publique du Canada* (Vol. 14, Automne, 1971), 344–53.

Reich, Robert, B., "An Industrial Policy of the Right," *The Public Interest* (No. 73, Fall 1983), 3–17.

Reinganum, Jennifer F., "On the Diffusion of New Technology: A Game Theoretic Approach," *Review of Economic Studies* (Vol. 48, 1981), 395–405.

"Technology Adoption Under Imperfect Information," *Bell Journal of Economics* (Vol. 14, No. 1, Spring 1983), 57–69.

Reschovsky, Andrew, "Residential Choice and the Local Public Sector: An Alternative Test of the Tiebout Hypothesis," *Journal of Urban Economics* (Vol. 6, No. 4, October 1979), 501–20.

Ricketts, Martin, *The Economics of Business Enterprise* (Brighton: Wheatsheaf Books, 1987).

Riker, William H., "The Senate and American Federalism," *American Political Science Review* (Vol. 49, No. 2, June 1955), 452–69. Reprinted in Riker, ed., *The Development of American Federalism* (Dordrecht: Kluwer Academic Publishers, 1987), 135–56.

"Federalism," in Fred I. Greenstein and Nelson W. Polsky, eds., *Handbook of Political Science: Government Institutions and Processes,* Vol. 5 (Memlo Park: Addison-Wesley, 1975), 93–172.

The Development of American Federalism (Dordrecht: Kluwer Academic Publishers, 1987).

Riker, William H., and Steven J. Brams, "The Paradox of Vote Trading," *American Political Science Review* (Vol. 67, No. 4, December 1973), 1235–47.

Riker, William H., and Jonathan Lemco, "The Relation between Structure and Stability in Federal Governments," in Riker, ed., *The Development of American Federalism* (Dordrecht: Kluwer, 1987), 113–29.

Robinson, Joan, *The Economics of Imperfect Competition* (London: Macmillan, 1933).

Roethlisberger, Fritz J., and William J. Dickson, *Management and the Worker* (Cambridge, MA: Harvard University Press, 1939).

Rogoff, Kenneth, "Can International Monetary Policy Cooperation Be Counterproductive?" *Journal of International Economics* (Vol. 18, No. 3/4, May 1985), 199–217.

Roll, Richard, "The Hubris Hypothesis of Corporate Takeovers," *Journal of Business* (Vol. 59, No. 2, Part. 1, April 1986), 197–216.

Romano, Roberta, "Law as a Product: Some Pieces of the Incorporation Puzzle," *Journal of Law, Economics, and Organization* (Vol. 1, No. 2, Fall 1985), 225–83.

Romer, Thomas, and Howard Rosenthal, "Political Resource Allocation, Controlled Agendas, and the Status Quo," *Public Choice* (Vol. 33, Issue 4, 1978), 27–43.

"Bureaucrats Versus Voters: On the Political Economy of Resource Allocation by Direct Democracy," *Quarterly Journal of Economics* (Vol. 93, No. 4, November 1979), 563–87.

"An Institutional Theory of the Effect of Intergovernmental Grants," *National Tax Journal* (Vol. 33, No. 4, December 1980), 451–8.

Rose-Ackerman, Susan, "Market Models of Local Government: Exit, Voting and the Land Market," *Journal of Urban Economics* (Vol. 6, No. 3, July 1979), 319–37.

Rosen, Harvey S., *Public Finance* (Homewood: Irwin, 1985).

Rosen, Kenneth T., "The Impact of Proposition 13 on House Prices in Northern California: A Test of the Interjurisdictional Capitalization Hypothesis," *Journal of Political Economy* (Vol. 90, No. 1, February 1982), 191–200.

Rottenberg, Simon, "The Baseball Players' Labor Market," *Journal of Political Economy* (Vol. 64, No. 3, June 1956), 242–58.

Rubinfeld, Daniel L., "Voting in a Local School Election: A Micro Analysis," *Review of Economics and Statistics* (Vol. 59, No. 1, February, 1977), 30–42.

"The Economics of the Local Public Sector," in Alan J. Auerbach and Martin Feldstein, eds., *Handbook of Public Economics,* Vol. II (Amsterdam: North-Holland, 1987), 571–645.

Ruggie, John G., "Collective Goods and Future International Collaboration," *American Political Science Review* (Vol. 66, No. 3, September 1972), 874–93.

"International Responses to Technology: Concepts and Trends," *International Organization* (Vol. 29, No. 3, Summer 1975), 557–84.

"Continuity and Transformation in the World Polity: Towards a Neorealist Synthesis," *World Politics* (Vol. 35, No. 2, January 1983), 261–86.

Salmon, Pierre, "La coopération internationale dans un monde sans hégémonie," *Analyses de la SEDEIS* (No. 53, Septembre 1986), 23–7.

"The Logic of Pressure Groups and the Structure of the Public Sector," in Albert Breton, Gianluigi Galeotti, Pierre Salmon, and Ronald Wintrobe, eds., *Villa Colombella Papers on Federalism, European Journal of Political Economy* (Vol. 3, Nos. 1 & 2, 1987a), 55–86.

"Decentralization as an Incentive Scheme," *Oxford Review of Economic Policy* (Vol. 3, No. 2, Summer 1987b), 24–43.

"Trust and Trans-Bureau Networks in Organizations," in Albert Breton, Gianluigi Galeotti, Pierre Salmon, and Ronald Wintrobe, eds., *Villa Colombella Papers on Bureaucracy, European Journal of Political Economy* (Vol. 4, Extra Issue, 1988), 229–52.

"Voters Comparing Performance Across Jurisdictions and the Case for Decentralization and Federalism," (Mimeo., 1993).

Salmon, Pierre, and Alain Wolfelsperger, "From Competitive Equilibrium to Democratic Equilibrium: Has the Analogy Been Fruitful?" Paper presented at the European Public Choice Society (Meersburg, 1990).

Samuelson, Paul A., "Dynamics, Statics, and the Stationary State," *Review of Economics and Statistics* (Vol. 25, No. 1, February 1943), 58–68. Reprinted in Joseph E. Stiglitz, ed., *The Collected Scientific Papers of Paul A. Samuelson,* Vol. I (Cambridge, MA: M.I.T. Press, 1966), 201–11.

Foundations of Economic Analysis (Cambridge, MA: Harvard University Press, 1947/1953).

"The Pure Theory of Public Expenditure," *Review of Economics and Statistics* (Vol. 36, No. 4, November, 1954), 387–9. Reprinted in Joseph E. Stiglitz, ed., *The Collected Scientific Papers of Paul A. Samuelson,* Vol. II (Cambridge, MA: M.I.T. Press, 1966), 1223–5.

"Arrow's Mathematical Politics," in Sidney Hook, ed., *Human Values and Economic Policy: A Symposium* (New York: New York University Press, 1967), 41–52. Reprinted in Robert C.

Merton, ed., *The Collected Scientific Papers of Paul A. Samuelson,* Vol. III (Cambridge, MA: M.I.T. Press, 1972), 411–21.

"Pure Theory of Public Expenditure and Taxation," in Julius Margolis and Henri Guitton, eds., *Public Economics: An Analysis of Public Production and Consumption and Their Relations to the Private Sectors* (London: Macmillan, 1969), 98–123. Reprinted in Robert C. Merton, ed., *The Collected Scientific Papers of Paul A. Samuelson,* Vol. III (Cambridge, MA: M.I.T. Press, 1972), 492–517.

"Schumpeter as an Economic Theorist," in Helmut Frisch, ed., *Schumpeterian Economics* (London: Praeger, 1982), 1–27. Reprinted in Kate Crowley, ed., *The Collected Scientific Papers of Paul A. Samuelson,* Vol. V (Cambridge, MA: M.I.T. Press, 1986), 301–27.

Sandmo, Agnar, "Income Tax Evasion, Labour Supply, and the Equity-Efficiency Tradeoff," *Journal of Public Economics* (Vol. 16, No. 3, December 1981), 265–88.

Saunders, Peter, "Explaining International Differences in Public Expenditure: An Empirical Study," *Public Finance/Finances Publiques* (Vol. 43, No. 2, 1988), 271–94.

Savage, Robert L., ed., "Policy Diffusion in a Federal System," *Publius: The Journal of Federalism* (Vol. 15, No. 4, Fall 1985), Entire Issue.

Scharf, Kimberley Ann, "Optimal Commodity Taxation with Increasing Returns-to-Scale Evasion Technologies" (University of Warwick, Discussion Paper 9433, 1992).

"International Capital Tax Evasion and the Foreign Tax Credit Puzzle" (University of Warwick, Discussion Paper 9437, 1994).

Schram, Arthur, and Frans van Winden, "Revealed Preferences for Public Goods: Applying a Model of Voter Behavior," *Public Choice* (Vol. 60, No. 3, March, 1989), 259–82.

Schumpeter, Joseph A., *The Theory of Economic Development,* First German Edition 1911. Translated by Redvers Opie (New York: Oxford University Press, 1934/1961).

Capitalism, Socialism and Democracy (New York: Harper Brothers, First Edition 1942/1975).

Schwartz, Richard D., and Sonya Orleans, "On Legal Sanctions," *University of Chicago Law Review* (Vol. 34, No. 2, Winter 1967), 274–300.

Schwartz, Thomas, "Vote Trading and Pareto Efficiency," *Public Choice* (Vol. 24, Winter 1975), 101–9.

Scitovsky, Tibor, "A Reconsideration of the Theory of Tariffs," *Review of Economic Studies* (Vol. 9, No. 2, Summer 1941), 89–110.

Scott, Anthony D., "The Evaluation of Federal Grants," *Economica* N.S. (Vol. 19, November 1952), 377–94.

"Piecemeal Decentralization: The Environment", in Robin W. Boadway, Thomas J. Courchene and Douglas D. Purvis, eds., *Economic Dimensions of Constitutional Change* (Kingston: John Deutsch Institute, 1991), 273–97.

Scott, W. Richard, *Organizations. Rational, Natural, and Open Systems* (Englewood Cliffs: Prenctice-Hall, 1981).

Scott, Thomas M., "The Diffusion of Urban Governmental Forms as a Case of Social Learning," *Journal of Politics* (Vol. 30, No. 4, November 1968), 1091–1108.

Selznick, Philip, *TVA and the Grass Roots* (Berkeley: University of California Press, 1949).

Sen, Amartya, "Development: Which Way Now?" *Economic Journal* (Vol. 93, No. 372, December 1983), 745–62.

Resources, Values and Development (Cambridge, MA: Harvard University Press, 1984).

"Individual Freedom as a Social Commitment," *New York Review of Books* (Vol. 37, No. 10, June 1990), 49–54.

Shapiro, Carl, "Premiums for High Quality Products as Returns to Reputations," *Quarterly Journal of Economics* (Vol. 98, No. 4, November, 1983), 659–79.

Shapiro, Carl, and Joseph E. Stiglitz, "Equilibrium Unemployment as a Worker Discipline Device," *American Economic Review* (Vol. 74, No. 3, June 1984), 433–44.

Sharkansky, Ira, "Regionalism, Economic Status and the Public Policies of American States," *Southwestern Social Science Quarterly* (Vol. 49, No. 1, June 1968), 9–26.

Shavell, Steven, *Economic Analysis of Accident Law* (Cambridge, MA: Harvard University Press, 1987).

Shepsle, Kenneth A., "Congressional Committee Assignments: An Optimization Model with Institutional Constraints," *Public Choice* (Vol. 22, Summer 1975), 55–78.

Shepsle, Kenneth A., and Barry R. Weingast, "Structure-Induced Equilibrium and Legislative Choice," *Public Choice* (Vol. 37, No. 3, 1981), 503–19.

Shoup, Carl S., *Fiscal Harmonization in Common Markets,* Vols. I and II (New York: Columbia University Press, 1967).

Public Finance (Chicago: Aldine, 1969).

Sidgwick, Henry, *The Elements of Politics* (London: Macmillan, 1919).

Simeon, Richard, *Federal-Provincial Diplomacy. The Making of Recent Policy in Canada* (Toronto: University of Toronto Press, 1972).

Simon, Herbert A., *Models of Man* (New York: Wiley, 1957).

The New Science of Management Decisions (New York: Harper, 1960).

Smiley, Donald V., "The Structural Problem of Canadian Federalism," *Canadian Public Administration* (Vol. 14, Fall 1971), 326–43.

Canada in Question: Federalism in the Eighties, Third Edition (Toronto: McGraw-Hill Ryerson, 1980).

Smiley, Donald V., and Ronald L. Watts, *Intrastate Federalism in Canada* (Toronto: University of Toronto Press, 1985).

Smith, Adam, *An Inquiry into the Nature and Causes of the Wealth of Nations* (New York: Random House, 1776/1937).

Smith, Bruce L. R., ed., *The New Political Economy: The Public Use of the Private Sector* (London: Macmillan, 1975).

Solzhenitsyn, Aleksandr I., *The Gulag Archipelago* (New York: Harper and Row, 1973).

Spencer, Barbara J., "Outside Information and the Degree of Monopoly Power of a Public Bureau," *Southern Economic Journal* (Vol. 47, No. 1, July 1980), 228–33.

Spicer, M. W., and S. B. Lundstedt, "Understanding Tax Evasion," *Public Finance/Finances publiques* (Vol. 31, No. 2, 1976), 295–305.

Srinivasan, T. N., "Tax Evasion: A Model," *Journal of Public Economics* (Vol. 2, No. 4, November 1973), 339–46.

Stanfield, Rochelle L., "'Defunding the Left' May Remain Just Another Fond Dream of Conservatives," *National Journal* (August 1, 1981), 1374–8.

Stigler, George J., "Production and Distribution in the Short Run," *Journal of Political Economy* (Vol. 47, No. 3, June 1939), 305–27. Reprinted in William Fellner and Bernard F. Haley, eds., *Readings in the Theory of Income Distribution* (Philadelphia: Blakiston, 1946), 119–42.

"The Division of Labor Is Limited by the Extent of the Market," *Journal of Political Economy* (Vol. 59, No. 3, June 1951), 185–93. Reprinted in Stigler, ed., *The Organization of Industry* (Chicago: University of Chicago Press, 1968), 129–41.

"Perfect Competition, Historically Contemplated," *Journal of Political Economy* (Vol. 65, No. 1, February, 1957a), 1–17. Reprinted in Stigler, ed., *Essays in the History of Economics* (Chicago: University of Chicago Press, 1967), 234–67.

"The Tenable Range of Functions of Local Government," in Joint Economic Committee, Subcommittee on Fiscal Policy, *Federal Expenditure Policy for Economic Growth and Stability* (Washington: U.S. Gov't. Printing Office, 1957b), 213–19.

"A Theory of Oligopoly," *Journal of Political Economy* (Vol. 72, No. 1, February 1964), 44–61.

The Theory of Price, Third Edition (New York: MacMillan, 1966).

"The Theory of Economic Regulation," *Bell Journal of Economics and Management Science* (Vol. 2, No. 1, Spring 1971), 3–21.

"Economic Competition and Political Competition," *Public Choice* (Vol. 13, Fall 1972), 91–106 [with p. 101 appearing in *Public Choice* (Vol. 14, Spring 1973), 166].

"Free Riders and Collective Action: An Appendix to Theories of Economic Regulation," *Bell Journal of Economics and Management Science* (Vol. 5, No. 2, Autumn 1974), 359–65.

The Regularities of Regulation (Glencorse: David Hume Institute, Hume Occasional Paper No. 3, 1986).

The Theory of Price, Fourth Edition (New York: Macmillan, 1987).

ed., *Studies in Chicago Political Economy* (Chicago: University of Chicago Press, 1989).

Stigler, George J., and Gary S. Becker, "De Gustibus Non Est Disputandum," *American Economic Review* (Vol. 67, No. 2, March 1977), 76–90.

Stiglitz, Joseph E., "Incentives, Risk, and Information: Notes Towards a Theory of Hierarchy," *Bell Journal of Economics* (Vol. 6, No. 2, Autumn 1975), 552–79.

"The Theory of Local Public Goods," in Martin S. Feldstein and Robert P. Inman, eds., *The Economics of Public Services* (London: Macmillan, 1977), 274–333.

"On the Economic Role of the State," in Arnold Heertje, ed., *The Economic Role of the State* (Oxford: Basil Blackwell, 1989), 9–85.

Strauss, George, "Tactics of Lateral Relationship: The Purchasing Agent," *Administrative Science Quarterly* (Vol. 7, September 1962), 161–86.

Strick, John C., "Conditional Grants and Provincial Government Budgeting," *Canadian Public Administration* (Vol. 14, No. 2, Summer 1971), 217–35.

Canadian Public Finance, Third Edition (Toronto: Holt, Rinehart and Winston of Canada, 1985).

Strotz, Robert H., "Two Propositions Related to Public Goods," *Review of Economics and Statistics* (Vol. 40, No. 4, November 1958), 329–331.

Subtil, Marie-Pierre, "Un casse-tête: la répartition des compétences entre la Communauté et les Etats membres," *Le Monde* (Vendredi, le 22 juin 1990), 7.

Summers, Lawrence, Jonathan Gruber, and Rodrigo Vergara, "Taxation and the Structure of Labor Markets: The Case of Corporatism," *Quarterly Journal of Economics* (Vol. 108, No. 2, May 1993), 385–411.

Sutherland, Edwin H., "The Diffusion of Sexual Psychopath Laws," *American Journal of Sociology* (Vol. 56, No. 2, September 1950), 142–48.

Taylor, Frederick W., *The Principles of Scientific Management* (New York: Harper & Row, 1911).

Telser, Lester G., "A Theory of Self-Enforcing Agreements," *Journal of Business* (Vol. 53, No. 1, January, 1980), 27–44.

Thirsk, Wayne R., "Tax Harmonization and Its Importance in the Canadian Federation," in Richard M. Bird, ed., *Fiscal Dimension of Canadian Federalism* (Toronto: Canadian Tax Foundation, 1980), 118–42.

Thompson, Earl A., "Book Review of *Bureaucracy and Representative Government,*" *Journal of Economic Literature* (Vol. 11, No. 3, September 1973), 950–3.

Tideman, T. Nicolaus, and Gordon Tullock, "A New and Superior Process for Making Social Choices," *Journal of Political Economy* (Vol. 84, No. 6, December 1976), 1145–59.

Tiebout, Charles M., "A Pure Theory of Local Expenditures," *Journal of Political Economy* (Vol. 64, No. 5, October 1956), 416–24.

Tirole, Jean, "Hierarchies and Bureaucracies: On the Role of Collusion in Organizations," *Journal of Law, Economics and Organization* (Vol. 2, No. 2, Fall 1986), 181–214.

"The Multicontract Organization," *Canadian Journal of Economics* (Vol. 21, No. 3, August 1988), 459–66.

de Tocqueville, Alexis, *Democracy in America*. Translated by George Lawrence (Garden City: Harper & Row, Anchor Books, 1835, 1840/1969).

Trzyna, Thaddeus C., *World Directory of Environmental Organizations. A Handbook of National and International Organizations and Programs, Governmental and Non-Governmental, Concerned with Protecting the Earth's Resources*, Third Edition, (Claremont: California Institute of Public Affairs in cooperation with the Sierra Club and IUCN, 1989).

Tullock, Gordon, "Problems of Majority Voting," *Journal of Political Economy* (Vol. 67, No. 6, December 1959), 571–9.

The Politics of Bureaucracy (Washington: Public Affairs Press, 1965).

"The Welfare Costs of Tariffs, Monopolies and Theft," *Western Economic Journal* (Vol. 5, No. 2, June 1967), 224–32.

"Federalism: Problems of Scale," *Public Choice* (Vol. 6, Spring, 1969), 19–29.

"A Simple Algebraic Logrolling Model," *American Economic Review* (Vol. 60, No. 3, June 1970), 419–26.

Usher, Dan, "The Growth of the Public Sector in Canada," in David Laidler, ed., *Responses to Economic Change* (Toronto: University of Toronto Press, 1986), 107–34.

Vaillancourt, François, *The Administrative and Compliance Costs of the Personal Income Tax and Payroll Tax System in Canada, 1986* (Toronto: Canadian Tax Foundation, 1989).

Vaillancourt, François, et Martine Hébert, "Les déclarations d'impôts personnels des Québécois pour l'année 1985: qui les complète et à quel coût?" *L'actualité économique, Revue d'analyse économique* (Vol. 66, No. 2, Juin 1990), 242–59.

Van Loon, Richard, "Ottawa's Expenditure Process: Four Systems in Search of Co-ordination," in G. Bruce Doern, ed., *How Ottawa Spends: The Liberals, the Opposition, and Federal Priorities* (Toronto: Lorimer, 1983), 93–120.

Vaubel, Roland, "Coordination or Competition among National Macro-Economic Policies?" in Fritz Machlup, Gerhard Fels, and Hubertus Müller-Groeling, eds., *Reflections on a Troubled World Economy: Essays in Honour of Herbert Giersch* (London: Macmillan, 1983), 3–28.

"A Public Choice Approach to International Organization," *Public Choice* (Vol. 51, No. 1, 1986), 39–57.

Vickrey, William, S., "One Economist's View of Philanthropy," in Frank G. Dickinson, ed., *Philanthropy and Public Policy* (New York: National Bureau of Economic Research, 1962), 31–56.

Viner, Jacob, "Power Versus Plenty as Objectives of Foreign Policy in the Seventeenth and Eighteenth Centuries," *World Politics* (Vol. 1, No. 1, October 1948), 1–29.

Vogel, Joachim, "Taxation and Public Opinion in Sweden: An Interpretation of Recent Survey Data," *National Tax Journal* (Vol. 27, No. 4, December 1974), 499–513.

Wagner, Adolph, "Three Extracts on Public Finance: i) The Nature of the Fiscal Economy; ii) The Basic Principles of Taxation; and iii) Justice in Tax Distribution," in Richard A. Musgrave and Alan T. Peacock, eds., *Classics in the Theory of Public Finance* (London: Macmillan, 1964), 1–15. Translated by Nancy Cooke from *Finanzwissenschaft*, Part I, Third Edition (Leipzig, 1883/1890), 4–16, 69–76.

Walker, Jack L., "The Diffusion of Innovations Among the American States," *American Political Science Review* (Vol. 63, No. 3, September 1969), 880–99.

"The Origins and Maintenance of Interest Groups in America," *American Political Science Review* (Vol. 77, No. 2, June, 1983), 390–406.

Walsh, Cliff, *Reform of Commonwealth-State Relations – "No Representation Without Taxation,"* (Canberra: Federalism Research Centre, Australian National University, Discussion Paper No. 2, 1991).

Fiscal Accountability, Vertical Fiscal Imbalance and Macroeconomic Management in Federal Fiscal Systems (Canberra: Federalism Research Centre, Australian National University, Discussion Paper No. 7, 1992).

Weber, Max, "Bureaucracy," in Hans H. Gerth and C. Wright Mills, eds., *From Max Weber: Essays in Sociology* (New York: Oxford University Press, 1946). Translated by Gerth and Mills from *Wirtschaft and Gesellschaft*, Part III, Chapter 6, Second Edition, 1925.

The Theory of Social and Economic Organization (Glencoe: Free Press, 1947). Translated by A. M. Henderson and Talcott Parsons from *Wirtschaft and Gesellschaft*, Part I, Second Edition, 1925.

Weingast, Barry R., and William J. Marshall, "The Industrial Organization of Congress; or, Why Legislatures, Like Firms, Are Not Organized as Markets," *Journal of Political Economy* (Vol. 96, No. 1, February, 1988), 132–63.

Weisbrod, Burton A., *The Voluntary Nonprofit Sector: Economic Theory and Public Policy* (Lexington: Lexington Press, 1977).

The Nonprofit Economy (Cambridge, MA: Harvard University Press, 1988).

Weldon, Jack C., "Public Goods (and Federalism)," *Canadian Journal of Economics and Political Science* (Vol. 32, No. 2, May 1966), 230–8.

Westhoff, Frank, "Policy Inferences from Community Choice Models: A Caution," *Journal of Urban Economics* (Vol. 6, No. 4, October 1979), 535–49.

Wheare, Kenneth C., *Federal Government,* Fourth Edition (London: Oxford University Press, 1963).

White, Tracy, ed., *Power in Congress* (Washington: Congressional Quarterly, 1987).

Whyte, John D., "Constitutional Aspects of Economic Development Policy," in Richard Simeon, ed., *Division of Powers and Public Policy* (Toronto: University of Toronto Press, 1985), 29–69.

Whyte, W. Foote, "Incentives for Productivity: The Bundy Tubing Company Case," *Applied Anthropology* (Vol. 7, No. 2, Spring 1948), 1–16.

Wicksell, Knut, "A New Principle of Just Taxation," in Richard A. Musgrave and Alan T. Peacock, eds., *Classics in the Theory of Public Finance* (London: Macmillan, 1964), 72–118. Translated by James M. Buchanan from "Ein neues Prinzip der gerechten Besteuerung," *Finanztheoretische Untersuchungen* (Jena 1896), iv–vi, 76–87, 101–59.

Wildavsky, Aaron, "A Cultural Theory of Expenditure Growth and (Un)Balanced Budgets," *Journal of Public Economics* (Vol. 28, No. 3, December 1985), 349–57.

Wilde, James A., "Grants-In-Aid: The Analytics of Design and Response," *National Tax Journal* (Vol. 24, No. 2, 1971), 143–55.

Williamson, Oliver E., "Hierarchical Control and Optimum Firm Size," *Journal of Political Economy* (Vol. 75, No. 2, April 1967), 123–38.

Markets and Hierarchies: Analysis and Antitrust Implications. A Study in the Economics of Internal Organization (New York: Macmillan, 1975).

The Economic Institutions of Capitalism: Firms, Markets, Relational Contracting (New York: Free Press, 1985).

Wilson, James Q., *Political Organizations* (New York: Basic Books, 1973).

"Does the Separation of Powers Still Work?" *The Public Interest* (No. 86, Winter, 1987), 36–52.

Wilson, James Q., and Edward C. Banfield, "Voting Behavior on Municipal Public Expenditures: A Study in Rationality and Self-Interest," in Julius Margolis, ed., *The Public Economy of Urban Communities* (Washington: Resources for the Future, 1965), 74–91.

van Winden, Frans, *On the Interaction Between State and Private Sector* (Amsterdam: North-Holland, 1983).

"Man in the Public Sector," *De Economist* (Vol. 135, No. 1, 1987), 1–28.

Winer, Stanley, L., "Some Evidence on the Effect of the Separation of Spending and Taxing Decisions," *Journal of Political Economy* (Vol. 91, No. 1, February 1983), 126–40.

"Taxation and Federalism in a Changing World," in Richard M. Bird and Jack M. Mintz, eds., *Taxation to 2000 and Beyond* (Toronto: Canadian Tax Foundation, 1992), 343–69.

Winer, Stanley L., and Denis Gauthier, *Internal Migration and Fiscal Structure: An Econometric Study of the Determinants of Interprovincial Migration in Canada* (Ottawa: Economic Council of Canada, 1982).

Winter, Ralph K., Jr., "State Law, Shareholder Protection, and the Theory of the Corporation," *Journal of Legal Studies* (Vol. 6, No. 2, June 1977), 251–92.

Wintrobe, Ronald, "The Optimal Level of Bureaucratization Within a Firm," *Canadian Journal of Economics* (Vol. 15, No. 4, November 1982), 649–68.

"Taxing Altruism," *Economic Inquiry* (Vol. 21, No. 2, April 1983), 255–70.

"The Efficiency of the Soviet System of Industrial Production," in Albert Breton, Gianluigi Galeotti, Pierre Salmon, and Ronald Wintrobe, eds., *Villa Colombella Papers on Bureaucracy, European Journal of Political Economy* (Vol. 4, Extra Issue, 1988), 159–84.

"The Tinpot and the Totalitarian: An Economic Theory of Dictatorship," *American Political Science Review* (Vol. 84, No. 3, September, 1990), 849–72.

Wintrobe, Ronald, and Albert Breton, "Organizational Structure and Productivity," *American Economic Review* (Vol. 76, No. 3, June 1986), 530–8.

Wittman, Donald, "Multi-Candidate Equilibria," *Public Choice* (Vol. 43, No. 3, 1984), 287–91.

"Why Democracies Produce Efficient Results," *Journal of Political Economy* (Vol. 97, No. 6, December, 1989), 1395–1424.

The Myth of Democratic Failure: Why Political Institutions Are Efficient (University of Chicago Press, 1995).

Wootton, David, ed., *Divine Right and Democracy. An Anthology of Political Writing in Stuart England* (Penguin Classics, 1986).

Yarbrough, Beth V., and Robert M. Yarbrough, "Reciprocity, Bilateralism, and Economic 'Hostages': Self-Enforcing Agreements in International Trade," *International Studies Quarterly* (Vol. 30, No. 1, March 1986), 7–21.

Young, Dennis, *How Shall We Collect the Garbage?* (Washington: Urban Institute, 1972).

Young, Robert A., "Tectonic Policies and Political Competition," in Albert Breton, Gianluigi Galeotti, Pierre Salmon, and Ronald Wintrobe, eds., *The Competitive State, Villa Colombella Papers on Competitive Politics* (Dordrecht: Kluwer, 1991), 129–45.

Zampelli, Ernst M., "Resource Fungibility, The Flypaper Effect, and the Expenditure Impact of Grants-in-Aid," *Review of Economics and Statistics* (Vol. 68, No. 1, February 1986), 33–40.

Zeckhauser, Richard, "Risk Spreading and Distribution," in Harold M. Hochman and George E. Peterson, eds., *Redistribution Through Public Choice* (New York: Columbia University Press, 1974), 206–28.

Name Index

Acheson, Keith, 163
Adams, John, 135n13
Adams, John Quincy, 91n12
Aharoni, Yair, 305
Aiken, Michael, 154
Akerlof, George A., 149, 175, 255, 297
Alchian, Armen, 177, 206, 215
Alesina, Alberto, 38, 315, 317
Allen, Douglas W., 8
Allingham, Michael G., 206n6
Anderson, Terry L., 291
Aoki, Masahiko, 173, 173n23, 174, 176
Aranson, Peter H., 284
Arendt, Hannah, 175
Arrow, Kenneth J., 11n5, 32, 40, 54, 150,
    156, 159, 206
Auerback, Alan J., 118
Auster, Richard, 124, 124n3
Axelrod, Robert, 268, 269

Bacharach, Samuel, 122
Bagehot, Walter, 14, 15, 90, 90n12, 125
Balladur, Edouard, 77n8
Banfield, Edward C., 39
Barrow, Robert J., 44n11
Barzel, Yoram, 222
Bateman, Worth, 244
Batey Blackman, Sue Anne, 294
Baumol, William J., 134, 162–3, 185,
    240n9, 288, 294, 294n6, 307–8
Becker, Gary S., 6, 8, 19–20, 20n11, 27,
    62n20, 250, 285, 291, 292n5, 300, 316,
    318, 318n1
Bélanger, Gérard, 164, 165n13, 166, 187,
    290, 301n10
Bella, Leslie, 218
Bénard, Jean, 163, 172n20
Bendor, Jonathan, 165, 167
Bennett, James, 62–3
Bennis, Warren G., 153
Bergstrom, Theodore C., 38
Berle, Adolf, 149, 177
Bernheim, B. Douglas, 300
Beveridge, William, 8, 9
Bird, Richard M., 97, 182n3, 183, 188,

212n12, 219, 220n14, 245, 254, 287,
    290, 299, 305
Birdsall, William C., 39
Bish, Robert L., 239n8
Black, Duncan, 40
Bloom, Howard S., 239
Beard, Charles, 138
Boadway, Robin, 198, 202, 255, 256
Borcherding, Thomas E., 13, 38, 222, 286,
    287, 288, 289n2, 305, 305n12, 306n13,
    307, 308
Bös, Dieter, 191–2
Bothwell, Robert, 107n9, 110n17
Boulding, Kenneth E., 7
Bradford, David F., 240n9
Brams, Steven, 120
Brean, Donald, 299
Brennan, Geoffrey, 12, 21, 126n6, 208, 215,
    220–1, 221n14
Breton, Albert, 28, 40n5, 86, 101, 110,
    111, 116, 165, 166, 167, 168–9, 168n16,
    169n17, 170, 170n18, 171–2, 173,
    173n23, 175, 178, 182n3, 184, 184n6,
    185, 186, 187, 188, 189, 198, 199–200,
    204, 209, 212, 221, 227, 228, 250, 251,
    254, 258, 259n16, 291, 296, 303
Breton, Margot, 63
Brontë, Charlotte, 9
Brown, Robert, 138
Brown, Wilfred B. D., 154
Bryant, Ralph C., 271
Bryce, James (Lord), 182n3
Buchanan, James M., 7, 9, 12, 21, 22, 23,
    43, 44, 45, 62n20, 97, 115, 120n28,
    126n6, 198, 208, 231, 232, 232n4, 243,
    254, 288, 298, 318, 319, 324
Buhofer, Heinz, 288
Burke, Edmund, 137n14, 140
Burns, Tom, 153
Bush, George, 34

Cairns, Alan, 260
Cameron, David, 306–7
Campbell, Colin, 100
Carey, William, 241–2, 243, 251n12

Chaban-Delmas, Jacques, 34
Chandler, Alfred, 153
Chapple, Elliot, 152
Charreaux, Gérard, 167, 167n15
Chernick, Howard A., 218
Cheung, Steven, 16
Chrétien, Jean, 107n12
Clarke, Edward, 39
Coase, Ronald H., 186, 187, 264, 288
Coleman, James S., 39n3, 115, 116, 236, 250, 297
Collier, Kenneth E., 27
Conybeare, John C., 264n2
Cooter, Robert, 101, 103
Corden, W. Max, 265
Courant, Paul N., 197
Courchene, Thomas, 239, 256, 304, 305
Cox, Donald, 300
Crain, Robert L., 235n5
Crain, W. Mark, 322n3
Crawford, Robert G., 215
Cross, Rod, 45n12
Crossman, Richard, 111
Crozier, Michel, 151, 153, 154

Dahl, Robert, 21n13, 24–5, 25n16, 26
Dales, John, 187, 188
Dalton, Melville, 152, 152n1
Darnton, Robert, 128
David, king of Israel, 128
Davies, David, 182n3
Davis, Ada J., 235, 235n5, 236
Davis, Otto A., 68
Day, Kathleen, 239
de Gaulle, Charles, 16
Deacon, Robert T., 38, 39, 222
Demsetz, Harold, 134, 306
Denzau, Arthur, 43
Dicey, Albert V., 14n7, 182n3
Dickson, William, 151
DiLorenzo, Thomas, 62, 63
Disraeli, Benjamin, 90n12
Dodd, Peter, 242, 243
Doern, G. Bruce, 99, 106, 107
Downs, Anthony, 27, 31, 33, 34, 115, 169, 170, 318n1
Drazen, Allan, 315, 317
Drummond, Tom, 107n9, 110n17
Dupré, Stéfan, 98n2

Eaton, B. Curtis, 8–9, 318, 319
Eavey, Cheryl, 165
Edel, Matthew, 238
Edwards, Corwin D., 335
Elazar, Daniel J., 191, 225, 228
Ellis, Richard E., 135n13

English, John, 107n9, 110n17
Epple, Dennis, 238

Fama, Eugene F., 177
Fayol, Henri, 151, 154
Ferejohn, John, xii
Finkle, Peter, 58, 62
Fiorina, Morris P., xii, 27
Fischel, Daniel, 241
Fisher, Ronald C., 219, 220
Flatters, Frank, 198, 202, 255, 256
Flowers, Marilyn R., 97
Forcina, Antonio, 38
Fortin, Bernard, 298
Fouché, Joseph, 132
Fourier, Charles, 290, 290n3
Frank, A. Gunder, 153
Fraschini, Angela, 199, 221
Fréchette, Pierre, 298
Frey, Bruno S., 34, 38, 39, 145, 206n6, 264n1, 267, 288, 304n11
Friedman, Milton, 319, 320n3
Friedrich, Carl J., 225

Galbraith, Jay, 152
Galeotti, Gianluigi, 28, 38, 40n5, 49n16, 86, 101, 174n24, 303
Gauthier, Denis, 239
George III, king of England, 193
Gibbins, Roger, 260
Gibson, Gordon, 260
Gilbert, Felix, 138
Gilpin, Robert, 265
Gingrich, Newt, 34
Goebbels, Joseph, 125n5
Goodman, Robert P., 38
Gordon, Roger, 191
Gordon, H. Scott, 41, 73n4, 75, 75n6, 138, 304, 305
Gouldner, Alvin, 151, 152, 152n2, 169
Gramlich, Edward M., 197, 219, 238
Gray, Virginia, 235n5
Grodzins, Morton, 228
Groves, Theodore, 39
Gruber, Jonathan, 328–9, 330

Hage, Jerald, 154
Hamilton, Alexander, 14, 193n7, 247
Hamilton, Bruce, 238
Hansmann, Henry, 279, 280, 281, 282, 284
Harris, Milton, 155
Hart, Oliver, 156
Hartle, Douglas G., 99, 100, 100n5, 102, 105, 107, 107n11, 108n15
Hashimoto, Masanori, 173
Hayek, Friedrich, 31

Hébert, Martine, 206n7
Heclo, Hugh, 110n18
Heiner, Ronald, 174n24
Henderson, J. Vernon, 198, 202, 255
Hettich, Walter, 45
Hibbs, Douglas A., Jr., 38
Hicks, John R., 29, 86
Hicks, Ursula K., 197
Hickson, David, 153–4
Hill, Peter J., 291
Hirshleifer, Jack, 300n9
Hitler, Adolf, 175
Hochman, Harold M., 7, 244
Hofferbert, Richard I., 235n5
Holmström, Bengt, 155, 156, 157
Hotelling, Harold, 31
Huchon, Jean-Paul, 16
Hughes, Jonathan R. T., 291

Iannaccone, Laurence, 299
Inman, Robert P., 44, 165n12
Ireland, Thomas, 297, 300

Jackson, Peter M., 151
Jay, John, 14
Jefferson, Thomas, 139
Jennings, Ivor, 14n7
Jensen, Michael C., 177
Johansen, Leif, 23
Johnsen, D. Bruce, 8
Johnson, David, 297, 300
Johnson, Harry G., 211n11, 245
Johnson, Lyndon B., 34
Johnson, Ronald, 174, 175
Johnston, Richard, 49n15

Kalt, Joseph, 33–4
Kaplan, Robert, 156n6
Katz, Elihu, 236
Kau, James B., 34
Kennedy, John F., 34
Kenyon, Daphne A., 229, 239
Keohane, Robert O., 264nn1, 2, 265, 266,
    267–8, 267n5, 271, 271n8, 272, 273
Key, Valdimer O., 27
Kincaid, John, 191
Kindleberger, Charles P., 240, 245, 270,
    271
Kirkpatrick, Jeane, 132n10, 133n11
Kirzner, Israel, 31
Klein, Benjamin, 149, 169, 208, 215
Knight, Frank H., 33
Kolm, Serge-Christophe, 23, 119n26
Kornhauser, Lewis, 102
Kotlikoff, Laurence J., 118
Kraan, Dirk-Jan, 115

Krashinsky, Michael, 280
Krasner, Stephen, 271
Krueger, Anne, 291

Ladd, Helen F., 239
Lafay, Jean-Dominique, 39n2, 53, 61, 61n19
Laffont, Jean-Jacques, 156, 161–2, 164,
    166, 167
Lammers, Nancy, 117, 118n25
Lancaster, Kelvin, 68, 78, 111, 240
Landa, Janet, 122n1
Landes, William M., 12, 141, 321, 322n3,
    324, 325
Landsberger, Henry, 152
Larkey, Patrick D., 287, 288
Laski, Harold, 182n3
Lawler, Edward, 122
Lazear, Edward P., 158, 189, 233
Lee, Judith A. B., 308n15
Leffler, Keith, 149, 169, 215, 326, 327
Leftwich, Richard, 242, 243
Leibowitz, Arleen, 116
Leland, Hayne, 149, 251
Lemco, Jonathan, 334–5, 334nn1, 2
Lenin, V. I., 132
Levinthal, Daniel, 156
Lévy-Garboua, Louis, 7–8
Lewis, Bernard, 14n6
Lewis-Beck, Michael S., 38
Libby, Orin, 137–8
Libecap, Gary, 174, 175
Lindahl, Erik, xii, 3, 23
Lindbeck, Assar, 291
Lipsey, Richard G., 68
Loewenstein, Karl, 260
Louis XVI, king of France, 125
Louvet, Philippe, 287
Lundstedt, S. B., 206

McCormick, Peter, 260
McCready, Douglas J., 188
McDonald, Forrest, 137n15, 138
MacEachen, Allan, 107n10
McGuire, Martin, 215, 220
Mackay, Robert, 43
McKee, Michael, 172n21, 176
McKelvey, Richard D., 27
McManus, Maurice, 68
McVoy, Edgar C., 235n5
Madison, James, 14, 25, 25n16, 26, 139,
    247
Main, Jackson, 137, 138
Major, John, 34
Manning, Ernest, 260
Mansfield, Edwin, 236
Marks, Stephen, 101, 103

Marshall, Alfred, 32, 188, 319, 320n2
Marshall, John, 92
Marshall, William, xii, 109–10, 115, 116–17, 117n24
Maslove, Allan M., 99, 106, 107
Mayo, Elton, 151
Meadows, George, 238
Means, Gardiner, 149, 177
Meckling, William H., 177
Meltzer, Allan H., 6, 305
Menger, Carl, 31
Menzel, Herbert, 236
Merton, Robert, 151
Mieszkowski, Peter M., 198, 202, 255
Migué, Jean-Luc, xi, 164, 165n13, 166
Mill, John Stuart, 25, 101
Miller, Gary J., 159, 165, 166
Miller, William, 137, 138
Mills, Edwin, 244
Mintz, Jack, 188, 219, 220n14
Mintzberg, Henry, 151, 153
Mirrlees, James, 155
Mises, Ludwig, 31
Mitterand, François, 34
Mnookin, Robert, 102, 103
Moe, Terry, 166
Moene, Karl O., 165, 165n13
Moore, Thomas J., 61
Morgenthau, Hans J., 265
Mougeot, Michel, 68
Mount, Ferdinand, 14nn7, 8, 15–16
Mueller, Dennis C., 38n3, 40, 53, 163, 286, 287, 305
Mueller, Frederick, 243n10
Mundell, Robert A., 184n5
Murphy, Kevin M., 8, 208, 300, 316
Musgrave, Peggy B., 97, 112, 184, 212n12, 219
Musgrave, Richard A., 23, 45n12, 97, 112, 160, 184, 198, 212n12, 219, 243, 254

Nalebuff, Barry, 233
Napoléon Bonaparte, 132
Nelson, Richard, 280
Newman, Peter C., 111
Niskanen, William A., Jr., 148, 162, 163, 164, 164n11, 165, 165n13, 166, 166n14, 167, 188, 288
Nixon, Richard M., 118n25
Nordhaus, William D., 38
Norrie, Kenneth, 239
North, Douglass C., 287, 289n2, 301, 301n10, 306
Nurske, Ragnar, 245

Oakland, William, 165n12
Oates, Wallace E., xi, 182n3, 184, 185, 186, 187, 198, 228, 239, 243, 244, 244n4, 254
Olson, Mancur, Jr., 44, 61, 62n20, 63, 171, 184, 185, 186, 187, 228, 269, 296, 297, 298
Ordeshook, Peter C., 27, 284
Orleans, Sonya, 206
Orzechowski, William, 163
Oster, Sharon M., 236
Ostrom, Vincent, 90, 142–3
Owen, Robert, 290, 290n3

Paldam, Martin, 38
Palmer, Matthew, 13
Panagopoulos, Epaminondas, 14, 41, 75, 83, 92
Panzar, John, 134
Pareto, Vilfredo, 318n1
Parkinson, C. Northcote, 175
Pasqua, Charles, 77n8
Pauly, Mark, 238
Peacock, Alan T., 182n3, 183, 286, 286n1, 288, 294n6
Pearson, Lester B., 34
Peltzman, Sam, 34, 171, 305
Percy, Michael, 239
Perrow, Charles, 152, 153, 154
Pfeffer, Jeffrey, 153
Pheysey, Diana C., 154
Phillips, Susan D., 60, 62
Pigou, Arthur C., 185
Pincus, Jonathan, 208, 215, 220-1, 220n14
Plott, Charles R., 40
Polinsky, A. Mitchell, 8
Polsby, Nelson, 73–4, 102, 112, 113n22, 114
Pommerehne, Werner W., 39, 182n3, 206n6
Popitz, Johannes, 182n3
Posner, Richard A., 12, 141, 321–3, 322n3, 324, 325
Potters, Jan, 58, 326
Prince, Michael J., 99, 106, 107
Pross, A. Paul, 58, 62, 63, 326
Pryor, Frederic, 182n3
Pugh, Derek S., 154

Quigley, John M., 236

Rabeau, Yves, 255n14
Radner, Roy, 159
Raisian, John, 173
Raviv, Artur, 155
Rawls, John, 22
Raynauld, André, 255n14
Reagan, Ronald, 260
Reich, Robert, 252n13
Reinganum, Jennifer F., 236

Reschovsky, Andrew, 238
Ricardo, David, 294
Rice, Tom W., 38
Richard, Scott F., 6, 305
Ricketts, Martin, 156
Riker, William H., 90, 92n13, 120, 139, 193n7, 228, 228n1, 259, 334–5, 334nn1, 2
Robinson, Joan, 128
Rocard, Michel, 16
Rodgers, James D., 7
Roethlisberger, Fritz, 151
Rogoff, Kenneth, 265n3
Roll, Richard, 41, 86
Romano, Roberta, 236, 242, 243
Romer, Thomas, 164, 165, 165n13, 197
Roosevelt, Franklin D., 34
Rose-Ackerman, Susan, 243
Rosen, Harvey S., 185, 186, 244
Rosen, Kenneth, 238
Rosen, Sherwin, 189, 233
Rosenthal, Howard, 164, 165, 165n13, 197
Rottenberg, Simon, 16
Roubini, Nouriel, 38
Rousseau, Jean-Jacques, 21n13
Rubin, Paul H., 34
Rubinfeld, Daniel L., 38, 39, 184, 186, 197, 238
Ruggie, John G., 267n6, 271, 272

Salmon, Pierre, 27, 28, 40n4, 62, 169n17, 189, 194, 233, 234, 261, 266, 318
Samuelson, Paul A., 11n5, 18, 24, 31, 32, 50n17, 184, 222, 240, 264, 269, 283, 284, 288
Sandmo, Agnar, 206n6
Saunders, Peter, 307
Savage, Robert L., 235n5
Sayles, Leonard, 152
Scharf, Kimberley Ann, 46, 206
Schneider, Friedrich, 34, 38
Schram, Arthur, 61
Schumpeter, Joseph, 31–2
Schwartz, Richard D., 206
Schwartz, Thomas, 120
Scitovsky, Tibor, 245
Sclar, Elliot, 238
Scott, Anthony, 183, 184n6, 186, 187, 188, 189, 197, 199, 200, 204, 209, 212, 251, 255n15
Scott, Thomas M., 235n5
Selznick, Philip, 151
Sen, Amartya, 29
Shapiro, Carl, 149, 158, 169, 284, 300
Shapiro, Perry, 39
Sharkansky, Ira, 235n5
Shavell, Steven, 187

Shaw, Keith, 45n12
Shepsle, Kenneth, xii, 115, 116, 117
Shipan, Charles, xii
Shleifer, Andrei, 300
Shoup, Carl, 45n12, 188
Sidgwick, Henry, 182n3
Silver, Morris, 124, 124n3
Simeon, Richard, 211n10
Simon, Herbert A., 153
Slack, Enid, 245, 254
Smiley, Donald V., 193n7, 228, 260, 261
Smith, Adam, 30, 142, 204, 312
Smith, Bruce, L. R., 58
Solzhenitsyn, Aleksandr, 132
Spencer, Barbara J., 165, 165n13, 166
Spicer, M. W., 206
Srinivasan, T. N., 206n6
Stalin, Josef, 132, 176
Stalker, G. M., 153
Stanbury, William T., 58
Stanfield, Rochelle, 62, 63
Stewart, Ian, 107n10
Stigler, George J., 6, 30, 48, 60, 61, 141, 142, 171, 204–5, 204n5, 208, 243, 248, 250, 292n5, 296, 297, 298, 308, 308n1, 333
Stiglitz, Joseph E., 13, 19, 155, 157, 158, 233, 243, 300
Stolp, Chandler, 287, 288
Strauss, George, 152
Strick, John C., 212n12, 218
Strotz, Robert H., 284
Subtil, Marie-Pierre, 185
Summers, Lawrence H., 300, 328–9, 330
Sutherland, Edwin H., 235n5
Swenson, Carol, 308n15
Szablowski, George, 100

Taylor, Frederick, 151, 154
Taylor, Serge, 165
Telser, Lester, 169, 250
Thatcher, Margaret, 182n2, 191, 196n1, 260
Thirsk, Wayne R., 188
Thompson, Earl, 164, 165
Tideman, Nicolaus, 39
Tiebout, Charles, 30–1, 188, 194, 230, 232
Tirole, Jean, 156, 159, 160, 161–2, 161n8, 162n9, 164, 166, 167
Tocqueville, Alexis de, 135, 182n3, 247, 286
Tollison, Robert, 116, 322n3
Trudeau, Pierre Elliott, 35, 335
Truman, Harry S., 34
Trzyna, Thaddeus C., 60
Tulkens, Henry, 188
Tullock, Gordon, 6, 7, 21, 22, 39, 115, 120, 148, 157, 162, 169, 185, 186, 222, 291, 324

Usher, Dan, 287, 305

Vaillancourt, François, 206n7
Van Gaalen, Roland, 165
Van Loon, Richard, 99, 108n15
Vaubel, Roland, 265, 271n7
Veil, Simone, 77n8
Vergara, Rodrigo, 328–9, 330
Vickrey, William S., 7
Viner, Jacob, 267, 268
Vischer, Michael, 238
Vogel, Joachim, 206

Wagner, Adolph, 286
Walker, Jack L., 62, 63, 183n4, 235n5, 236, 241
Walsh, Cliff, 197, 199n3, 211
Washington, George, 135n13
Watts, Ronald, 193n7, 260, 261
Webb, Kernaghan, 58
Weber, Max, 151
Weingast, Barry, xii, 109–10, 115, 116–17, 117n24
Weisbrod, Burton, 64, 279, 280, 281, 281n3, 282, 297, 299–300
Weldon, Jack, 185
Westoff, Frank, 243
Wheare, Kenneth C., 94, 182n3, 208, 228
Whinston, Andrew B., 68
White, William D., 8–9, 318, 319
White, Tracy, 113n22
Whyte, John, 223
Whyte, W. Foote, 153
Wicksell, Knut, xii, 3, 21–2, 23, 88, 89, 119, 119n26, 311, 328

Wildavsky, Aaron, 305
Wilde, James A., 197
Williams, Kenneth C., 27
Williamson, Oliver, 153, 157, 169, 215
Willig, Robert, 134
Wilson, James Q., 39, 62, 90, 91
Winden, Frans van, 58, 61, 326
Winer, Mark, 287, 288
Winer, Stanley, 45, 197, 212, 239
Winter, Ralph K. Jr., 241
Wintrobe, Ronald, xi–xii, 110, 111, 116, 132n10, 133n11, 134n12, 143, 154n4, 165, 166, 167, 168–9, 168n16, 169n17, 170, 170n18, 171–2, 173, 173n23, 174n24, 175, 176, 178, 188, 250, 297, 300n9
Wiseman, Jack, 182n3, 183, 286, 286n1
Wittman, Donald, 20, 20n12, 28, 60, 61, 61n19, 64
Wolfelsperger, Alain, 40n4
Wolff, Edward N., 294
Wootton, David, 125, 129

Yarbrough, Beth V., 264n2
Yarbrough, Robert M., 264n2
Yinger, John, 239
Young, Dennis, 239n8
Young, Robert A., 58, 62

Zampelli, Ernst, 215, 220
Zechhauser, Richard, 8
Zelenitz, Allan, 238
Zupan, Mark, 34

Subject index

adverse selection, 156, 158
advertising, 326
agencies, governmental, 260, 261
agency problem(s), 109, 149–50; demand lobbies and, 59, 61–7
agency theory, 149, 150
agenda-setting/agenda control, 115–16, 164–5
agenda structure, 20
agent-agent networks, 152
agents, 149; and asymmetric distribution of information, 150; power of, 153
aggregation: and interaction of demand lobbies with centers of power, 59–61
agricultural employment, changes in, 306
agricultural subsidies, 318
allocation functions, 198
allocation powers, 184
altruism, 7, 300
American Confederation of 1781, 247
American exceptionalism, 14–15, 90–3
American federation, 229
American Republic: political structure of, 135, 137–41
announcements: by centers of power, 85
antidistortion and control devices, 166, 177
appointment, selection by, 142
appointments, 94; to congressional committees, 113; power to produce, 77; by Prime Minister, 99
aristocracy, 14, 92
arm's length agencies, 73, 74
Articles of Confederation, 139
assignment of functions/responsibilities, 184–6, 187, 209–10; constitution(s) and, 223
assignment of powers, 184–90, 199, 200–2, 228; changing, 225–6; constitutionally entrenched, 190, 247; income redistribution, 243–4; optimal, 228; theory of, 186–7
assignment of taxation powers, 191
assignment problem, 184–8
Australia, 97, 220n14, 231
Austria, 306
Austrian model, 31

authority: in centers of power, 71–2, 150, 153, 165
autocracy, 130, 202
autocratic regimes/rule, 29, 128, 129, 130–1; Wicksellian Connection in, 146; under *Vox Dei* and *Vox Populi* dispensations, 132–4
autonomy: in congressional governments, 93–4; loss of, in tax harmonization, 211–12
autonomy/quasi autonomy: and separation of powers, 72, 75
average cost curves, 203, 205, 206, 207, 243, 333

backbenchers, 15, 101, 102
balance, 75, 86; and checking, 83, 92, 93
balanced budget, 44; constitutionally prescribed, 120
balanced governments, 93–4
balances, analysis of, 93–4
balancing: relationship with checking, 74, 75–6
bargaining, 36, 41, 188, 303; and equilibrium outcomes, 102–6
bargaining breakdown, 106, 119
"Bargaining in the Shadow of the Law," 102, 114
"bargaining in the shadow of the Prime Minister" model, 102–6
bargaining strategies, 103–4, 105, 106, 107, 108
Bayesian-Nash equilibrium, 103, 118
beggar-thy-neighbor policies, 210, 251
Belgium, 306
benevolence, 128
benevolent despots, governments as, 11, 40, 46
bicameralism, 259–60
bounded rationality, 153
bourgeoisie, 140, 141
branches of government, 72, 73–4; U.S., 91–2
budget, meaning of, 97; *see also* balanced budget

budget-constrained model, 164
budget deficits, long-term, 315–17
budget maximization, 163, 164, 165
budget secrecy, 96, 99–100, 105–7; Canada, 111; explanations of, 106–7
budgetary decision-making, 35
budgetary equilibria, 96
budgetary processes, 96–121, 146, 303; in congressional governments, 96–7, 98, 111–18, 119–20, 121; models of, 35; in parliamentary governments, 96–7, 98–111, 118–19, 120, 121; Wicksellian Connection in, 118–21
bundling, 222–3
bureaucracy(ies), 35–6, 147–8, 287; competition between bureaus in, 167, 176–8; model(s) of, 148, 188, 288; in principal-agent model, 155; relationship with consumers, 149; study of, 151; see also efficient bureaus/bureaucracies
bureaucracy, senior, permanent, nonpartisan, 96, 101; in enforcement of equilibrium allocations, 110–11
bureaucratic capture models, 11, 27
bureaucratic manipulation, 226
bureaus: discretionary power analysis of, 162–7; horizontally/vertically situated, 149; internal organization of, 167–76; see also inefficient bureaus
business and political budget cycles, 38–9
business enterprises: and free-riding, 300; as suppliers of goods and services, 279, 289, 291, 292, 293, 302, 305, 308, 309, 311

Cabinet: in parliamentary systems, 98, 99, 100, 102
cabinet government, model of, 102–11
cabinet shuffle, 104, 108–9
cabinets, 73, 119
Calculus of Consent, The (Buchanan and Tullock), 7
Canada, 17, 70, 110, 212, 231, 232, 276, 288, 290, 306, 312; broadcasting industry, 86; budgetary processes in, 35, 111; Cabinet, 72, 74; centers of power, 40, 72; Charter of Rights and Freedoms, 15, 83; checking in, 76n7; coordination in, 211n10; Department of Finance, 111n19; Department of National Revenue, 111n19; Equalization Payments, 258; equalization programs, 256–7; Established Programs Financing, 258; grants programs, 219–20; House of Commons, 15, 40, 74, 91; intergovernmental competition, 245; legislature, 324–5; lobbies in, 62, 63; macroeconomic management policy, 332; Minister of Finance, 107n12; Office of the Auditor General, 98n1; parliamentary government in, 15, 91, 96, 97; reform of expenditure budgetary process, 108–9; regional policy in, 252; Senate, 40, 74, 260; Supreme Court, 40; Tax Collection Agreements, 212, 214, 258

Canada Assistance Plan, 258
Canada Council, 260
Canadian Constitution, 324
Canadian federalism, 229, 335
canvassing the electorate, 139, 223
capital asset, trust as, 178
capital mobility, 189, 191, 192, 207, 230, 257–58
capture, 86, 94
cartels, 208, 249
caucuses, 96, 101–2, 115
centers of power, 34, 181, 321; agency problem, 149; aggregation and interaction of demand lobbies with, 59–61; aggregations of, 70; Canadian government, 40; and checks and balances, 70–95; in dictatorships, 132–3, 134; goods and services supplied by, 43; information needs of, 57–9; interaction of, 26–7; managers of, 333; maximizing expected consent, 52–7; multiple, 124, 129; number of, 142; and private goods, 68–9; support for lobbies, 62–3, 64; types of, 134–5; see also competition, between/among centers of power; elected centers of power; nonelected centers of power
central banks, 74, 85, 98n1
central governments, 193–4; competition and stability in, 228–63; and competitive outcomes, 248; enforcer role of, 193, 195; and equity, 198; as monitors, 229, 248–62, 263; monopoly by, 208; omniscient, 185, 187; role of, 198, 199–202, 209
centralization, 183, 184, 190, 224, 225, 229; and competitive instability, 244; of constitutional powers, 258; federal states, 334–5; and transaction costs, 187
centralization equilibria, 194
characteristics: in government-supplied goods and services, 78, 79, 81, 82, 83, 84, 85, 87, 95; informal payments take form of, 111
charity, institutionalization of, 304
Charlottetown Consensus, 34
cheating, 59, 249–50, 282
checking: relationship with balancing, 74, 75–6, 83; competitive, 70
checking behavior, 35, 75–6; Wicksellian Connection, 87–90

checking game: zero-sum/positive-sum, 84
checking instruments, 71, 74, 76–9, 87, 95; model of, 79–87
checks and balances, 14–15, 26, 28, 35, 36, 146, 321; American government, 91–2; foundations of, 41; literature on, 75; model of, 70–95, 121, 141; in parliamentary governments, 15–17; theory of democracy based on, 28–9
China, 274
choices: of principals and agents, 150, 164
churches, 30, 279, 285, 299, 305, 308, 311
"circular flow" equilibrium, 31, 32, 33
citizens, 14; assessment of government performance, 233, 234; in international competition, 267–8, 272; relationship with center heads, 149
classical federalism, 94, 208
clubs, 30, 44, 62n20, 279, 311
coalitions, 201
coercion, 13; in control of free-riding, 304; government control over, 292–3
coercion model, 13
coercive organizations: exit from, 13
collapse, 240, 246
collective action, model of, 264, 296
collective choices, 39; demand functions for, 37–8
collective ownership of political power, 124, 125; in *Vox Dei* dispensation model, 125–9; in *Vox Populi* dispensation model, 129–34
collectivities, 10, 11
collusion, 33, 34, 59, 65–6, 69, 79, 94, 123, 141–5, 146, 226, 268, 312; of agents, 166; among centers of power, 85–7, 293; and division of functions, 222, 223; forestalling, 105; inefficiencies deriving from, 176; reducing gains from, 106; between subsets of centers of power, 76; between supervisors and agents, 160–1; in *Vox Dei* dispensation, 129
collusion in hierarchies, model of, 159–61
commissions of inquiry, 77
committee system, 20, 113–18; *see also* standing committee system
common-good doctrine, 10–11
communist regimes, 124, 125
comparative advantage, 283, 289, 294, 304; in control of free-riding, 301–2; of nonprofit organizations, 282; *see also* relative efficiency
competition, 3–4, 146, 148, 311–12; breakdown of, 123, 141–5, 146–7; in budgetary processes, 96, 108–9; between bureaus in bureaucracies, 167, 176–8;

between/among centers of power, 30–4, 35, 50–1, 53, 54–5, 56, 59, 61, 62, 64, 65, 66–7, 69, 79, 94, 95, 134, 136–7, 139–40, 176–8, 279–80; concept of, 30–4; in congressional and parliamentary systems, 35; consent and repression under, 130; constraints on, 190, 223–6; as destructive force, 260; and duplication, 331–3; inducements for, 229–35; in industry, 229; international, 264–5, 266, 267–70; and market for consent, 146; between ministers, 106; models of, 14, 17, 30–1; in nonmarket sector, 280, 293; organization of, 109, 114–15, 118, 120, 121; political structure and, 135; in politics, xi–xii, 5; and relations of centers of power, 5; and repression, 127–8, 130; and stability: central governments, 228–63; structural consequences of, 331; suppliers and demanders in, 122; suppressed/imperfect/ perfect, 69; suppressing, 249; in use of checking instruments, 84; weak, in small governments, 142; and Wicksell-Lindahl efficiency, 24; *see also* horizontal competition; intergovernmental competition; intragovernmental competition; rules of competition; vertical competition
"competition for the field," 134
competitive equilibrium: in military takeovers, 144–5
competitive federalism, 188
competitive governmental systems, 188–90
competitive governmental systems, theory of, 192, 194, 200, 259, 260; and intergovernmental competition at international level, 265–76
competitive instability, 254, 262
competitive outcomes: with failure problem, 264; stability of, responsibility of central governments, 248
competitive stability: grants and, 257–8
complementarities, 210, 226
compliance: in tax collection, 205–6
composite structures, governments as, 11, 13–14, 17, 25–6
compound governments, 14, 17, 34, 70, 71–4, 84, 95, 98, 122; centers of power as, 72–4, 75; checking behavior in, 35; checks and balances in, 93–4; collusion in, 87; competitive, 24; intragovernmental competition in, 5; study of, 148
compromises, 59, 65, 70, 77–8, 87, 88, 89, 95
concealment, 160
concentration, 183, 189, 225
concentration equilibria, 194, 225

concession functions, 315–16
concessions, 70, 77–8, 87, 95
confederal government systems/states, 226,
    227, 311; constitutions, 261–2
confederalism, 224; and stability, 245–7
Congress: in congressional governments, 98
"Congress of Opinions?," 101
Congressional Budget Committee (U.S.),
    112
Congressional Budget Reform Act (U.S.), 97
congressional governments/systems, 16; ab-
    sence of budget secrecy in, 107; budgetary
    processes in, 35, 96–7, 98, 111–18, 119–
    20, 121; checks and balances in, 91–2;
    equilibrium allocations in, 110; utility
    losses in, 227; Wicksellian Connection in,
    303
consent, 41, 69, 85, 95, 122–47, 233; mea-
    sured by elections, 94; in military take-
    overs, 144; price for, 123–4; probability
    of, 48–9; substitutes for, 130; withhold-
    ing, 246; see also expected consent
consent mechanisms, 49–57
conspiracies, 222, 223, 226
constituencies: and checking instruments, 83,
    84, 85, 86; consent of, 95; informational
    problems of, 87
constituency mobilization, 77
constituent assembly(ies), 199, 200, 203,
    324; omniscient, 187–8
Constitution (Britain), 15
Constitution (Canada), 258, 324
Constitution (U.S.), 14, 91, 92, 112, 138,
    139, 193, 194, 259, 308
constitution-making stage, 21, 22
constitutional amendments, 225, 226, 248,
    261
constitutional efficiency, 21–3
constitutional entrenchment, 259, 261–2,
    271
constitutional factor, 223–6
constitutional monarchy, 5n2
constitutions, 22, 148; constraints imposed
    by, 223–6; international, 275, 276
constraints: binding nonprofit organizations,
    282–4, 285; constitutional entrenchment
    as, 262; on monitoring, 259–62
consumption behavior, 46–7, 284–5
contingency plans, 103, 106
contingency theorists, 153
contracts, 155, 158, 159, 296; incomplete,
    implicit, 8, 214–15, 221, 316–17; self-
    enforcing, 227
contract(ual) enforcement, 28, 169, 204,
    214–16, 248

contractual enforcement costs, 194, 197,
    213–21, 222, 223, 225, 226, 227
contractual relations, 214–16
control-loss, 157
conventional inputs: differential productivity
    growth of, 293–5
conventions, 71; of international regimes,
    272, 274
cooperation, 33, 191, 201, 202; internation-
    al, 264, 265, 267, 268, 271, 272; and sta-
    bility, 249–50
cooperative federalism, 191, 228, 249
cooperative governmental systems, 191
cooperatives, 30, 279, 285, 289, 290, 292,
    302, 305, 309
coordination, 33, 206, 210, 227, 248, 312
coordination costs, 191, 197, 203, 204, 208,
    209–13, 222, 223, 225, 226, 227
corporate enterprises: agency problem in,
    149
corporate law, 241–3
corporation-stockholder relations, 241–3
corporatism, 328–9
cost minimization, 187–8, 199, 200, 227
costs: of monitoring and enforcing, 46; in
    tax avoidance/evasion, 45
costs/benefits: in monitoring and enforce-
    ment, 273–4; Pareto-optimal link between,
    311; and political process, 319; Wick-
    sellian Connection, 118–19
Council of Economic Advisors (U.S.), 112
coups d'état, 143–5
Cournot-Nash equilibrium, 30, 35, 80
courts, 141; see also judiciary
covenants, 249–50, 261
Creative Destruction, 31–2, 33
Crown Corporations (Canada), 325

Dales critique, 188
debt, 43–4
decentralization, 182, 183, 246
decisionmakers: and consent, 134; military,
    144; and modes of competing, 269; politi-
    cal power of, 122
decisionmaking: congressional governments,
    114–15; governmental, 96; in organiza-
    tions, 163; in parliamentary governments,
    100, 101
decision structures, 150–1, 156, 162, 163
deconcentration, 246, 271
defense, 6, 247; and federalism, 334–5
defense expenditures, 252
Defense Intelligence Agency, 73
Delaware, 241–3

demand, 37–69, 287, 288; elastic/inelastic,
83; model of, 181; price and income elasticities of, 305; supply and, 304–8
demand, theory of, 34–5, 41–2, 69
demand curve for consent, 130
demand curves, 50–1, 87, 89; long-run, 90,
95; Wicksellian Connections, 52
demand functions, 3, 23, 28, 29, 37–8, 52,
53, 70, 121; aggregation of, 60–1;
changes in, 54; consent mechanism in,
49–57; cross-elasticities of, 57, 58, 59–
60, 302; free-riding and, 45; individual
and nominal, 42; information about, transmitted to centers of power, 63, 64, 65,
101; maximizing constrained utility functions in obtaining, 41–2; neoclassical, 46;
nonprofits and, 282; own-elasticity of, 57,
58, 59–60, 302; partial equilibrium, 38;
revelation of, 39, 68, 227; unstable, 44;
and utility losses, 222–3
demand lobbies, 34–5, 41, 57–66, 69, 78,
87, 101, 223; aggregation and interaction
of, with centers of power, 59–61; and collusion, 87
demand price of consent, 124, 128
demand revelation, 3, 34, 48–57, 311, 328
demand revelation mechanism, 39–40, 41,
42, 46, 57–9, 90
demand side: of consent market, 124, 125,
129
demobilization: restrictions on, 144–5
democracy(ies), 4, 5, 6, 14, 17, 92, 146;
centers of power, 48; checks and balances,
70; competition among, 268; consent in,
134; jurisdictional levels, 191–2; multilevel, 181–2; organizational features of,
13; preferences of citizens in, 29; requisites of, 24–9; rules for, 70–1; as suppliers of goods and services, 34
democratic theory, 24–5
dependency hypothesis, 266
derived demand, theory of, 319–20
desirability of cooperation, 264, 265
despotic regimes, 29
deus ex machina, 188
development policies, 251–2, 253–4
dictatorships, 6, 87, 131–4; classes of,
132–4
differential growth: in ability to acquire information, 302–4; in capacity to control
free-riding, 295–302
differential productivity growth: of conventional inputs, 293–5
diffusion of policies and programs, 235–7;
stability and, 241–3

dilemma of mobility, 191–2
direct democracy, 39, 164, 303
discretion, 177
discretionary budgets, 164
discretionary power model, 155, 162–7, 168
diseconomies of scale, 205, 213
dismissal, 158, 159
dispensations, 124, 125; *Vox Dei,* 125–9;
Vox Populi, 129–34, 146
dissent, 126–7
distortion, 160, 200
diversification: of supply/demand, 280–1,
282–3; of supply sources, 289, 304
divided sovereignty, 276
divine right of rulers, 125, 128–9
divine will: as foundation of political legitimacy, 124, 125–9
division of functions, 189, 194, 196, 203,
216–17, 226, 227; characteristics of, 208–
9; and contractual enforcement costs,
218–19; in European Union, 275; factors
in, 222–3; international, 271; optimal,
219; technology and, 203, 204–9
division of labor, 306
division of powers, 184–6, 188, 190, 193,
194, 196, 199, 201, 226, 228, 249; challenging, 248; constitutionally entrenched,
203, 226, 227; constraints imposed by,
223–6; and division of functions, 223; in
European Union, 275; international, 271,
275; interstate federalism and, 260; model
of, 187
doctrine of instruction, 92n13, 139
doctrines, 9–11
duplication, 209, 331–3
dynamics, 32, 33

Eastern Europe, 17
Economic Constitution of Federal States, The
(Breton and Scott), 187, 204
economic integration, 299, 307
economic nationalism, 291
economic policy, 332–3
economic regulation, theory of, 6
*Economic Theory of Representative Govern-
ment* (Breton), xi
Economics of Politics, xi, 4
economies of scale, 130, 131, 201, 204–5,
207, 209, 212, 216, 283, 307; and coordination costs, 213; differential, 295; in
information gathering, 223; in tax collection, 214, 217, 218
efficiency, 202; bureaucratic behavior and,
178; concepts of, 4–5, 17–24; cost of enforcing property rights and, 9; distinct

efficiency (*cont.*)
from stability, 240; and diversification of demand, 283–4; exogenously improved, 19; grants in, 257; of long-term budget deficits, 316–17; problem of, 248; redistribution and, 9; of regional policies, 253
efficiency argument, 198, 201–2
efficiency wages, 175, 196, 300
efficient bureaus/bureaucracies: models of, 167–78
efficient management, 185
elected centers of power, 5, 29, 48, 74; balance and, 93–4; and checking instruments, 85
elected governing party(ies), 53
election, selection by, 142
election forecasting/postcasting, 38
elections/electoral contests, xii, 25, 26–7, 28, 34, 83–4, 94, 110, 148, 281; demand functions revealed in, 38
electoral competition, 291–2
electoral platforms, 27, 281
endogenous factors: in growth of governments, 287–8
endowments, 54; distribution of, 138, 140–1, 145, 146
enforcement, 45, 194, 207, 262, 272; costs/benefits of, 203, 273–4; in free-riding, 301; in networks, 169; of resource allocations, 109–10; tax collection, 205–6; third-party, 215, 217
enforcement mechanisms, 9, 193
enforcement of contracts, 204
enfranchisement, 135–7
England, 15–16; *see also* Great Britain
English Constitution, The (Bagehot), 14–15, 125
entitlements, 146, 304, 305; distribution of, 138, 139–40
entrenched assignments: constraining competition, 190
entrepreneurial competition model, 31–4
entrepreneurs, political, 33–4
entrepreneurship, 31–4, 70, 238; *see also* Schumpeterian entrepreneurship
equalization payments, 198, 219, 256–7
equilibrium(a), xi, xii; budgetary, 35; and growth, 304–8; in market for consent, 35; neoclassical, 31; stable, 240; under *Vox Populi* dispensation, 131
equilibrium allocations: commitment to existing, 111; enforcement of, 109–10
equilibrium assignment of powers, 187
equilibrium division of functions, 191, 197
equilibrium division of powers, 191
equilibrium information structure, 150

equilibrium organization of governmental systems, 187
equilibrium outcomes, 3, 191, 213; bargaining in, 102–6; consent market, 146; first-best, 68, 69
equilibrium price of consent, 124–5, 146
equilibrium volume: of tax avoidance/evasion, 45, 46
equilibrium volume of consent: *Vox Dei/Vox Populi* dispensations, 132–4
equity, 198, 202, 257
equivalence principle, 161
ethical codes/norms, 301
European Parliament, 275, 276
European Union, 266, 275–6; Council of Ministers, 275
excess burden (tax payments), 55–6, 221
exchange relations: family relations as, 300–1, 316–17
exclusive territories, 208
Executive (the): in Congressional systems, 102
executive branch, 72
Executive branch (U.S.): and budgetary process, 112–13, 117–18
executive federalism, 228
exit: threat of, 13, 237
exogeneity assumption, 197–8
exogenous events/shocks, 117, 246; and budget deficits, 316, 317; and competing centers of power, 129; and efficiency of checking instruments, 82–3; and ownership of functions, 224, 225; in growth of governments, 287–8
expected consent, 41, 48, 80, 83, 84, 122; maximization of, 49, 52–7, 61, 63–4, 74, 79, 86, 87, 181, 237
expenditure and regulatory functions, 203, 205, 213
expenditure budgets, 97, 100, 120, 121; U.S., 112, 113, 118
expenditure budgetary process: Canada, 108–9
expenditure budgeting, 111
expenditure concentration, 183, 184, 190, 216, 217, 221, 226, 247; equilibrium, 224; information costs and, 223
expenditure decisions, 3, 21, 22, 23, 197, 198
expenditure responsibilities, 200, 201
expenditures: relationship with revenues, 44, 226
extended franchise, theory of, 6
external benchmark mechanism, 233–5
external secrecy, 106–7
externalities, 186–7, 240; and coordination,

210; and free-riding, 295; internalized, 201; and world order, 265
externalities, theory of, 264, 287
externalization, 84

factions, 25
factors of production: demand curves for, 130
falsification of information, 59, 64, 65
falsification of preferences, 13, 18, 45
families, 30, 308, 309, 311; change in, 301–2; and free-riding, 300–1; suppliers of goods and services, 279, 285, 289–90, 292, 293, 297, 302, 305, 306
families (houses): holding political power, 124
Family Compact (Canada), 143
family relationships: as exchange relationships, 300–1, 316–17; government intervention in, 300
Fathers (Mothers) of the Governmental System, 224
Federal Bureau of Investigation, 73
Federal Corporate Uniformity Act (proposed), 251n12
federal governmental systems, 193, 199, 201–2, 226, 227, 311; assignment of powers, 228; constitutional amendments, 225; constitutions, 261–2; structure and stability of, 334–5
federalism, xi, 94, 182, 184, 186, 224, 225; competitive, 188; and grants, 257; intrastate, 260–1, 274; and stability, 245–6
Federalist, The, 14, 25, 139–40, 193, 194, 195, 246–7, 248, 262
federations, 218–19; centralized/decentralized, 229
feeling of moral obligation to obey, 125, 126
fiscal change: and population migration, 235, 238–9
fiscal illusion, 197, 200, 220, 226
fiscal imbalance, 196, 197–23, 226, 227, 254–5, 315
fiscal residuum, 198
fiscal variables: and political mobility, 239
flow of funds, intergovernmental, 197–8, 199, 209, 214, 221, 226, 227; contracts in, 215; explanation of, 220–1
flypaper effect, 219, 220, 221
force: consent and, 122; place of, in politics, 35
formal structures, 150–3, 154–5, 159; authority derived from, 165; manipulation of, 172–3, 174, 176
Founding Fathers, 92; of American Constitution, 193–4

Founding Fathers/Mothers, 224
France, 70, 107n12, 181, 182, 206, 261, 306; Constitution of the Fifth Republic, 16; Executive Branch, 16
franchise, 35, 138, 146; effect of, on distribution of entitlements, 137–8, 139–40; size of, 25; universal, 140, 145
fraud, 45, 284
free-riding, 4, 41, 54, 63, 137, 319, 328; capacity to control, 283–4, 306, 307, 308; differential growth in capacity to control, 295–302; in nonprofit organizations, 281, 282, 304, 305; in small groups, 318; and utility maximization, 42, 44–6
freedom of information laws, 87
French Revolution, 125
functions, 194, 222, 224; assignment of, 184–5, 187, 209–10, 223; coordination costs and, 212–13; distinct from powers, 183–4; *see also* division of functions

games, theory of, 8–9, 264
Germany, 231
gifts/bequests, 8, 316–17
gifts by rulers, 128
global economic integration: and tax evasion, 299; *see also* world order
global instability, 240, 241
God: as source of all authority, 125
goods and services, xii; alternative suppliers of, 121; complex, 59; defined, 5–9; demand for, 217; entry for, 66; distribution of supply flows of, 190; as Lancasterian characteristics, 57; link between taxprices and valuation of, 23–4 (*see also* Wicksellian Connections); nonmarket-provided, 3; partial equilibrium demand functions for, 38; production of, 63–4; provision of, through redistribution, 9; quantities of, desired by households, 37; relationship with taxation, 19; supplied by centers of power, 34; supplied by nonprofit organizations, 280–2; supply of, 70, 148; *see also* government-supplied goods and services
goods are goods assumption, 284–5, 288, 293
governability, 127; production of, 130, 131; repression and, 134
government(s): balanced, 93–4; competitive, 3–5; models of, 4, 9–17; as monopolies, xi, 12–13, 281, 292–3; role of, 10; size of, 142, 143
government expenditures, growth of, 307–8
government funding: of demand lobbies, 62–3, 64

government-supplied goods and services, 12,
40, 192, 260, 288, 289, 307, 311; aggregated into classes, 184; demand functions
for, 38–9; imposed on population, 46–7;
international, 270, 271; intragovernmental
competition as revelation mechanism for,
147; jurisdictional levels and, 209; revelation of demand for, 330; supply of, 148
government transfers, 305–6
governmental contributions: to special-
interest groups, 141
governmental organizations, 40
governmental production and supply, 70, 72,
83–4, 87, 90, 95; definitions and assumptions, 74–9
governmental system (the), 181
governmental systems: competitive, 188–90;
doctrines of, 194; equilibrium organization
of, 187; ideal, 185; organization of, 196–
227, 229; theory of, 182–3; vertical relations in, 183; and world order, 265–6; see
also competitive governmental systems,
theory of
governments, 181; and free-riding, 299;
growth of, 286–309; and income redistribution, 291–2; and intergenerational
contracts, 316–17; and international competition, 267–8; and market failure, 265;
as monopolists, 281, 292–3
grants, 43, 185, 196, 198, 219–21, 227,
253, 254–8; conditional, 215, 258; and
horizontal competition, 250, 254–8; inefficiency of, 255–6; and political mobility,
239; substitution/income effects, 215, 220;
unconditional, 258
Great Britain, 90–1n12, 97, 181–2; House
of Lords, 260
Gresham's law, 241
growth: equilibrium and, 304–8
growth of competitive governments (model),
280
growth of governments: and changes in agricultural employment, 306; models of, 305

hegemonic powers/hegemons, 265, 266,
272–5
hidden action model, 156–7
hidden information (problem), 158
hidden information models, 156
hierarchy(ies), 148–78; of governmental systems, 186; models of, 148; organizational,
36; in principal-agent relationship, 161;
problem of, 149–54
Holland, 267
horizontal competition, 189, 190–4, 228,

229, 246, 247; central governments monitoring, 248, 250–8, 262, 263; monitoring
international, 274–6; potential entry and
exit mechanism, 230–2; and stability, 229,
240–5
horizontal/lateral networks/relationships, 152,
162, 164, 167, 169, 171, 172, 176, 183
horizontal trust networks, 173
hostile takeovers, 41, 94
House: in Congressional systems, 102
House of Commons: in parliamentary governments, 98, 99, 110
households: consumption behavior, 50, 51,
284–5; demand responses of, 37, 40
housing policy function, 213
hubris, 41, 69, 259
human capital, 9, 43; intergenerational contract for, 316–17; trust as, 169, 173
human relations, 151
Human Relations school, 161n8

ideal form of government, 202
"ideal type," 151
ideological constituencies, 84
ideologies, 33–4, 130, 131
imitation/imitators, 31, 32, 33, 34
imperfect information, model of, 30, 31, 155
imperfect markets, 30
imperfect monitoring, models of, 155
imperialism, 266
impersonal dictatorships, 133, 134
impoundments, 118, 120
incentive-compatible contract(s), 157
incentive contracts, 155, 162
incentives: insurance and, 157, 160
income(s), 50; changes in, 37, 40; property
rights and distribution of, 8–9; spent by
governments: rich and poor countries,
305–6; see also income redistribution
income insurance, 7, 9
income redistribution, 4, 5, 18, 243–4, 254–
5, 284–5, 305; and free-riding, 295; multisource supply of, 289–91; preference-
based rationale for, 7
income redistribution argument, 202–3
income redistribution policy, 255–6
incomplete information, 156
India, 17
individual ownership of political power, 124,
125; in Vox Dei dispensation model, 125–
9; in Vox Populi dispensation model, 129–
34
indoctrination, 130, 131
industrial psychologists, 151
industry, organization of, 229

inefficient bureaus: models of, 148, 155–67
informal services, 169–70
informal structures, 150–3, 154, 159–60, 161–2, 167, 168–9, 176; defined, 151; horizontal relations in, 164, 165–6; networks and, 172
informal trades, 111
informal transactions, 152–3
informal transactions model, 167–72, 173–4, 176
information, 23, 28, 306; ability to obtain, 106–7, 284, 308; asymmetric, 65–6, 251; asymmetrically distributed between principals and agents, 150, 162, 164, 168; conveyed to ministers, 101, 102; differential growth in ability to acquire, 302–4, 308; incomplete, 156; junior governments and, 223; lack of, 27; need for, 57–9; needed by principals, 169–70; planting, 77; about preferences and utility losses, 101, 102; power to obtain, 77; and pressure, 326–7; transmitted by demand lobbies, 35, 58, 59, 60, 63–4, 65; used to evaluate performance, 233; and Wicksellian Connection, 67–8
information costs, 222–3
information falsification, 59, 64, 65
information gathering, problem of, 308
information leakages, 169
information problems, 50–1, 55, 57; and collusion, 87
information structures, 150–1, 156, 157, 160, 162, 163–4, 166, 168–9, 171; characteristics of, 163, 165, 168
infrastructure projects, 252
innovation, 31–3, 34, 41
instability, competitive, 249
institutional factors: constraining vertical competition, 194
institutional instability, 240–8
institutions (government): and budgetary equilibria, 96
insurance: and incentives, 157, 160
"interest function" approach, 61
interest-group capture models, 11–12
interest groups, 4, 48, 58, 62, 148, 171, 223, 287; competing over spoils, 316; in demand revelation process, 34–5
interests/issues: of demand lobbies, 60
intergenerational social compact, 316–17
intergovernmental competition, 3, 181–95, 202, 226, 227, 262–3, 311, 312; as central organizing principle, 194; empirical evidence of, 235–40; external benchmark mechanism, 233–5; at international level,

265–76; mechanisms motivating, 229–35; models of, 191; organization of government and, 229; and productive capacity, 203; unstable outcomes, 194–5
intergovernmental interactions, 228–9; competitive, 239
intergovernmental relations, 227; horizontal/vertical, 249; jurisdictional levels in, 182–95; political mobility and, 239; theory of tournaments applied to, 234
intergovernmental transfers, 201, 202–3
interjurisdictional spillovers, 198, 228, 254–5; efficient management of, 185–6, 187; international, 265; see also jurisdictional spillovers
internal competition, 132, 143
internal organization of single bureaus, 167–76
internal relationships of centers of power, 149–55
"internal" secrecy, 106–7
international arena: competitiveness of governments in, 195, 239–40; see also world order
international organizations, 264, 270, 271, 272
international political economy literature, 265
international regimes, 265, 266, 271–5
international trade, theory of, 293–4
interpersonal transfers, 202, 255, 256–7
intragovernmental competition, 3, 16, 24, 34, 35, 69, 181, 226, 311; breakdown of, 143–5; in compound governments, 5; organization of, 121; as revelation mechanism, 147
intraorganizational problem, 149–55, 162
intrastate federalism, 259, 260–1, 274
Israel, 17
Italy, 70, 181, 182, 306; *mani pulite* (clean hands) operation, 73n3

Japan, 17
"Japanese firm," 172–3, 174, 175
Jevons Law of Indifference, 54
judicial reinterpretation, 225, 261
judicial review, 76, 92, 225, 248, 324
judiciary(ies), 72–3, 74; independence of, 321–5
junior governments, 188, 193, 202, 208, 259; efficiency of, 246; goods and services supplied by, 198, 222; information for, 223; ownership of functions, 224; and revenue collection function, 214, 215–21; and tax harmonization, 211

jurisdictional domains, 182, 184, 185, 186, 189, 191–2, 193, 200, 229; assignment of powers to, 199; competition between, 244, 247; and division of functions, 208–9, 223–6; and division of powers, 228; in intergovernmental relationships, 183–95; and tax avoidance/evasion, 207
jurisdictional spillovers, 199, 200, 201, 202, 209–10, 221, 226; see also interjurisdictional spillovers
jurisdictions: diffusion of policies and programs, 235–7

Keynesian macroeconomics, 198
kinship networks, 289–90, 308

labor mobility, 202, 257–8, 302, 306, 308
labor market tournaments, 233–4
labor policy function, 205, 210
labor productivity, growth of, 294
labor unions, 30, 279, 311, 328–9; power of, 319
Lancasterian characteristics of goods and services, 40, 57
"Law of Increasing State Activity," 286
Law of Indifference, 54
leaders/leadership: in economic life, 32
legislation, 321–3, 324
legislative assemblies, 23–4, 73
legislative branch, 72
legislative policies: and programs implementing and enforcing, 77; indices of diffusion of, 235–7
legislators: benefits received by, 321, 322–3, 324, 325
leviathan model, 12, 13
Lindahl prices, 43n10
lobbies, 35, 102; see also demand lobbies
lobby managers, 59, 65; reverse shirking by, 59, 62, 64
lobby members: shirking by, 59, 61–4
lobbying, 58, 326–7
local governments: collusion in, 87; competition between, 30–1; and undesired potential entry and exit, 232
local instability, 240, 241
local public goods, 188, 230–2, 238
locational/spatial competition theory, 31
logrolling, 20, 39, 41, 115–16, 303; in congressional governments, 120, 121; restricted, 117; stable equilibrium, 115–17
loyalty, 175

machine politics, 142–3
macroeconomic variables, 38
Madisonian democracy, 25–6

Madisonians, 28
majoritarian principle, 281
majority rule, 25–6
management: of demand lobbies, 64, 65; problems of, 36
management-worker problem, 149
managerial competition, 177–8
Marbury v. Madison, 92
marginal taxprices, 43, 45, 46, 54, 81; changes in, 54–5, 214
marginal utility losses, 126, 305
marginal utility of wealth, 134
market competition, 307
market economy: excess capacity, 332–3
market failure, 264–5, 270, 271, 287
market for consent, 35, 123–4, 146–7; early American republic, 139; polar models of, 124–34; U.S. House of Representatives and, 135–9
market for managers, 177
market-provided goods and services, 37, 46, 47, 49; demand functions for, 38–9
market size: and specialization, 204–5
markets, 66, 306, 308; and free-riding, 296–7, 298–9
markets, theory of, 16
master-servant relationship, 201, 221, 259
maximization of sales theory, 163
maximization procedures, 41
median voter model/theory, 38, 221, 287
megalomania, 41, 69
merger, 129
Mexico, 17, 252
microeconomic theory, 69, 281–2, 288
military dictatorship, 143–4
military regimes: unstable, 143–4, 145
military takeovers, 143–5, 146–7
Minister of Finance, 99, 100, 103, 105, 106, 120; power of, 107, 108; in parliamentary governments, 110, 114, 118, 119
ministers, 103, 104, 105–6, 110; bargaining strategies of, 108; in parliamentary systems, 98–9, 100, 101, 118, 119; relationship with senior bureaucracy, 110–11
minorities, 12, 85; "passionate," 83
misrepresentation-of-costs strategy, 165, 166
misrepresentation of information, 165
mixed governments, 71, 72
mobility, 254; capital/labor/technology, 189, 191, 254–5, 257–8; interjurisdictional, 254
mobility of persons: as competitive force, 191–2
model(s) of government, 5, 9–17
"modified Westphalia system," 267n6
monarchy, 14, 92

monitoring, 45, 157, 158, 166, 262, 272; costs/benefits of, 273–4; effectiveness of, 158–9; of international competition, 270, 271–5; by junior governments, 215; responsibility for, 193; vertical competition, 258–62

monitoring function of central governments, 248, 249–62, 335

monitoring responsibilities of governments: international, 270

monitor(s), 193; central governments as, 229, 248–62, 263; reasons to use, 249–50

monoliths, governments as, 11, 12, 40

monopolistic competition, 283

monopolists, 166; governments as, 281

monopolists (oligopolists), 54

monopoly, 12–13, 208, 237, 312; by central governments, 208; governments as, xi, 12–13, 292–3; over coercion, 13

monopsonists (oligopsonists), 54, 126–7

monopsony, 127, 129, 130, 146

moral codes, 301; and free-riding, 296, 297

moral hazard, 156, 251, 296

motivation(s), 69, 122; to use consent mechanism, 49–52

multitier governmental systems, 246; centralization in, 184; vertical imbalance and flow of funds in, 198

Nash equilibrium, 61, 64, 119, 315

Nash equilibrium outcomes, 103, 106, 107–8

national sovereignty, 271

natural entropy, 169–70, 171

negotiations, 225, 226, 248, 303

neoclassical economics, 7, 54, 264

neoclassical paradigm, 33

neoclassical theory, 28, 30, 33; equilibrium in, 31, 32

neo-Madisonian theory of democracy, 5, 6, 25, 28

network exchanges, 174

network of trust relationships: bureaucracy as, 111

networks, 169–70

neutrality: in tax reform, 19

New Harmony, Indiana, 290

New Principle of Just Taxation, A (Wicksell), 22

New Zealand, 110

nondistribution constraints, 282–4, 285

nonelected centers of power, xii, 29, 40–1, 48, 49, 74; balance and, 93–4; and checking instruments, 95

nongovernmental agencies, 47; supplying goods and services, 288, 289–91

nongovernment-nonmarket institutions, 279–80, 283, 306

nonmarket sector: size of, 279–85

nonprofit organizations, 280–4

nonprofit sector, 279

norm of beneficence, 152n2

norm of reciprocity, 152n2

norms, 152n2, 169

North American Free Trade Agreement, 252

Office of Management and Budget (OMB) (U.S.), 112

old-age pensions, 284–5, 289

oligopoly theory, 86, 237

oligopsony, 129, 146

omniscient decisionmakers, 187, 188

openness of economy, 306–7

opposition parties, 53, 61, 72, 189; Canada, 15; in parliamentary systems, 72, 91, 102

optimal contract theory, 64

optimal currency areas, 184n5

optimal tax theory, 18–19

optimum tariffs, theory of, 211n11

Orbiston (Scotland), 290

organicist model (government), 10, 11, 12, 17, 40

organizations, agency model of, 155, 156

output: measurement of, 294–5

overlap, 209, 331–3

ownership: divided, 193–4

ownership of functions, 224–6, 227

ownership of powers, 261

parents/children relationship, 8, 316–17

Pareto efficiency, 87; supply of goods and services, 23

Pareto optimality, 311; in legislative decisions, 23–4; Wicksellian Connection, 68, 69, 95

Parkinson's law, 175–6

Parliament, 98–9

parliamentary debates, 101

parliamentary governments/systems, 15–17, 114; budgetary processes in, 35, 96–7, 98–111, 118–19, 120, 121; checks and balances in, 90–3; opposition parties in, 72, 91, 102; party discipline in, 185; Prime Minister in, 92–3; utility losses in, 227; Wicksellian Connections in, 303

parliamentary monarch, 5n2

parliaments, 311

partial equilibrium frameworks, 127, 130

party discipline, 102, 115

party leadership, 113, 117; control of, 96; control of committee agendas, 115–17

payments, 177–8; and vertical trust, 174–5

perfect competition, 43, 129, 130, 133, 178
perfect competition model, 30–1
perfect competition in prices (paradigm), 55
perfect markets (concept), 30
personal dictatorships, 133–4
Philadelphia Convention, 91
Pigovian subsidies, 185, 198, 221
planning, 332
policing function, 193
policy(ies): slanting, 77
Policy and Expenditure Management System
    (PEMs) (Canada), 108–9
policy and program diffusion: stability in,
    241–3
policy harmonization: European Union,
    275–6
political consent: market for, 146–7; model
    of, 123–34
political equilibria, 125; suffrage and, 139,
    140, 141
political information, 86–7
political legitimacy: foundations of, 124,
    129–30; *Vox Dei* dispensation model,
    125–9; *Vox Populi* dispensation model,
    129–34
political market failure, 20
political media, 86–7
political mobility, 191–2; estimates of, 238–
    9; and stability, 243–5
political parties, 28, 61, 73n4, 101; checking
    instruments used by, 84; and collusion,
    142; enforcing equilibrium allocations,
    109–10; rivalry of, 31; *see also* opposition
    parties
political power, 48, 122–3; dispersion of,
    75; individually or collectively owned,
    124, 125; of military, 144, 145
political pressure, 207, 318
Political Science literature, 4
political scientists, 58–9, 191
political structures: U.S., 135
politicians, 149
politico-economic approach, 38–9
politics, 7, 123, 281; bureaucratic, 269;
    competitive, xi–xii, 5, 77; economic anal-
    ysis of, 3–4; entry/exit, 140; equilibrium
    outcomes, 3; essentials of, 26–7; game of,
    41; model of, 321; motives in, 122; power
    and, 48; theory of, 27; as zero-sum enter-
    prise, 6–7
Politics and Public Finance theory, 3, 26n18
Politics and Public Finance: Wicksellian the-
    ory of, 4
poll and survey data, 58
polls/polling, 49, 58, 223

popular will: as foundation of political legit-
    imacy, 124, 129–34
population: equilibrium partition of, 230–2,
    234
population migration: elasticity of, 235,
    238–9
potential entry and exit mechanism, 230–2,
    233, 237
power: in centers of power, 150, 153; and
    politics, 48; and repression, 127; of small
    groups, 318–20
power to obstruct, 77
powers, 184, 194, 224; distinct from func-
    tions, 183–4; *see also* division of powers
Preface to Democratic Theory, A (Dahl),
    24–5
preference revelation device(s), 230–2
preferences, 54, 107, 222; and budget(s),
    102; for characteristics of goods and ser-
    vices, 59, 60; and competition, 234; falsi-
    fication of, 13, 18, 45; identical, 255;
    imperfect information on, 50–1; informa-
    tion in, 59, 64, 223; intensity of, 83–4,
    303; and international competition, 267,
    268; and jurisdictional levels, 78, 192;
    misrepresenting, 44, 45; and principle of
    responsiveness, 186; in/and redistribution,
    7–9
preferences-based rationale for redistribution,
    318–20
presidency (the), 96; role of, 117–18, 121
Presidency (U.S.), 138–9
President (the): in congressional systems, 98
President (U.S.), 135, 322n3; and budgetary
    process, 112–13
pressure, political, 101; information and,
    326–7
pressure groups, 4, 19–20, 58, 62; in de-
    mand revelation process, 34–5; theory
    of, 6
pressure politics, 4, 48
price competition, 56–7, 240; *see also* price
    rivalry
price formation and adjustment, 235; lack of
    theory for, 54
price of consent, 133, 146
price rivalry: analysis of, 239–40; and stabil-
    ity, 245
prices: influences on, 54–5
Prime Minister, 101, 103–4, 108; in parlia-
    mentary governments, 99, 100, 110
prime ministerial power, 96, 102, 105, 106,
    107, 108, 119; limits of, 104
prime ministerial shadow, 119

principal-agent model, 155–62, 163, 166, 167, 168
principal-agent networks/relationships, 41, 61, 152, 154, 208, 296; implications for, of competition between centers of power, 177–8
principal-agent problem, 157
principals, 149; active, 167–76; and asymmetric distribution of information, 150; and informal structures, 152; passive, 162, 166–7, 177, 178; role of, 148
principle of responsiveness, 185–6
principle of subsidiarity, 185, 186
Prisoners' Dilemma problem, 24, 161, 264, 268–9
private goods: and free-riding, 295–6; government-supplied, 68–9
probabilistic voting, 61, 26n18
probabilities, externalization of, 48–9
probabilities of consent: information regarding, 60, 63
process of federalism, 225–6
product differentiation, 281–2, 283
prohibitions and standards, 250–1
proletariat, 140–1
property rights, 270; and distribution of income and wealth, 8–9; enforcement of, 273
property rights theory, 264, 271, 272
proportional representation, 86
provincial/state governments, 200–2, 249; competitive stability, 257–8; as conduits for transfers, 255; and excess immigration, 232; values and interests of, 261
Public Choice, xi, 312; literature, 4, 18, 20, 25, 26, 36, 230
Public Economics, 4, 5; literature, 18; Public Finance, 19, 205–6, 226, 230, 239; model, 3
Public Finance (Public Economics), 196
public finances: of real-world governments, 4
public goods, 4, 13, 68, 184–5, 222, 284; and free-riding, 295, 296; international, 265, 269–70; and misrepresentation of preferences, 19
public goods, theory of, 18, 264, 287
public sector, 49–50, 181, 281; institutional makeup of, 121

quasi-rents, stream of, 216–17, 218–19
Quebec, 212, 219
"Queen's model," 202
Queenwood (England), 290
Quiet Revolution (Quebec), 290

Ralahine (Ireland), 290
rank-order tournaments, economic theory of, 189
reciprocity, 152
redistribution, 4, 6–9, 12, 19, 66; rationale for, 318–20; see also income redistribution
redistribution functions, 198
redistribution powers, 184
referenda, 39, 303
regimes, 271–2
regional policies, 250, 251–4
regulation, 9, 141, 286
regulatory function, 203, 205, 213
regulatory process, 96, 311
relative efficiency, 283–4, 289, 291, 303; determinants of, 293–304; market forces and, 307; of supply sources, 292–3, 305, 308–9
religious, humanitarian, and other eleemosynary organizations, 279, 285, 289, 290, 292, 293, 297, 301–2, 305, 309; and free-riding problem, 299–300
remittances, 214, 216–18, 224, 258
Renaissance Venice, 15, 138
rent-seeking, 59, 65–6, 69, 291–2
rent-seeking, models of, 27, 35; theory of, 6
rents, 12, 178; accruing to dictators, 133; accruing to public sector, 131; lobbies and, 35
reorganization, 171, 173, 176
Report of the Royal Commission on the Economic Union and Development Prospects for Canada, 188
representative democracies: utility losses, 303
repression, 127, 129; amount used to produce governability, 131, 132, 134; under autocratic rule, 130–1; consent and, 122; monopoly over, in military takeovers, 145

republican principle, 25–6
reputation, 149, 159, 284; theory of, 264
resale price maintenance, 208
research and development, 252
resource allocation: in monitoring and enforcement, 272, 273–4; structural changes and, 109; and utility losses, 226
resources: consumed in production of goods and services, 43
responsiveness, 185–6
revelation mechanisms, 37–8; analysis of, 38–9; intragovernmental competition as, 147; see also demand revelation mechanism

revenue budget/budgeting, 97, 99, 106, 107, 111, 120, 121; U.S., 112–13, 118
revenue concentration, 183, 184, 190, 206n8, 207, 208, 209, 212, 213–14, 217, 221, 226, 247; equilibrium, 224, 225; information costs and, 223
revenue function, 203, 205–7, 209, 212, 213–14
revenue payments, 214, 216–18, 219, 224, 258
revenue responsibilities, 200, 201
Revenue Sharing (U.S.), 258
revenues: relation with expenditures, 226
reverse cheating, 215, 219
reverse shirking, 59, 62, 64, 69
Rotten Kid Theorem, 300
Rousseauesque social contract, 8
routine/nonroutine dichotomy, 150, 154–5
Royal Commission on Dominion-Provincial Relations (Canada), 242
rules, 93, 124, 125; bureaucratic, 175; for democratic governments, 70–1
rules of competition, 70–1, 192–3, 223–4, 246; central governments as monitors of, 229, 248–62; enforcing, 195, 272–3, 274, 275–6; monitoring and implementing, 248, 249, 250, 335
Russia, 17, 132

Salmon mechanism, 189, 192, 194, 229–30, 233–5, 237, 257, 262, 266, 267, 276
Schumpeterian entrepreneurship, 31–2, 70, 78, 88, 269
scientific management, 151, 154
secrecy: breach of, 102; and collusion, 142; rule of, 101–2; *see also* budget secrecy
secularization, 301–2, 306, 308
Sedition Act (U.S.), 138–9
selective behavior, 168, 170–1, 177–8
self-enforcing agreements, 264
self-enforcement, 215–16, 227, 249–50
self-interest, 23
self-interest doctrine, 10, 11–14, 17
Senate: in Congressional systems, 102
senators, 101
senior government(s), 201–2; goods and services provided by, 222; ownership of functions, 224; revenue collection by, 214, 215–21; revenue policy function of, 207; and utility losses, 246
seniority, 20, 113, 116
separation of ownership and control, 149, 177
separation of powers, 14–15, 26, 71–3, 75; literature on, 72–3; in parliamentary governments, 15–17; U.S. government, 91

services: supplied by nonprofit organizations, 284–5, 304–5; *see also* goods and services
shirking, 282, 296; by agents, 155, 157; by lobby members, 59, 61–4, 69; monitoring and, 158–9; by senior governments, 215, 216
Shirley (Brontë), 9
"simplifiers," 14n7, 15
simultaneity, 21, 22, 23, 24, 89; in budgetary processes, 119, 120; in valuation of costs and benefits, 119
situational factors: and formal/informal structures, 152, 153
size of governments, 287
small groups: power of, 9, 318–20
social change: and free-riding, 302
social compact, 8
social contract, 8, 21n13
social disruption, 319, 320
social institutions, 311
social interaction, 151
social insurance, redistribution as, 8
social norms, 300
social pressures: and free-riding, 296, 297, 299, 301
Social Sciences and Humanities Research Council (Canada), 260
social services, delivery of, 289–91
social welfare, maximization of, 23
social welfare function (SWF), 18, 19
sociological literature, 150, 151, 152, 153, 161–2, 174
South America, 17
sovereignty, 271, 272, 276
sovereignty, theory of, 228
Soviet Union, 132, 176, 225, 229, 266, 273, 274; *see also* Russia
Spain, 181, 206
span(s), 184n6, 198
special interest groups: government contributions to, 141; *see also* interest groups
special-interest legislation, 141, 145, 321–2, 323, 324, 325
specialization, 190, 194, 200, 203–5, 226, 227, 304, 306, 331, 332; insufficient/excessive, 226; marginal benefits of, 212; of supply sources, 289
"Speech to the Electors of Bristol" (Burke), 137n14
spillovers model, 260; *see also* interjurisdictional spillovers *and* jurisdictional spillovers
stability: competition and: central governments and, 228–63; of federal states, 334–5; under horizontal competition, 229,

240–5; international, 275–6; securing, 248–62; and vertical competition, 229, 245–8

stability problem: use of monitors in, 248–62

stabilization functions, 198

stabilization powers, 184

stabilizing grants, 253, 258

standards: as monitoring device, 251

standing committee system, 96, 110, 115, 116–17

strategies: of principals and agents, 150, 164, 165–6

structure of governmental systems, 184, 185, 225–6; of federal systems, 334–5

stylized structure(s): budgetary processes, 111, 112–14; parliamentary governments, 98–101

subsidiarity, 186

subsidies, 252–3; agricultural, 318; to nonprofit organizations, 283–4

substitution, 41, 42, 46–8

suffrage, 122–3, 134–41; demand for, 144; volume of, 146

supervisors, 154, 160

supervisory hierarchy, 157–8

supply, xii, 26, 54; competition among sources of, 30; and demand, 304–8; determinants of, 288–304; theory of, 28, 286, 287, 288

supply outcomes, 65, 66; active principals in, 176

supply price of consent, 123–4, 126, 128–9, 132, 136; in Vox Populi dispensation, 130

supply responsibilities, 226; international, 270

supply side, xii, 4, 27, 28, 37n1; of consent market, 124, 125

supply sources: competition among, 292; relative efficiency of, 290, 302, 308–9

support, 122–3, 134–41; in military takeovers, 144; volume of, 146

surrogate Vox Dei dispensation, 129

Swiss Confederacy, 247

Switzerland, 231, 303

"tagging," 255, 256

take-it-or-leave-it choices, theory of, 164, 165, 166

takeovers, 41, 143–4; see also military takeovers

takings, 160, 164, 166, 167, 170, 171, 177–8; and horizontal trust, 174

tax administration/collection, 205–7

tax avoidance/evasion, 45–6, 54, 206–7, 216, 298–9

tax bases/rates, 43, 45, 207, 210, 245, 298, 328

tax collection, 213, 214

Tax Collection Agreements (Canada), 212, 214, 258

tax competition, 188

tax enforcement: and free-riding, 296, 297–8, 302, 307

tax harmonization, 188, 189, 191, 211–12, 221; costs of, 217

taxation/taxes, 18, 43, 120, 298, 328; and budget deficits, 316; deadweight costs of, 316, 318; distortive function of, 46–7; and expected consent, 54–7; relation of goods and services to, 19

taxation decisions, 3, 197, 198

Taxation Economics, 46

taxprices, 18, 37, 39, 50, 53–4, 67, 70, 201, 202, 311; changes in, 40, 55–7; definition of, 41; and quantities of goods and services, 96, 146, 226; and utility maximization, 42, 43–4; and valuations of goods and services, 23–4, 95; variance in, 90

technological change, differential, 295

technological factors: constraining vertical competition, 194

technology mobility, 189, 191, 192, 230, 257–8

technology(ies): as constraint on competition, 197, 213; constraints on, 223–6; to control free-riding, 45; and division of functions, 203, 204–9; and formal/informal structures, 152, 153, 154; variations in, 54

temporary monopolists, 32

tenure, 295n7

"Theory of Clubs," (Buchanan), 231–2

theory of second-best, 68, 69

Third world countries, 129, 290

tie-ins, 296–7, 301

Tiebout: equilibrium, 238, 243; mechanism, 192, 194, 229, 230–2, 233, 234, 238, 239, 262, 266, 267, 276; model, 244

tit-for-tat strategy, 268–9

trade barriers, 331–2

trades, 111; as enforcement mechanism, 169

traditions, 9, 11

transaction costs, 18, 186, 187

transaction-costs efficiency, 20–1

Transaction Costs Economics, 20

transfer pricing, 207

transfer(s), 9, 66, 160, 161n8; as ratio of aggregated measured income, 305–6; services treated as, when supplied by governments, 280, 284–5, 295, 304–5; of tax burdens, 228

transfers of funds, 194, 198, 200

Treaty of Rome, 275, 331
trust, 20, 172, 215, 261; and cooperation, 250; horizontal, 172, 173, 174; informal trades and, 111; long-term trading, 116; measurement problem, 173–4; in networks, 169, 170–2; in principal-agent relationship, 159; vertical, 171–2, 173, 174, 175–6
trust, theory of, 264
trust networks: competition for membership in, 177, 178
trust relationships, 176
two-part pricing models, 39
tyranny/tyrants, 25, 26, 134

unanimity, 21–2, 23, 24, 87, 89, 119; in budgetary processes, 119, 120
unbalanced growth, 307; model of, 287, 294
uncertainty, 156
unitarianism, 224; and stability, 245–6, 247–8
unitary states systems, 193, 199, 201, 203, 224, 226, 227, 311; constitutional amendments, 225; constitutions, 261–2; as ideal form of government, 202; power of central governments in, 229; tax administration, 206
United Kingdom, 107n12, 306
United States, 17, 70, 212, 276, 306; branches of government, 74; budgetary processes, 35, 111, 112–18
–Congress, House of Representatives, 74, 92, 112–14, 117, 135–9; Appropriations Committee, 112, 120; Rules Committee, 114n23; Ways and Means Committee, 113, 119–20
–Senate, 74, 112–14, 117, 135, 139, 259, 260; Appropriations Committee, 120; Finance Committee, 113, 119–20; congressional government, 96, 97; demand lobbies in, 63; Electoral College, 91, 92, 194; executive, 74; General Accounting Office, 98n1; gun lobby, 86; intelligence services, 73; monitoring international competition, 272–4; President, 91, 92; Revenue Sharing, 258; Supreme Court, 91–2, 135; Treasury, 112; urban crisis in, 244–5, 254
urban crisis (U.S.), 244–5, 254
Urban Public Finance in Canada (Bird and Slack), 245
urbanization, 306
utility functions, 6, 32, 37, 267, 268; interdependence of, 7; maximization of, 23, 37, 41
utility losses, 23, 50–1, 53, 55, 81, 82, 101,

222–3, 246, 308; and budget deficits, 315, 316; change in, 146; compensation for, 128; direct/representative democracies, 303; government structure and, 227, 303; information on, 59, 64, 69, 121; minimization of, 60, 61, 67, 85, 87, 167, 214, 302, 306; resource allocations and, 226; responsiveness to, 86; sensitivity to, 84; and volume of consent, 123–4
utility maximization, 42–8

vertical competition, 184–90, 193, 194, 227, 228, 229; central governments monitoring, 248, 262, 263; international, 271, 274–5; monitoring, 258–62; and stability, 229, 245–8
vertical disintegration, 205
vertical fiscal imbalance, 197–204, 214–15, 221, 226, 227
vertical integration, 205
vertical networks, 162, 169, 171–2, 175–6
vertical relationships, 152, 183
vertical trust networks, 173
veto power, 76, 118
Villa Colombella Seminar, 188–9
voluntary organizations, 292, 293, 297, 299–300, 301, 305, 308
vote intention data, 57–8
voting, 35, 41, 49, 85; prospective/retrospective, 27–8; theories of, 4; *see also* suffrage
voting mechanisms, 40
voting models, 27, 48
Vox Dei dispensation model, 124, 125–9, 146
Vox Populi dispensation model, 124, 129–34, 146

war-of-attrition game, 315–16
wealth redistribution, 3, 4, 8–9; *see also* income redistribution
Weldon critique, 185, 186, 187, 188
welfare, 304, 305
welfare economics, 4, 11n5, 18, 19, 44, 69, 185, 188, 198, 200, 201, 202, 203, 258, 265; theories of market failure, 287
welfare-economics efficiency, 18–21
welfare programs, 255
West Germany, 306
Western Electric, Hawthorne plant, 151
Western Europe, 17
Wicksell-Lindahl efficiency, 23–4, 26, 28, 29, 35, 39, 178, 226, 262
Wicksellian Connection, 3, 25n15, 35, 42, 52, 66–9, 197, 229, 302–3, 306, 308, 311–12; budget outcome and, 96, 98; in

budgetary processes, 118–21; in bureaucracies, 167; bureaucratic behavior and, 178; central governments' monitoring role and, 262, 263; checks and balances in, 70, 87–90; empirical, 328–30; in governmental systems, 226–7; and political consent, 123, 146, 147

Wicksellian model, 4; concept of efficiency and, 22
world federalism, 270, 275, 276
world order, 264–76
world order failure, 264, 265

zoning, 232